# Atlantic Salmon Chronicles

*E. Richard Nightingale*

This book is dedicated to my grandsons, Joseph, Peter, Keenan, and Connor. *The Atlantic salmon crisis is but a small window on the future of our planet. It's your planet now, boys. Husband it well.*

# Atlantic Salmon Chronicles

## The Fish, the Rivers, the Fly-Fishing Techniques and Equipment

E. Richard Nightingale

Sycamore Island Books · Boulder, Colorado

*Atlantic Salmon Chronicles:*
*The Fish, the Rivers, the Fly-Fishing Techniques and Equipment*
by E. Richard Nightingale

Copyright © 2000 by E. Richard Nightingale

ISBN 1-58160-104-2
Printed in the United States of America

Published by Sycamore Island Books, a division of
Paladin Enterprises, Inc.
Gunbarrel Tech Center
7077 Winchester Circle
Boulder, Colorado 80301 USA.
+1.303.443.7250

Direct inquiries and/or orders to the above address.

**Publisher's Cataloging-in-Publication**
*(Provided by Quality Books, Inc.)*

Nightingale, E. Richard.
    Atlantic salmon chronicles : the fish, the
 rivers, the fly-fishing techniques & equipment /
 E. Richard Nightingale. -- 1st ed.
    p. cm.
    Includes bibliographical references and index.
    ISBN: 1-58160-104-2

    1. Atlantic salmon fishing.  2. Fly fishing.
 I. Title.

SH685.N54 2000          799.1'756'097
                QBI00-500058

Neither the author nor the publisher assumes
any responsibility for the use or misuse of
information contained in this book.

Front cover: *Canoe and Salmon* by Thomas Aquinas Daly (6365 East Arcade Road, Arcade, NY 14009).

Back cover: Photo courtesy of Paul Schmookler.

Illustrations by Larry Largay.

Visit our Web site at www.sycamoreisland.com

# Table of Contents

# Foreword
## *by Bill Taylor*

Wild Atlantic salmon have always been an important part
of my life. My father introduced me to the pleasures of
trout fishing with a worm not long after I was old enough
to walk, and as a youth, I spent every possible moment
during my summer vacations fishing. Many of my fondest
memories are of the wonderful summer days we spent
tramping through the woods and along the streams of
New Brunswick in search of beaver ponds where big
brook trout often lurked. As a teen, I graduated to fly
fishing, which elevated to new heights the pleasure of my
days spent on the streams.

But Atlantic salmon always filled my dreams, fueled
by the stories I heard and read about fishing on the
legendary salmon rivers of Quebec, Newfoundland, and
my home province of New Brunswick. As soon as I
received my driver's license, I began living my salmon
dreams. New Brunswick's mighty Miramichi, with all of
its wonderful tributaries, and Nova Scotia's beautiful
Margaree River, as well as lesser known Maritime rivers,
such as the Big Salmon, the Kennebacasis, and the

Stewiacke, became my regular weekend haunts. Often, my good friend and fishing partner Hank and I would drive all night to be the first anglers on our chosen pool at daybreak.

As a fanatical young salmon angler, I read and re-read every book on the art of salmon angling I could lay my hands on. I studied the books of such salmon legends as Joe Bates, George Frederick Clarke, Dana Lamb, and, of course, Lee Wulff, intent on learning all I could about Atlantic salmon. If only *Atlantic Salmon Chronicles* had been available to me then.

The Atlantic salmon is considered by many accomplished fly fishers to be the ultimate challenge and justly deserving of its title "King of Gamefish," first crowned by Izaac Walton in his 1653 treatise *The Compleat Angler*. Rarely are such descriptions applied objectively; however, in the case of the Atlantic salmon, there is much that lends credence to Walton's claim.

The Atlantic salmon is perhaps the most difficult of all gamefish to entice to the fly, for it ceases to feed upon returning to freshwater from its ocean migration. While trout and bass offer plenty of challenges to fly fishers, at least they aren't fasting when we fish for them. Once hooked, the Atlantic salmon's long, powerful runs and aerial acrobatics are legendary. Strong and powerful swimmers, the Atlantic salmon travel thousands of miles from their birth rivers to their North Atlantic feeding grounds and then return to the same stretch of river where they were hatched to repeat their miraculous cycle of life. Unlike their Pacific cousins, which all die after spawning, Atlantic salmon are able to survive the rigors of their spawning to return to the ocean and repeat their amazing journey, where they must again avoid a host of natural predators and man-made devices bent on their destruction. It's not uncommon for the Atlantic salmon to repeat its amazing spawning run two or three times, and the record is an incredible seven times by a salmon from New Brunswick's once prolific Big Salmon River. Unfortunately, the salmon runs of the Big Salmon River and the 30 other wonderful little streams that empty into the Bay of Fundy are fighting against a tidal wave of threats pushing them ever closer to extinction.

The rivers where Atlantic salmon live are some of the wildest and most beautiful places on earth. Atlantic salmon need clean, cool, well-oxygenated water; they thrive in rivers that often begin as a trickle in the mountains or uplands and tumble to the sea through forested valleys rich in bird and wildlife. The great salmon rivers of eastern Canada, Europe, and Scandinavia are treasures, as valuable and vital to man's survival as they are to the salmon's.

Not surprisingly, there has been much written about the Atlantic salmon, both from angling and natural history perspectives. Richard Nightingale's contribution to this important body of literature is a comprehensive and perceptive take on the subject that captures both perspectives equally well. Richard understands that the salmon's best friend in its struggle against gill-netters, hydro dams, clear-cutting, pollution, and a host of other threats is the conservation-minded angler. The more aware we, as anglers, are of the serious threats facing wild salmon, the more likely we are to lend our support to conservation groups to clean up rivers and write letters to government officials.

From the angling perspective, *Atlantic Salmon Chronicles* provides plenty of helpful advice for beginner and experienced salmon fishers alike. There is much insightful information about equipment, fly selection, knots, and fishing strategies learned over the more than 30 years that Richard has pursued Atlantic salmon throughout the North Atlantic rim. His chapter on the "Sacred Rivers of the Salmon" is captivating. We are introduced to the great Atlantic salmon rivers of the world, and there is no better guide than Richard. Throughout this book are offered fresh approaches to angling for Atlantic salmon that are as interesting as they are effective.

Through his fishing travels, Richard has seen first-hand how the Atlantic salmon is being pressured by the heavy hand of man (too many years of over-fishing, pollution, habitat destruction, industrial development, and changing environmental conditions that in many rivers have forced the wild Atlantic salmon to the brink of extinction) threatening the very survival of the species in many rivers that just a decade ago were filled with bright, beautiful fish. Richard's advice on the steps that must be taken to conserve this magnificent fish is right on the mark. As caring and thoughtful anglers, we have an obligation to do our part to ensure that wild Atlantic salmon are here for our children and grandchildren to enjoy.

The Atlantic Salmon Federation (ASF) has been leading the fight to save the Atlantic salmon and safeguard its habitat for more than 50 years. While the conservation and environmental threats facing the Atlantic salmon are many, we are making progress in our quest to protect and restore this irreplaceable natural treasure. Our conservation message is being heard by more and more anglers and by people concerned about wild salmon and the health of our rivers and oceans. People are beginning to understand and appreciate the importance of wild salmon as a barometer of the health of our own world. Most importantly, politicians and elected officials are finally recognizing the intrinsic, as well as the economic, value of wild salmon.

*Atlantic Salmon Chronicles* reaffirms the ASF message. Wild Atlantic salmon define the North Atlantic ecosystem, and their return to our rivers is a symbol of hope. They are the "canaries in the coal mines" of our lives, signaling to us the health—and sometimes the malaise—of our forests, rivers, and oceans.

When we stand in a wild river casting for Atlantic salmon, we immerse ourselves in the natural world. We see sights and hear sounds that heighten our senses and soothe our souls. We also become participants in nature rather than spectators, and we become players in a sport that is rich in centuries of tradition and lore.

And when, after thousands of casts, we finally connect with a wild Atlantic salmon, a connection is made that blesses our day and sometimes enriches our lives. To be connected to a fresh-run Atlantic salmon as it tears across a pool, catapults itself from river to sky, and runs back downriver toward the sea is for many fly fishers the ultimate experience. We feel a wild energy that is both electrifying and humbling. And when we cradle a wild Atlantic salmon in our hands, carefully pointing its head into the oxygen-rich current before releasing it back to the river, we feel the very pulse of the wilderness through a creature that has been to the far corner of the North Atlantic Ocean and overcome seemingly insurmountable odds to rise and take our fly in the very river where it was born. To hold that same wild salmon in our hands; stroke its sleek, muscular body; and feel its wild heart pound is an experience that continues to capture the hearts and minds of fly fishers around the world.

As exhilarating and thrilling as hooking a wild Atlantic salmon is, there is so much more to Atlantic salmon angling than catching salmon. As with Richard, many of the most enjoyable and memorable days of my life have been spent with family and friends on salmon rivers. And while the thrills of landing a great salmon or a fish under particularly challenging conditions are forever burned into my memory, it's the experiences between salmon that I remember most vividly: the rich fragrance of the balm of the Gilead tree in June along the Restigouche; our annual family camping trips on the sweet little Cains River; seeing the wonder in my daughter's eyes as she watched awestruck as an osprey plucked a salmon from the river or she listened to the haunting call of a loon late at night; and the hours spent around campfires and in lodges with good friends. These are experiences that have enriched my life beyond measure. And always, it's the Atlantic salmon that has drawn us to the river and is the common thread that binds these experiences together.

*Atlantic Salmon Chronicles* is an important addition to the tradition of great books covering Atlantic salmon. Richard Nightingale joins the ranks of angling and literary greats such as Lee Wulff and Joe Bates, who brilliantly wove the angling and conservation themes throughout their fine books.

Bill Taylor, President
Atlantic Salmon Federation
St. Andrews, New Brunswick

*Pool and Riffle*
Etching and Aquatint
8 1/2 x 6 inches
Author's Collection

# Foreword
## *by Dr. Alex T. Bielak*

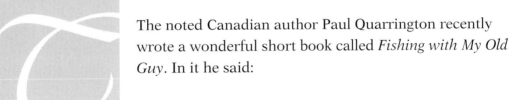

The noted Canadian author Paul Quarrington recently wrote a wonderful short book called *Fishing with My Old Guy*. In it he said:

> *I have a theory about the transitional nature of a human life, how one needs someone to facilitate passage, how this is often accomplished by an elder under the pretense of imparting the minutiae of some art or craft. Some anglers, near the end of their days, have acquired that knowledge which they can share with the young ones. Fishing is an area that can, even in this decidedly unmagical day and age, still produce magi. I call them Old Guys.*

After flogging the waters of the salmon world for 20 years while researching the ways of the salmon, I have found my own "Old Guy." It is my honour to have been asked by him to provide this foreword to his book.

In April 1996, a letter arrived on my desk shortly after I had made a presentation at a Miramichi Salmon Association Annual Meeting in Boston. Politely flattering, it informed me that the writer, one E. Richard Nightingale, was putting together "some unique concepts" in a book he called *Atlantic Salmon Chronicles*. The writer requested some assistance regarding his chapter on the "life of the salmon, its conservation, and its future."

Over the course of the following months, through letters exchanged, draft chapters read and commented upon, and a number of extended phone conversations, I came to the conclusion that Dr. Nightingale's book was indeed going to be unlike any other in its scope and treatment of the subject. To understand why, one has to know something about Richard. A tall, fit, distinguished, and methodical gentleman, he has been fly fishing for 50 years and has been an active salmon angler for more than 25. He also has a doctorate in physical-analytical chemistry and runs a technology consulting firm. It should not come as a surprise that he has written extensively in the technical journals and holds no fewer than 12 U.S. patents. (Since chemistry was one of my weakest subjects, I've hesitated to ask what they may be for, in case he tells me!) His professional rigour permeates every aspect of his book.

One only has to look at the chapter on knots to see what I mean. Most anglers, and likely most writers on the subject, have been content to find a knot (or knots) that they are comfortable with (usually this translates to one they can tie reasonably competently) and stick with it for that reason. Not Richard! Richard personally tested every popular knot and then some, calculated average deviations for the tests, reported the percentages of leader or knot breaks, and ascertained which knots are actually stronger than others. This level of detailed analysis is typical of this and the other chapters. That is not to say that his writing is in any way dry or difficult. In fact it is compelling, and one senses that Richard always has an ultimate goal of ensuring that the practical nature of this technical information is obvious to the angler reading it.

For instance, his observations led him to develop the "Sixteen-Twenty loop knot," which he terms "the strongest knot [he] ever tested." (To my knowledge, this is the only angling book to include "before and after" photomicrographs illustrating how a knot gets its strength.) He also details the little-appreciated fact that many knots are material specific. In some instances, a properly constructed knot may be more secure than the leader itself. Richard concludes that the security of a knot is indicated by the percentage of leader breaks and that a high percentage of leader breaks indicates that a knot is easily formed to near maximum strength.

This is probably one of the more important pieces of angling-related analysis in recent times, given that most of us have lost more than one salmon when a common or garden piece of leader gave way, rather than having a several-hundred-dollar rod or reel let us down at the moment of truth, so to speak. However, for those of you concerned by the latter, Dr. Nightingale is equally thorough in other chapters, in which he describes the inner workings of fly reels (which he admits is his primary hobby); critiques fly rods, lines, tackle, and equipment; and discusses ways of fishing the wet fly.

The mention of the knot above also deserves mention from another standpoint. Richard is the fifth member of the Sixteen-Twenty Club, one of the most exclusive fellowships in angling. Simply put, he, together with only a handful of other Moisie fishers (notably the late Lee Wulff, who founded the club), has landed a 20-pound or larger salmon on a size 16 single-hook fly. That this feat was achieved at the great pool where the Ouapetec River flows into the Moisie is a splendid coincidence that helped draw Richard and me together. The pool—in what Richard describes as his "sacred river" in a chapter of the same name—is as much a special place for me as it is for him, since it was there that I spent a considerable amount of time developing some of the ideas that were central to my doctoral thesis.

Richard Nightingale brings the same approach to his fishing as he does to his writing. I had the pleasure of fishing with Richard at Grog Island on the Restigouche in the early season a couple of summers back. Fresh fish were still scarce, but Richard covered every bit of fishable water for as long as there were light and hope. He practiced what he preaches in his book, too, using an assortment of flies. Too often in North America, we think only in terms of integral-body hairwing flies. Richard broadens our horizons to define and classify flies according to form (the type of hooking device) and style (the type of body and wing), with a good section on tube flies commonly found in Iceland and Europe. Why we have been so slow to adopt these relatively simple-to-construct flies is a mystery to me. Perhaps this book will help stimulate their wider adoption by the angling community.

In the evenings, as we sampled some of Richard's own salmon pastrami, he grilled me endlessly with insightful questions related to salmon biology and conservation. A chance comment relating to the Fifth International Atlantic Salmon Symposium scheduled for Galway, Ireland, in 1997 led to Richard's attending the meeting. There—apart from adding to the already considerable list of rivers he has fished throughout the salmon world—he secured, at first-hand, much of the material for his chapter on salmon conservation. The chapter attempts—rather well—to deal with some of the complex and pressing issues facing *Salar*. In doing so, it goes well beyond the usual cursory discussion of life cycle and description of threats that one too often finds in angling books.

As I sit fine-tuning this foreword, I've re-read a couple of the draft chapters and have been reminded just how good and involving Richard Nightingale's writing can be. For instance, the important chapter devoted to Richard's undisguisedly personal discussion of "sacred rivers" is both detailed and informative, yet manages to transport the reader's mind to the riverbank, tickling the fancy to explore waters yet to be experienced and remembered. And that is the crux of this captivatingly written book. It is one very experienced, technically oriented man's take on salmon fishing. Whether critically evaluating the various equipment and clothing on the basis of functionality and applicability, speaking to the importance of physical conditioning, comparing European and North American techniques for fishing the wet fly, or tempting the reader with his favourite gastronomic renditions of salmon, Richard Nightingale does it unlike anyone before him.

It is in this sense that Richard has become my "Old Guy." Through this enjoyable and informative book, I think he can do the same for any reader, no matter how long he or she has been fishing.

Dr. Alex T. Bielak
Fall River, Nova Scotia

# Introduction

This book was conceived on the banks of the Grímsá River in Iceland. It was there in 1977 that I first experienced a week of serious salmon fishing, serious as compared to occasional days on the Penobscot or the Miramichi or the St. Mary's in Nova Scotia. That experience—and successive weeks in 1978 and 1979—taught me two important lessons. First, the way to learn salmon fishing is to become immersed in it. In seven days, fishing 12 hours each day, I not only learned how and what to do, but also how not and why not. Second, I learned that much of the mystique of salmon fishing lies in its heritage. Salmon fishing, particularly the sport of the fly, is rooted in Old World culture, with concepts that were designed to impress, awe, and even intimidate.

I had gone to Iceland that first year well-read and thought I knew what to expect. Thanks to Lee Wulff's classic book *The Atlantic Salmon*, I was well versed in technique, but I was almost overwhelmed by the aura of the eclectic group of anglers I encountered.

Contrary to the mystique, salmon are easy to land. It's inducing them to strike that's hard. Much as I hate to admit it, compared to the wary old brown trout, salmon are dumb. Maturing in expansive oceans, salmon know only to jump or flee when hooked, and the larger fish usually bear down instead of expending energy with repetitive jumps. Certainly, they don't rush for streamside shelter the way a wily trout does. The knowledgeable angler with modern tackle can subdue any salmon that swims, if only he can hook it.

Initially, the purpose of this work was to draw aside the mystique and divulge to the neophyte elementary concepts for capturing the salmon. That is still a primary concern. Repeatedly, I speak to the beginning salmon fisherman, knowing that there is also much for the advanced angler to master. But beware. Salmon fishing is an art form unto itself. It is as different from trout fishing as stalking the bighorn sheep is from quail hunting. The technique of salmon fishing is much more akin to saltwater flats fishing, and repeatedly throughout this chronicle I emphasize the obvious comparisons, particularly with respect to rods, reels, rigging your tackle, and even how you fight the fish.

In the years that have intervened since my concepts were first developed, I have come to recognize a second purpose, which now may be almost as important. That is to critique, for the beginning salmon fisherman and others more advanced, some of the conceptions and misconceptions that prevail in our sport. The explosive growth of fly fishing in the past decade tends to becloud our appreciation of the art of angling. Perhaps that is a polite way of saying that this growth has become market driven. While this has resulted in technological advances, many have been at the expense of reason and good sense. Marketing palaver is often substituted for usefulness. More choices and higher prices do not necessarily produce better or more useful equipment. Some of these issues I address herein, accepting where appropriate the role of contrariant.

I have on occasion suggested in jest that anyone who writes another salmon book is of questionable sanity. No one can contribute more to the salmon fishing literature than have Lee Wulff, Hugh Falkus, and Joseph Bates with their monumental treatises (58, 16, 03). [NOTE: Citations 01–59 in parentheses refer to bibliographical entries.] For this reason I have tried to be selective in choosing subjects for this manuscript, emphasizing those of which I can speak with authority. This book is organized so that each chapter presents an informative and instructive overview of its subject. Several of the chapters commence with narratives designed to illustrate the subject or convey a message. All of these are based on actual fishing experiences. Two books in recent years, neither about salmon, have impressed me with their unusual format and exceptional content: Trey Combs' monograph on saltwater angling, *Bluewater Fly Fishing* (12), and the second in a seminar series by Bernard "Lefty" Kreh (29). It is my wish that this volume may be similarly received.

*Atlantic Salmon Chronicles* is for the dedicated angler, however inexperienced he or she may be. The first half of the book offers totally new insights and evaluations, especially for rods and reels, flies, knots and leaders, and other equipment. Where appropriate I identify exemplary products and in a few cases flawed or inadequate ones. Such commendations and condemnations are my opinions. I have no ties to, nor have I received consideration from, any tackle manufacturer, camp operator, or purveyor. For me, it is much like a young scientist reviewing scientific manuscripts. You try to be objective, complimentary where possible, and critical only if necessary. Regrettably, much of our current angling literature is not objective and warrants a more critical review.

Several of the chapters are unique in presenting detailed analyses of subjects too often treated in a mundane or cursory manner. Chapter 3 presents a comprehensive review of modern fly reels—their drags, clutches, and operating features—with a view to enabling the angler to make a reasoned selection.

Chapter 4 attempts to answer the ageless question,

"What flies do I really need?" Flies are examined in a totally new context: that of form and style. In examining the form and style of the Atlantic salmon fly, it is impossible not to recognize the metamorphosis from feather-wing flies to hairwings to bug, shrimp, and eel patterns traced with fluorescence and glitter. Inexorably, it forces us to acknowledge that we fish for salmon with lures designed specifically to attract and induce.

Chapter 5 presents an in-depth study of knots unlike anything heretofore published. Not only do we accurately measure the relative strengths of common knots used by the salmon angler, but for the first time we achieve insight into the significance of the leader's breaking instead of the knot. The practical consequence is that the three new knots developed from this study are stronger than any others, as strong as or marginally stronger than the Bimini Twist.

The second part of *Atlantic Salmon Chronicles* opens with an eclectic chapter on the conservation of the salmon, a chapter that, in true epic tradition, derives its unity from our concern for the central hero. The better we understand the response of the salmon to stresses imposed by man and by nature, the better we may be prepared to alter those factors that endanger the species. We then examine the salmon fishing experience: the most appropriate techniques and tactics for fishing the wet fly, how to get started, and the assistance you will need. Chapter 11 presents thoughts on world-class rivers and where to go for the very best salmon angling. It has become my favorite chapter, for it summarizes the salmon angling experience: the rivers and the wilderness environment, the people and their culture, the memories you retain forever.

Throughout these discussions I strive to be enlightening as well as educational, recognizing that no one understands the enigmatic Atlantic salmon. For dessert, I conclude the manuscript with some of my favorite salmon and related recipes. That's the way I savor my salmon trips. It seems an appropriate manner in which to conclude this chronicle.

Obviously, any effort such as this has many collaborators, some unknown and a few unintentional. My wife once accused me, with wry humor, of having too many fishing friends. This work would be incomplete without acknowledging the influence and assistance of some of those friends, including the Moisie gang of Tom Clark, Lloyd Gang, Jim Harquail, and Clem Kaupp. I am indebted to Lavinia Beard, Paulette Blanchette, Tom Duncan, John Dughi, Jaakko Erkinaro, Ed Jaworowski, Mike Fitzgerald Sr., Thorpe McKenzie, Alan McNaughton, Pat Moffitt, Bob Nicholson, Jim Williams, Earl and Margit Worsham, and Rod Yerger, who reviewed various sections and chapters and offered invaluable commentaries.

Valuable information, insight, and suggestions were offered by Bill Bewsher of the Atlantic Salmon Trust, Glenn Crowther of W.C. Gore & Associates, Kevin Davidson of the Canadian Department of Fisheries and Oceans, Jerry Doak of Wallace W. Doak & Sons, Richard Kondak of Shimano, Robbie Jansen of Seamaster, Jim Lepage of Orvis, Tom McCullough of Cortland Line, Bob Rackley of DuPont/Stren, Bruce Richards of Scientific Anglers, Roberto Sacconi of STH Reels, Doug Smith of Korkers, Jim Vincent of RIO Products International, Ken Whelan of the Salmon Research Agency of Ireland, and Fred Whorisky of the Atlantic Salmon Federation (ASF). The assistance of Paul Schmookler of The Complete Sportsman, Jaako Erkinaro of the Finnish Game and Fisheries Research Institute, Teemu Makinen of the Teno River Fisheries Research Centre, and Sue Scott of the Atlantic Salmon Federation in providing extraordinary photographs is gratefully acknowledged. I must also express my appreciation to a most thoughtful friend, Tom Hakes, for access to his extensive library.

Gratitude and special recognition go to Alex Bielak, one of Canada's premier salmon authorities, who helped to guide me through the complexities of salmon research and its impact on conservation. Alex has been an active researcher representing both recreational and commercial fishing interests; he continues to be involved in salmon management at senior levels in both the provincial and federal levels of the Canadian government. He encouraged me to the point that I dared not fail.

A very special note of recognition goes to Thomas Aquinas Daly, one of America's most admired landscape and sporting artists, for allowing me to reproduce 14 of his magnificent watercolors and oil paintings, without which the visual appeal of this project would be inadequate. I am pleased to acknowledge the Atlantic Salmon Federation for permission to reprint maps of the Matapedia and Grand Cascapedia Rivers by the late Pierre Lutz, the Alta Laksefiskeri Interessentskap for permission to reproduce the map of the Alta River by David Eley, and Larry Hunt for permission to reproduce the map of the Miramichi River system by Erin M. Hunt.

All of us who labor for the benefit of the Atlantic salmon owe gratitude, recognition, and support to the leadership of the ASF for its unstinting devotion to the cause. For my part, I am pleased to cite for his advice and counsel Lucien Rolland, Chairman Emeritus of the ASF (Canada), who presided at my induction into the Sixteen-Twenty Club, and to express my gratitude to Bill Taylor, ASF president, who so graciously has accommodated my requests in search of fact and verity. I am honored to have him write a foreword for this book.

To those who assisted in the production of this book, I owe much: Brendan Banahan, who pointed the direction; Phil Monahan, who first edited the book; and Larry Largay, who prepared the illustrations. It is a pleasure to acknowledge the manufacturing team at Sycamore Island Books: Jon Ford, editorial director; Donna DuVall, editor; and Fran Milner, art director. It was a rare privilege to work with such collegial comity that even difficult decisions were easily resolved.

Finally, I wish to remember the lifelong influence of my boyhood friend, Arthur Lowell Price Jr. (1927–1978), who shared with me so many of the outdoor experiences of our youth. We first met as Tenderfoot Scouts; our paths eventually diverged as Eagle Scouts of Troop 17,

Arrowhead Council. Art never caught a salmon, but his numerous contributions to scouting captured the hearts of many youths.

E. Richard Nightingale
Summit, New Jersey

*St. Jean Salmon Returned*
Oil on Board
14 x 20 inches
Private Collection

# *Chapter* 1

# *Salmo Salar:* The Paradigm of Sporting Pisces

King of fishes, the fish of kings; the world's glamour gamefish; the quintessential fish (14). By such exalted appellations is the Atlantic salmon known. That the Atlantic salmon has captured the imagination of man is undisputed. The power and beauty and grace of this fish have awed men for countless millennia. Petroglyphs drawn by cave dwellers 20,000 years ago prominently feature the Atlantic salmon. The scientific name, *Salmo salar*, is derived from the name accorded by the Roman legions who encountered the species during their occupancy of Spain, France, and Britain. *Salar* means "to leap." And leap it does: with joy as it ascends its natal rivers, with power to surmount the falls that hinder its passage, with grace and beauty to enter the hearts of those who would paint it or capture it.

The Atlantic salmon is the consummate fish for the sportsman. It's strong to overcome obstacles and resist capture. It's graceful to entice the photographer and painter. And to its everlasting malevolence, it's among the most prized of foods on earth. Furthermore, the salmon is angled only in the cold, freshwater rivers of the northern forests and pre-Cambrian plateaus. Its pursuit engenders an outdoor experience unmatched by any other in North America, save that of the Western steelhead. Fishing for Atlantic salmon combines the art of the tier, the skill of the angler, and the lure and the lore of rivers.

This book is derived from one man's adventure with the Atlantic salmon. The narrative sections are based on what I have learned chasing that elusive creature and what I have observed about others who join the chase— their questions and their incertitudes. As a young teenager, I began fly fishing for bass and panfish in Illinois and then for brook trout in Ontario. Fifty years later, I pursue the Atlantic salmon as ardently now as I did bluegills then. But much has changed.

Ours is an age of technological revolution. The tiny transistor has had a greater impact on our civilization in 50 years than all previous inventions combined. It enables us to perform invasive, life-saving medical miracles; to wage mass destruction at intercontinental distances; and to fly to the moon and beyond. Yet the price paid, and still to be realized, is unfathomable. Everything about our lives is organized, categorized, and scrutinized, frequently for purposes other than utility, and often to a degree that defies reason.

Even the subjects of our sporting affection are organized. Virtually every species of freshwater fish and game is represented by a federation or association, and many have their own magazines or journals. That's good when it comes to advancing awareness and cultivating conservation. Unfortunately, it too often leads to competition whose purpose is to shoot the most birds, bag the biggest game, or catch the largest fish. Such contests are unethical, ill advised, and unworthy of anyone who calls himself a "sportsman." Certainly, they are contrary to all principles of conservation.

The impact of modern technology on the wild creatures of our planet is devastating, and the Atlantic salmon has not escaped the onslaught. We have learned how to track salmon to their oceanic feeding grounds, only to have high-tech netting on the high seas nearly annihilate the wild species. We have developed salmon farming to supplement the dwindling species, only to learn that the progeny are physically and genetically inferior, sometimes incapable of reproducing themselves, and detrimental to the wild fish they were bred to supplant. Most sad is the realization that the destruction caused by salmon farms is irreversible. Too many strains of wild salmon have disappeared from the majestic rivers of the world for the trend to be reversed at this late date.

Other forces also have changed the angling experience. A recurrent theme in the several chapters on equipment is the extent to which egoistic and erroneous, even false, advertising has supplanted utility in our selection of angling tackle and equipment. All too frequently "best" is measured solely by price. It no longer just means functionally superior.

I am old enough to have seen bamboo rods supplanted first by fiberglass and now by graphite, silk lines by polymeric fibers with elastomeric coatings, and gut leaders by nylon and other hydrocarbon fibers. The cotton canvas so prevalent in canoes, packsacks, and tents a half century ago has been replaced by synthetic fabrics and composites of every description. Few rivers today have canoes that are not powered by outboard motors. On one river I fish, the canoes have neither paddles nor oars for locomotion. Either you motor or you walk. Certainly, our equipment is more efficient and effective than in days of yore, but is the angling experience more pleasurable or as exhilarating? Is not that the true test of the outdoor adventure?

It is time to acknowledge the changing nature of Atlantic salmon angling. Not just by discussing the development of new "lures" and improved equipment, nor in deploring the marketing of useless gadgetry and the shameless self-promotion of "fishing professionals." I prefer to emphasize the romance of the river and the skill required to contest this "Paradigm of Sporting Pisces."

Today we angle for an endangered, if not a vanishing, species. If we are to continue to fish for the species, we also must adopt individually the same strict conservation measures we expect of others. Currently, cock grilse may still be taken without significantly affecting the species, but no multi-sea-winter (MSW) salmon should be killed by anglers. However, there is great economic pressure by some camp operators and guides, fearful their business and employment will suffer, to resist such conservation practices. Yet for 15 years such has been the practice in the Province of New Brunswick, and the Miramichi is one of the few rivers in North America where the salmon fishery is flourishing.

We need to return to first principles. Why in today's society do we fish? How better can we enjoy the adventure? I still cling to the belief, tenuous as it may be, that fishing is a hobby to be savored with leisure. It should not be a commercialized expedition in which you traipse behind a guide, much as you would follow a sherpa up a great Himalayan mountain.

The greatest change I have noticed in the half-century of my experience is the dramatic increase in "time pressure." Eighty-five percent of our population is said to be "clock-locked." We live in a time warp where our every activity is compressed into the most meager of time slots. We accumulate too many "toys" and enjoy too little leisure. A very recent survey reveals that the average worker enjoys only 1.4 hours of leisure time per week. All too frequently fishing is no longer a casual activity. We rush to the river and rush home again. Too few of us take time to enjoy the people we meet, the wildlife we pursue, or the scenery we so admire. For 20 years I wanted to return to the tiny hamlet of Rossport, Ontario, on the north shore of Lake Superior, where I spent so many summers of my youth. But I was always rushing somewhere else. As I enter retirement, I am learning that time pressure is not just for the employed. It has become a way of life and is not easily put aside, even when you do not have to "be there today."

Why then do we pursue the salmon? Philosophers may have answers. I do not. I only know that I enjoy fishing.

Being outdoors in the solitude of the river is my *raison d'être*. I love to spend time alone on our local trout stream, distracted only by a sunning water snake, the honking geese, a fleeting mink, or the Hendrickson hatch of late afternoon. But I love even more the grandeur of a pristine salmon river, unspoiled by civilization and often devoid of it. I never fully comprehended the romance of the river until I fished the Alta in Norway. As I relate in Chapter 11, the experience of fishing a long run of that majestic river, being swept by skilled guides back and forth across the hissing current, without a word being spoken for half hours at a time, with only a distant eagle to divert my attention, can only be described as magnificent.

This book is organized to enable the angler to master any one of its subjects in a single chapter, but the soul of the book is contained in Chapter 8 on conservation and Chapter 11 on great rivers of the world. Conservation on the one hand and the sublime experience of the capture on the other. The dichotomy between protecting and capturing parallels so many of life's conflicts. How better can we illuminate the angling of *Salmo salar* in today's world? Perhaps we may even find purpose as well as satisfaction in our angling adventures.

*River Shadow*
Watercolor
14 x 10 1/4 inches
Private Collection

# Chapter 2

# Selecting
# Fly Rods,
# Matching
# Fly Lines

### PART I. FLY RODS

Fly fishing is the art of angling the fly. You become
proficient at fly fishing by learning fly casting. Fly casting
is the skill of throwing a thin, very long mass on the end
of a long, very flexible stick. If your throw is proficient,
the line mass unfurls uniformly and lands on the water
gently, carrying with it whatever fly you may have
attached to its end. As unflattering as this description may
seem to the artful angler, we need to emphasize at the
outset that fly casting is an acquired skill that does not
come naturally to many.

Fly casting is not difficult. In fact, it is fairly easy to
become rather accomplished if you use balanced
equipment and take the time to practice the fundamentals.
How much concentration and practice you put into getting
started will determine, to the exclusion of all else, the
satisfaction you will receive. It's just like life, *n'est-ce pas*? In
my opinion, experienced spin- or bait-casters making the
transition to salmon fly fishing have an advantage over
trout anglers for one important reason: they understand the

15

concept of casting a straight line, of not lobbing, flipping, or *whipping* [Charles Ritz (46)] their line as do many trout fishermen, particularly dry-fly trout fishermen. Dry-fly fishermen are frequently the worst of salmon casting students because they are accustomed to concentrating on a fly floating at the end of a limp leader, not on the technique of casting and mending a straight line. Now, experienced fly-casting instructors may react with consternation at my use of "lobbing" as an introduction to fly casting, but sometimes you best make the point by telling students what not to do, or how not to proceed.

The purpose of this chapter is to assist beginning salmon anglers and others to select the appropriate fly rod and a matching line. I assume that even the rankest beginner is aware that fly rods are rated according to the weight of the fly line that best matches the casting action of the rod. A heavy, stiff rod will not lob a gossamer thread, nor will a light, flexible rod lob a small cable. *Rule one: You must match the weight of your line to the action of your rod.*

Let's assume that you are about to enter the wonderful world of salmon angling. You have only limited experience as a fly fisherman and need a new salmon rod. You enter your local fly tackle shop and inquire about salmon rods. After some brief pleasantries, you are informed, "Here is the perfect outfit." Now it is your turn to react. Have you ascertained that this shop really knows anything about fishing for Atlantic salmon? Are any of the employees active salmon fishermen? Most importantly, before receiving the recommendation were you asked about your fly-fishing experience? Were you invited outside, perhaps to the parking lot, to try out several rod-and-line combinations? Did anyone ask about your casting ability or observe or comment on your casting proficiency? If you purchase the recommended outfit, may you return it after a day's trial if you find you cannot cast with it? If the answer to more than one of these questions is "no," I suggest you respectfully postpone any decisions until you have had a chance to reconsider your options.

Today there are a myriad of fly rods on the market.

Some are long, some short; some relatively stout, some flexible; some very expensive, others of modest price. No one can recommend the proper rod for you until he has seen you cast. Even then it is an inexact art. The proper rod for you depends on your casting style, particularly whether you prefer a flexible rod or a relatively stiff one. Until you have determined that, all else is guesswork. The wise angler never buys a rod without having first tried it.

In 1987 I lost my then-favorite salmon rod, one of the original Orvis Presentation models (later renamed the Rivermaster). On a trip to Oregon, I met a knowledgeable fisherman who urged me to try a new model of rod from a western manufacturer, which I did. I took the rod home, fished it part of one summer, and discarded it as a piece of junk. That rod sat untouched in a closet for six years. In 1993, I came across that forgotten "junk" and decided one day to take it to the casting pond. Surprise, surprise. As if it were a fine wine that had mellowed for six years, I discovered a truly fine fly rod with which I could cast a full 30-yard fly line. Now I can reveal that it was a Loomis rod. Obviously, the rod had not changed, but I had. My casting capabilities had improved significantly. I was a much more proficient caster, better able to handle rods of differing flexibilities. *Rule two: You must match the flexibility of your rod to your casting style.*

To select a rod, you must first know what weight of fly line you intend to use. I have caught salmon on line weights from 5 through 10, and even 11-weight lines are not too heavy for the large, boisterous rivers of Norway. Fighting a salmon on a light rod is very exciting, but most salmon rivers are much too windy for the lighter-weight lines. Your rod and line must be suitable for the wind and river currents that you will encounter.

The majority of the single-handed fly rods used for Atlantic salmon in North America are 9 or 9 1/2 feet long and are designed to cast either an 8- or a 9-weight fly line—i.e., a fly line whose first 30 feet weigh between 202 and 250 grains, or about 1/2 ounce, the same as a medium-weight freshwater spinning lure or bait-casting plug. The difference, of course, is that 1/2 ounce is distributed over 30 feet of line. It should be obvious that a peculiar casting motion must be used to propel such a mass. But with what rod of what flexibility? There are approximately 50 rod manufacturers in the United States, many of which offer two or three flexibilities, often in two or more grades. Is it any wonder that we are so thoroughly confused as to rod selection?

## Fly-Casting Fundamentals

*Pierre and I are positive that anyone who is taking up fly fishing . . . must, at the beginning, completely forget everything that has to do with dry fly casting and fishing. He must first fish wet fly at least one season.*[1]

Charles Ritz
*A Fly Fisher's Life*

Fly fishing is somewhat like bird hunting, which is an exciting sport if you are sufficiently accomplished to hit an occasional bird. But if you buy a shotgun and go afield without any practice, the results can devastate your ego. Fortunately, these days there are good fly-casting instructors readily available to assist you in learning correctly. The two best, in my opinion, are Joan Salvato Wulff and Ed Jaworowski, both of who have written excellent books on the subject, *Joan Wulff's Fly-Casting Techniques* (55) and *The Cast* (24). I tend to associate more with Ed's style than with Joan's, because Ed is interested in pursuing the larger fish, such as striped bass along the eastern seaboard or great northern pike in our northern lakes. Casting to and playing such fish are more akin to Atlantic salmon fishing than to trout fishing.

One of the reasons that Ed Jaworowski is the premier instructor is that he has reduced fly-casting fundamentals to four principles, which he summarizes in one sentence:

---

1. Charles Ritz, *A Fly Fisher's Life*, Revised edition, 1972, p. 284.

*Eliminate the slack from your line, constantly*
*accelerate your hand to a quick stop, in the direction you*
*want the line to go, making your stroke longer for large flies,*
*[greater] distance and [in the] wind.*[2]

To properly understand Ed's principles, you must
recognize how they are applied. Imagine that you have
borrowed a friend's 8- or 9-weight rod and line and are
ready for some preliminary practice. Start by stretching
out 30 feet of fly line, together with a leader and hookless
fly, on the pond or across the lawn in front of you. Now,
let's examine the principles, one by one, and the actions
required to demonstrate the principles.

1. *You can only load the rod (i.e., make it bend) after you*
   *have removed all the slack from your line.* Action:
   Lower your rod tip to the surface of the water (or
   grass) and strip in all the slack line. You cannot cast
   slack line any more than you can throw a wad of
   loose string. For an efficient cast, your line must lie
   in a line straight out from the tip of the rod. The
   closer the rod tip is to the water's surface, the easier
   it is to pick up the line. As we shall discuss in Chapter
   10, a low rod tip is also the proper position in which
   to fish out your cast and fight large salmon. The high
   rod of the dry-fly trout fisherman is taboo in salmon
   country. The higher the rod tip, the more difficult it is
   to initiate and elevate your back cast.
2. *You can only load the rod quickly by moving your hand*
   *increasingly faster (i.e., increasing the acceleration of*
   *your forearm); you can quickly unload the rod only by*
   *abruptly stopping your hand and forearm.* Action:
   Begin the pickup of up your cast slowly and increase
   the speed of your forearm until the fly leaves the
   water. Abruptly stop the back cast precisely at the
   moment the fly leaves the water and allow the rod to
   unload (recoil), projecting the line behind you. Your

---

2. Used by permission of Ed Jaworowski.

upper arm should remain relaxed and move as your forearm and elbow dictate. A short cast will require little upper arm movement. For a long cast, start your pick-up more slowly and use a longer arm action to increase the velocity of your back cast. The maximum loading or bending of the rod occurs only when the acceleration of your casting hand (and forearm) is ever increasing. The minute your hand starts to decelerate, the loop in your cast widens and your line sags.

The forward cast is the reverse of the back cast. Allow the line to *almost* straighten behind you. Start your forward cast slowly just before your line fully straightens and then accelerate rapidly. Stop your forward motion abruptly, and the line will unfurl before you in a tight loop. Joan Wulff calls this the power snap, "the thrust-to-a-stop ending of the acceleration" (56). If you wait until the line completely straightens before starting the forward cast, the line literally stops moving and starts to fall.

One of the better descriptions of this facet of casting is presented in the revised edition of Charles Ritz's book (46). In his later years, Ritz developed what he and others refer to as the high-line-speed concept of casting. High line speed can only be achieved by rapid acceleration during your casting motion. Ritz describes the casting motion as akin to wielding a heavy hammer. You start moving your forearm slowly, increasing the velocity of the hammer until the motion stops abruptly when the hammer strikes the nail.

3. *The direction of the line is determined by the direction the tip is moving when the rod straightens.* Action: Move the tip of your rod in the direction you want your cast to go at the very instant your rod straightens. Regardless of the direction of your back cast, the forward cast must follow in the direction that the tip is traveling at the time the cast straightens. This corollary may be Jaworowski's

greatest contribution to casting theory. If you have any doubts about this, you should see Ed make a hook cast. Ed can place a fly behind a rock or around either end of your canoe by merely moving the tip of his rod in the desired direction as the cast straightens. Few of us are so accomplished.

4.  *You can make casts easier only by lengthening the stroke of your cast.* Action: For greater distance or with heavier flies or in high wind, lengthen your casting stroke. When you need extra momentum, use more arm motion; do not try to overpower your cast. A longer stroke gives you more time to accelerate, which yields a higher line speed without requiring more "arm power." Try it; it really does work.

Throughout this introduction, I have emphasized that proper casting is a forearm movement, not a wrist motion. Your wrist should remain relatively straight throughout the casting stroke. If you concentrate on hand movement instead of a forearm movement, invariably you will start casting with wrist movement that severely limits your power and your control.

It should be clear that the purpose of this introduction is not to teach fly casting in two easy pages. Hopefully, it will alert the beginning angler to the principles of efficient fly casting and thus assist his selection of the proper fly rod.

### Fly-Rod Fundamentals

The modern graphite fly rod is a technological wonder. It is strong, resilient, and energy efficient, and it enables all of us to cast far better than with the bamboo of our grandfathers or the fiberglass of our fathers. The secret lies in the stiffness of the graphite fibers from which the rods are made. Modern graphite fibers used for rod building have a stiffness factor, or modulus of elasticity, ranging from 33 million to more than 51 million pounds per square inch (psi). The lower modulus graphite

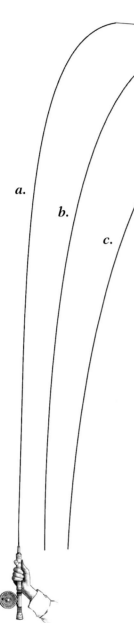

*Figure 2-1. Casting action for three rod profiles: (a) extra-fast action (tip flex), (b) fast action (mid-flex), (c) moderate action (full flex).*

is used primarily in lightweight trout rods. In general, intermediate- and high-modulus graphite are used in stiffer rods and for casting heavier lines. However, there is no relation between the modulus of the graphite and the quality or price of a rod. In fact, there is no direct relation between the modulus of the graphite fibers and that of the finished rod. The manufacturing methods and the adhesive resins used may result in a higher modulus in the finished rod using 33 million psi graphite than in a rod made from 51 million psi graphite. Different graphite products produce rods for differing uses.

The art of manufacturing a graphite rod lies in the design of the bending or flexing profile. Do you want fast tip action for casting or a more gradual taper better adapted for fighting large fish? Virtually all of the advances in the last half-dozen years have resulted from better design profiles. Most of the large manufacturers produce rods of three flexibilities or casting profiles, as shown in Figure 2-1. The casting action of these profiles is generally referred to as extra-fast (tip flex), fast (mid-flex), and moderate (full flex) respectively. No one, it seems, wants to admit to slow casting actions.

Rods with full-flex profiles are frequently manufactured from low-modulus (33 million psi) graphite. Most such rods are too soft for the efficient casting of the heavier lines used for salmon, although playing a small salmon or grilse on such a rod is great fun. The majority of salmon rods today are manufactured from medium-modulus (42 million psi) graphite, such as the well-known IM-6 graphite, which offers an excellent balance between casting and fighting actions. Rods of this type are recommended for all but the truly accomplished fly caster. A few of the newer single-handed rods, such as the Loomis GLX and the Sage SP series, use high modulus (51 million psi) graphite. This produces a relatively stiff rod with a very fast tip that is not well suited for the average angler.

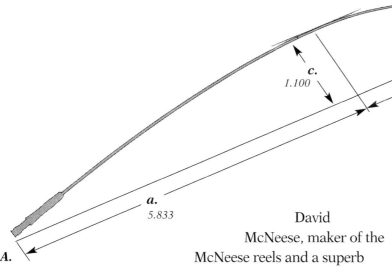

*Figure 2-2. The Orvis Flex
Diagram. (Courtesy of The
Orvis Co.)*

*(a) represents that portion of
the rod that increases in slope
to a maximum point along
the rod length.*

*(b) represents that portion of
the rod that decreases in slope
from the flex point to the tip
of the rod.*

*(c) represents the apex of the
curve or the highest point
drawn perpendicular from the
base line (a and b) to the
curve's apex. This point is
known as the Flex Point.*

***a/b** = the flex indicator, which
is the number used to
establish our Flex Indicator
Number.*

***Flex Index** = (1.781-1.0) x 10
= 7.81 rounded to the nearest
.5. This rod would be an 8.0
Mid-Flex Rod.*

David
McNeese, maker of the
McNeese reels and a superb
caster in his own right, has described these ultra-fast
rods as suitable only for those who can cast a full 30-yard fly
line in a wind. David can do just that.

One of the most perplexing problems for anglers is
how to compare rods of differing flexibilities and how to
select from among rods of different manufacturers. Until
recently there has been no basis for comparison. Each
manufacturer subjectively classifies its rods according to
its own deflection profiles that define how a given line will
cast when the rods straighten. The subjective nature of
such testing has led to widely differing interpretations of
flexibility among the various manufacturers.

In the fall of 1997, as the result of a multi-year study,
Orvis introduced a new rod-rating system that suggested
the obvious: we should rate rod flexibility according to
how far down from the tip the rod flexes. If a rod is flexed
as shown in Figure 2-2, the apex of the deflection curve
determines the flex point.[3] Orvis defines the flex point as
"the apex of the curve or the highest point drawn
perpendicular from the baseline AB to the curve's apex."
Perhaps a more exacting definition would be the tangent
of the curve as determined by a line parallel to the
baseline AB.

---

3. Orvis measures the flex index parameters by mounting the rod at a 30-degree incline, secured only at the
handle. The rod tip is loaded with weights until the handle/tip line A-B is horizontal, from which the distances a,
b, and c are measured and the apex tangent is determined.

The flex index is defined by the ratio of lengths **a** to **b**, and is calculated as:

$$\text{Flex Index, F.I.} = 10\,(a/b - 1)\ \text{or}$$
$$\text{F.I.} = 10\,(5.833/3.274 - 1) = 7.81$$

In the example shown, the flex index is 7.81 rounded to the nearest 0.5, or 8.0, a mid-flex rod by Orvis standards. Orvis defines tip flex as having flex indices from 9.5 to 12.5, mid-flex from 6.0 to 9.0, and full flex from 2.5 to 5.5. While Orvis is careful to avoid the traditional *tip, mid,* and *butt* nomenclature, these flex categories correspond to extra-fast, fast, and moderate actions, respectively.

The dimension **c** shown in Figure 2-2 has no meaning with regard to calculating the flex index but is meaningful regarding rod stiffness. The flex point corresponds to the basic or first vibration node of the rod. The distance ratio **c/b** is a measure of the rod stiffness; the smaller the ratio, the stiffer the rod. It might appear that the next step in rating rods would be to develop a stiffness index based on the **c/b** ratio.

The Orvis flex index provides the angler with the means to compare rods of different flexibilities irrespective of manufacture. It does not, however, define for the angler which fly line is best suited to his use. That subjective determination must be left to each fisher individually.

Anglers generally think of the rod profile only in terms of its casting qualities. They fail to recognize the significance of the profile in determining the rod's fish-fighting qualities. Visualize a fly rod as comprising three sections, as shown in Figure 2-3 (p. 26): the top one-third to one-half of the rod is the casting segment, the middle half is the fighting segment, and the lower 12 to 18 inches is the handle segment.

The difference between fast-, moderate-, and slow-action rods is determined by how far down into the midsection the rod bends during the cast. The top third or half of your rod, the portion that easily flexes, determines the casting action. The upper half of the rod so predominates in casting that many instructors recommend that you practice casting using only the upper half of the rod until you have mastered the timing of the cast. Again Ritz's insight of 40 years ago is incisive: "This method [using only the upper half of the rod] has the advantage of preventing a beginner from using the rod as a whip. It is almost impossible to whip the line when casting with a rod tip [because] the casting arm reaches upwards to compensate for the missing butt section" (46). The reason this half-rod technique is so effective is that it forces you to use your forearm instead of your wrist.

You cannot fight a strong fish well with a flexible, relatively weak tip section. That's why you must fight large fish with a low rod in order to utilize the middle portion of the rod. You simply cannot apply sufficient force to fight a large salmon with a high rod as does the trout fisherman. Try this simple experiment. Strip out 2 or 3 feet of line from the tip of an 8- or 9-weight rod and lock the drag so the line cannot slip. Attach a 1/2-pound weight to the end of the line, hold your rod horizontally, and attempt to lift the weight. Are you surprised by how much the rod bends? Now attach a 1-pound weight and again lift your rod. (*Caution*: Do not attempt this with a 5-weight or lighter rod; it might break.) The bend represents the force of fighting a fish with 1 pound of force. But we use 8- and 12-pound leaders so we can fight with more force. The only way you can apply 2 or 3 pounds of force without bending double (and thus breaking) most rods is to hold your rod in such a position that the tip does not bend excessively. Clearly, this cannot be done by lifting your rod tip high.

To understand how to best use the midsection of your rod for fighting fish, tie the end of your line or leader to a small scale. With your line straight, pull on the rod handle until the scale registers 2 pounds. Keep the tip of the rod pointed at the scale and slowly rotate the rod handle *horizontally* while maintaining 2 pounds of force. Note

*Figure 2-3a & b. The action segments of the fly rod: (a) casting, fighting, and handle segments and (b) the casting action utilizing the tip segment.*

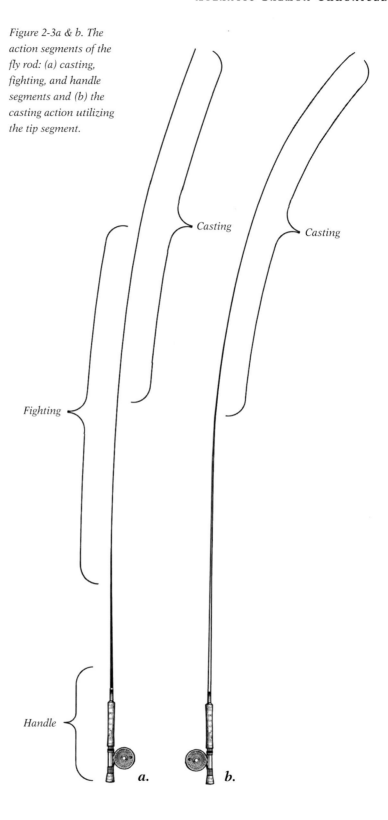

Casting

Casting

Fighting

Handle

*a.*　　*b.*

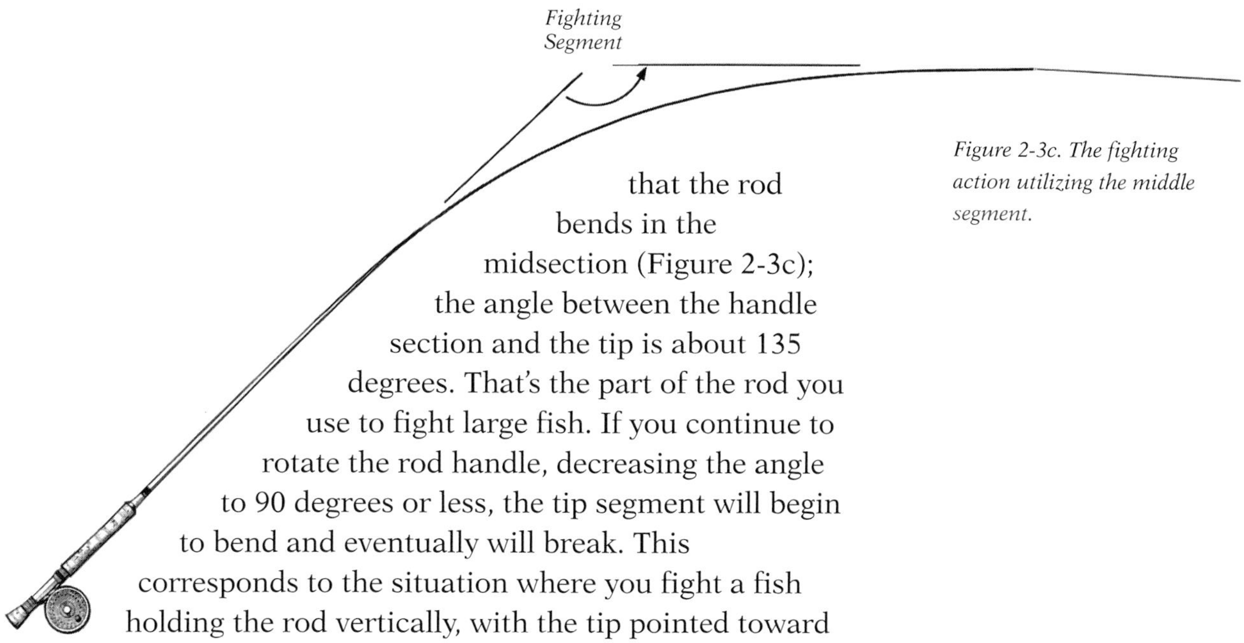

*Fighting
Segment*

*Figure 2-3c. The fighting
action utilizing the middle
segment.*

that the rod bends in the midsection (Figure 2-3c); the angle between the handle section and the tip is about 135 degrees. That's the part of the rod you use to fight large fish. If you continue to rotate the rod handle, decreasing the angle to 90 degrees or less, the tip segment will begin to bend and eventually will break. This corresponds to the situation where you fight a fish holding the rod vertically, with the tip pointed toward the water.

Designing a rod profile for a particular casting action is not difficult, but reducing the design to practice is artful. After a profile has been defined, it is necessary to grind a hardened-steel mandrel whose shape is the inside contour of each rod segment, including the ferrule if the rod has integral or swelled ferrules, as those used by Loomis and Orvis. Scott and Winston, on the other hand, use internal spigot ferrules that are fitted and assembled after the rod blank has been cured.

The typical manufacturing process is rather simple. A tapered section of graphite fiber material (called a *flag*), approximately 0.010 inch thick and impregnated with a tacky one- or B-stage epoxy adhesive, is cut from a large roll of material. Typically, the material is 90-percent graphite, whose fiber runs lengthwise, and 10-percent fiberglass scrim, whose fiber runs across the grain, perpendicular to the graphite. The fiberglass (or sometimes graphite) scrim serves to hold the graphite in place and provide hoop strength in the finished rod section. The type of epoxy resin used and its curing properties are as important as the graphite, since resin composes about 40 percent of the total material.

The edge of the flag is aligned along the stainless-steel mandrel, and the graphite flag is then rolled, under pressure, around the mandrel to produce an uncured rod section. Depending on the rod, the section may contain five to eight layers of graphite cloth in a butt section, two to five layers in a tip. The rod sections are then tightly wrapped with cellophane tape (rod makers formerly used string) and hung in a temperature-controlled oven at 250°F for two hours, during which time the graphite cloth is fused with the epoxy resin. The sections are then removed from the oven, the mandrel withdrawn, the tape removed, and the ends trimmed. The fishing quality of the rod has been defined at this stage. Now the blanks are ready to be finished, which includes sanding them to remove tape or string marks (some blanks are purposely left unsanded), painting them with a two-part epoxy coating, and attaching the fittings. An excellent pictorial review of the manufacturing process is presented in L.A. Garcia's book, *Handcrafting a Graphite Rod* (19).

The real cost of a rod is in its design, development, and marketing. The actual production costs are minimal. Strange as it may seem, it is the fitting and finishing of the rod blanks that determine the price of the finished rods. And therein lies one of the problems with the marketing of fly-fishing equipment today. The past decade has seen a tremendous growth in the popularity of fly fishing. Increasing demand has led manufacturers to develop new and greatly improved products, but the economies of scale have not been passed along to the customer. Annual price increases have been routine to the point that many anglers cannot afford the premium rods, many of which are now priced from $500 to $700. Dare I whisper, "Overpriced, sometimes grossly so"?

As this is written, we are witnessing a leveling off of the rapid growth that fly fishing has seen in the last decade. Some are even predicting no growth or a modest decline in the immediate future. For the first time in a decade, the major manufacturers are becoming value-conscious, and many are offering less expensive grades of rods, often at half the price of the premium rods, in order to compete with the large number of new manufacturers whose rod prices are generally less than $200. The problem for the angler is how to choose among the superabundance of rods of varying price ranges. The answer lies in differentiating between price and quality.

Not all manufacturers design separate profiles for first- and second-line rods, and indeed there is no reason to do so, although some use different graphite materials or a prior year's profile. The answer for some of the large rod companies has been to ship unfinished rod blanks to Korea or Taiwan for fitting and finishing. The finished rods are returned to the United States and sold as second grade or offered to resellers under private labels. In casting quality, such rods may be identical to the premium models; however, the fittings and finish are seldom of top quality.

### Rod Components and Finish

The perceived quality of a rod is defined by the components used and the finish applied to the rod. If all rod manufacturers used the components best suited for their intended purpose, there would be no story. But they do not. A couple of years ago, I won a premium fly rod in a Trout Unlimited raffle. Since it is one of the finest casting rods I have ever used, I don't mind identifying it as a Winston three-piece model LT 9 foot for a 7-weight line. It handles either a 7- or 8-weight line magnificently. But it has, in my opinion, some of the least appropriate fittings I have seen on any rod priced at more than $400, to say nothing of a brilliant green color whose reflection is guaranteed to alarm fish. I use it as an example because it is such a fine fishing tool in spite of its shortcomings.

The fitting of a rod involves the following components:

A.  the reel seat and, if desired, a fighting butt
B.  the cork grip
C.  the stripping guides, line guides, and the tip guide

Let's examine the various components with a view toward discriminating between appropriate and less satisfactory fittings.

The handle is the operating mechanism of your rod. Its design is far more important than most anglers realize. Figure 2-4 illustrates four handle sections similar in design but differing in detail and dimensions. The top handle is from my Winston LT rod, the second is from an Orvis HLS rod, while the third and fourth handles were installed by the author on Sage RPL+ and Thomas & Thomas blanks, respectively. The Sage blank has a 1 1/2-inch fighting butt permanently attached. The others are shown with their detachable butts.

Consider first the reel seats. The Winston reel seat with a detachable fighting butt is, in my opinion, simply inadequate. It has only a single locking ring, loosely fitted over coarse locking threads (10/inch), which is easily lost if the fighting butt is removed. The Orvis reel seat also contains a single locking ring, but it is more tightly fitted over fine threads (16/inch) and holds the reel more securely. Perhaps the *best* freshwater reel seat on the market is that shown on the Sage blank. It is a model A8L2 seat manufactured by Pacific Bay (113) of machined aluminum. [NOTE: Citations 101–119 in parentheses refer to the Referenced Trade List in the back of the book.] It is 4 inches long with two locking rings, each of which contains a rubber O-ring embedded within, and is available in three colors. The double rings ensure that the reel will not loosen on the seat; the O-rings prevent accidental back-off of the rings, something sorely needed on the Winston rod. The extra length of the up-locking reel seat aids in keeping the rod away from your body when you're using a fighting butt. Priced at about $15, one-third that of comparable seats, it is among the least expensive reel seats available.

A small fighting butt is desirable should you need to rest your rod at your waist during a long fight. If the fighting butt is there, you will use it more than you might imagine. The size and shape are up to you or your rod

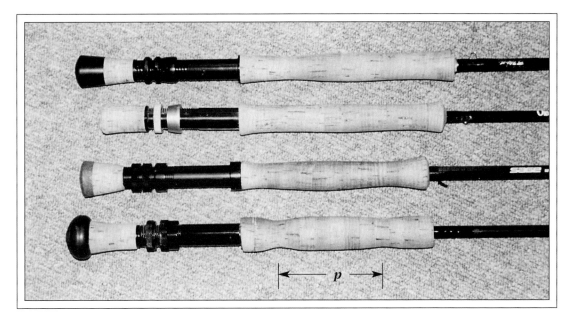

maker. I prefer a butt l to 1 1/2 inches long permanently attached to my rod, as shown on the Sage blank in Figure 2-4. A permanent butt is never in the way and can't get lost. If you buy a rod with a separate butt, examine the rod case. Some manufacturers supply rod cases that will not hold the rod with the fighting butt attached. That's a sure invitation to a lost butt.

The design and shape of the cork grip are very important. Cork grips are designed to fit everyone and, as a result, often fit no one. The common feature of all the grips shown in Figure 2-4 is a large cork upper ring about 1 1/8 inches in diameter, against which you press your thumb in casting. The dainty grip with extended forefinger has no place on the salmon stream. A full Wells grip, 7 1/2 inches long and containing fifteen 1/2-inch cork rings, is shown on the Winston rod. The problem I find with all grips of this type is that the portion actually held by your hand, dimension "p" in Figure 2-4, is too long for most people. On most such grips the "p" dimension is 4 1/4 to 4 1/2 inches. Try enclosing a 4 1/4-inch banana within your hand; you can't do it. The result is that most people shift their hand back and forth on the grip as they cast. If the "p" dimension is shortened from 4 1/4 inches, as on the Winston and Orvis rods, to about 3 1/2 inches,

*Figure 2-4. Four rod handles. Top to bottom: Winston LT, Orvis HLS, Sage RPL+ blank fitted with Pacific Bay A8L2 reel seat, and Thomas & Thomas blank fitted with grip with "p" dimension of 3 1/2 inches.*

as shown on the Thomas & Thomas rod in Figure 2-4, and the heel indentation is of smaller diameter than the thumb indentation, you alleviate the tendency to shift your hand. It took me some years to sort this out. Finally, I realized that when the grip fits your hand properly, you obtain full control and proper leverage from your hand to your rod. Improperly fitted grips do not allow you to exert leverage over the entire rod grip. To demonstrate this, I removed the old grip from the Thomas & Thomas blank and installed a new, shorter, and somewhat fatter one as an experiment. I now find it near perfect, particularly when used with a progressive reel foot that places the reel up under the cork grip (see Chapter 3). More recently I have noted that the "p" dimension on the new Winston BL5 series of saltwater rods is about 3 3/4 inches. That's a tremendous improvement by Winston; it makes the grip much easier to hold.

Fly rod handles should be gripped lightly, even when you are casting, to prevent vibration and shock waves in your cast. The slightly fatter grip that I installed on the Thomas & Thomas blank enables me to hold the grip securely but loosely. Recently Orvis has developed a new and controversial approach to minimizing rod vibrations: the damped rod grip. The portion of the rod butt inside the grip is covered with an elastomeric sleeve before the rod butt is inserted into the cork grip. Floating on an elastomeric core, the grip is said not to transmit the low-frequency casting vibrations from your hand to the rod. Technical vibrational analysis indicates that the concept works, but the industry is very suspicious of such new ideas, and the extent to which this concept will be validated by the industry remains to be seen.

Many people like a fly keeper inserted at the top of the cork grip. For a custom-built rod I recommend either the folding fly keeper or the newer slip-on design, both by Fuji. The folding keeper is advantageous in that it stays out of the way until you need it.

One thing the salmon angler, indeed any angler, does not need is an upper or fore grip, as is sometimes seen on saltwater fly rods. It serves no useful purpose and is nothing but a marketing gimmick. The idea of a fore grip is attributed to Stu Apte, who designed it to reduce the effective rod length and thus increase the leverage for lifting giant fish from the deep. But a fore grip shortens the fighting segment of your rod. That's exactly what the salmon angler does not want.

Most rods have two or three stripping guides between the handle and the line guides. They serve to funnel line smoothly to the line guides during your cast or when the fish is running. The stripping guides take much wear, and the material from which the rings are manufactured should be very hard. The best ring guides are those plated with titanium nitride. Titanium nitride is one of the hardest materials known and resists the grooving that will fray and eventually destroy your fly line. However, large titanium nitride stripping guides are new to the industry and currently extremely expensive. The silicon carbide stripping guides used by most rod manufacturers are satisfactory. You should avoid the softer aluminum oxide or titanium oxide guides. Many factory rods use stripping guides that are too small to be effective. Large stripping guides are advantageous in reducing the angle between the line and your stripping hand and hence reduce the stripping friction. Do not use stripping guides smaller than number 16 with an inner diameter (ID) of about 10.9mm. The stripping guide just ahead of your rod handle should be a number 20 with an ID of about 13.3mm. Even a number 25 guide with an ID of 17.4mm is not too large if the rod is intended for saltwater use. Unfortunately, some manufacturers resist the cost of the larger guides and seem to feel that the smaller guides, like those used on trout rods, are more attractive to the average angler.

The proper number, size, and spacing of the upper line guides are essential to ensure a smooth flow of line. On many salmon rods, the line guides, whether of snake or single-footed design, are also too small. That's a problem with my Winston rod, whose guides are among the smallest in the industry—a fact that one authority attributes to Winston's bamboo lineage. The snake guides on the tip section of my Winston rod have IDs that range from 0.215 to 0.25 inch, whereas a more appropriate range would be 0.27 to 0.30 inch.[4] That may seem like a small difference, but it's very meaningful in improving the flow of your line.

The choice of material for the tip guide is very important because the tip is subject to great friction as the line and backing pass back and forth through the tip. Most rods are fitted with chromium-plated tips, which are adequate for the casual angler. Serious anglers, especially those using the new gel-spun polyethylene (GSP) backings that are more abrasive than Dacron or Micron (see Chapter 4), should replace the tip on any new rod with a large loop tip (0.30 inch ID) plated with titanium nitride, such as the Tigold tips sold by Pacific Bay. At this time, only two rod manufacturers offer titanium nitride guides as standard equipment on their premium rods.

Your rod's worst enemies are nicks and cuts, which eventually lead to fracturing of the graphite and rod failure. The epoxy coating applied to the rod by virtually all manufacturers except Loomis helps to protect the rod from nicks and scratches, as well as hiding cosmetic imperfections in the cured rod sections. I am a firm believer that the rod finish should not be so brilliant as to announce your presence to all the fish. Prior to assembling a rod for themselves, knowledgeable anglers frequently remove the sheen from a coated rod blank with fine emery cloth.

Having reviewed the options available, how do you avail yourself of quality fittings? There are two solutions: purchase a factory-finished rod fitted with acceptable components or purchase a rod blank and either assemble it yourself or have it assembled by a qualified artisan. We shall examine both routes.

The largest, best-known rod manufacturers include

---

4. These inner diameters correspond approximately to snake-guide Nos. 4 and 5. However, the exact dimensions differ according to manufacturer. You should ascertain the actual dimensions before you order any guides.

Loomis, Orvis, Sage, Scott, Thomas & Thomas, and Winston, all of which offer rods selling upwards of $500. Reflecting the trends in the marketplace, all of these companies also offer a second, less expensive line of rods, sometimes manufactured from the same blanks as the premium rods. All of these companies produce some excellent rods, but not all rods from a given manufacturer perform equally well. I urge you not to be swayed by testimonials from fly-fishing professionals or guides who are compensated to promote a manufacturer's product. I own rods from each of the above companies. Some are excellent; some are not well designed and are unsatisfactory.

In recent years, as the fly-fishing market has matured, a number of new companies have entered the rod market with rods that cost less than half the price of the premium rods of the major manufacturers. Some of these rods are outstanding, offer exceptional value, and present an excellent choice for the beginning salmon angler. Modest-priced rods are available from Fenwick, Penn, Pfleuger, Redington, St. Croix, and Versitex, among others. Rods in this price category are also available from major sporting companies such as L.L. Bean, Cabela's, and Bass Pro Shops. Many of the rods from this group, but again not all, are fully equivalent to the higher-priced models.

Whatever price category you select, never, never buy a rod without first having cast it. If you decide to purchase a factory-assembled rod, I recommend that you first borrow three or four rods from your friends, take them to a casting pond, and try casting with each of them. Here's the catch: You should try each rod with at least three different fly lines, since, as we shall see, fly lines differ as much as do fly rods. Each rod should be cast with a weight-forward line of the recommended weight, as well as with lines one weight heavier and one weight lighter. The modern graphite rod easily handles such a range of line weights, particularly when you adjust the length and velocity of your cast. In addition, you should try each rod with at least two different weight-forward lines of the rated weight, since the length of the rear taper of the fly line may affect your casting every bit as much as a change in line weight. Four rods with four lines each; yes, you will have a busy but very satisfying afternoon at the casting pond.

Enter the custom rod. The price difference between a factory-finished rod and a rod blank is so large that there is merit in having a rod assembled to your specifications or assembling the rod yourself. Consider a premium rod whose retail price is $500. You can buy the blank from which that rod was finished for about $200. You may also purchase a blank for one of the modest-priced rods mentioned above for about 40 percent of the price of the rod itself. If you are inclined to tinker or have a friend who does, you may have a rod assembled to your specifications, often at a considerable savings.

The opportunity to offer custom rods finished to your specifications has created a whole new industry, custom rod assembly. *Black's 2000 Fly Fishing* guide (08) lists 99 custom rod builders, many of who assemble graphite rods upon request. Among the large companies, Orvis has taken the lead in offering to assemble to your specifications a rod built on any of its premium blanks, at prices only marginally higher than its standard rods. It's a fine way to obtain a premium rod fitted to your needs. Other custom purveyors such as The Saltwater Angler (116) have adopted a similar approach for rods built on Loomis, Sage, and other blanks. Most locales have well-qualified artisans who specialize in finishing rod blanks to your specifications. Many advertise their skills in local fishing publications; a few occupy booths at fly-fishing shows. Your local fly shop can generally recommend a local craftsman who is skilled in such crafts. If you do choose this route, the best sources of information on components are the catalogs by Angler's Workshop (101), Dale Clements Custom Tackle (104), and Pacific Bay (114). Excellent how-to-do-it books on building fly rods are offered by the Flex Coat Company (49, 106) and L.A.

Garcia (19). The latter offers step-by-step instructions for assembling graphite rods.

Two caveats about custom rod assembly: inexperienced craftsmen can damage a rod blank by applying excessive thread pressure while wrapping guides, and occasionally they fail to properly secure the cork grip to the rod blank. But then I had the grip on one of my $500 factory rods work loose after only two weeks' use. Most premium rods and many of the less expensive ones now come with lifetime warranties against breakage for any reason. Some rod blanks do not carry any warranties. Choose carefully if this feature is important to you.

## Two-Handed Rods

In North America, unless specified otherwise, "fly rod" means the single-handed rod. In Europe, at least for salmon, it means a two-handed rod frequently 14 to 17 feet long. For many years, the egos of the North American anglers did not permit them to acknowledge the advantages of the two-handed rod, nor would the European fishers admit that single-handed rods had any role in "their" sport. What both sides failed to acknowledge was that one- and two-handed rods were invented to accommodate different geographies. By European standards, many North American salmon streams are small, somewhat flat, and relatively windless. By North American standards, many European rivers are broad, tumultuous, and windswept, but such generalizations only serve to fan the flames of controversy.

All this has now changed, and we are beginning to see numerous two-handed rods on the larger, windier rivers such as the Miramichi, the Restigouche, and the George in Quebec. The two-handed rod is of distinct advantage for long casts, for fishing in the wind, for mending casts in quirky currents, and for ease of casting for those with physical limitations and disabilities. It is the only viable option for Spey-type casting. My friend John D., an accomplished trout angler, was first introduced to salmon on the Restigouche River, for which

he chose a two-handed rod. After two days, he changed
back to his single-handed rod for a dozen casts. He laid
down the single-handed rod and returned to the two-
handed rod. Now he questions whether he will ever use a
single-handed rod for salmon again. "It's that much
easier," he declares emphatically.

The two-handed rod is frequently called a Spey rod,
named for the River Spey in Scotland, where the trees and
high embankments prevent back casts and where a type of
roll cast, the so-called Spey cast, is the norm. For
simplicity, we often adopt the Spey name in referring to
such rods, but we must recognize that the great majority
of such rods are used in North America only for overhead
casting, which requires a much stiffer action than for a
true Spey rod. The Spey rod has a softer, more limber
action that is better suited for roll casting. The softer
action also acts as a shock absorber (you don't have to
bow to a jumping salmon), is more forgiving, and makes
it much easier to play a salmon.

A 14- or 15-foot two-handed rod can be unwieldy on
a small stream and is unnecessarily long for simple
overhead casting. A shorter two-handed rod, 11 or 12 feet
long, is a joy to use on any stream, particularly in the
wind, and greatly lessens the physical fatigue of one-hand
casting. Overhead casting with a two-handed rod is
similar to casting with a single-handed rod. After each
cast is played out, you lengthen your line another 3 to 5
feet for a subsequent overhead cast. At the longer
distances, it may be necessary to strip in line before
repeating the cast, just as with a single-handed rod. The
difference is that the leverage generated by the longer
two-handed rod enables you to pick up a much greater
length of line from the water and to shoot a longer cast.
An accomplished angler using a 14- or 16-foot rod can
pick up 80 or more feet of line and can easily cast an
entire 150-foot Spey line, far more than the angler can
control. With such casting, however, you can cover a lot of
water before you need to move downstream and
reposition yourself for another series of casts.

Other than its ease of casting, perhaps the greatest advantage of the two-handed rod is its ability to achieve very high line speed that greatly aids in cutting the wind. For this reason, the shorter two-handed rods using 8- or 9-weight lines are most popular for overhead casting. They are the ideal solution for windswept rivers. If you need to convince yourself of the two-handed approach, try using your single-handed rod with two hands, one at the top of the grip and the second on the rod butt below the reel. Immediately you will notice how easy it is to achieve a high line speed with very limited arm movement. It's the ideal way to cast a single-handed rod in a heavy wind. Some even equip their single-handed rods with a 6-inch detachable fighting butt in order to better cast in the wind.

The principal advantage of the two-handed rod is that you have better control of the fly. As I discuss in Chapter 9, while fishing the single- and two-handed rods side by side in the same pool, I obtain about twice as many strikes on the two-handed rod. I am convinced that this is the result of better presentation of the fly with the two-handed rod and the enhanced control of the fly as it courses through the water.

For true Spey or roll casting, the distance that may be covered effectively with a two-handed rod is not greatly different than for the one-handed rod. Mike Maxwell, North America's premier proponent of the two-handed rod and proprietor of Gold-N-West Flyfishers of Vancouver, British Columbia (109), suggests that the effective range is from 20 to 70 feet for rods up to 14 feet long using 8- and 9-weight lines. Most Spey lines are rated for the equivalent of two or three line weights such as Rio's WWF7/8/9F Windcutter line. However, if presentation, not distance, is your primary objective, it is easier to make a Spey or roll cast with a 10/11-weight line than with a lighter line.

The longer 14- and 16-foot two-handed rods do play an important role on windswept rivers, such as those found in Iceland and Scandinavia. In a howling gale, nothing places your fly as well, and as easily, as a long rod. When fishing Iceland I always take both my 11- and 14-foot rods: the longer rod for the wind and the shorter rod for finesse in placing my fly.

I predict that the popularity of two-handed rods, particularly the shorter 11- and 12-foot rods, will increase dramatically in North America as anglers begin to appreciate the joy of casting with rods that are physically less demanding than are our traditional one-handed rods. For overhead casting, the shorter two-handed rods are ideally suited for even the largest of our North American rivers.

The two best sources of information on two-handed rods and the technique of Spey casting are the excellent books by Mike Maxwell (36) and the late Hugh Falkus (17). Maxwell of Gold-N-West and Jim Vincent of Rio Products International (109, 115) also offer instructional videos on Spey casting.

## PART II. FLY LINES

Sometimes I long for the good old days when our fly line options were size and sometimes color. Today, in addition to the all-purpose lines, we have lines designed for casting to specific species of fish, for casting delicacy, for distance, for power in the wind, for mending long casts, with tips of varying sink rates, for virtually any conditions that may be envisioned. For a given line weight, we must consider the front taper of the line, the length of the belly, the back taper, the profile and total length of the line head, the length and density of a sinking tip (if there is one), and even the buoyancy of the line itself. For fifteen line classes, of which only eight are truly significant, there are well over 1,500 lines from which to select. How does one choose?

Fortunately for the Atlantic salmon angler, the choices are restricted and the selection greatly simplified by the habits of our fish, which cause them to hold in relatively shallow water and to rise readily to take flies at or near the surface. Rarely, if ever, are we forced to cast to fish holding in more than 8 feet of water. When we do, special tactics and tackle must be adopted.

## TABLE 2-1

## AMERICAN FISHING TACKLE MANUFACTURERS ASSOCIATION
## FLY-LINE RATING STANDARDS
## (WEIGHT IN GRAINS)

| Line Weight | AFTMA Standard | Manufacturing Range |
|:---:|:---:|:---:|
| 1 | 60 | 54–66 |
| 2 | 80 | 74–86 |
| 3 | 100 | 94–106 |
| 4 | 120 | 114–126 |
| 5 | 140 | 134–146 |
| 6 | 160 | 152–168 |
| 7 | 185 | 177–193 |
| 8 | 210 | 202–218 |
| 9 | 240 | 230–250 |
| 10 | 280 | 270–290 |
| 11 | 330 | 318-342 |
| 12 | 380 | 368–392 |
| 13 | 450 | 435–465 |
| 14 | 500 | 485–515 |
| 15 | 550 | 535–565 |

Fly lines are defined by the weight of the first 30 feet of line exclusive of any short, level tip. The current weight-based rating system for fly lines shown in Table 2-1 was established in 1961 by the American Fly Tackle Manufacturers Association (AFTMA). There are no comparable standards for fly rods, although the new Orvis system described above may eventually lead to uniform flexibility and stiffness ratings among the different rod manufacturers.

With great hindsight, it is obvious that this rating system demonstrates a significant bias in favor of the trout fisherman, where 30 feet plus the leader length may represent a typical cast. For the salmon, steelhead, and saltwater flats fisherman, 30 feet is a short cast, and the rating system is inadequate in predicting the performance of a rod that is typically cast with 40 or 50 feet of line beyond the tip of the rod.

In recent years, rod manufacturers have recognized the obvious shortcomings of the AFTMA system as applied to the heavier line weights, particularly classes seven through eleven. The result has been a tendency for manufacturers to beef up their rods to better accommodate longer casts. Thus the typical 8-weight rod, instead of being designed to cast perfectly a 210-grain section of line, may actually be built to cast 275 grains, corresponding to the first 40 feet of an 8-weight line. The result is that the rod is designed for what, by definition, is a 275-grain *10*-weight line; the so-called 8-weight rod is underrated. In recent years, most graphite rods designed for 7- to 11-weight lines have been underrated to such an extent that knowledgeable anglers frequently use lines one size larger than that recommended by the rod manufacturer in order to fully utilize the power of the rod. Now you begin to see why, to achieve a balanced outfit, I have previously emphasized the need to try out rods with lines of different weights and differing tapers.

To correct the obvious deficiencies in the present rating system, Bruce Richards, chief line designer for Scientific Anglers, has proposed a length-compensated revision to the rating system that takes into consideration the longer average casting distance for the heavier lines. It is anticipated that this new line rating system will be adopted by the AFTMA within the next year.

Line construction affects your casting efficiency, since the weight distribution in a line depends upon its profile. The profile of a typical weight-forward line is represented by Figure 2-5. The line *head,* which constitutes the predominance of the weight to be cast, comprises the tip, the forward taper, the belly, and the rear taper. Special-purpose lines are developed primarily by adjusting the lengths of the belly and the forward and rear tapers.

*Figure 2-5. Profile of a weight-forward line: (a) tip, (b) forward taper, (c) belly, (d), rear taper, and (e) running line.*

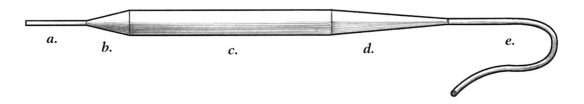

a.       b.            c.              d.              e.

*Figure 2-6. The casting action: (a) start of the cast, (b) unfurling of the line, (c) line slowing due to air resistance, and (d) line falling to the surface.*

The typical casting motion is represented by the four figures shown in Figure 2-6. As the angler casts his line (Figure 2-6a), he imparts momentum to the line. *You cast momentum*, which is defined as mass multiplied by velocity. For a given line mass, the initial velocity of the line is determined by the efficiency of the effort you put into your cast. Note that I avoid the word *energy*. We often work with the misconception that if you work harder and put more energy into your casting effort you can cast farther. That is the major fallacy of casting. On a 50-foot cast, almost all of us employ enough energy to throw a full 30-yard line! We use several times as much energy as is actually needed for the cast, but most of our effort is wasted in inefficient motion. The trick to becoming a good caster is to become efficient.

As the line unfurls during the cast (Figure 2-6b),

momentum is conserved. The velocity of the line that has unfurled remains constant relative to the rod tip. The velocity of the line yet to unfurl increases as the mass of the line yet to unfurl decreases. The energy carried by the line diminishes as it unfurls, primarily because of air resistance.

To make a good cast, you need to impart enough momentum to straighten the line. A line with a long front taper assists by reducing the mass at the end of the cast (Figure 2-6c), which, conserving momentum, increases the velocity of the unfurling line. This increases the air resistance, which dissipates the energy of the line more quickly and results in a delicate delivery of the fly as it falls to the surface of the water (Figure 2-6d). A short or blunt front taper has the opposite effect. Blunt tapers are particularly effective in conserving the momentum needed to cast into a strong wind or to turn over a very heavy fly.

The length of the line head affects casting and mending. Consider Figure 2-7, which illustrates the casting of three 8-weight lines, the first with a typical 36-foot head, the second with a 40-foot head, and the third with an extra-long head, say 65 feet. At 30 feet, all three lines will cast well. At 40 feet, the lines with the longer heads will cast better because the head of the line is in contact with the tip of the rod, which controls the cast. The line with the 36-foot head (Figure 2-7a) will not cast as well because the thin running line between the head and the tip of the rod will not impart sufficient momentum to the heavier head. The shorter head causes you to progressively lose casting control as the line extends beyond 36 feet because of the hinging effect between the thin running line at the tip of the rod and the heavier head beyond.

In this example, the 40-foot head is the optimum (Figure 2-7b). The 65-foot head will cast well at 40 feet (Figure 2-7c), but if you need to shoot additional line, that portion of the belly remaining in the guides is too heavy to pull additional line though the guides. In addition, its large size increases the friction in the guides, which further reduces your casting distance.

Lines with extra-long rear tapers are extremely useful

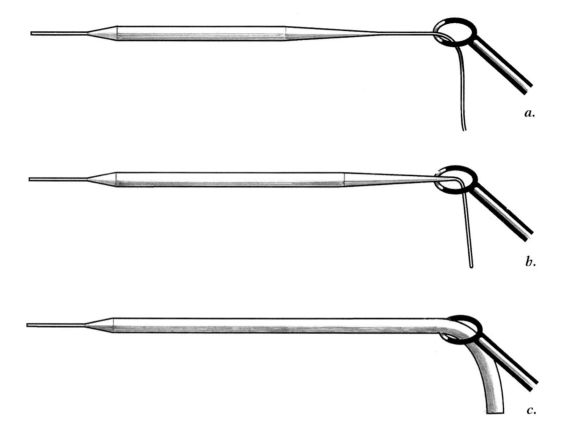

to the salmon angler who needs to mend his line on the water (see Chapter 9). Mending cannot be accomplished satisfactorily with the thin running line extending from the tip of the rod. You must have sufficient line mass to generate the momentum to mend. Figure 2-7c represents the situation using a line with an extra-long head that extends back through the tip and down to the reel. Clearly you maintain line control in such a situation, but as you cast more line, the casting mass increases and the line may feel too heavy for your rod. Logically, the solution would be to purchase a line one size lighter. But one size lighter than what—the rod-rated size or the pragmatic size used for short-distance casting?

The weight-forward floating line is the proper line for 98 percent of all salmon anglers, if they resist the temptation to use sinking tip lines. As discussed more fully in Chapter 6, short lead heads that may be looped to the tip of your floating line are a much better way to fish a

*Figure 2-7. Three weight-forward lines with different heads: (a) short head causes hinging, gives poor control; (b) optimum head in contact with tip, gives good control; (c) an extra-long head causes friction in guides, is difficult to shoot, and reduces casting distance.*

sunken fly. Few salmon anglers need anything but a
floating line. Mending the line to maintain the proper fly
speed in the current is an integral part of salmon fishing,
so lines with an extra-long rear taper are highly desirable.
Such lines are designated "long head" or "steelhead" lines
and usually have a rear taper of about 25 feet, with overall
head length of 65 feet.

For those who wish to pursue in more detail the
techniques of line design, casting behavior, and control, the
best—indeed the only—book on the subject is *Modern Fly
Lines* by Bruce Richards (45), issued as a volume of *Lefty's
Little Library*. Richards also discusses the construction,
physical parameters, and selection of fly lines.

No discussion of lines is complete without the
controversial question of color. Many trout fishermen are
adamant about the necessity for dull-colored lines. New
Zealand guides are famous for their predilection for dull
lines. With that in mind, on my first trip to New Zealand,
I dutifully dyed the ends of my lines a muddy olive gray
only to find the guides, at least those on the Tongariro
River, completely indifferent to the color of the line. For
salmon fishermen, the answer is simple. The salmon don't
care either. Choose whatever color of line pleases you. I
prefer light orange or white—something that contrasts
with the background, is easy to follow in the currents, and
is visible at dusk. One of my trout-fishing friends chooses
line colors based on his ability to see the line in the air.
For photography, a bright orange is best.

Finally, a word about fly-line care. The modern
PVC fly line is a minor manufacturing miracle that we
often take for granted. It casts extremely well, requires
minimal care, and usually lasts for years. PVC has a
hydrophobic surface, and a new line floats high on the
water. However, plasticizers and lubricating
compounds slowly leach from the line and form a film
on the surface that picks up dirt, destroys the
hydrophobic coating, and causes the line to float low in
the water or even to sink. You should clean a floating
line frequently to remove the dirt film and restore its

floating properties. Commercial line cleaners are fine, but Armor All, designed for cleaning PVC automotive fabrics, is even better. A few cleansing tissues and a small cake of hand soap will do the trick and are always readily available. Do not, however, use strong detergents that may attack the surface of your line. A clean line casts better because of reduced friction with the line guides.

## LAST CASTS: A RECOMMENDATION

Alas, as we have seen, there is much more to selecting a balanced fly-casting outfit than asking for someone's recommendation. For some, working their way through the plethora of options is part of the sport; for others, it's an annoying process that only interferes with their getting on the river.

There is, however, another view. Most of us, over a period of time, accumulate a great quantity of equipment, much of which is peripheral if not downright superfluous. I carry some 500 flies around the world with me and in a week of fishing use perhaps a dozen patterns. I have accumulated so many fly lines for my various rods that each spring I spend half a day sorting and sifting for the three that I really want for a specific river.

Throughout this book, I urge a simpler, more restrained approach to salmon tackle. Start with one rod, one reel, one floating line equipped with a couple of lead heads (see Chapter 6), and two dozen flies. You will have plenty of time later to contemplate the many temptations ahead. I am convinced that all of us would benefit, and enjoy our salmon angling more, if we concentrated on the art of presenting our fly to the fish. Why else do we stand in cold water for four hours at a stretch to cast 400 times, hoping to hook one fish?

The beginning salmon angler would do well to start his salmon adventures by procuring a single-handed, modestly priced rod. For around $200, you can buy rods offered by Redington, St. Croix, Versitex, or perhaps one of the second-line rods by one of the major companies. Use that rod for your first two seasons and give no thought to replacing it until you have landed five salmon. I strongly recommend a four- or five-piece rod, 9 feet long for an 8- or 9-weight line. Modern three-, four-, and five-piece rods cast every bit as well as do two-piece rods.[5] Never again will I buy a two-piece rod, and I urge you to think likewise. Two-piece rods are difficult to transport by any means and a liability when you are traveling by air. Three-, four-, and five-piece rods may be carried aboard most airplanes, so you do not risk lost or stolen equipment.

The conventional carry-on case usually holds three rods and comes equipped with a variety of outer pockets for reels and other equipment. Thirty-one-inch cases will not accommodate four-piece 9 1/2-foot rods. A 38-inch case is a better choice, since it will also accommodate three-piece 9-foot rods. However, prior to purchasing any carry-on case, check the latest airline regulations. There is presently a move afoot by the airlines to strictly enforce the regulations that prevent any carry-on luggage from exceeding 22 inches in length. Only five-piece rods would be permitted under the proposed restrictions.

A new concept is the Genesis case manufactured by Boulder Landing Rod Cases. This case is manufactured of extruded PVC tubing and is lined with foam to cushion interior vibration. An attractive feature of this case is that it is fitted with movable foam cradles and can hold three or four rods. If the cradles are properly spaced, one such case can accommodate both one- and two-handed rods. While these cases are too long to be carried in the cabin of an aircraft, they provide security for your checked luggage.

Assuming it balances with your chosen rod, your first fly line should be a WF8F (or WF9F) long-head or steelhead-type line. The 25-foot rear taper will make the

---

5. Very recently, five-piece rods have been introduced by Winston and subsequently by Sage that may revolutionize the market. Much more convenient to carry than three-piece rods, the five-piece rods avoid the mid-rod ferrule, which is the weak spot in some two- and four-piece rod construction.

line easier to mend, and the extra weight of the rear taper will help to compensate for the inevitable underrating of the rod. Since most neophyte fishermen are not adept at long casts, this line may be nearly ideal for you. As your casting ability improves, you may then consider adding a standard head WF9F for windy conditions or a long-head WF7F steelhead line that, when cast with a high line speed, will not overload the rod on long casts. In essence, the latter line gives you the best of both situations but is desirable only if you are comfortable delivering high-velocity casts. Be cautious in selecting long-head lines; choose only those with long rear tapers. A 35-foot belly is of limited use if accompanied by only a 3-foot rear taper.

I cannot stress too strongly the need to ascertain periodically that your fly line is balanced to your rod's action and your casting style. It is the key to successful casting, a necessity for proper fly presentation, and essential for inducing the salmon to strike. As an accomplished angler, I still spend more time selecting, testing, and balancing lines than I spend on any other facet of my equipment. Sometimes it's fun, sometimes a chore, but always it's a productive use of my time.

Now it's time to think about reels.

*Twilight Salmon*
Oil on Board
14 x 20 inches
Private Collection

# Chapter 3

# All About Reels

Depending on your viewpoint, the modern fly reel is either a simple winch on which to wind your fishing line or a complex tool that stores your line, controls the rate at which it may be unwound from the spool, and enables you to play and land fish larger and stronger than previously believed possible. Fishermen today, particularly those who would fight with very light tackle or land very large fish, often eschew the simple pawl-and-check reel for something more sophisticated. Defining the degree of sophistication is the problem. Which features are functional and necessary, which may be desirable or optional, and which only constitute form and beauty?

There are two types of manually operated fly reels, direct-drive and anti-reverse. Direct-drive reels are those in which the handle rotates in both line-out and line-in modes. The spool rotates one or more turns for each revolution of the handle. If the spool rotates more than one turn per handle revolution, the reel is said to be a multiplier, the most common multiplying ratios being 1.7:1, 2:1, and 2.5:1. The demand for direct-drive, multiplying reels—such as the salmon reels by Bogdan and Godfrey—is very limited.

Anti-reverse reels are those in which the reel handle is disengaged while line is being withdrawn from the spool. Anti-reverse means that the handle does not rotate unless the line is being retrieved. It is not synonymous with the friction-coupled drags to be discussed subsequently. Until 1996, anti-reverse multiplier reels were available, primarily from Orvis. However, the demand for such reels was negligible, and they are no longer made.

## TYPES OF DRAGS

**PAWL AND GEAR CHECK.** This oldest type of "drag" consists of a pawl held by spring tension against a

*Figure 3-1. The Hardy Perfect Reel.*

gear on the reel spool (Figure 3-1). Upon rapid withdrawal of line, the pawl exerts tension on the gear, which prevents the line from overrunning the spool and creating a snarl or "bird's nest." The pawl check is not a drag per se but serves to retard a free-running spool. The development in America of the pawl "click reel" is attributed to Charles F. Orvis, whose Orvis Click Reel was first introduced in 1876. The drag on reels with pawl checks is properly applied to the face or rim of the spool by your thumb, fingers, or palm. It's a very simple, reliable, and foolproof system. One limitation of such reels is that it is not possible to apply even drag pressure with your fingers or palm. Invariably, the finger pressure will fluctuate, creating a pulsing resistance that the fish may feel. With small fish it doesn't matter. With large anadromous fish it may be the signal to fight on.

**DRUM DRAGS**. Drum drags are derived from the Silent Check first introduced on the Hardy Perfect Reels in 1908. In 1920, Hardy expanded the concept to incorporate in its Saint George reels a Silent Check drag much like the external drum drag described below, except that the drag arm pressed directly against the spool and did not employ a separate clutch plate.

There are two types of drum drags in current use—those operating on a clutch plate external to the reel spool, much in the manner of automotive drum brakes; and the newer, internal drag operating inside a clutch drum, which is centered inside the spool. The best known example of the external drum drag is that used in the Pfleuger Medalist reel and its numerous copies (Figure 3-2). As the line plays out, the clutch plate turns with the spool, thus engaging the drag. The drag arm(s) encircles the clutch plate, and pressure is applied to the arm by adjusting the tension spring. Using modern materials, this design is very reliable. The primary disadvantage of the external drum drag is that, if the drag surfaces are not perfectly mated, it is subject to excessive start-up drag. However, several expensive, handmade reels use this type of drag, including the Bogdan reels, those by Ballan and Godfrey, and the new Governor reels.

The internal drum drag in the Ryall and Ross (Gunnison) reels utilizes a split piston that expands to apply force to the clutch drum. The Ryall system is illustrated in Figure 3-3. As the drag knob is turned, the tapered pin is forced into a split piston, which applies pressure to the inside of the clutch drum, thus increasing the drag. One of the advantages of this drag is that it is easy to seal the drag surface from exposure to dirt and water.

**CALIPER DRAGS.** Caliper drags operate much like an automotive caliper brake to apply pressure to one or both sides of a clutch plate. The Scientific Anglers System

*Figure 3-2. The Olympic reel, one of numerous copies of the Pfleuger Medalist.*

2 reels use pressure pads on both sides of the clutch plate
(Figure 3-4); the Lamson reels use one or two small
pressure pads on one side of the clutch plate. Both drag
types are reliable, as long as the pressure pads are not
exposed to excess moisture.

An interesting aside about the Lamson reels: many
manufacturers have jumped aboard the recent disc-drag
mania, each bragging that their disc drag is in one way or
another superior to that of the competitors. At one point, the
Lamson reels were incorrectly advertised as having a disc
drag, only because the drag pad is in the shape of a circular
disc 1/4 inch in diameter, even though it doesn't operate in the
manner of a disc drag. While each Lamson drag pad has an

*Figure 3-3. The Ryall reel. In
the top photo, note the tapered
pin (indicated by the arrow)
on the stem of the drag knob.*

*Figure 3-4. The Scientific Anglers System 2 reel.*

area of only 0.05 square inch, it is a very dependable drag. One prominent fly shop in Red Bank, New Jersey, has reported selling hundreds of these reels for saltwater use without ever returning one reel to the factory for repairs.

**DISC DRAGS**. The disc drag is the most significant development in the last half century for fly reels. The origin of the disc drag is not well documented, but Ted Jurasik Sr., designer of the Billy Pate and Tibor reels, attributes the disc drag to the cork-faced clutch used during the 1920s in the early Ford automobiles. The concept of cork discs or washers was initially adapted for use in the larger sizes (Nos. 2 1/2, 3, and 4) of the Fin-Nor Big Game trolling reels during the late 1940s. In its simplest form, the drag is a ring of cork, polymer, or composite material fastened to one side of the clutch plate. Tension is applied by tightening a spring or torsion disc, which forces the drag disc and the spool face together. In line-out operation, the drag disc typically bears against the back face of the rotating spool or against the back side of the frame, as in the Orvis Odyssey (Figure 3-5) and Precision reels. With line-in retrieve, the drag is relieved as the clutch plate rotates with the spool. Perhaps the biggest disadvantage of disc drags is the inability to easily seal the system from moisture and grit.

*Figure 3-5. The Orvis Odyssey, 1st model, reel.*

This reliable drag system appears to have been first used for fly reels in 1950 by Seamaster in its anti-reverse reels and later in 1972 when its direct-drive models were introduced. Fin-Nor adopted the cork disc drag in its direct-drive "wedding cake" reels, introduced in 1968. That drag was later chosen for its Classic series of direct-drive and anti-reverse reels introduced in 1977. The same drag (and clutch) system was adopted for the anti-reverse Billy Pate reels introduced in 1976 and also for the Billy Pate direct-drive models introduced seven years later. The disc drag has been adopted by many of the new reel manufacturers because of its simplicity and dependability.

An offset disc drag is used by Orvis in its Battenkill, CFO, and DXR Disc reels and in the new Elite reels, among others. The Orvis drag is composed of two Rulon polymer discs separated by a brass disc and sandwiched between stainless-steel discs. These drag discs are contained in a flat cylinder geared to the clutch. An advantage of this system is that the drag surfaces are fully enclosed (but not truly sealed) and thus effectively shielded from dirt and water.

**TURBINE IMPELLER DRAG.** The newest type of drag is the turbine impeller drag developed by the Argentine firm STH and introduced into the U.S. market in 1997 jointly by STH and

*Figure 3-6. The Orvis Battenkill Disc reel.*

Cortland. The drag consists of an impeller geared to the spool and immersed in a small oil bath positioned on the outer frame, opposite the handle. As a fish takes line, the impeller revolves in the oil chamber, creating a viscous drag. The magnitude of the drag is determined by the angular velocity at which the spool, and hence the impeller, rotates as the fish runs. During a long run, as the diameter of the line on the spool diminishes, the force required to strip line increases, thus providing additional drag force for a given angular velocity. A multi-viscosity oil is employed to minimize drag fluctuation as a result of changing temperatures. The size of the impeller, the gear ratio, and the viscosity of the oil employed are optimized to provide as much as 1 1/2 pounds of drag for a fast-running

*Figure 3-7. The Cortland large-arbor turbine-drag reel.*

fish. No clutch is required, since the angler does not retrieve fast enough to encounter appreciable drag resistance.

While the turbine creates resistance to snub a running fish, it is not a drag in the usual sense of the word. Technically, it is a "momentum check" because the resistance is proportional to the rate at which the spool revolves and the angular momentum it generates. Many large fish will run slowly, in which case the turbine will revolve slowly and provide insufficient resistance to snub such a fish. In testing one of the new Cortland models, I found that the reel could not generate nearly enough drag to check the run of even a 16-inch trout.

At present, turbine drag reels are available from STH and Cortland in both machined and injection-molded models in either the STH or Cortland brands with standard or cassette spools. All models have palming rings. The various sizes of reels use oils of differing viscosity to provide different drag ranges. In a few models, the turbine is geared to the spool through a reversed-detent plate clutch (described in the following section), which adds a modicum of drag to the retrieve to prevent the spool from overrunning during the retrieve. Without the reversed clutch, a sharp tug on the line may cause the spool to overrun and create a nasty bird's nest or snarl on the spool.

At this stage of development, the turbine drag is an interesting curiosity. Its simplicity certainly is attractive to the neophyte angler, particularly those trout fishermen who prefer a very light drag. In my opinion, the reel would be more useful if it possessed a minimal drag of several ounces or was equipped with dual gears from which the angler could select the minimum drag desired.[1]

## TYPES OF CLUTCHES

In some respects, the clutch on a reel is as important as the type of drag. The clutch serves to engage the drag surface in line-out operation and to disengage the drag for line-in retrieve. Instantaneous  engagement and disengagement are desirable, although some of the most popular clutches have periodic arcs of engagement. At present, there are three types of clutches widely employed in modern reels: the detent plate, the gear and pawl, and the one-way bearing. In addition there are a number of clutch variations that are used by only one or two manufacturers. All employ a separate plate or drum that may be engaged or disengaged from the reel spool. In as much as there is no industry agreement on nomenclature, I have adopted the following terminology as most descriptive.

**DETENT-PLATE CLUTCH**. The plate in this clutch contains a series of inclined grooves, or "detents" around the face of the plate that engage a retractable pin protruding from the spool face. In the line-out position, the pin locks into one of the grooves and prevents the spool from revolving without engaging the clutch plate and hence the drag. During the retrieve, as the clutch plate turns in the reverse direction, the pin slides up the inclined ramp and falls into the next detent, thus preventing the drag from engaging. Modern clutch plates are made from Teflon or other wear-resistant polymers to provide frictionless operation. One advantage of this type of clutch is that the detent plate may be formed with grooves of opposite hand on either side of the clutch

---

1. In 1999, STH greatly improved its turbine reels by adding a small disc drag. But if you rely on the disc drag, does the turbine serve any useful purpose?

plate. The reel retrieve may be changed from right to left hand by simply reversing the plate on the reel spindle. The detent plate clutch is frequently used in conjunction with the external drum drag operating on the rim of the clutch plate. The best-known example of this clutch is that used by Medalist-type reels (Figure 3-2). A minor annoyance is that the sliding pin mandates a line-in click.

**GEAR-AND-PAWL CLUTCH**. The use of the external gear-and-pawl clutch for fly reels originated in the 1950s and has been widely used by Fin-Nor, Billy Pate, and Seamaster for their saltwater reels. In the last decade, it has been copied by many of the new reel manufacturers. In its most common form, the clutch plate is a large-toothed gear with a pawl stop, which prevents the plate from turning in the line-out position, thus engaging the drag—usually a cork or composite disc. During the retrieve, the gear rotates in the opposite direction and the pawl slides freely over the gear teeth, permitting drag-free retrieve. The Abel clutch shown in Figure 3-8 is identical to that used by McNeese, Islander, and others and is representative of all gear-and-pawl clutches, most of which are copied from the Seamaster design. Simple and very dependable, the gear-and-pawl clutch can be designed to be reversed from right- to left-hand retrieve without changing clutch plates. A major disadvantage is that this clutch is not easily shielded from water and sand. Like the detent-plate clutch, it provides a line-in click whether you want it or not. If I am reeling in line, I don't need a click to tell me so. Because this clutch is so simple, many reel manufactures do not bother to install a line-out click, even on expensive, hand-crafted reels.

In a different adaptation, the internal gear-and-pawl clutch is enclosed in a flat, geared cylinder. The cylinder fits over the reel spindle, and the internal gear is keyed to the spool. The geared cylinder engages an offset drag. This results in a very small clutch that is shielded from the elements but not truly sealed. This type of clutch was used extensively in the British-made Leeda reels. It is currently

*Figure 3-8. The Abel reel.*

employed by Lamson, Orvis (Battenkill Disc and CFO Disc reels), and Scientific Anglers (System 2 reels), among others.

All clutch designs have their limitations. The internal gear-and-pawl clutch is limited by the torque that a small gear may sustain. In large, heavy-duty reels such as those used for tarpon or billfish, the internal gear is replaced by an expandable spring, which fits inside the geared cylinder and wraps snugly around a bushing keyed to the spool. As the spool turns in the line-out mode, the spring wraps tightly around the bushing and forces the clutch cylinder to turn, thus engaging the drag. For line-in retrieve, the spring is unwound and expands slightly, thus freeing it from the bushing and preventing the clutch from engaging. This wound-spring clutch is currently used by Orvis in its DXR tarpon reels.

**ONE-WAY-BEARING CLUTCH**. In recent years, many reels have adopted a one-way bearing that allows the clutch plate to revolve against the drag surface in only one direction. The bearing housing is restrained by the drag force or keyed to the spool as in the Danish Modern Art (DMA) reel shown in Figure 3-9. When engaged in line-out mode, the clutch plate rotates against the drag surface as the spool revolves; when the clutch plate is disengaged, the one-way bearing permits the spool to rotate freely. A significant advantage of this clutch system is that it is relatively easy to seal the bearings from moisture and grit. If properly designed, the drag surface also may be sealed within the bearing housing, as in the Ari Hart "F" and "S" reels. However, at the present time there are no completely rustproof one-way bearings available. If the bearings are not properly sealed, salt water may eventually corrode even Type 400 stainless-steel bearings. The one-way bearing clutch is used in the DMA reels, the inexpensive Elite reels, the Fin-Nor FR series, the Fly Logic Optimum, the Hardy Disc Ultralite, the Ari Hart "F" and "S" series reels, the Ross San Miguel series, and the Streamline reels, among others. The DMA reels, the Elite reels, the Fin-Nor reels, and those by Ross are unique. By reversing the bearing housing on

*Figure 3-9. The Danish Modern Art reel.*

the spindle, the retrieve is changed from right to left hand. The one-way-bearing clutch is an excellent design because it is very small and operates concentrically with the reel spindle. This type of clutch is likely to predominate as new reel designs are developed.

Two new clutches, while used at the present time by only two manufacturers each, are so outstanding that they warrant special consideration.

**SPRAGUE OR ROLLER CLUTCH**. One of the better new clutches, if not the best, is the Sprague or roller clutch. Long used for the fail-safe operation of machinery, it utilizes the old principle of a ball or roller moving between two inclined planes. Moving in one direction, the ball bearing is rolled "up" between the two planes, forcing one to engage and move the other. Moving in the opposite direction, the ball is free and the two planes are not engaged.

The first fly reel to effectively utilize this principle was

*Figure 3-10. The Bauer reel.*

the Odyssey reel introduced by Orvis in 1993.[2] With its disc drag, this reel would be state of the art if only Orvis had incorporated a sealed drag. A newer entrant whose innovative design was voted best-of-show at the 1995 International Fly Tackle Dealers show in Denver, the Bauer reel uses a simplified and ingenious version of the roller clutch shown in Figure 3-9. The Bauer clutch uses stainless-steel roller discs, which are held in place by cellular urethane spring pads or discs. The drag disc is mounted on the clutch plate. When the clutch plate rotates in the line-out direction, the urethane spring discs force the stainless rollers to engage the spool, thus applying the drag. When rotated in the opposite direction, the stainless discs move freely inside the spool well and the drag is not engaged. To change from right-to left-hand retrieve, you need only interchange the positions of the stainless-steel and urethane spring discs. The Sprague clutch is not likely to supplant the one-way bearing clutch, but it holds considerable promise for the future development of moderately priced dual-mode reels (see page 87).

**PAWL-ENGAGEMENT CLUTCH.** The pawl-engagement clutch was introduced in 1997 by Scientific Anglers in its Mastery reels and simultaneously by Orvis

2. In 1997, the clutch in the Orvis Odyssey reel was changed to the pawl engagement clutch shown in Figure 3-11.

*Figure 3-11. The Orvis
Odyssey+, 2nd model, reel.*

in its redesigned Odyssey reels (Figure 3-11). In concept, this clutch is similar to the one-way pawl-and-gear clutch used in the highly regarded Fenwick World Class series of reels, circa 1984–91. The clutch operates much like an inverted or reversed gear-and-pawl clutch, with two or three uni-directional pawls fastened to the rear face of the spool and operating against a geared clutch plate centered on the reel spindle between the spool and the frame. The pawls in this simple clutch are easily inverted to change the hand of the retrieve. Like the gear-and-pawl clutch, this system is not easily sealed, although it would be easy to shield this system in the manner of the Bauer reels.

## TYPES OF REEL

**DIRECT-DRIVE REELS**. The direct-drive reel is well-known to all anglers. It is available in numerous styles, from the inexpensive Pfleuger Medalist to the extravagant Governor, with prices ranging from $35 to $6,000 respectively. For salmon, indeed for all strong fish, it is important that the drag be smooth and easily adjusted with minimum start-up torque. It is important that the drag surface be protected from water and contamination by sand and dirt. (Table 3-1 correlates drag and clutch types for a number of current or well-known reels.)

# TABLE 3-1
## DRAGS AND CLUTCHES USED ON SELECTED REELS

| TYPE OF DRAG | TYPE OF CLUTCH | | |
| --- | --- | --- | --- |
| | Detent Plate | Gear and Pawl | One-Way Bearing |
| External Drum | Pfleuger Medalist | Bogdan<br>Godfrey<br>Governor/Staub<br>TiborLight | Ballen |
| Internal Drum | Ari 't Hart<br>Ross Gunnison<br>Ryall | | |
| Caliper | | Lamson (e)<br>Marriott (e)<br>Pfleuger Supreme (e)<br>Sci. Anglers System 2 (e) | |
| Disc | Ross Cimarron<br>Teton/Tioga<br>Valentine | Abel<br>Billy Pate<br>Fin-Nor<br>Islander<br>McNeese<br>Penn International<br>Orvis Battenkill Disc<br>Orvis CFO Disc<br>Seamaster | Ari Hart F & S<br>Danish Modern Art<br>Elite<br>Fly Logic<br>Fin-Nor<br>Hardy Disc Ultralite<br>Henschel<br>Redington Disc<br>Right Angle<br>Ross San Miguel<br>Streamline |

**Other Combinations:**

Arnold reel (d)—caliper drag, no clutch
Bringsén reel—handle-controlled disc drag, no clutch
Bauer reel—disc drag, roller clutch
Orvis Odyssey reel (1st model) (d)—disc drag, Sprague clutch
Orvis Odyssey+ reel (2nd model)—disc drag, pawl-engagement clutch
Orvis DXR reel—disc drag, wound-spring clutch
Redington-Hart reel—cam driven disc drag, wound-spring clutch
Scientific Anglers Mastery reel—disc drag, pawl-engagement clutch
STH Turbine reel—turbine drag, no clutch
(d) discontinued reel model; (e) enclosed gear-and-pawl clutch

*Figure 3-12. The Arnold reel.*

**ANTI-REVERSE REELS**. There are two types of anti-reverse reels: those in which the reel handle is mechanically engaged and disengaged and those with the handle coupled through a friction drag.

In the postwar era, the first attempt to produce a mechanically coupled anti-reverse handle was the Arnold Reel introduced in the late 1940s by the Bivans Manufacturing Co. of Los Angeles. A ball bearing was contained in an inclined groove (Figure 3-12) under the handle cover. For line-in retrieve, rotating the handle forward rolled the bearing up the incline, engaging the spool surface, thus forcing the spool to revolve. In line-out mode, the rotating spool was intended to disengage the ball bearing and the handle. In about 1946, my father and I purchased two of the first Arnold reels available in Illinois. To our great disappointment, the anti-reverse mechanism was unreliable, as was the pressure pad or half-caliper drag.

In 1952 J.W. Young & Sons introduced the Landex salmon reel with pawl checks and an anti-reverse handle. The handle was connected to the spool by a cam and pawl (Figure 3-13). In retrieve mode, the cam actuated the pawl, which engaged and rotated the spool. The spool was disengaged only by rotating the handle backward one-quarter turn, after which the spool rotated freely,

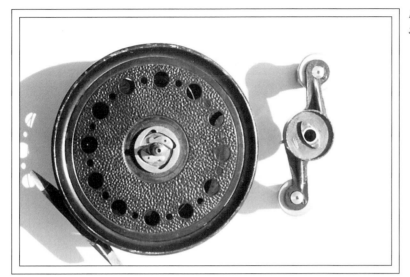

*Figure 3-13. The J.W. Young & Sons Landex reel.*

independent of the handle. The obvious disadvantage of this system was the need to disengage the handle after each cast and every retrieve. In the give-and-take of fighting a strong fish, it was often difficult to complete that reverse quarter turn as the fish surged.

Another method for achieving the anti-reverse effect is the gear system used in the Valentine Planetary gear reels. This system is based on the handle's being geared to the spool through a cover plate. During retrieve, the handle rotates about its own axis as it precesses in a circle around the rim of the reel (Figure 3-14). When a fish runs and the line is withdrawn, the spool gear rotates the handle rapidly on its axis at twice the rate of the spool rotation. However, because the inertia of the handle and cover plate is insufficient, the handle does not precess around the rim of the reel in the line-out mode. The advantage of this system is that by grasping the handle with your fingers, you can immediately slow or stop the out-running line. You must remove your fingers from the reel handle to permit free out-running as the fishes surge, but it is much easier to control the spinning reel handle than to palm the rim of a reel. It is surprising that this simple system has not received wider application in a well-machined reel, since this design is not subject to the drag limitations of the friction-coupled reels discussed below. In several respects, this is the ultimate anti-reverse design.

*Figure 3-14. The Valentine reel. Note planetary gear on back side of the cover plate.*

In 1989, Seamaster introduced the patented Dual Mode reel, which overcame the deficiencies of the previous mechanically coupled anti-reverse designs. Based on the cam-and-pawl design of the Landex reel described above, the Seamaster Dual Mode reel is a tribute to the genius of the late Captain Robert McChristian. Through the simple but masterful solution of pinning the cam to the reel spindle, "Cap'n Mac" succeeded in forcing the pawls to retract as the line begins to play out (Figure 3-15). No longer is it necessary to reverse the handle one-quarter turn, as with the Landex reel. Since its introduction, the Seamaster Dual Mode has become the workhorse of saltwater fly

Figure 3-15. The Seamaster
Dual Mode reel.

*Figure 3-16. The Henschel
dual-mode reel.*

fishermen, dominating the market for everything from bonefish to billfish. The original models of this reel had a tendency to chatter if the cams were inadvertently positioned between the in and out modes, but this problem has since been resolved. Not available in takedown models, the reel is well protected against moisture and grit, although not completely sealed.

The newest dual-mode reel is the Henschel, manufactured in Germany and introduced in 1996 (Figure 3-16). The friction-coupled handle is activated by a proprietary version of the ball bearing-and-inclined-plane principle described for the Arnold reel. A unique feature of the Henschel mechanism is that the handle housing bears against the drag washers. Rotating the handle forward produces additional pressure in the axial direction, which further increases the drag force. The Henschel reel may be a prototype for reels of the future.

The second type of anti-reverse reel is the friction-coupled reel, which operates in a manner similar to a direct-drive reel with disc drag and gear-and-pawl clutch except that the handle is not attached to the spool. The handle revolves around the reel spindle and is coupled to the spool only by the friction of the drag. A typical friction-coupled reel, the McNeese, is shown in Figure 3-

*Figure 3-17. The McNeese reel.*

17. If the tension on the line is not too great, the line may be retrieved in the usual manner. Under heavy tension, as with a strong running fish, the drag friction may be insufficient, which means that the drag may slip and the line can play out while you are reeling in. The major disadvantage of friction-coupled anti-reverse reels is that you can only overcome a slipping drag by tightening the drag knob. If you tighten the drag sufficiently to snub a running fish, you risk a broken leader.

Perhaps the biggest problem with this style of reel is that the slipping drag too frequently becomes a crutch for the inexperienced angler and permits him to play the fish

*Figure 3-18. The Bringsén reel.*

too long. By setting a very light drag, the neophyte can "worry" the fish to death. I once watched a friend play a 22-pound salmon so gingerly that it required an hour and fifteen minutes to land. That is four times the norm. The fish was so exhausted that, had it been released, it would have had no chance for survival.

A completely new type of anti-reverse reel was introduced in 1996 by Bringsén Reels of Mörrum, Sweden (Figure 3-18). This reel operates much like other friction-coupled reels except that it does not have a separate drag knob. The drag is built into the retrieve mechanism. As you retrieve against a running fish, the handle causes a threaded inner sleeve to draw the drag washer against the spool, thereby increasing the drag sufficiently to overcome the resistance of the fish. If the fish suddenly starts a stronger run, you may lessen the drag by reversing the reel handle a half-turn. Control is always within the reel handle. The advantage of this design is that you can instantaneously increase or decrease the drag without shifting your hand from the handle.

The Henschel and Bringsén reels are unique in that each may operate in either a direct-drive or anti-reverse mode. The Henschel operates in anti-reverse mode at very low drag force, the Bringsén at high drag force. This feature is discussed on page 94.

## REEL PARAMETERS AND DESIGN

The drag and the clutch are the predominate factors that determine the functioning of a reel. However, other parameters contribute significantly to the operation and appearance of a reel. Consider the following:

a.  *Frame*. Should the frame fully enclose the spool, as in the Bogdan and Seamaster reels, or is a partial (open) frame adequate? Should the frame be solid or ventilated to reduce weight?

b.  *Spool*. What diameter and width of the spool are best? Should the spool be solid or ventilated? Do you need interchangeable spools?

c.  *Handle*. Should the reel have one or two handles? What should be their shape?

d.  *Drag adjustment*. Should the drag adjustment be on the handle side or the obverse side of the reel? Do you want knob or lever adjustment? Do you want or need rim control?

e.  *Reel foot*. Do you want a regular or canted (offset or progressive) reel foot?

f.  *Click*. Do you want an outgoing click, incoming click, both, or neither?

g.  *Color*. Any color will do as long as it's a dull black!

These design parameters are strongly influenced by the intended use of your reel. The preferences of salmon and saltwater anglers will differ significantly from those of trout fishermen, who are more likely to be influenced by appearance and tradition. Focusing here on salmon and saltwater use, the following are my design selections based on logic and my opinions, which are based on well-developed prejudices.

A frame that fully encloses the spool protects the reel during a fall or from carelessness. You may note that many of the premium reels mentioned above, as well as most of the newer reels (Bringsén, DMA, Fin-Nor FR series, Henschel, Maurice Noël, Penn, Ryall, Scientific Anglers Mastery series, and Teton, among others) all possess enclosed or fully caged frames. I take good care of my equipment; yet over the years I have bent the handle on one reel and the frame on another by falling over rocks. Experience has taught me that it may be unwise to purchase any expensive reel that does not have a fully enclosed or caged frame, even though some of the newer reels have stout open frames (also called *partial frames*, *partial cage frames*, or *C-frames*). Obviously, this logic is not widely shared by many of the newer reel manufacturers.

My view is that, for both freshwater and saltwater use, the frames and even the spools should be solid and unventilated, primarily to keep out moisture and dirt. Reels are sufficiently lightweight today that a half-ounce less weight for a perforated or ported frame is meaningless. Keeping dirt out is not. In 1995, one of the major West Coast reel companies introduced, amid great fanfare and extra cost, ported or ventilated frames for its reels (which utilize exposed cork drags). Why anyone would pay an extra $60 to deliberately expose the working surfaces of their reel to moisture, let alone dirt or saltwater, is beyond me. Certainly it's a disservice to unknowing customers. It completely ignores the fact that the start-up torque of cork drags is affected by water films. By contrast, Lamson Reels has adopted a customer-friendly approach. Its models LP-3.5 and larger have "non-ventilated cases to prevent the intrusion of sand and salt."

The advantage of unventilated frames was well illustrated several years ago by Bob Popovics, a well-known New Jersey saltwater flyrodder, who buried a Charlton reel in the sand and repeatedly stepped on it. Then he dug it out, rinsed it in the surf, and without further fanfare proceeded to fish with it. You wouldn't even consider such a stunt with a ported Abel or other reel with ventilated frame and without a sealed drag.

Tradition, not weight, has much to do with one's preference for solid or ventilated frames and spools. For a century, trout reels manufactured in the United States have favored ventilated spools. Until the 1960s, solid frames and spools were the rule in Great Britain for both trout and salmon reels. Until the last decade or so, the premier American salmon reels—such as the vom Hofes and the Bogdans, as well as the Fin-Nor, Billy Pate, and Seamaster saltwater reels—utilized solid, unventilated spools. However, as more reels feature sealed drags and bearings, the argument against ventilated frames and spools will become moot.

For salmon reels, interchangeable reel spools are irrelevant. For trout fishermen they're a nice touch, in which case the partial or C-frame may not be so objectionable. Most of the newer premium reels designed for salmon and saltwater use do not incorporate quick release or instantly interchangeable spools. Obviously, if your reel does not have readily interchangeable spools, you won't be able to easily reverse the retrieve. The reversible retrieve feature is really only important in minimizing a dealer's inventory. Buy your reel with whichever retrieve you prefer and forget it.

The minimum size of a reel is determined by the line size and the backing capacity you employ. The maximum size is limited by weight and by appearance—yes, by cosmetics. But size, or volume capacity, is measured by both the diameter and the width of the spool. In general, the larger the diameter of the spool, the better. Not only is the line capacity greater, but the amount of line retrieved per revolution of the handle is also greater. This can be a very significant factor in fighting strong fish. For instance, a spool 4 inches in diameter filled to capacity retrieves 23 percent more line per revolution than does a 3 1/4-inch spool.

So we have two parameters to balance: line capacity and retrieval rate. A 4-inch spool that is an inch or more in width when filled to capacity holds more backing than necessary for freshwater use, yet the large diameter provides a very desirable retrieval ratio. Recently the fly-reel industry discovered the large-arbor reel as one solution. By increasing the minimum diameter of the reel arbor, manufacturers can reduce the line capacity without decreasing the retrieval rate of the larger diameter spool. At the 1995 International Fly Tackle Dealers show, new large-arbor reels were introduced

by Abel, Bauer, Islander, and Tibor, and since that time these
reels have become increasingly popular as anglers put aside
their prejudice against large-diameter reels and discover the
advantages of a more rapid retrieve.

Large-arbor reels are one means of increasing the
rate of line retrieval. Another solution, if retrieval rate is
your prime concern, is using multiplying reels. A 3 1/4-
inch-diameter spool with a 2:1 retrieval ratio winds in 62
percent more line per handle revolution than does the 4-
inch spool with a 1:1 retrieval ratio. That's why the
Bogdan and Godfrey multiplying reels have been popular
with salmon fishermen. But why only salmon fishermen?
It has always puzzled me that such reels have not found
favor with saltwater fly fishermen. One answer is that
such reels contain too many parts, which inevitably
results in a higher rate of failure. A second answer may be
the same reason I don't use them: I do not like the feel of
the retrieve when using a multiplying reel. I used one for
several seasons and always felt as if I was winching in the
fish, which literally I was. I would much prefer to make
additional revolutions of the handle than to fight that
extra torque, but not all agree with me on that view.
Multipliers, like large arbor reels, may be advantageous in
fighting anadromous or saltwater species that tend to run
toward you trailing large loops of line.

The width of the spool is also important, not because
of line capacity but because of the change in the rate of
retrieval as line is removed from the spool. Consider a
spool 4 inches in diameter and 7/8 inch wide, which when
filled to capacity has an initial retrieval rate of 12.6 inches
per revolution. If a fish runs 100 yards, the line removed
from the spool has reduced the effective diameter to 2 3/4
inches, a 31 percent reduction in the diameter and
retrieval rate. If, however, the spool was 1 1/4 inches wide,
the retrieval diameter would be reduced to only 3.3 inches,
since the volume of line removed remains constant. In this
example, the retrieval diameter, and hence the rate of
retrieval for the wider spool (3.3 inches), has been reduced
17.5 percent, compared with a 31-percent reduction for the

narrower spool. Why has no one applied such volumetric concepts to either reel capacities or line and backing volumes? Reel manufacturers would do well to report the volumetric capacity (in cubic inches) of spools. Line manufacturers could report the volume required for a given line size and backing capacity. You could then match the volume of your line and backing to that of the reel. The line and backing capacities might need to be averaged to account for people winding lines with differing degrees of tension, but average volumes would be better than having none. The first thing I noticed when examining the descriptive literature for the Henschel reels was that the volumetric capacities of their spools were tabulated.

If you choose a reel strictly on functionality, it is best to use a large-diameter reel with a wide spool, completely filled with line and backing. Except for the additional weight it adds, the amount of excess backing required to fill the spool is irrelevant.

Another thing that has puzzled me is why no one has introduced arbor fillers to reduce the capacity of large-diameter reels. As a youth, I was active in a bait-casting club. Our reels were equipped with cork bushings, which fit over the arbor to increase arbor diameter. Applied to fly reels, one large-diameter spool could be fitted with different arbor bushings to reduce the reel capacity as desired.

The closest approach to variable spool volume, albeit an expensive one, is the system introduced by Charlton in 1996 offering spools of differing capacity for use with one frame. For instance, its Model 8850C reel is offered with four spools of differing capacities, the new model 8450C with three different spools.

There is no reason for either a direct-drive or an anti-reverse reel to have two handles. Even with the S-shaped handle bar of the classic salmon reel, a well-designed counterweight is preferred to a second handle, since it will not entangle your line. Shaped reel handles look great and feel fine, but if you are using a direct-drive reel, where it may be necessary to remove your fingers quickly, a smooth, tapered wooden handle not more than 1 inch long is preferable.

Drag adjustment is a controversial subject. The drag knob or lever must be easily accessible. Most accomplished anglers favor the drag adjustment on the handle side of the reel, where it is readily available to the hand with which you reel. With anti-reverse and dual-mode reels, this is clearly the preferred position. If the drag handle is on the obverse side, it does not mean that you must switch hands to change the drag. Simply rotate the rod 90 to 120 degrees to your right (if you are right-handed), reach under the reel with your right hand, and adjust the drag. I prefer drags that feature large knobs, since they provide a wider range of control than do preset lever drags. Lever drags are satisfactory for single-purpose reels (e.g., salmon), but most do not have a sufficient range of light drag settings to suit me.

Palming rims or rim control is a nonissue with me, unless I am using a pawl-and-check reel. When fighting strong fish, you should always get the fish "on the reel" as quickly as possible and avoid any loose line. Then you control the fish with the drag of the reel. Nevertheless, some anglers seem to feel that a reel is incomplete without a palming ring, even though they may seldom use it. For reels with only a pawl check, a palming rim is a distinct advantage for applying heavy drag pressure to a strong-running fish.

In 1994 I gave a talk on reels for chapters of Trout Unlimited in which I predicted that canted (offset or progressive) reel feet would soon become popular. Such feet are now offered by Abel and Henschel, as well as by Ari Hart, which first introduced them. Abel charges an extra $80 for the canted foot, and Henschel charges an extra $20. This feature is included in the price of the Ari Hart reels. On medium to heavy rods, I find the canted foot to be a distinct advantage in shifting the balance point of the rod forward, up under the handle, particularly with reels that are somewhat heavier than average. It helps me resist the tendency to move my hand up and down the handle for casting and retrieving, and makes casting much less tiring.

According to a recent survey by Ed Jaworowski, 75 percent of fly fishermen prefer reels with a click of some type. Some people like an outgoing click if for no other reason than to announce to their friends that they have hooked a fish. I like a soft outgoing click because it tells me what the fish is doing. Guides like them for the same reason. However, some Alaskan guides prefer that you remove or silence your drag in bear country. Bears, it is said, learn to associate the click sound with a hobbled fish. Saltwater fishermen tend to regard clicks as just one more part that may fail under pressure. It's hard to imagine expensive precision reels' being manufactured without at least the option of line-out clicks, yet the list of such is very long. I like a silent reel for line-in retrieve, for which reason I tend to avoid detent-plate and gear-and-pawl clutches.

Color or finish is not a frivolous consideration. More reels are sold on appearance than on technical parameters. One of the problems with the current market for fly-fishing tackle is that so much equipment is sold with disdain for the well-informed customer. Recently one of the trade magazines strongly advised merchants not to provide much detail to their customers. "Convince them that you have a good selection and let them choose," the magazine argued, and the choice will be strongly influenced by aesthetics. In essence, the attitude seems to be that almost anything will do, so why be selective? The finish of a reel is a prime example. Dull finishes catch fish, but bright finishes reel in the fishermen. A dull, nonreflective finish is best for both your rod and reel. It avoids spooking the occasional salmon and all of your bonefish. Manufacturers respond in diverse ways to this dichotomy. In 1995, Orvis concluded that the finish on its excellent Odyssey reel was insufficiently alluring and introduced a brighter finish. As a result, a number of dealers cleared their inventories of reels with the older finish at bargain prices. During this same period, recognizing that the duller "guide's" finish was preferable, Abel charged an extra $25 to $45 for the more desirable nonreflective finish. Charlton also has had many requests by serious anglers for a duller finish. Since the duller finish requires much less hand polishing, Charlton charges $40 to $50 less for such models. So much for reel marketing.

The Europeans strongly favor reels with nonreflective surfaces. Many of the reels manufactured in Germany, the Netherlands, Scandinavia, and the United Kingdom (such as those by DMA and Henschel and the black Hart reels) feature nonreflective finishes.

## REEL SELECTION

Selecting the proper reel for your particular use requires making bewildering choices as to type, design parameters, and aesthetics. In early 1995 there were more than 85 makes of fly reels offered in the United States, to say nothing of the thousands of models and sizes. I have since lost count. It's easy to note new entrants, but those who go out of business because of excessive competition seldom advertise the fact. The three most important decisions you must make, other than your price range, are the type of drag, the type of clutch, and whether or not you desire a fully enclosed frame. Then you begin to compare individual reels.

To enhance reel merchandising, much has been made in recent years of the perceived advantages of machined frames and spools over cast and stamped ones. In general, machined and cast frames are fitted more precisely than stamped parts, but you need not shy away from a well-finished cast frame. Properly cast frames are very strong and require some of the same machining as do totally machined frames. The Orvis Battenkill Disc and the Scientific Anglers System 2 reels are among the best values in today's reels, and their cast frames are quite satisfactory, although the partial or open frame of the Battenkill reels and the smaller System 2 reels will not withstand a heavy fall. Interestingly, Scientific Anglers recognizes that enclosed frames are important to the salmon angler but not to those chasing trout. The 8/9, 10/11, and 11/12 sizes of reels in both System 2 and the new Mastery series utilize fully enclosed (the manufacturer calls them "fully caged") frames.

Similarly, there has been much ballyhoo about the

use of bar-stock aluminum for reel frames and spools. The use of Type 6061-T6 or other aluminum is one of the least critical factors in the manufacture of a reel. Reel manufacturers would do far better to advertise the use of dove-tailed reel feet, Type III anodizing, or an optional click mechanism. Have you noticed that reel advertisements always show photos of attractive reels and beautiful women but seldom of the inside of a reel or its workings? Until one-way bearings and roller clutches came into vogue, the advertising literature rarely mentioned such features. Even now the ads may reveal the material used for the disc drag but often force you to guess the mating surface. Does the drag surface bear against stainless-steel, brass, Teflon, Rulon, composite graphite, or the aluminum spool frame?

Disc-drag reels are very popular because they are simple and most of them offer a dependable drag at both very light and heavy settings. Much has been made about the area of the drag surface. In theory, the larger the drag surface, the less the start-up torque. Actually there is little, if any, relation between area and the performance of the drag. Not having personally evaluated all the materials being used for disc drags, I can only comment from the vantage point of the user. Drags utilizing soft cork, with its high coefficient of friction, generally bear against a hard surface, such as the anodized face of the aluminum spool, and work under relatively low pressure. Drags with composite cork or polymeric drag surfaces with a lower coefficient of friction work under higher compression. I tend to favor a plain cork drag (lubricated with Neats Foot oil or a dispersion of micronized Teflon or PTFE) operating against a Teflon or Rulon surface. That combination was first incorporated, to my knowledge, in 1984 in the now discontinued Orvis SSS reel and was one of the smoothest drags I've ever used. Variations on this theme, such as cork or impregnated cork versus Rulon, continue to be used by Orvis and others, especially for large-arbor and saltwater reels, whose drags may be severely tested by hard-running saltwater species.

However, cork is a natural product and varies greatly in density and compressibility. In addition, quality cork is increasingly difficult to obtain. Some is soft and spongy; some is so hard it does not hold lubricant well. For this reason, many reel manufacturers are beginning to switch to synthetic or composite drag components. Charlton's proprietary carbon-fiber drag is excellent, as is the graphite-impregnated cork used by Islander. The cork-and-nitrile-rubber material currently used in the Orvis Odyssey drag is likewise very satisfactory. Properly lubricated, it is unusually smooth with negligible start-up torque.

There is one subject on which there should be no argument. When fishing for any species that has the ability to strip a hundred yards off your reel, you must retrieve with your dominant hand. If you are right-handed, reel with your right hand. After years of discussion, most experts now concur in this view. The reason is simple. If your fish has taken out 100 yards of backing, you must retrieve at least 130 yards, including the fly line. Even with a large-diameter spool that regains, say, 10 or more inches per revolution, you must make 500 revolutions of the reel handle—not counting the additional line the fish takes back out, which must be retrieved a second or third time. Few casual anglers can retrieve with the necessary dexterity using their nondominant hand. Fighting a strong fish for 20 or more minutes requires more than casual hand strength.

A careful angler does not allow dirt to enter his reel. Whether or not both the drag and clutch should be completely sealed from dirt and moisture is arguable. Such newer performance reels as the Bringsén, the Charlton, the Henschel dual-mode, and the Ross San Miguel are sealed. Reels such as the Bogdan, McNeese, and Seamaster are not truly sealed but are effectively shielded by an enclosed frame.

One very large reel company is resisting this trend because it does not believe it can offer a truly sealed system that may be serviced by the angler if necessary. I concur that the serviceability of a well-shielded drag is

more important than having to return a totally sealed reel
to the factory for repair. However, sealed or even well-
shielded drags may effectively exclude moisture without
requiring a pressurized seal.

Beginning in 1997, the Bauer reels incorporated a
urethane washer, which encloses the clutch disc and
presses against the back of the spool, thus barring all dirt
and casual moisture. Ross Reels has introduced sealed
drags for its new line of San Miguel reels. The McNeese
anti-reverse reel copies the original Seamaster design by
machining a small flange on the front rim of the spool,
which engages a similar flange on the frame. The clearance
is so slight that a 7X tippet cannot fit between the spool
and frame. Several years ago while chasing a pod of small
permit in the Yucatan peninsula, I snarled my line on the
tip of my rod. My options were to wade a quarter mile to
shore, disassemble my rod where I stood, or lower my
McNeese reel into the water so I could reach the end of the
rod. I chose the last option, since time was of the essence
in casting to those elusive creatures flirting about me. That
evening, after dismantling the reel for cleaning, I found to
my amazement only one very tiny drop of water inside the
drag chamber. The tight fit of spool and frame had
effectively excluded water during that brief immersion.

A semi-technical study of drags was published in the
*Orvis News* in April 1993, concurrent with the introduction
of the Odyssey reel. Nine well-known reels were run at 400
rpm, half-submerged in water, and the effect of water on
the drag was measured over a period of one minute. Half
the reels showed a modest increase in drag force and half a
significant decrease. The two reels with caliper drags
showed very large decreases in drag force, which was
attributed to "hydroplaning" of the drag pads. Only the
Orvis Battenkill Disc reel showed negligible change in the
drag force, undoubtedly because its well-shielded
cork/Rulon drag was never really wet. We never fish with
our reels in the water, but the lesson is clear. Keep your
drag as dry as possible. If your drag does become wet,
tighten the drag and strip out line to dry out your drag pad.

Most people prefer direct-drive reels. Control is always at your fingertips, but you do need to release the handle when a fish surges. There are circumstances in which the anti-reverse reel is advisable. People who perform with their fingers, such as surgeons and artists, frequently use them. So do those of us who fish for large billfish whose run of several hundred yards is a true knuckle buster.

The introduction of the Pfleuger Supreme Model 577 and 578 reels, the Shakespeare 1898 EC reels in the early 1970s, and the Fenwick World Class reels in 1984 did much to enhance the popularity of anti-reverse reels, especially for saltwater use. The Pfleuger and Shakespeare reels were similar in using a friction-coupled drag in an anti-reverse mode. By flipping a lever on the back of either reel, the handle was shifted into what was called a "direct-drive mode," the purpose of which was to permit line to be stripped freely, without working against the heavy drag often used for saltwater fly fishing. This "direct-drive mode" was a misnomer. Even though the handle rotated as line was withdrawn, the friction-coupled drag still allowed line slippage during the retrieve. It was not a true direct-drive in as much as forward rotation of the handle did not inevitably result in line retrieval.

The design of the Fenwick World Class reels, produced between 1984 and 1991, was a decade ahead of its time. These reels utilized a fully caged frame, a shielded drag composed of graphite-impregnated bronze discs working against stainless-steel washers, and a unidirectional pawl-and-gear clutch not unlike the newer pawl-engagement clutches introduced by Orvis and Scientific Anglers in 1997 (see pages 65–66).

The development of the friction-coupled drag introduced a new dimension to anti-reverse reels, and there is now a whole generation of fishermen who associate the anti-reverse concept with the friction-coupled drag instead of with a nonrotating handle. Neophytes like the slipping-drag feature because, when it is lightly set, they can retrieve when the fish allows but they can continue to "wind in" while the fish is taking out line. Dan Blanton, a well-known West Coast guide, explained his choice of an anti-reverse reel with friction drag while fishing alone for king salmon. Once a Chinook was hooked, he had to weigh anchor and row out of a line of boats in order to retrieve the fish without tangling the lines of others. If his rod slipped while rowing, the reel handle on a direct-drive reel might snag, resulting in the loss of the fish.

The epitome of reel design is the dual mode. In the line-out mode, the handle is stationary, but control is instantly regained by merely grasping the handle. The dual mode avoids the major deficiency of friction-coupled drags: you're trying to reel in while the fish is running out. At this time, dual-mode reels are offered by Henschel, Herron, Seamaster, and Sievert. I predict that within five to seven years, dual-mode reels will replace many of the friction-coupled anti-reverse reels and will dominate the market for premium anti-reverse reels. Designs are now available that enable a dual-mode reel to be manufactured at the same cost as for a direct-rive reel.

## THE "BEST REELS"

The British gunmakers have a long tradition of "best guns" that incorporates the very finest in design and construction available from the world-renowned houses of Boss, Holland and Holland, Purdey, and others. With best guns, function and form are blended as one.

Fly reels have not reached the same level of distinction. The design emphasis for reels during the past decade has placed form before function, appearance ahead of utility. Despite the excellent designs available, reel construction still lags behind what is achievable. Only very recently have developments begun to reemphasize function and value. The new Fly Logic reels, introduced at the 1996 International Fly Tackle Dealers show, are a good example. The Fly Logic Optimum model has an open or partial frame machined from bar stock; is equipped with a disc drag, a sealed one-way bearing clutch, and optional clicks; and is priced around $200.

More recently, a new lightweight series by Elite Products offers a cast-and-machined open frame, a composite cork-and-Rulon disc drag, a reversible one-way needle-bearing clutch, and optional clicks. Its salmon-sized Andros model holds a WF9F line and 200 yards of backing and is priced at about $130.

Other entries in the value sweepstakes include the well-proven Ryall reels and their look-alike cousins from Teton. The Teton reel offers a sealed disc drag, a reversible detent-plate clutch, a fully caged and machined frame with Type 3 anodizing (which is Teflon coated to accommodate extended saltwater exposure), and is available with interchangeable large-arbor spools. All this at prices on either side of $200. No wonder that, in only four years, the Teton has become the best-selling reel in the world. A simpler version, the Tioga model with Type 2 anodizing and without detents on the drag knob but otherwise functionally identical to the Teton, retails for $100 to $160.

The best reels, in my view, are identified by the extent to which they fulfill their intended purpose. The price of a reel is frequently unrelated to its utility as a fishing tool. The $6,000 Governor reel, with its 180 parts and gold-inlaid and engraved frame, is certainly not the most functional fishing tool on the market. Whether its garish exterior is the most attractive is for someone else to determine.[3]

There can be little doubt that the best value in a reel today is the simple Pfleuger Medalist, the patent for which was issued on August 9, 1934. Sixty years later, it is still the most widely used reel in North America and at one time was the most popular reel in the world. In the 1980s, Medalist reels were said to have landed more salmon in North America than all other reels combined. It was so popular that, until a few years ago, custom

---

3. New models of the Governor reel, now renamed the Staub reel, made in Canada without inlays or engraving, were introduced in 1997–98. Featuring type 7075 aluminum, Vespel drag shoes, and aluminum bronze gears, these reels are available in three sizes and two retrieve ratios; the list prices vary from U.S.$1,114 to $1,671.

spools were machined for it. For the beginning salmon angler who wants to get started at minimal cost, it's the ideal choice. The Model 1495 1/2 or 1498 Medalist, 3 1/16 or 3 11/16 inches in diameter, will hold 150 yards of 30-pound Dacron backing and an 8- or 10-weight line—more than enough capacity for salmon. After you have fished with that reel for two years and are ready to invest in a more elegant reel, you can retain your Medalist as a backup or use it with a line of different weight. For an initial outlay of less than $50, you simply cannot go wrong.

As mentioned previously, there is an increasing number of direct-drive reels currently selling for between $100 and $250 that warrant consideration as a separate subset of outstanding values. These include the Lamson LP series, the Orvis Battenkill Disc reels, the Ryall reels, the Scientific Angler System 2s, and the Fly Logic, Elite, and Teton and Tioga reels discussed above. As a result of recent price reductions, the outstanding Mastery reels by Scientific Angler have also joined this subset of values. While not incorporating all the features of the state-of-the-art reels, these reels represent outstanding value for all but the most demanding anglers. In my judgment, the price and performance of these reels make a mockery of $500 reels with ported frames and unshielded drag surfaces.

My current nomination for the best direct-drive reel, irrespective of price, may arouse the ire of many devotees of the Bogdans and Seamasters. A "best" reel today should possess a superb drag and a dependable clutch, and it should be sealed against dirt and moisture. Prior to 1999, those honors most certainly went to the Charlton reels, in spite of the fact that these reels do not utilize fully caged frames. Their totally sealed drag and clutch, the innovative carbon-fiber disc drag, and interchangeable spools of varying capacity represent industry leadership. The newer large-arbor Charltons are a joy to behold. As these words are revised in October 1999, it appears that the new Van Staal reels, each with a fully machined frame

*Figure 3-19. The Charlton reel.*

and a sealed drag and clutch, may have joined Charlton as the premier direct-drive reels.

Experienced salmon anglers may question my overlooking the Bogdan reel. The Bogdan has a panache like none other along the salmon rivers of North America. This is a tribute to a fine gentleman, Stan Bogdan, who for more than 50 years has produced the "salmon angler's reel." For four generations, the Bogdans and the vom Hofes have defined the form and style of a premium fly reel. However, new design features, much simpler construction, and a wider range of drag force have made some newer reels better suited for critical use, including saltwater fly fishing. Nevertheless the Bogdans will long be remembered, like the vom Hofes before them, as the best of their generation.

My choice for the best among the friction-coupled anti-reverse reels is more difficult because all of the candidates use essentially the same drag and clutch systems. Refusing to choose on the basis of appearance, I am inclined to cite the McNeese reel as the best among a comparable crowd of standard-arbor U.S.-made reels. Utilizing a fully caged frame, David McNeese's innovative use of a Vespel bearing, a graphite-impregnated Teflon (which simply does not wear and never needs lubrication), and clever touches such as the flanged spool rim and Type 7075 aluminum with Type III deep anodizing are evidence of a very thoughtful design.

Depending on your priorities and style preferences, an alternative selection might be the new Islander anti-reverse reel, which has "everything" except a fully caged frame and a sealed drag. Made in Canada, its features include a cork disc drag, a counterbalanced spool with a palming rim, sealed bearings, a reversible retrieve, an adjustable outgoing click, and a bonded and screwed reel foot. This reel is now also available in the large-arbor configuration with a titanium clutch gear. The problems are its weight and an insufficiently dull finish. Like the Charlton, it is an extremely well-designed reel and is offered at a very competitive price.

*Figure 3-20. The Bogdan reel.*

## THE BEST OF THE BEST:
## ALL-MODE FLY REELS

When Captain McChristian coined the term *dual mode* for his Seamaster reels, his intent was to distinguish clearly a class of direct-drive reels with an anti-reverse handle. That term, of course, also pertains to the Young Landex and Valentine Planetary gear models. However, a few anglers prefer the friction-coupled design, because it permits line slippage if the drag is not set too tightly. Two new reels, the Bringsén and the Henschel, combine the best features of dual-mode and friction-coupled reels into a new class I have defined as All-Mode reels.[4] The Henschel and Bringsén reels adopt different approaches to accomplish the same purpose, that of providing an anti-reverse handle with both a friction-coupled, anti-reverse mode—to permit line slippage and minimize tippet failure—and a direct-drive mode to assert control as needed.

The Henschel reel incorporates some unique design features, including a friction-coupled drag. The drag consists of dual Teflon drag washers, one on each side of the spool, working against stainless-steel washers. The clutch is composed of one-way bearings contained in a housing that is pinned to the back side of the frame. Both the clutch bearings and the drag discs are sealed and never need lubrication. In retrieve mode, if you reverse the handle a few degrees, the drag is reduced to about 1 ounce, thus introducing what is essentially a free-spool mode of operation. If your fish makes a sudden surge, you can reverse the handle and avoid trouble. The drag reverts to its prior setting as you again reel in line. When set for a drag less than a predetermined minimum, the reel operates in the line-slipping, friction-coupled anti-reverse mode. As you increase the drag beyond that predetermined value, the reel shifts into direct-drive mode. Unfortunately, that predetermined minimum is usually about 1 1/2 pounds of drag. Thus you have an

---

4. All-Mode is a trademark of Salaris Tackle Division, Resin Resources, Inc., Box 19, Summit, NJ 07902.

anti-reverse mode under 1 1/2 pounds and a true direct-drive mode over 1 1/2 pounds. This reel would be more useful if the drag in anti-reverse mode was limited to 4 ounces or less, since you can always reverse the handle and have a free-running spool if less drag is needed. Upon request, the factory will reduce the range of the anti-reverse drag and is now considering adopting a lower preset minimum value for all reels. The anti-reverse drag on my own Henschel was reset to 2 ounces. The Henschel reel is available with either a regular or canted (progressive) reel foot (Figure 3-16), with or without an outgoing click. Its dull black finish is undoubtedly the toughest finish on any reel made. Clearly, the state-of-the-art dual-mode reel of this day is the Henschel.

The second All-Mode reel, which is advertised as an anti-reverse reel, is the Bringsén reel. As described previously, the drag adjustment for this reel is built into the handle, and you need only advance or reverse the handle to instantly adjust the drag. The advantage of this design is that you can increase the drag from free-spool to a preset maximum or decrease the drag without shifting your hand from the handle. The maximum drag you can achieve is preset, depending on the model. My Model 3 Bringsén is preset to release at about 2 1/4 pounds, beyond which the reel shifts into the line-slipping, friction-coupled mode. The purpose of this release is to prevent lock-ups and broken tippets, and it serves that purpose well. If you fail to reverse the handle, you know that the drag will slip and may release in time to save a running salmon. Most knots will hold against 2 pounds of steady pull, although a quick 2-pound jerk may cause the knot to slip and break. Two and a quarter pounds is an extremely heavy drag for any freshwater use, including salmon, but it may be insufficient for large tarpon, for instance. Upon request, Bringsén will set the drag release to any value you specify.[5]

The Bringsén reel is lightweight (8 to 10 ounces),

5. A detailed description of the Bringsén reel with schematic drawing may be found in U.S. Patent 5,626,303.

and the sealed drag is exceptionally smooth and functions flawlessly. This concept of a single drag-and-retrieve control shows great promise for large salmon and saltwater species. I have used a Bringsén reel to land a number of large salmon, and it is rapidly becoming one of my favorite reels because it's extremely easy to vary between a very light and heavy drag. For those who like to play their fish by palming (or thumbing) the reel, it's the perfect choice. My impression is that experienced anglers appreciate and greatly enjoy the single drag-and-retrieve control but novices may find it a bit intimidating.

## LAST CASTS: A SECOND RECOMMENDATION

In presenting this review of current reel design, undue emphasis has been placed on the newer premium reels because that has been the trend over the past decade. No beginning salmon angler should feel compelled to join the high-stakes game of expensive precision reels. Indeed, I strongly advise against it. The price-to-performance relationship of most premium reels is unrealistically skewed, and the majority of anglers simply cannot afford the luxury. To accompany that modestly priced rod recommended in Chapter 2, I strongly urge a beginning angler to purchase an inexpensive Pfleuger Medalist and use it for two seasons. (Somewhat more sophisticated options might be the reasonably priced Orvis Battenkill Disc 8/9, the Scientific Anglers System 2 Model 8/9, or one of the Elite, Fly Logic, Teton, or Tioga reels.) Later you will be better prepared to choose a performance reel that incorporates the features you desire.

A good reel needs good care. For that matter, any reel requires minimal attention. If you are not going to use your reel for a few days, strip out the fly line and allow the backing to dry out. Dry off the reel and the fly line as you rewind it onto the reel. If used in saltwater, your reel should be thoroughly rinsed in fresh water each evening to dissolve any residual salt. Don't overlubricate. Follow the manufacturer's directions. Reels with sealed or Vespel bearings never need lubrication.

Despite inferences to the contrary, cork drags do need attention. Responsible manufacturers provide a small vial of cork lubricant, be it Neats Foot oil or one of the new polymeric dispersions. If in doubt, call the manufacturer and request a small sample of the recommended lubricant. It puzzles me that many manufacturers fail to include a 50¢ vial of oil (or a decent reel case) with a $500 reel. If your reel has a composite drag of any type, you must follow the manufacturer's recommendation, which may simply be "do not lubricate." The biggest problem with cork drags is that many come from the factory improperly lubricated. The unknowing angler tries out the reel, finds that the drag does not function properly, and curses the manufacturer for putting out a piece of junk. My friend Charlie F., a very accomplished saltwater fisherman, took with him to Exuma a new large-arbor bonefish reel, which I had recommended. The first evening we examined the reel and found that the drag was poorly lubricated and erratic. I removed the old lubricant, worked new lubricant into the drag surface, and declared the reel ready for action. Two days later, Charlie hooked the largest bonefish he has ever seen. The first run took out a solid 125 yards of backing. The drag worked perfectly in landing that 10 1/2-pound bone, all because we took the time to hone the drag.

In 1995, I identified five trends in reel development, four of which are now clearly in vogue: large diameter spool arbors, sealed drags, canted reel feet, and the dual-mode mechanism. (My fifth trend, simplicity, remains an elusive goal.) For salmon or saltwater angling, the dual-mode construction is ideal, but it may not be for everyone. A few anglers prefer an anti-reverse reel with friction-coupled drag for special applications. Many of us are enamored with the direct-drive reel with its spinning handle. It's simple and straightforward, and we have always done it that way. One of the finest salmon anglers I know, a gentleman who has landed more salmon on a size 16 single-hook fly than any living person, frequently employs a direct-drive Bogdan steelhead reel without any drag, with only a pawl check.

For general use, I alternate between a direct-drive and one of the All-Mode reels. I greatly enjoy the large-arbor, direct-drive configuration for bonefish and similar flats fishing. However, I do not find the large arbor an advantage for fighting very strong fish because you seldom spool much line at a time. For salmon, I prefer one of the All-Mode reels, depending on the rod I have chosen and the water to be fished. When fishing the tiny size 16 hooks described in Chapter 10, I occasionally find myself gravitating back to the Valentine Planetary reel in spite of its aggravating line-in click because it is so easy to control a running fish by lightly grasping the handle. (If only someone manufactured a well-machined planetary reel.) A Bringsén reel is outstanding for use with a two-handed rod, because the long, limber rod provides additional resilience with which to fight the fish.

I like all my "toys," but for particular purposes some are more appropriate than others. Not being a serious collector of old reels, I think of my collection as current history, a record of developing reel technology. It's as Arnold Gingrich said in *The Well Tempered Angler*, "*Sunt ornamenta mea*" (21). They are my jewels.

*Bon Mouche*
Watercolor
9 1/2 x 13 3/4 inches
Private Collection

*Chapter*

# The Form and Style of the Atlantic Salmon Fly

### ALTON'S RED BUTT

We were fishing the upper Miramichi River out of the Porter Brook Camp near Bloomfield Ridge. Owned by a friend of John M., this camp encompasses almost a mile of water, including several fine dry-fly stretches on the lower beats. A lovely camp majestically set among tall fir trees, gorgeous weather, and excellent water with long runs interspersed with stunted rapids, it was everything you could wish for, except an abundance of salmon. On September 30, the last day of the season on the upper river, the fishing ambiance was unexcelled, but the catching left much to be desired. We had caught a fair number of fish earlier in the week, but this day was slow. The September run of MSW salmon was later than usual, and now even the grilse seemed to be hiding.

Our rotation for the evening session found me at the top of the camp's waters, just below the bridge, with John and Charlie on the middle stretches. To start the evening, I had brought along a new 14-foot, two-handed rod with which to experiment. My first pool, which we called

Beaver Run, was a long, deep glide on the far side of the river through which the main current courses before it sweeps back to the left, following the channel along the camp side.

For fall fishing on the Miramichi, my favorite bright-weather fly is the Chief Needahbeh, an orange-red streamer with jungle cock eyes. Although little-known except along the Miramichi, it is an exceptional attractor pattern for fall fishing. Carefully knotting a size 6 Chief to my leader, I began to fish the run. My skill with the two-handed rod was limited in those days, and it was not easy to keep my fly well positioned in the water. Recent rains had raised the river enough to require careful wading as I attempted to maneuver down the gravel bar into the faster water. Frequent attempts to lengthen my line resulted in drooped backcasts, which I was to learn later would lead to failure.

As I worked down the run, my casting improved, probably because I was now working with a constant length of line. On my last cast in that run, my fly hit the water's edge on the far side and properly swung down and across to my side. Just as the fly touched the lip of the pool before spilling over into the gentle rapids below, I felt the most savage strike I have ever experienced. The fish hung on the hook for the briefest of moments and was gone. That two-handed rod was almost torn from my hands. I was left shaking. Incredulous, I slowly stripped in my line, not believing what had just occurred. Then I examined the fly and found, much to my everlasting regret, that one of the hook points was broken, undoubtedly by those drooped casts that had allowed the fly to strike the stones on the island behind me. I never saw the fish, but if the ferocity of the strike was a meaningful indicator, I had lost the biggest salmon ever to strike my fly—because of failure to obey my own rule and check the hook periodically.

Meanwhile Alton, our guide, had picked up John in the canoe and poled him to mid-river, where he was casting campside, back toward the left shore. As I stood on the end of the island wallowing in my sorrow, my attention was diverted by the sight of a bend in John's rod. After a brief struggle, John landed his second grilse of the day and was through for the season. Alton poled him ashore and motioned for Charlie to join him in the canoe.

I crossed over the tip of the island and began fishing the left side, knowing that my options were limited. The high water had covered the shoals to the point that I could not wade out. I was forced to await Alton and the canoe. My wait was short-lived, for within 8 or 10 minutes, within a few feet of where John had hooked his fish, Charlie's rod was likewise bowed. Another brief struggle and Charlie went ashore with his grilse.

Alton now turned his attention to me, knowing that I needed a ride from the island. Darkness was upon us, and it looked as if my fishing for the season was over. As I climbed into the canoe, I casually mentioned to Alton the coincidence of landing two running grilse in the same spot along the shore. With the wisdom of a northwoods guide who has seen it all, Alton allowed as how it was not that much of a coincidence. "You see," he said, "I've noticed that in the fall when the grilse are running upriver, we often catch them at dusk right along the shore in about a foot and a half of water." That was exactly where he had positioned John and Charlie.

For the third time that evening, the canoe was now anchored just off the left shore, and even in the rapidly fading light it was obvious that Alton intended to give me a final chance as well. "Here, you'll need this," he said as he handed me a size 10, single-hook Red Butt. "It's what them other fellers used," he explained. Changing to my one-handed rod, I dutifully attached his fly, even though I thought there was no chance to land another fish before total darkness enveloped our season. But within 10 or 12 casts, my line tightened, and I too had my evening's grilse, the last fish of the year at Porter Brook.

As we trudged up the path to camp, I queried Alton about our three grilse, all caught within the last 30 minutes of the season. His answer was classical New Brunswick-ese: "They like the Red Butt, eh?"

## WHAT IS A FLY?

The preceding vignette illustrates well the axiom that
the right fly at the right time will catch fish. It is the other
permutations of fly and time that frustrate us beyond
reason. How do you design a fly that will attract salmon?
Fortunately for the salmon, there is no answer to this
question. Salmon are enigmatic creatures. Until they have
spawned, they do not eat while in fresh water. Yet they
have been known to strike at pieces of bark, bottle caps,
bread crusts, cigarette butts, coins, live insects, dead
insects, twigs, even knots on a leader. They regularly strike
at all sorts of lures and bait, including casting spoons,
spinning plugs, worms, and prawns, all of which are often
legal outside North America.

However, fishing the fly is the established method of
choice for North American anglers, and fly fishing is by
far the preferred method as catch-and-release becomes
the watchword in a world of declining resources. But lest
we fly fishers become too smug with our craft, we must
realize that fly fishing offers numerous opportunities for
abuse: large hooks fished on short, sunken leaders with
the intent to snag fish; opportunistic fishing to salmon
penned by low water; killing "oversized" grilse; reusing
salmon tags. There seems no end to the methods by which
the determined can cheat the system.

When I began salmon fishing in the 1960s, flies were
still primarily defined by the standard British feather
wings, a class that for fishing purposes is all but extinct
today due to rising labor costs and more innovative
techniques. Today we have a great variety of other fly
styles from which to choose: hairwings, streamers, Spey
and Dee styles, dry flies, bugs, and a variety of lesser
creations. Each of these styles may be formed on a variety
of hooks. The permutations are innumerable. Let us first
review the most important forms and styles, after which
we'll consider a basic selection appropriate for anglers in
North America. Finally, I shall temper the basic selection
based on my own experience and prejudices.

## FORM

The form of a fly is defined by the hook or hooking arrangement. For flies whose bodies are integral with the hook, the most common forms are single and double hooks, such as those found in the typical hairwing fly. Tube flies with bodies separate or detached from a single, double, or treble hook are becoming increasingly common and in Europe have largely replaced the detached-body articulated hook or Waddington shank. But a hook is not just a device for impaling a fish. It may be the medium on which to assemble your attractor materials, a keel for steadying your fly, or a weight to sink the fly (or to prevent it from floating). These and other considerations often influence your choice of hooks.

**SINGLE HOOKS**. The most common single hook is the Mustad 36890, which is offered in sizes 12 through 3/0. A description of this and other hooks discussed herein is presented in Table 4-1. Unfortunately, there are no uniform standards as to the sizes of salmon hooks, even among different models by the same manufacturer. Unlike trout hooks, there are not even comparative standards for short or long shanks or extra-fine or extra-heavy wire. My hook box contains five different size 8 singles with shank lengths from 0.67 inch (Reddich) to 1.00 inch (Partridge Wilson).

Two other Mustad single hooks are common among salmon-fly tiers—the 9049 dry fly hook, offered in sizes 8 through 4, and the 90240 low-water hook, in sizes 10 through 4. Low-water hooks are by definition made of extra-fine wire, usually have an extra-long body, and are designed to provide good holding power. They are used with a smaller-than-usual fly body built on the front of the single hook. Dry fly hooks are of intermediate or fine wire and have a long body and a wide gape to provide good hooking ability.

Partridge makes outstanding single salmon hooks: the M, the company's standard single hook in sizes 10 through

5/0; the N, a low-water hook in sizes 10 through 8/0; the CS10/1 Bartleet Traditional with sizes 10 to 3/0; the CS10/2 Bartleet Supreme with sizes 10 to 1/0; the well-known Wilson 01 dry-fly hook, available in sizes 16 through 2; and the CS42 bomber/dry-fly hook in sizes 2, 4, and 6. The Partridge M hook has a shorter body than the Mustad 36890 and thus offers a useful option, particularly for the smaller sizes. Partridge advertises the Bartleet Traditional hook as "a beautiful hook for both display and fishing." Its dropped point makes it very effective at hooking fish, but the point is prone to breakage and very difficult to keep sharp. The CS10/1 Bartleet is often used for long-hackle Spey-style flies. I like the shorter, heavier CS10/2 in the smaller sizes for use with heron-type hackles. Perhaps the chief disadvantage in stocking the two Bartleet hooks is that their sizes are not related to those of any other hooks nor to each other. For instance, a size 6 Bartleet Supreme is much larger, both in length and gape, than a standard size 6 hook. You cannot order Bartleets without prior knowledge as to their actual dimensions.

Several lesser-known makes of single salmon hooks are also available, including the Gaelic Supreme hooks by Sprite of Redditch and newer entries by Daiichi and Tiemco. The Bob Ververka salmon hook and the Alec Jackson Spey hook, both by Daiichi, are popular on the West Coast for steelhead flies and are available in gold, silver, and black.

The selection of a particular hook by the fly tier is often compromised by availability. Most dealers do not stock an adequate selection of any but the most popular brands and sizes, and anything out of the ordinary usually must be specially ordered. Whether you tie your own flies or have them custom tied, you should become familiar with the basic hooks. A useful, if somewhat incomplete, cross-reference on hooks has been compiled recently by Bill Schmidt, *Hooks for the Fly* (47). The second part of his pamphlet lists the characteristics of the hooks by the major manufacturers but omits a number of hooks of interest to the salmon angler, including all the Kamasan hooks and

# TABLE 4-1
## DESCRIPTION OF SELECTED SALMON HOOKS

| Hook Form | Make & Model | Description | Sizes |
|---|---|---|---|
| Single hooks | Mustad 36890* | Limerick Bend, forged, Dublin point turned-up looped oval eye, black | 12-3/0 |
| | Mustad 9049 | Extra-long shank, fine wire, forged, Dublin point, turned-up looped oval eye, black | 8-4 |
| | Mustad 90240 | Extra-long shank, 2X fine wire, short hollow point, turned-up oval looped eye, black | 10-4 |
| | Partridge M | Standard-weight wire, looped up-eye, black | 10-5/0 |
| | Partridge N | Low-water hook, extra-long shank, looped up-eye, black | 10-8/0 |
| | Partridge O1* | Wilson single, long shank, looped up-eye | 16-2 |
| | Partridge CS2 | S.E.B. salmon/steelhead hook, long shank, looped down-eye | 8-2 |
| | Partridge CS10/1 | Bartleet traditional, Dublin style (dropped) point, looped up-eye, black | 10-3/0 |
| | Partridge CS10/2 | Bartleet Supreme, short version of CS 10/1 | 10-1/0 |
| | Partridge CS42 | Bomber hook, long shank, wide gape, looped down-eye, bronze | 6-2 |
| Double hooks | Mustad 3582F* | Standard-weight wire, oval up-eye, black | 12-2 |
| | Partridge P | Standard-weight wire, looped up-eye, black | 12-2 |
| | Partridge Q | Low-water hook, extra-long shank, looped up-eye, black | 12-3/0 |
| | Partridge O2* | Wilson double, long shank, looped up-eye, black | 16-2 |
| Drury-type treble hooks | Veniard Esmond Drury hook | Wide gape, outpoint, nickel (sizes 6, 8, 10) or black (14-2) | 14-2 |
| | Mustad 80550BL | Forged, micro barb, turned down-eye, black | 4-1/0 |
| | Partridge X2B | Long shank, outpoint hook, up-eye, black | 6-2 |

## (TABLE 4-1 CONTINUED)

| Hook Form | Make & Model | Description | Sizes |
|---|---|---|---|
| | Partridge CS12 | Extra-long shank, outpoint hook, up-eye, black | 12-2 |
| | Partridge GRSX2B | Long shank, outpoint hook, up-eye, Grey Shadow finish | 10-6 |
| Tube fly hooks | Mustad 9174 | Extra-strong single hook, extra short shank, straight ring eye, bronzed | 10-9/0 |
| | Partridge MM3ST | Extra-strong single hook, short shank, straight ring eye, black | 8-2 |
| | Partridge R3HF* | Falkus outbarb double hook, straight oval eye, black | 14-6 |
| | Loop SZ6 | Straight oval eye, short shank, black nickel | 6-2 |
| | Partridge GRSX8 | Falkus outbarb treble hook, oval eye, Grey Shadow finish | 10-4 |
| | Partridge X1 | Outpoint treble hook, extra strong, round eye, black, silver, or Grey Shadow | 16-3/0 |
| | Partridge X3 | Oval/needle eye treble hook, straight eye, black or silver | 12-2 |
| | Partridge CS9 | Rob Wilson extra-strong, outpoint treble hook, round eye, black, silver, or Grey Shadow finish | 10-2 |
| | Kamasan B990 | Extra-strong treble hook, oblong eye, bronze | 12-2 |
| | Mustad 3551 | Treble hook, ringed eye, bronze | 20-5/0 |

* Recommended for a fly tier's basic inventory of hooks.

the Loop hooks, as well as the Alec Jackson and Bob Verveka styles from Daiichi. With adequate notice, either Wallace W. Doak and Sons (105) or Hunter's Angling Supplies (110) can obtain almost any hook you desire.

**DOUBLE HOOKS**. No double hook dominates the market as does the Mustad 36890 single, but the Mustad 3852 series, now offered in only two styles, is one of the

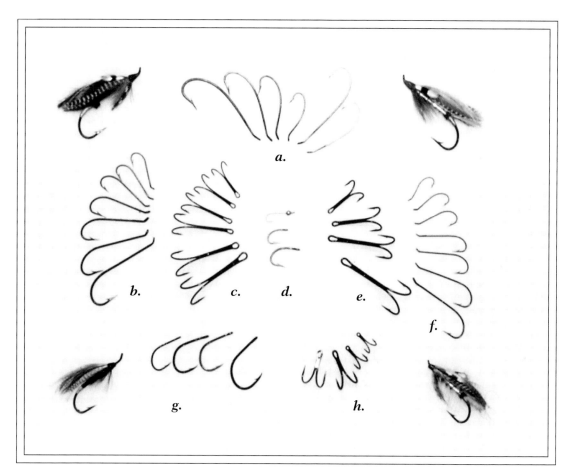

most prevalent. The 3852F with turned-up tapered eye is the preferred form and is available in sizes from 12 to 2. Larger double hooks are available from Sprite of Redditch. If you are interested in large double hooks, examine the included angle between the two barbs. Some hooks have an angle that is excessively large, almost as if one of the barbs of a treble hook had been cut off, which diminishes the effective gape of the hook.

Partridge makes several of the most popular double hooks. The P double salmon (sizes 12 to 2) and the Q low-water double (sizes 12 to 3/0) are their standards. The O2 Wilson double hook (sizes 16 to 2) is a superlative hook, especially in the smaller sizes, and is the preferred hook for sea trout in Europe. It is made of extra-fine wire, has a long body, very fine points, and is tempered very hard, as are all Partridge hooks. The Wilson sizes are unrelated to

Figure 4-1. An assortment of salmon hooks. Top to bottom, left to right:

(a) Partridge CS10/2 sizes 1/0, 2, 6, 10; Partridge CS42 sizes 2, 6

(b) Mustad 36890 sizes 1/0, 2–12

(c) Partridge Wilson O2 sizes 4–14

(d) Gaelic Supreme nymph size 16 with bead head; Mustad 9174 sizes 6, 10

(e) Mustad 3852F sizes 2–8

(f) Partridge Wilson O1 sizes 4–16

(g) Partridge Nordic MM3ST sizes 2, 4, nickel 4, 6

(h) Loop SZ size 6, Partridge Falkus R3Hf sizes 6, 10, 14

other standard-hook sizes; a size 16 Wilson is the same size as a size 12 standard. For all these reasons, the Wilson doubles are superb for very small flies, especially those tied low-water style.

**TREBLE HOOKS**. Treble hooks are illegal for salmon fishing throughout North America, except for portions of Quebec where trebles sizes 6 and smaller are permitted. In Europe, trebles are still used in the form of the Esmond Drury-type long-shank treble hooks with up-turned eye, and, of course, with the Waddington shank. However, Drury-type treble hooks are rapidly being replaced by tube flies. The advantage of Drury and Waddington trebles over tube flies is their weight, which may be a consideration in fast, boisterous waters where aluminum or brass tubes are not permitted. The Drury-style treble is fine in the smaller sizes, but for large flies the Waddington shank is preferred since it enables you to use small treble hooks (sizes 6 and 8), which hold better than do the larger hooks. The true Esmond Drury outpoint hook with long shank and upturned eye is available from E. Veniard Ltd. (117) in sizes 14 through 2. Mustad now offers a Drury-type, long-shank treble hook (No. 80550) with a turned-down eye in sizes 8 through 2. Partridge offers three Drury-type hooks. The X2B long shank with an upturned eye, in sizes 16 to 2, is very similar to the Esmond Drury hook described above. Also available are the CS12, with a 6X long shank and upturned eye, in sizes 12 to 2, and the GRSX2B long-shank outpoint, in sizes 10 to 6. Several other straight-eye trebles are also available from Partridge.

**HOOKS FOR TUBE FLIES**. The idea for tying a fly body around a tube, initially a turkey quill, is said to have originated about 1945 with Winnie Morawski, a well-known fly tier at Charles Playfair & Co. in Aberdeen, Scotland. Spreading slowly at first, the concept has gained momentum in recent years to the point that tube flies are universally used in Iceland and in Europe on the big-fish rivers of Norway, Sweden, and Russia. Tubes have the unique advantage that the style of the fly body can be built independently of the hooking arrangement. Several tube fly bodies can be strung together to create different effects. A skittering head may precede a conventional body. An additional advantage is that, because the hook is independent of the fly body itself, you need only a small inventory of hooks.

The hook for a tube fly should have an eye shaped to permit easy insertion in the rear of a plastic tube or into a supplemental piece of tubing slipped over the rear of a plastic or metal tube. Until recently, hooks with properly shaped oval eyes have not been readily available in the United States. For small flies, many of us have managed with small treble hooks with round eyes, but the eyes of most domestic trebles are too large for standard plastic tubes.

For those who wish to use single hooks in tubes, as is required in Sweden, there are two options—the Mustad 9174 and the Partridge MM35T Nordic hook. The Mustad 9174 has an extra-heavy, extra-short shank with a ringed eye and is available in sizes 10 through 9/0. The Partridge MM35T has a short shank with ringed eye in sizes 8 through 2.

Partridge makes a superb double hook with a straight, oval eye for use with tubes, the R3HF Falkus Outbarb double hook, which is available in sizes 14 through 6. As the name implies, the barbs on these hooks are on the outside of the bend, which assists in secure hooking. By bending down these outbarbs, you can make the ideal barbless hook. I use these hooks, particularly sizes 6 and 10, for all my tube flies in North America and have found them very satisfactory. To my knowledge, the only other double hook a with straight eye designed specifically for tubes is the new Loop SZ hook manufactured by Mustad. It is available in sizes 6, 4, and 2.

Partridge offers several short-shank treble hooks suitable for tube flies. My favorite is the GRSX8 Falkus Outbarb treble, offered in sizes 10 through 4, with an oval eye and Grey Shadow finish. Their standard treble, the X1, is very strong and is available in four finishes, including the silver finish much in demand in Iceland. The X3 tube fly treble, available in sizes 12 through 2, possesses an oval/needle eye for easy insertion into the tubes and is offered in both black and silver finishes. For very fast, tempestuous rivers, such as those found in Norway, the CS9 Rob Wilson double-strong outpoint treble is available in sizes 10 through 2 in four finishes. It is an excellent hook for large flies in heavy water but is too heavy for use with small flies or in slow water.

When fishing with aluminum or brass tubes in Europe, you must use a silicone, vinyl, or polyolefin plastic sleeve to connect the hook and tube, since the hook cannot be inserted into the rigid body of the tube. Since the tubing must be large enough to encompass the tube body, hooks with needle or tapered eyes usually must be crimped into place to prevent the hook from slipping out and tangling the wing of the fly. Rod Yerger supplies crimped plastic connectors with his tube flies, but he prefers a round-eye hook, such as the Partridge X1, which will not slip from its connector. If you do use plastic connectors, be certain that the material is tough enough and the tube wall thick enough to withstand the constant flexing that occurs during casting. Many of the silicone and vinyl connectors commonly supplied with tubes simply fall apart after an hour's casting. Of those that I have tried, flexible nylon tubing seems to be the best, although the new heat-shrinkable polyolefin tubing may be even better.

The Kamasan B990 treble hook, distributed by E. Veniard Ltd., is little known except among serious anglers fishing tube flies in Europe. Available is sizes 12 through 2, this hook is very strong, with an oblong eye and chemically sharpened needle points. While I find little need for treble hooks except when fishing tube flies in Europe, the B990 is my personal favorite among the treble hooks.

Mustad offers several treble hooks that may be adapted

for tube flies, although none are specifically designed for that purpose. The 3551 short-shank with ringed eye is a fine hook in the smaller sizes (it's available in sizes 20 through 5/0), but some anglers do not find the larger sizes sufficiently strong. Short-shank hooks are desirable for tube flies, since they do not allow leverage for the fish to work free as do the very long shanks. Choose a treble hook carefully because the ringed eye of most trebles not specifically designed for tubes is often too large for insertion into a tube, unless a separate section of larger tubing is used to join the tube body with the hook.

## STYLE

While the form of the hooking device determines the hooking ability and holding capacity of the fly, it is the style of the fly (and the manner in which it is fished) that determines your success in inducing a salmon to strike. One of the oddities of salmon fishing is that certain locales will adopt or use certain styles to the exclusion of all others. Guides are notorious for their capricious choices of fly styles. Should the fly body be fat or slender, the wing full or sparse, upright or laid back on the hook body, tied on a long hook or short? Should a tube fly be tied "upright," as with a hairwing, or symmetrical "in the round." Once you start introducing variations in coloration, sparkle, and fluorescence, the options are infinite. The best advice for the beginning salmon angler is to adopt a few standard patterns, whatever the style, and learn to fish them well.

I am firmly of the school that says the size and presentation of your fly is far more important than the specific pattern. This has been demonstrated on a number of occasions by respected anglers who have fished an entire season with only one fly pattern, but of any size: A.H.E. Wood with the March Brown, Neil Graesser with the Mar Lodge, Frank Griswold with the Griswold Gray, and especially Hugh Falkus, who fished three successive seasons, each with a single pattern. Falkus used a Blue

Charm the first year, Thunder and Lightning the second, and a Stoat's Tail (a buttless Black Bear) the third. In each case, the number of salmon landed during the season did not differ significantly from the angler's usual yearly averages using an unrestricted number of patterns, perhaps because greater care was taken with the presentation of the fly.

Neglecting a myriad of minor creations, there are five primary styles of salmon flies: (1) the feather wing, (2) the hairwing, (3) Spey and Dee styles, (4) streamers, and (5) dry flies and buck bugs, examples of which are shown in Figure 4-2. Joe Bates' excellent treatise on the art and history of the Atlantic salmon fly, *The Art of the Atlantic Salmon Fly* (04), describes the development of the colorful, classic feather wing during the latter part of the 18th century and continuing throughout the 19th century. During that period, feather-wing flies were the dominion of British and Scottish anglers who, with their gillies, developed fly tying into the fine art it is today.

In the 1930s the process of substituting animal hair for feathers in the winging of flies began to evolve. The transition was hastened by two major factors: hairwings display better fly action in the water, and they are easier and less expensive to tie. Bates relates his experience of watching an elderly gentleman on the Matapedia River gently separate with a pin all the wing fibers of a new Jock Scott fly. When asked why, the gentleman explained that as much as he loved the traditional feather-wing flies, the separated fibers pulsated in water and thus provided a better action to attract the salmon. Today, hairwings have totally replaced feather wings for all but the most traditional of salmon anglers. Some, and I count myself among them, believe that the profile and color of certain traditional feather wings remain unmatched. For that reason, I still carry a few Silver Greys in my fly box.

The Dee-strip-wing and Spey-style flies both originated in Scotland, from the River Dee in Aberdeenshire and the River Spey. While they look similar, they are constructed differently (26). The hackle of the Dee fly is tied in by the tip at the rear of the body and is palmered forward over the body, after which the narrow strip wings are applied. The Spey fly also has short strip wings, usually brown mallard, but the body hackle is applied differently. A heron or pheasant feather is tied in by the butt at the rear of the body and is spiraled forward in a clockwise direction between two body tinsels, after which a third body tinsel is wound counterclockwise forward to the head without binding any of the hackle fibers. It sounds complicated, but the construction results in a durable fly with the longest hackle fibers extending from the rear of the body. Properly constructed, the Spey fly has a slightly rounded or humpback shape with the wings set very close to the body. This style was developed to provide lots of fiber action in the fast, boisterous waters of the River Spey. At one time Dee and Spey flies were tied on special "Dee" hooks that were similar to low-water hooks. Such hooks are no longer available, but the Partridge N low-water, the CS10/1, or the Mustad 36890 makes an acceptable substitute. Dee- and Spey-style flies are popular on the steelhead rivers of the West Coast but are used only occasionally for Atlantic salmon in North America.

Most anglers are very familiar with streamer flies such as the Mickey Finn hairwing streamer or the Gray Ghost feather-wing. They are used primarily in the cold waters of spring and for dour fish holding in deep holes during high water. I include shrimp and prawn patterns in this category because their construction and use are somewhat similar. Interestingly, prawn and shrimp patterns are being used with increasing frequency under all conditions in North America.

The dry-fly-and-buck-bug category includes Bombers, Irresistibles, the Wulff series, the heavily hackled Whiskers and MacIntoshes, and the buck bugs, now offered in the colors of the rainbow. The similarity in styles among the principal dry flies and the bugs, which are mostly fished wet, lies in the use of deer hair bodies and bucktail.

The various fly styles may be tied directly onto a hook, in which case the body is said to be integral with the hook. A detached fly body is one tied onto a tube or Waddington shank to which a hook is fastened separately. Integral-body flies are adaptable to all styles, although large streamers and dry flies are seldom tied on double hooks. Esmond Drury-style treble hooks have been used for feather-wing flies, but today such hooks seem restricted to hairwing flies and shrimp and prawn patterns. The demand for Drury-style trebles is decreasing every year, although they find some use on Quebec's north shore, particularly on the lower Moisie River.

Tube flies comprise the vast majority of detached-body flies today because, among its other advantages, the tube usually separates from the hook when the fish strikes, which makes it much easier to play and land the fish. The Waddington shank with an articulated double or treble hook is extremely popular on the big fish rivers of Europe but finds only limited application for Atlantic salmon in North America, although its use is growing for West Coast steelhead. Surprisingly, Waddingtons do find some use in New Brunswick, where, despite the prohibition against weighted flies, the Waddington is accepted as a normal hook shank for use with a single or double hook. They are also used in very small sizes for low-water conditions on the Matapedia and other Gaspé Peninsula rivers. Rod Yerger, a prominent custom tier, believes that "when fishing deep, in the larger sizes the Waddington shank fishes better than any fly ever invented." He particularly favors a 2 1/2-inch Waddington with a size 6 double or treble hook. The primary areas for the Waddington shank flies remain the heavy waters of Norway and Scotland.

## THEORIES OF FLY SELECTION

We acknowledge that we don't understand why a salmon strikes a fly. Yet more effort is spent in developing the proper fly than on any other phase of salmon fishing. If only we spent half as much effort developing our presentation! When you open your fly box, you have several decisions to make: what form of fly, what style, what color, and what size hook, usually in that order. The selection of form and style is often made with little thought. But oh, what anguish we enjoy in selecting color and size. There are at least four concepts of color selection worth consideration.

**DARK DAY/DARK FLY; BRIGHT DAY/LIGHT FLY**. The simplest and most basic concept of fly selection states that you should use a dark fly on a dark day and a bright or silvery fly on a bright, sunny day. Against a dark sky, the salmon can easily determine a profile but not the color. Strive to make the silhouette of the fly stand out. On a bright day, the salmon easily discern colors and sparkle. Take advantage of this and present brightly colored flies with tinsel and sparkle.

**LA FONTAINE COLOR THEORY**. In his 1990 book, *The Dry Fly—New Angles* (32), Gary LaFontaine developed a "Theory of Attraction" for dry-fly trout fishing. The theory states that the color "of surrounding light affects the intensity of a fly's color" and that "flies with intense colors attract trout when trout are *in a mood to be attracted*" (italics by author). Note that it is the intensity as perceived by the fish that counts, not just how you and I might view the fly. LaFontaine's theory purports to explain why flies like the Royal Coachman are so effective. Under most light conditions, at least some parts of that fly appear bright, other parts dull. For instance, in reddish light the red floss of the body and the brown hackle appear bright while the peacock herl body is seen as a dull green. In greenish light, the herl body is a bright green while the floss body and hackle appear as dull colors. It is important to emphasize the need for "a mood to be attracted." For salmon, that's the most important requirement of all.

LaFontaine explains that his theory is not applicable to wet flies. Nevertheless, in *Atlantic Salmon Fishing* (13)

Bill Cummings examined the LaFontaine theory for its relevance to salmon. Cummings suggests that this concept may explain the effectiveness of the Butterfly, which is similar to a Royal Coachman but with white wings. Except when under a very dark sky, at least part of the Butterfly will appear "intense." This concept is similar to Art Lee's proposal in *Atlantic Salmon Journal* (33) that the better the fly color contrasts with the color of the sky (against which the salmon views the fly), the more attractive the fly will be to the salmon. He suggests that the fly should "jump out" at you. But doesn't that bring us back to the dark-sky/dark-fly concept?

LaFontaine's theory would be easy to test for salmon. Why not compare the effectiveness of similar red-and-green flies in both the reddish light of a late evening or autumn sun and in the greenish waters of the Gaspé Peninsula? We know that reddish orange flies are very effective in the tannic waters of autumn and that greenish flies such as the Green Highlander and the Cosseboom are successful in the Gaspé. At least this would give the angler a new concept to ponder

**HUBERT'S GUIDE FOR BRITISH PATTERNS.** In a privately printed book entitled *Salmon-Salmon* (23), Joe Hubert presented a color guide for British patterns, which may be summarized by the chart on page 117.

This guide is very useful in that it represents the consensus of a majority of anglers today for all styles of flies. Hubert's love for the traditional feather-wing flies is betrayed by the various examples he chose, even though in 1975, when his book was published, hairwing and tube flies were very popular in Iceland, which is the focus of the book. Anticipating the discussion to follow, equivalent hairwing patterns for his four categories might include the Silver Rat, the Blue Charm or hairwing Night Hawk, the Rusty Rat, and the Black Bear-Green Butt.

While not rich in technique, Hubert's compilation offers some incisive comments, including the fact that you "should consider the light on the fly" as it appears to the

## COLOR GUIDE FOR BRITISH PATTERNS

| Type of Sky Examples | Pattern Overall Color |
| --- | --- |
| Bright, sunny Silver Gray | Light colors, silver or gold bodies |
| Partly cloudy Night Hawk | Medium colors, aided by black flies with silver bodies |
| Overcast, diffuse light Jock Scott | Medium colors, with reds, blues, and greens, minimum tinsel |
| Dark, rain Black Dose | Dark flies with blues and browns, little or no tinsel |

salmon. It was more than a decade before this concept became popular. Hubert also emphasized that a slightly overcast sky with diffused lighting is perfect for salmon angling. With that most of us will agree.

**POSITION-OF-THE-SUN THEORY**. That the position of the sun affects how salmon discern a fly is unquestioned. That we can make meaningful use of this concept, attributed primarily to Preston Jenning, is arguable. The most succinct summary of this theory is presented in Joe Bates' and Pamela Bates Richards' recent book, *Fishing Atlantic Salmon* (05). I paraphrase as follows. If the salmon is facing the sun low in the sky, it can easily discern the silhouette and shape of a fly but not much in the way of its color. Thus it is desirable to use a very dark fly (Black Bear-Green Butt or Black Rat) on a dull or cloudy day and a somewhat brighter fly (Silver Rat or Night Hawk) on a sunny day. When the sun is high overhead, the salmon easily discern color, and you should consider a bright fly (Blue Charm or Hairy Mary) on a sunny day and a similar fly with less tinsel (Rusty Rat or Muddler) on a dull day.

When the salmon is facing away from a sun low in the sky, as in very early morning or late evening, consider a light, bright fly in sunny weather (Silver Grey or Silver Blue) or an extra light or white fly for dull days (Priest or Gray Rat). The flies listed in parentheses are suggestions offered by Bates. Anyone considering this concept should review Bates' discussion carefully.

Like the preceding theories, this position-of-the-sun concept has elements of truth and concepts that are questionable, if not simply wrong. Part of the problem lies in discerning how dim is dull and how dark is cloudy. On a very dark, rainy day salmon cannot discern much, if anything, in the way of color, and a dark fly with a good silhouette such as the Green Butt works best. If a salmon lies facing the rising sun or setting sun on a brilliant day, the backlighted silhouette of a Night Hawk with its black wing should be much preferred to the Silver Rat with its gray-and-white wing, since both possess essentially the same tinsel bodies. For a sun high overhead in decent light, I would choose either the Blue Charm or Rusty Rat, switching to a much darker fly, not the Muddler, as the light fades. The criterion for selecting a very light fly when the salmon is facing away from a sun low in the sky is likewise questionable. Would the all-white Priest be better than a Blue Charm or Silver Rat? I seriously doubt it. I would never choose a white fly under such conditions.

## A BASIC FLY SELECTION

Whenever a new member joins our salmon group, invariably his first questions are about fly patterns—what patterns and sizes to order, how many do you really need? The following are my recommendations for a minimal, basic selection for a week's fishing in most of North America. Additions and exceptions we'll discuss later. The dressings for the lesser-known or unusual fly patterns are presented at the end of this chapter.

Five basic patterns, four wets and a dry fly, will cover 85 to 90 percent of your needs. The wet flies are the Black

*Figure 4-2. The five basic styles of salmon flies, top to bottom: Green Highlander hairwing (courtesy of W.W. Doak & Sons Ltd.), antique Black Dose feather wing (Hardy Bros.), Rat-Faced MacDougall dry fly (courtesy of W.W. Doak & Sons Ltd.), Elver streamer (by author), and Lady Caroline Spey style (courtesy of Rod Yerger).*

*Figure 4-3. Left: Black Bear–Green Butt (by the author).*

*Bottom: Kola Rat (by the author).*

Bear-Green Butt, the Silver Rat, the Blue Charm, and the Rusty Rat. This selection includes a dark fly, a silver fly, and two bright flies, one with tinsel and one with little or none. The dry fly is the Bomber.

The Green Butt is your basic black fly, and the fluorescent green butt is marginally better than other colors. If I could choose but one fly to use all season, it would be the Green Butt, although I would modify it slightly by mixing into the wing three or four strands of very fine fluorescent orange or green winging such as Dan Bailey's Wing Fiber. Black flies are the ideal selection for dark, cloudy days. There is a second black fly that I have come to appreciate almost as much as the Green Butt—the Kola Rat. This fly has a peacock-herl body through which are palmered long furnace and grizzly hackles, side by side. These hackles' fibers come alive in even the slowest water to provide an enticement that salmon find difficult to resist. The wing is black squirrel or bear hair, finished with furnace and grizzly hackles wound together to form a collar at the head. I have become so confident of this pattern that I now carry it in sizes 2, 6, and 10.

No silver fly provides better flash and sparkle than the Silver Rat. It is an excellent choice for all but the darkest of skies and waters. My preferred alternate, although not as attractive on bright days, is the classic Silver Grey feather wing. It has better colors than the Silver Rat, and I like its profile.

The Blue Charm and the Rusty Rat are two of the most popular flies today. These are so good that it is hard to know which to choose in a given situation. The Hairy Mary—either the light, dark, or Irish badger variation—is fully equivalent to the Blue Charm in an overhead sun. For intermediate light bordering on the dull, nothing quite matches the Rusty Rat.

These four basic hairwing wet flies, in three sizes each, provide an ample arsenal for anyone. The three basic fly sizes are 4, 6, and 8. If you purchase two flies of each size of each pattern, you have a basic two dozen, an adequate assortment for your first week's trip. If you wish to expand beyond this basic group, purchase first some size 10 Green Butts; small black flies are always in demand. My five basic patterns and the two options are shown in Figure 4-3.

Do you start with single or double hooks? There are good arguments for each, but I strongly recommend double hooks for flies smaller than size 2. They ride better in the water and are more dependable in hooking the salmon. Remember, hooking the fish is the hardest part of salmon fishing. I do not accept the oft-repeated arguments about one barb of a double hook working against the other and eventually pulling loose. Besides, more often than not, only one barb penetrates the fish's jaw.

Your basic fly assortment is completed with the addition of two Bombers each in sizes 2 and 8, tied on the Partridge CS42 hook, if you have a choice. Salmon seem to prefer very large or very small Bombers. The in-between sizes are often less effective. I like the basic brown Bomber with white horns and tail. The color of the palmered hackle is immaterial, although orange is attractive.

## ALTERNATIVE SELECTIONS

Few North American salmon anglers will take issue with the universality of the five patterns I have recommended for a basic inventory. However, as you seek to expand your selection, individual preferences and prejudices begin to predominate, particularly with patterns peculiar to specific rivers and regions. Joseph Pulitzer, the publisher and former owner of the Grog Island Camp on the Restigouche, summarily dismissed the worshipping of specific fly patterns as a "pagan form of religion." The fact is that we choose flies based on what appeals to us or our guide.

My alternative selections are biased by experience. I know how and where to fish specific patterns. In new or unfamiliar waters, these alternates are the patterns I try first if the basic patterns fail to produce fish. Other anglers undoubtedly would suggest different patterns.

*Figure 4-3 (continued). Top: Silver Rat (courtesy of Rod Yerger).*

*Middle: Silver Grey (Hardy Bros.).*

*Bottom: Low-water Blue Charm (by the author).*

*Figure 4-3 (continued). Top: Rusty Rat (courtesy of W.W. Doak & Sons Ltd.).*

*Middle: Bomber tube fly (courtesy of Rod Yerger).*

*Bottom: Sili-leg Bomber (Matt Grobert).*

**STREAMERS**. You may note that the basic wet flies were predominantly black, silver, blue, and yellow—all well-recognized salmon colors. What about the missing red and green? My theory is to incorporate some of these desirable colors into other styles of flies, thus broadening my selection. Three streamer patterns stand out: the Chief Needahbeh (sizes 6 and 8); either the Black Sheep or preferably Bryson's Sheep (sizes 2 and 6); and a prawn pattern, the General Practitioner (sizes 2 and 6). For fall fishing in bright weather on the Miramichi, the orange-red Chief is unsurpassed. One possible explanation for its success is that cock fish view this streamer, in fact most streamers, as a potential spawning rival, just as they do small parr (which can fertilize eggs), and readily attack it. I carry Chiefs dressed with a short feather wing in the style of a traditional feather-wing fly and also with a long feather wing dressed on a typical streamer hook. If the water temperature is above 50°F, the shorter feather wing is the better choice.

I find a goat-hair or sheep pattern such as Bryson's Sheep effective, especially in size 2 or 4 for high water. Its long tail imitates a small eel or elver. Contrary to the teachings of Lee Wulff, I do not experience many short strikes on the long tail of a fly. As discussed in Chapter 11, long tube flies are very popular in Europe. If salmon want a fly, they will strike at the head or the eyes, just as they take a small fish. If they want to play, they will perform all sorts of tricks, including balancing the fly on their nose. The occasional short nip may merely be the fish hitting the fly with its tail.

Of all the shrimp and prawn patterns, the General Practitioner is among the best and is certainly the best known. To further expand my assortment of styles, I carry and recommend the version tied with marabou hackle. Marabou fibers introduce an action unequaled by any fiber, natural or synthetic. That's the reason the Woolly Bugger is so effective for trout.

Streamers are often an excellent choice as a change of pace for jaded fish that show no interest in your favorite

patterns. The second year that I fished the Grímsá River
in Iceland, the weather was unusually cold for mid-July,
and the fishing was lousy. In the first 3 1/2 days, 10 rods
caught only three fish. My assigned beat on the morning
of the fourth day was Laxfoss, the enormous pool
underneath the falls. That pool was full of dour salmon,
which for the first hour refused all my offerings. Finally,
in utter disgust, I searched my fly boxes for something
truly different and found several Olive Matuka trout
streamers. "Might as well try one," I reckoned. "Can't do
any worse." On the fourth cast, I hooked my first fish of
the week, and by lunchtime I had landed five salmon. I've
never caught a salmon on a Matuka since.

**DRY FLIES AND BUCK BUGS.** I recommend that
you increase your inventory of dry flies slowly, because
the Bomber is the best dry fly and you need only a few
patterns. Beyond Bombers, my choice is the White Wulff,
a very effective searching pattern in sizes 4 and 8. With
these two patterns you never need Rat-Faced
MacDougalls or Goofus Bugs.

Do I really need a Green Machine, either wet or dry?
Wet, yes; dry, no. Buck bugs tied with deer-hair bodies fill
an important niche since, depending on their
construction, they may be fished either dry, skittered, or
wet. I believe that the reason for the popularity and
success of any of the bugs is that as the hair becomes
water-logged, the fly almost sinks and is thus fished
"damp," as some people say, just beneath the surface in
the top 2 inches of the water column, the best depth for
attractor patterns. The problem I find with any of the
buck bugs tied with deer-hair bodies is that they float just
when I want them to sink. This is particularly
troublesome with the small size 8s and 10s, which I like to
fish just under the surface. Jerry Doak, proprietor of
Wallace W. Doak and Sons, which sells thousands of bugs
each season, has suggested that a single-hook bug sinks
better than the double, that there is a tendency for double-
hook bugs to ride up. Another solution, of course, is to

*Figure 4-4. Selected
alternative fly patterns.*

*Top to bottom: White Wulff
(courtesy of Rod Yerger),
Chief Needahbeh (courtesy of
W.W. Doak & Sons Ltd.), and
Bryson's Sheep (by the
author).*

*Figure 4-4 (continued). Selected alternative fly patterns.*

*Top to bottom: Marabou General Practitioner (Ted Godfrey), Green Machine (courtesy of Rod Yerger), and Butterfly (courtesy of W.W. Doak & Sons Ltd.).*

have your small bugs tied with wool bodies, which readily absorb water. Alternatively, you may use a fluorocarbon leader to help sink the small flies.

The history and development of the buck bug are convoluted. The original brown bugs became popular in the early 1970s. Shortly thereafter various anglers began experimenting with color. Jerry Doak, in a whimsical article entitled "The Green Machine" published in *Fly Tyer* (15), attributes the development of the green bug to Evelock Gilks and others fishing at Nelson's Hollow, just upriver from Doaktown, where the name *Green Machine* was coined in l977. This euphonious name took hold in 1978, and the rest is history.

I carry a few Green Machines sparsely tied on lightweight Wilson double hooks in sizes 10 and 12, since they offer me a different style in another color. (Remember, a Wilson 10 is about the size of a standard 6.) However, I am convinced that it is not the green color that makes the difference. Four years ago, I witnessed a large hen salmon captured on a Green Machine (fluorescent green butt) in the tannic-red waters of the Miramichi on a gray, overcast morning. None of the color theories would have suggested the use of that fly under those conditions. Later the same afternoon, I observed a 20-pound cock fish landed on the same fly under the bright, reddish light of a clear October evening. So much for the color theories.

Other colors have their devotees. In the early 1980s, the black bug (Shady Lady) sprang to life and has now become the second most popular bug on the Miramichi River. If you like buck bugs, don't overlook the black bugs with fluorescent green and/or red butts in sizes 8 and 10. They can be effective when other black flies are ignored. A hot-orange bug (the Bitch) with a fluorescent orange tag and tail is also popular for use just at dusk, particularly on the Moisie. A bug of any color fished just below the surface can be deadly.

The manner in which a hook is dressed may contribute more to the success of buck bugs than we realize. Rod Yerger ties thousands of bugs on a variety of hooks each year for demanding customers. Rod relates the story of fishing unsuccessfully at Sutter's Pool on the Miramichi with a Green Machine tied on a standard Partridge M single hook. He happened to notice that the fly was swinging through the water with its tail tipped down. The hook was too heavy for the dressing given the moderately slow current. His guide, Wavell Price, offered him another Green Machine tied on an identical hook except that bug had a tail of golden pheasant crest fibers. Switching flies, Rod found that this second fly rode properly in the current; he subsequently caught five grilse on that fly during the next two days. These kinds of details sometimes make the difference.

Standard green flies such as the Green Highlander and the Cosseboom are not on my list only because my early salmon fishing occurred in venues with tannic waters where green flies are little used. For clear rivers such as the Restigouche, the Matapedia, and those of the Gaspé Peninsula, I certainly would add a green, yellow, and gold fly to my inventory, preferably the Green Highlander.

**COMMOTION FLIES**. The concept of commotion flies is attributed to Father Elmer J. Smith, a Miramichi legend from Prince William, New Brunswick. He believed that salmon are attracted by the commotion of the fly as it is moved across the surface of the water. Taken literally, this suggests that only flies riffled or skittered on the surface create commotion. In my view, the concept of commotion needs to be interpreted more broadly and should include flies whose very construction results in commotion, as well as the commotion introduced by the manner in which the fly is manipulated in the water. (Manipulated or induced commotion is discussed in Chapter 9.)

The Butterfly, developed by Maurice Ingalls, is certainly a commotion fly. This pattern is ubiquitous on the Miramichi for good reason: it catches fish. Fished in typical wet-fly manner, the white wings quiver and sway in the water like those of no other wet fly. Again Rod

*Figure 4-4 (continued).*
*Selected alternative fly*
*patterns.*

*Top to bottom: Willie Gunn*
*(courtesy of Rod Yerger),*
*Lady Mary (by the author),*
*and Gray Monkee (by the*
*author).*

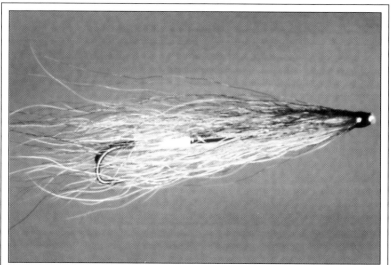

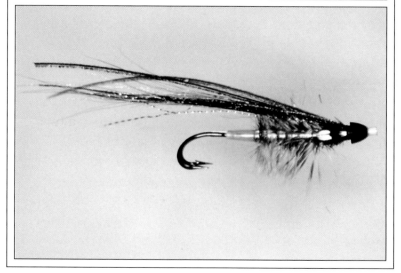

Yerger's experience tying hundreds of Butterflys each year is instructive. As he states in his catalog, "This is one fly I think fishes better on a single hook." Rod believes that the single hook rides better and displays more action.

Generally, the motion of Spey hackles or long rooster hackles palmered through a fly body creates action but not commotion. However, some dry flies create commotion without manipulation. My favorite is the Sili-leg Bomber, a regular Bomber with three pairs of white or black legs tied through the body, much like the Girdle Bug trout fly. Even in a quiet current, those legs quiver enticingly.

Lastly, the body action of very long flies, such as the sheep patterns and especially the Sun Ray Shadow tube fly, creates a type of underwater commotion. If you have ever observed such flies undulate in a very clear river or manipulated them on the end of a long, two-handed rod, you would recognize just how much commotion a sunken fly can create.

**TUBE FLIES**. Integral-body flies, mostly hairwings, dominate my selection of recommended flies, but as the years pass I find that I spend more and more time fishing tube flies, even in traditional rivers such as the Moisie and the Matapedia. They are highly effective, may be assembled in countless configurations and colors, and, most importantly, relieve me of carrying dozens of hairwing patterns, each with its own hook. Two, or at most three, sizes of hooks are all that are required for all your tube flies. Suddenly, the selection of flies becomes simple again. Using tube flies means that I don't have to carry integral-body flies larger than size 4. In high water, if I need a fly larger than size 4, I usually slip on a tube of the appropriate size with a size 6 or 8 double hook. If necessary, a short lead head (see Chapter 6) will help to sink the light hook.

Many anglers recommend that you start your collection of tube flies with the usual hairwing patterns, such as the Green Butt, Silver Rat, etc. I suggest a different approach: broaden your inventory by adopting totally different patterns. In my experience, three or four tube patterns stand above all others. The best tube fly, without question, is the Willie Gunn, named after its originator who was the river keeper at Sutherland Estates on the River Brora. It has been so successful in Scotland that they say you only need three flies: a Willie Gunn, a Willie Gunn, and a Willie Gunn. Tied with black hair over red-and-yellow, its overall coloration is similar to the Thunder and Lightning or the Phoenix and Comet tube flies. I think of it as a Mickey Finn layered with black hair.

My principal bright tube fly is the Lady Mary, the pattern on which I landed my first Sixteen-Twenty Club fish and for which I admit a definite prejudice. While no more outstanding than many other patterns, its hot-orange underwing and purple hackle offer an interesting change of pace. Somewhat by coincidence I have carried this pattern tied with an upright or "top-side" wing, as well as tied in the round like the Willie Gunn. I had much better success with the upright wing, perhaps because of its thinner, slimmer profile.

Black and silver flies play an important role in salmon fishing, and there are a dozen well-known patterns such as the Night Hawk, the Collie Dog, and the Stoat's Tail. My third favorite tube fly is a nondescript but very effective black, gray, and silver eel-like pattern that I call simply the Gray Monkee. It borrows from the Sunray Shadow, Gunnar's Monkey, and the Silver Stoat.

Tube flies are a welcome diversion to me. They free me from the rigid hierarchy of integral-body flies. But you will notice that my three tube favorites are a dark fly, a bright fly, and a silver fly, the same basic choice as for hairwings. One of the things that impresses me is that people who use tube flies do not seem compelled to carry dozens of fly patterns. Four or five patterns, each in two lengths, will generally suffice. It seems that without the historical precedence for a multiplicity of patterns simplicity reigns.

When you select tubes, unless you are going to use bead- or coneheads (see below), purchase only the double or lined tubes. They are stiffer than unlined tubes and much easier to work with. More importantly, long goat-hair tails will not wrap around the tube as easily as it does with the flexible unlined tubes. When you purchase or tie tube flies, examine the head carefully. Small tube flies with large heads have a tendency to ride high and skim the surface, particularly in strong, fast currents. A short, 1- or 2-foot lead head between the line and the leader is often desirable to correct this problem (see Chapter 6).

Very recently a new dimension has been introduced into tube fly construction—the conehead system—which is particularly effective for increasing the depth at which your fly fishes. The concept is simple. Secure a metal conehead (or a brass or tungsten bead) to the front end of the tube fly. The added weight helps to counterbalance a heavy hook, particularly for small flies or in slow currents. A properly balanced fly fishes better and hooks more fish. Some say that a weighted fly also casts better and helps to turn over a long leader, although I have reservations on that point. But, clearly, a tube fly with a weighted head will not skim the surface. The weight and color may be varied by using aluminum, brass, or tungsten cones or beads of varying sizes. I believe this new system will further render obsolete the Waddington shanks of yore. The most perplexing problem is fitting properly sized cones or beads to the varying diameters of the tubing. Except for the very largest sizes of coneheads, a proper fit usually requires inserting a short length of small-diameter tubing into the head of an unlined tube onto which the cone or bead is affixed with CA glue. Håkan Norling published an article in the Winter 1998/99 issue of the *Atlantic Salmon Review* (27b) that describes a variety of conehead combinations for tube flies. But a word of caution: tube flies with coneheads just may be considered weighted flies, which are prohibited in all salmon jurisdictions in North America. It's best to check with local authorities first. On the other hand, if Waddington shanks are legal in Quebec and New Brunswick, coneheads certainly should be.

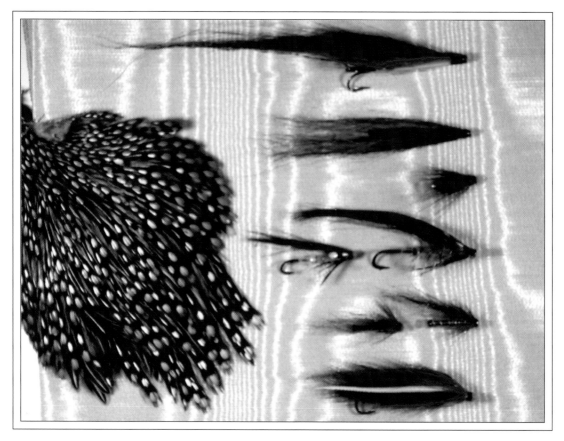

*Figure 4-5. An authentic Sun Ray Shadow (top, courtesy of Margit and Earl Worsham) and an assortment of tube flies.*

## SELECTED FLY DRESSINGS

Of the 17 patterns discussed in this chapter, 10 are well known. The Sili-leg Bomber is an obvious extension of the standard pattern, the development of which was attributed to Maurice Ingalls and Father Elmer Smith by Jerry Doak in a telephone conversation with me (15). For the legged version, be sure to use Sili-Legs, not the round rubber legs. The action of the silicon rubber is much livelier, presumably more seductive to the salmon. The dressings for the six lesser-known patterns are presented below. A word of advice about fly dressing. Tie or purchase your flies with slender profiles. I am convinced, as have been many before me, that slim flies with sparse wings fish better than do flies with heavily dressed wings. Size 6/0 tying thread, fine or extra-fine tinsel, and fine animal hair such as fitch tail or goat hair all contribute to sleek flies with excellent action in the water.

**KOLA RAT**. The rat series of flies is attributed to Roy Angus Thomson, who developed the Gray Rat in 1911. The "rat" name reflects Thomson's initials. The Kola Rat was developed for use in the Ponoi River on the Kola Peninsula of northwestern Russia. Traditionalists will argue that the Kola Rat is not a true rat fly in that the wing is black, usually squirrel or bear, instead of the gray fox guard hairs used in all other rat patterns. Be that as it may, it's an extremely effective fly.

| | |
|---|---|
| Thread | Black |
| Tag | Narrow oval silver tinsel |
| Tail | Peacock sword fibers |
| Body | Large peacock herl, usually reinforced with very fine gold or silver wire |
| Body hackle | Grizzly and furnace hackles, with fibers stripped from one side of each feather, palmered together over the peacock herl body |
| Wing | Black squirrel or bear |
| Hackle | Grizzly and furnace hackles, with fibers stripped from one side, wound together for two or three turns |
| Head | Black |

For the body, I prefer the bronze herl found at the top of the tail feather near the eye. To easily strip the hackle feathers, grasp them by the tip with the bright side facing away from you. With your thumb and forefinger, gently strip the right side of each feather. Tie in the feathers by the tip and wind the hackles in the usual manner. Furnace hackles are less common than other "trout" hackles. They are reddish brown with a black center.

**CHIEF NEEDAHBEH**. This fly was developed by Roland Nelson, better known as Chief Needahbeh, a Penobscot Native American who operated a tackle shop on Moosehead Lake in Maine. Nelson was an excellent fly caster and was often featured at sportsmen's shows in the 1950s. The Chief fly was originally intended for brook trout and landlocked salmon. It has since become one of the best fall patterns for sea-run salmon in Maine, New Brunswick, and Nova Scotia when dressed on a standard-length salmon hook.

| | |
|---|---|
| Thread | Black |
| Tag | Narrow oval silver tinsel |
| Tail | A few fibers of red duck or goose |
| Body | Bright red floss or silk |
| Ribbing | Narrow oval silver tinsel |
| Wing | Two yellow saddle hackles, tied back to back, outside of which are tied red saddle hackles on either side. Depending on the style, the saddle feathers may be quite long, as in a feather-wing streamer, or short as in a feather-wing fly |
| Throat | Red and yellow saddle hackles, with fibers stripped from one side of the feathers, wound together, dressed rather fully |
| Cheeks | Short jungle cock |
| Head | Black |

The original Chief was dressed by Nelson on a long streamer hook. Nelson used long saddle-hackle wings, a flat tinsel tag and ribbing, and only a red hackle for the throat collar. Dressed on salmon hooks such as the Partridge CS2 S.E.B., a shorter wing, not more than 1 1/2 times the hook length, is now more popular, as are the red and yellow throat hackles. Some tiers have switched to a gold tag and ribbing, feeling that it better accents the tones of the fly.

**BRYSON'S SHEEP**. The sheep patterns have been widely used in Iceland and Europe and finally are beginning to find a home in North America. The sheep series was developed by Joe Hubert, who was intrigued by the immature eels, or elvers, on which salmon sometimes feed while in the ocean. The best known of the series is the Black Sheep, which, with its blue hackle, silver tag, and red head, was developed for the rivers of Iceland, where blue is a desirable color. For use in the tannic, tea-colored waters found in much of North America and also on the Kola Peninsula of Russia, yellow and gold are better colors. Bryson's Sheep (so named by Ernie Schweibert) is based on a fly developed by William Bryson, former Director of Outdoor Recreation of the Province of Nova Scotia, for use in the dark waters of that area. It may be tied with an integral body on single or double hooks or as a tube fly.

| | |
|---|---|
| Thread | Black |
| Tag | Fine oval gold tinsel |
| Body | Black floss or wool |
| Ribbing | Fine or medium gold tinsel |
| Wing | Fine black hair, two to three times the hook length, tapered to imitate an eel-like body. On top of the black hair, tie one-third as much canary-yellow winging. |
| Throat hackle | Canary yellow |
| Cheeks | Short jungle cock |
| Head | Black |

The wing material may be bucktail, bear, goat, or a suitable synthetic such as Big Fly Fiber. If goat is used, a black bucktail underwing as long as the hook should first be tied over the body to provide a platform for the goat and to prevent it from wrapping around the hook. This is a very effective fly in sizes 2 and 4 for big rivers. It may also be tied as a tube fly 3 to 5 inches long.

**WILLIE GUNN.** This is one of the many tube flies designed to be tied in the round, symmetrical from any angle. It is effective in all sizes, although the larger sizes should be tied with a slim profile while the small tubes may be fuller and fatter. With this fly, it pays to experiment with body style.

| | |
|---|---|
| Thread | Black |
| Tube | 1/2- to 2-inch plastic |
| Ribbing | Small oval silver tinsel |
| Body | Black floss |
| Underwing | Mixed red and yellow bucktail, sparsely tied completely around the tube |
| Wing | Black bucktail or squirrel hair applied over the underwing |
| Collar | Blue-dyed guinea fowl (optional) |
| Head | Black |

Tie in the ribbing and body floss, leaving ample room for the hook to be inserted at the rear. If the ribbing is tied in at the very rear of the tube, the tube may not stretch sufficiently to permit insertion of the hook. Wind the floss forward. Spiral the tinsel forward over the body. Apply a thin layer of mixed red and yellow hair completely around the tube and tie in about 1/4 inch back of the eye. If sparkle is desired, mix a few strands of Krystal Flash or Bailey's Wing Fiber into the underwing. Now cover the underwing with a thin layer of black hair tied in just forward of the red-and-yellow layer. This makes for a neater head. The fly should appear dark, but not black. The red and yellow colors should be clearly seen at the tail of the fly but not at the head. The guinea collar is often omitted. An interesting, if less intensely colored, variation may be obtained by mixing red- and yellow-dyed gray squirrel tail.

**LADY MARY**. Tube flies with complex or multiple wings, as well as throat hackles, are best tied upright, not in the round. I prefer flies that are not excessively gaudy but with some sparkle. For those reasons, I designed the Lady Mary to be bright, but with restrained glitter.

---

| | |
|---|---|
| Tube | 1/2- to 1 1/2-inch plastic |
| Thread | Black |
| Tag | Fine oval gold tinsel |
| Body | Flat silver tinsel, wound clockwise |
| Ribbing | Fine oval gold tinsel, wound counterclockwise |
| Underwing | Hot orange polar bear or bucktail interspersed with a few strands of Bailey's fluorescent orange Wing Fiber |
| Wing | Brown-black or black fitch tail or squirrel |
| Throat hackle | Purple hackle, dressed as a sparse collar |
| Cheeks | Very small jungle cock (optional) |
| Head | Black |

---

Tie in the gold ribbing and the flat silver tinsel 1/8 inch from the end of a 1/2-inch tube or 1/4 inch from the end of a longer tube. Wind the body tinsel forward, clockwise. Wind the gold ribbing forward, counterclockwise. Now tie in the underwing, which should not extend beyond the end of the hook. Body veilings or underwings should be positioned to reveal a trace of fluorescence or a touch of tinsel. Tie in the wing, spreading the hairs slightly to add bulk. Long flies should be sleek and slender. I like short flies to be bushy and bug-like. In any event, however, if it is attached, the wing on a tube fly should cover the hook. Add the throat hackle. If jungle cock eyes are desired, keep them very small.

Polar bear fur is a very interesting material. While it appears white, if you hold the fur up to the sunlight, you will find that each of the long guard hairs is a clear hollow tube. These guard hairs are not wetted as is ordinary hair. Along with musk ox and wolverine, polar bear is one of the few hairs to which ice crystals will not adhere. That's why the Inuits and Eskimos used a piece of polar bear fur for icing their sled runners. When finished, they have merely to shake the fur free of ice and it is ready for subsequent use.

**GRAY MONKEE**. Tube flies such as the Collie Dog and Sun Ray Shadow tied without a body on a bare plastic tube intrigue me. They are very simple and very effective. My Gray Monkee is a smaller version of the Sun Ray Shadow but with a body hackle similar to Gunnar's Monkey.

| | |
|---|---|
| Tube | 1/2- to 2-inch plastic |
| Thread | Black |
| Tag | Small or medium round silver tinsel, two turns |
| Ribbing | Small or medium round silver tinsel |
| Body hackle | Grizzly hackle |
| Wing | Black hair or Big Fly Fiber overlaid with three or four strands of Bailey's fluorescent green Wing Fiber on top of which are tied three or four strands of peacock herl |
| Throat hackle | Sparse black bucktail or hen hackle, extending to the end of the tube (optional) |
| Cheeks | Short jungle cock (optional) |
| Head | Black |

Tie in the silver ribbing about 1/4 inch from the rear of the tube. Wind the tag and then tie in the grizzly hackle. Twist together the tinsel and tying thread and wind forward in spirals spaced 1/8 to 3/16 inch apart and tie it off. Now wind the grizzly hackle forward to just ahead of the tinsel. The tinsel provides protection for the hackle and keeps it from slipping on the tube. On top of the tube, clip the hackle so it won't interfere with the wing, and tie in a small bunch of winging material, tapering the ends. I find that Big Fly Fiber works well for this application. Tie several strands of Bailey's Wing Fiber on top of the wing, and then add several strands of peacock herl. If desired, add the optional throat and jungle cock cheeks and cement the head.

As with many tubes tied with upright wing, this fly fishes extremely well with a Falkus outbarb double, size 6 or 8 (Partridge R3HF). Even where treble hooks are legal, I much prefer the double hook since it acts as a keel to prevent the fly from twisting.

**SUN RAY SHADOW**. A tube fly that is used in Norway—to the virtual exclusion of all others on the Laerdal River—is the Sun Ray Shadow. This fly was developed about 1970 by the late Ray Brooks. He and his wife, Margit, were substantial leaseholders on the Laerdal in those days. Designed to imitate small eels, the fly is tied on a clear plastic tube 1 1/2 to 2 inches long. The wing is of long black hair, originally of Colobus monkey. The underwing may be blue or brown deer hair or gray-white squirrel tail. Blue is the most popular. Flies such as these, with tails up to 6 inches long, are particularly adapted to fast currents and high waters, where, fished close to shore, they are often deadly. The dressing for the Sun Ray Shadow is very simple:

| | |
|---|---|
| Tube | 1/2- to 2-inch double-walled plastic tube |
| Underwing | Blue or brown deer hair, or gray-white squirrel tail |
| Wing | Long black goat, black bear, a black synthetic such as Big Fly Fiber, or even human hair, topped by strands of peacock herl |
| Head | Black |

The length of the tube is usually one-quarter to one-third the length of the wing. A 1-inch tube would typically yield a fly 2 1/2 to 3 1/2 inches long. The 1 1/2-inch tube is generally used with 5- to 6-inch hair. In high or fast water, an aluminum or copper tube may be used where legal. Double-walled plastic tubes are desirable to add rigidity and prevent the long tail from curling around the tube. The underwing is tied in about 1/4 inch behind the head of the tube. I like to add a few strands of Dan Bailey's fluorescent green or orange Wing-Fiber on top of the underwing. Then tie in the wing just ahead of the underwing. Make certain that the tail is well tapered, not blunt. Tied in this manner, the head of the fly is small and neat. Add jungle cock eyes if you prefer, although the original Shadows did not use them. If goat hair is used for the wing, make the underwing a bit fuller than usual to provide a platform for the goat hair and to prevent its curling about the tube.

## LAST CASTS

Less attention is paid to size than any other aspect of fly selection. It's something you are expected to learn by trial and error, experience, assimilation. As we have seen, the most common sizes of wet flies in North America are 4, 6, and 8. The problem I have with that selection is that there is insufficient variation among the sizes. I infrequently fish flies as large as size 4 and very often fish size 10s and 12s. An ideal selection might include sizes 4, 7, and 10; but, of course, size 7 no longer exists. One option would be to retain size 4s for cold and high-water conditions, to dress size 7 fly bodies on size 6 hooks, and to adopt size 10 flies in place of 8s.

The British sometimes pay exacting attention to fly size. Undoubtedly, this stems from the fact that they experience a much wider range of water temperatures than do we in North America. Some Scottish rivers, such as the Oykel and Helmsdale, open as early as January 11, where low-water temperatures dictate very large flies. By contrast, during summer in the Highlands, the spate rivers are subject to very low water and unusually high temperatures, which require small flies, size 14 not being uncommon. Carrying size selection to an extreme, Richard Waddington once suggested starting with size 4 flies for water temperatures 48–50°F and decreasing your fly by one size for every 2° rise in water temperature. That's a bit too dogmatic for my taste.

The best discussion on this subject I have seen is contained in a charming little book entitled *Fly Fishing for Salmon* (22) by Neil Graesser, a member of the management committee of the Atlantic Salmon Trust. His first chapter offers one of the best short summaries available of how we fish for salmon. Much can be learned from such books by authors from other cultures. Hugh Falkus' treatise, *Speycasting: A New Technique* (17), is another outstanding example. The only better way to learn is to actually fish the European and Icelandic rivers.

For the beginning salmon angler, where to purchase flies is often a major problem since an adequate selection of salmon flies is seldom available at your local fly shop. One of the very best sources is Wallace W. Doak and Sons of Doaktown, New Brunswick (105). It publishes an illustrated catalog and also offers duty-free shipping. The premier custom-tiers of fishing flies in the United States are Ted Godfrey (108) and Rod Yerger (119). Either can assist you with recommendations, and they both offer special patterns for rivers around the world. Yerger is unique in that he personally ties all the flies he sells—on almost any hook you specify. The quality of his flies is outstanding.

For those so inclined, I urge that you learn to tie your own salmon flies, at least the basic hairwings and the simple tube flies. As you explore different rivers, you will learn of local pattern variations that merit consideration. It is a simple matter to tie a few such patterns and try them. Not only will it enhance your enjoyment of the angling experience, but it also contributes to your understanding of the enigmatic salmon.

Tread lightly when you enter the wonderful world of flies. It a stunning, complex, beautiful, bewildering maze from which you may never exit.

*A Salmon in Fast Water*
Watercolor
9 5/8 x 14 inches
Private Collection

# Chapter 5

# Knots: Their Contruction and Testing

## CASA BLANCA TARPON

It was my first attempt to catch a tarpon on a fly. We were fishing out of Casa Blanca, a charming camp on the small coastal island of Punta Pajaros, on the south side of Ascension Bay some 100 nautical miles south of Cancun, Mexico. The entire area is within the Sian Ka'an Biosphere Reserve, an extensive and well-protected ecosystem that encompasses the bay and 1.3 million acres of the surrounding coastal swampland. The area is alive with small bonefish and, under normal conditions, has a good supply of small- and medium-sized permit.

Baby tarpon (15 to 25 pounds) and a few larger fish are found in the brackish inland lagoons, the access to which is an adventure in itself. A 40-minute drive south of camp along a rough coastal trail brings you to the thin arm of one of the inland lagoons. You pole your boat into a series of mangrove swamps and up what can generously be described as a mangrove canal. Suddenly you make a right turn into the mangroves and follow a very narrow

**145**

archway cut into the swamp above a rivulet of water flowing toward an unrevealed destination.

After 10 minutes of poling along an incredibly twisted path, you emerge into the lagoon, which is fed by several saltwater springs called *zenotés*. It's a beautiful, isolated world perhaps three miles long and a mile across, banded by mangroves on all sides and alive with flamingoes and pelicans, a few alligators, and even the occasional swamp deer.

My partner Charlie, an experienced tarpon fisherman, had just completed his first turn that sunny morning. Now it was my turn to attack those brutes. I was using a 9-foot rod with 9-weight line and a modified salmon leader. That leader was to be my undoing.

Standing in the prow, I was casting 30 to 35 feet into the edges of the mangroves, particularly into any deep pockets. Sometimes it required a sidearm cast to place my fly under the overhanging mangroves. One particularly long cast into such a pocket resulted in a sudden boil. Instinctively, I tried to strike the fish and set the hook. But this fish had other ideas. Instead of turning away as to flee, the tarpon swam straight toward me. I could not strip in line rapidly enough to set the hook. About 15 feet from the boat, the tarpon veered sharply and turned its head to escape; at the same instant I did set the hook. The leader parted above the bite tippet. My first tarpon was lost.

Upon examining the leader, it was obvious that I had goofed badly. I had taken a knotted salmon leader, cut off the tippet, and tied a perfection loop, to which was looped the class tippet and a short bite tippet. But the leader had parted at the first blood knot above the tippets, at a knot on the old salmon leader. My ego was badly bruised. As an experienced, knowledgeable fisherman, how could I have been so dumb?

A presumably strong knot had failed. A fish was lost. I had relearned one of the oldest lessons in fly fishing: fish don't break leaders; jerks do.

## WHAT IS A KNOT?

Imagine you are thrown a rope and asked to grasp it and describe how you can secure your end of the rope. There are two obvious ways. First, you may grasp it in your hands with your fingers wrapped around the rope, much as in climbing a rope. Your fingers are analogous to coils of rope wrapped around the main rope. If you have enough fingers or sufficient coils, you can hold the rope against a sizable force (Figure 5-1). Coils or wrappings of one rope around another constitute a very important class of what in sailing terminology are called *hitches*. The Bimini Twist is the best known of the fisherman's hitches.

The second manner in which you can fasten the end of a rope is to secure it to another object, perhaps making a loop around a stake or through

*Figure 5-1. Camel hitch. Your fingers are analogous to the coils of rope in a hitch.*

the eye of an anchor. These types of loop hitches are the means by which we secure flies to leaders.

There is a third class of major importance to the fisherman—bends—which are defined as those fastenings that secure the ends of two ropes. The best known examples are the square knot and the sheet bend. Bends are most important to the fisherman in forming knotted leaders, with such well-known examples as the blood knot and the double or triple surgeons knot.

In addition to hitches and bends, nautical parlance recognizes two additional categories—splices and knots, the latter being defined as anything that is not a hitch, bend, or splice. Such subtleties are lost on the fisherman. To us, they are all simply knots. What is important to us is the manner in which knots are formed and used.

To illustrate and understand the discussion to follow, it is necessary to recognize the basic parts of a rope, line, or leader as shown in Figure 5-2. The standing part (a) is the main, inactive portion of the line. The bight (b) is the central, usually curved, part of the line. For our purposes we shall assume that our knots will be formed in the bight. The extremity or termination of the line is the end (c). We fishermen call it the *tag* or *tag end*. Tags are always clipped short to avoid catching foreign matter. For forming loops, the standing line is frequently bent back and the knot formed around it. We shall refer to this as the returned standing line (d).

Those interested in knots should consult the knot bible, *The Ashley Book of Knots* (02). First published in 1944 by Clifford W. Ashley and subsequently reprinted 40 times, this book is a true tour de force, listing an incredible 3,850 types of hitches, bends, splices, and knots. Reflecting the age of specialization, the International Guild of Knot Tyers was established in 1982 to unite the interests of knot aficionados. Membership is open to anyone interested in knots; information may be obtained from the secretary of the guild.[1]

---

1. Nigel Harding, Honorary Secretary, 3 Walnut Tree Meadow, Stonham Aspal, Stowmarket, Suffolk, IP146DF, England. E-mail: igkt@nigelharding.demon.co.uk.

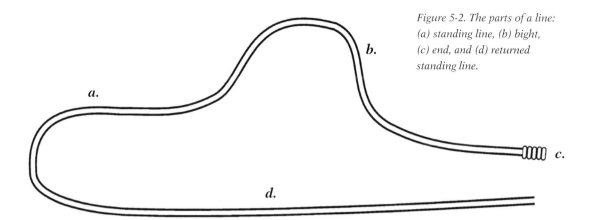

*Figure 5-2. The parts of a line: (a) standing line, (b) bight, (c) end, and (d) returned standing line.*

## KNOTS IN NYLON AND OTHER SYNTHETICS

In the years immediately following World War II, monofilament nylon replaced gut as the standard leader material. Just as nylon rope presented a much slicker surface than the hemp ropes it replaced, the very smooth, slick surface of nylon leader material offered new challenges to those who would knot it. Two books, *Fly Fishing in Salt Water* by Lefty Kreh (28) and *Practical Fishing Knots* by Kreh and Mark Sosin (31), provide excellent summaries of knots in nylon for the fisherman. Bob McNally's book, *Fishermen's Knots, Fishing Rigs, and How to Use Them* (38), also offers practical information on a large selection of knots although it by no means includes "all known practical knots." A more recent book by Geoffrey Budworth, *The Complete Book of Fishing Knots* (10), offers an excellent pictorial guide for the tying of fishermen's knots, including vignettes on the history of selected knots.

In the past several years, new super-slick backing and leader materials that further challenge the fisherman have been introduced. Some of the traditional knots for nylon will not hold these new synthetics. New knots have been prescribed, and at least one manufacturer even advocates the use of CA glue to achieve good knot strength. As we shall see, with a clear understanding of how to properly form knots, such drastic measures are unnecessary.

A knot must meet three criteria: (1) it must be appropriate to the intended use, (2) it must be properly formed, and (3) it must be easily tightened to its maximum strength. The last is the most important criterion.

The appropriateness of a knot is hard to define, since new adaptations are constantly being refined. Examples may make the point. How many of us in haste to replace a fly have tried to secure the hook with a series of half hitches? Such measures are wholly unacceptable, for the knot is no better than the first overhand knot adjacent to the hook eye, which is itself a very weak one. In the tarpon example above, it was totally inappropriate (and inexcusable) to use any knot in that leader. Looped leader segments (described in Chapter 6) would have averted the entire incident.

A good knot must be easy to form properly. If the knot calls for turns or coils, use the number of coils appropriate to the strength of the leader material. If you use too many coils, you cannot properly tighten the knot. If you use too few, the knot may not hold. Carefully form the coils adjacent to one another so that, when tightened, they align themselves to provide maximum strength. The angle at which the leader material lies over or against itself can be critical. At certain angles, the nylon may cut itself and weaken an otherwise strong knot. Consider the figure-eight knot, which, if tied in a single strand of nylon, is not particularly strong. However, tied around another strand of nylon, it results in a strong and useful knot.

The manner in which you tighten the knot is most critical. Even inappropriate knots may be rescued if properly tightened. All knots should be lubricated, with either water or saliva, prior to tightening. (I do not concur that saliva should be avoided because it contains a digestive enzyme that might weaken the knot.) The lubrication both facilitates the tightening and also dissipates the considerable heat generated during tightening. If the standing leader and tag ends are tightened in the proper order, at the proper speed, you will form a strong knot.

No knot will break until it begins to slip. If it slips, it

will almost always break. Our aim is to form a knot that is as strong as the leader material itself. This we call a full-strength or 100-percent knot, which means that the leader will break because of minor imperfections in the material itself more often than will the knot. Obviously a knot cannot be stronger than the material from which it is formed. But a perfect knot will break less often than the strand of leader material from which it is formed. The concept of 100-percent knots is most important in tying leader tippets and is discussed in detail in a later section on the testing of knots. If you are using 40-pound material for the butt of the leader, a 70-percent knot still provides adequate knot strength. However, when fishing a 6-pound tippet, a 70-percent knot would weaken your leader to 4.2 pounds test, unacceptably weak for salmon.

Now comes the fun. What are the best knots for the beginning salmon fisherman to use to join backing, line, and leader? What knot can you depend on to hold your fly? Throughout the discussion that follows, we shall put primary emphasis on the knots that are most useful and are easily tied to maximum strength. These are knots that I use. A salmon, for that matter a tarpon, is much too precious to lose because of a faulty knot.

## LOOP HITCHES

**BIMINI TWIST**. Aside from the specific knot used to form knotted leaders, the Bimini Twist is perhaps the most important knot for the fisherman. This hitch is a virtual 100-percent knot that can be tied in any size of monofilament, as well as in Dacron and other synthetic backing materials. In addition, the Bimini Twist provides stretch and resilience found in only one other knot, the tournament knot described below. Unfortunately, the Bimini Twist is often considered too complicated for freshwater fishermen. Nonsense. If you can tie a decent clinch knot, you can form the Bimini.

Many years ago, when I first started using the Bimini, I was perplexed, somewhat stymied, by instructions to form a 3-foot loop around your knee or foot. Why? I only needed a small loop, about 12 inches in circumference. The answer, of course, is that the Bimini was designed to provide bluewater fishermen a doubled line specifically for billfishing. International Game Fishing Association (IGFA) rules permit a doubled line up to 30 feet long for line classes heavier than 10 kilograms. Freshwater fly fishermen use the Bimini for its strength and resiliency. The following steps are offered for the right-handed tier, as illustrated in Figure 5-3 (p. 154).

1.  Grasp the tag end of your line or leader 10 inches from the end and cross it over the standing line 24 inches from the end. You now have a loop about 14 inches in circumference, which will result in a Bimini loop about 6 inches long (12 inches in circumference), just the right length to slip over any spool when you're attaching a fly line to your backing.

2.  Grasp the intersection with the thumb and second finger of your left hand, insert your right hand into the loop, and twist it 20 to 22 times (Figure 5-3a). Trey Combs, whom I accept as the most lucid authority on this subject, suggests that any number of turns exceeding 15 will suffice (11).

3.  Now place the loop over a nail or peg. At home I frequently use the finial on the back of a kitchen chair. Keeping your left hand in place, hold the tag end in your right hand. With your left index finger, reach into the loop and pull the twisted pair toward you, which tightens the twist.

4.  As the twist tightens, slowly relax your hold on the tag end and allow it to wrap around the twisted pair (Figure 5-3b). It is not necessary that the wrappings be coiled perfectly adjacent to one another as shown in my figure and in every Bimini picture I have ever seen. It is the total number of well-spaced wrappings that really counts.

5.  When the twisted pair is completely wrapped by the tag end (Figure 5-3c), grasp the wrappings with the

thumb and forefinger of your left hand and close the knot with one half-hitch on the nearest leg of the loop. The half-hitch secures the wrappings.

6. Now wrap both strands of the loop with two half-hitches (Figure 5-3c).

7. Complete the wrappings with three reversed hitches as shown (Figure 5-3d). These latter hitches lock the knot, so tighten them carefully, being certain that they do not overlap one another. The finished knot is illustrated in Figure 5-3e.

Trim the tag end to 1/16 inch, and your knot is ready for use. Never use any adhesive to secure a Bimini. To do so will destroy the resilience built into the knot.

We have demonstrated that coils around a standing line are an excellent way to form a strong knot. Loops within a knot are another method, particularly if the line or leader reverses direction within the knot, as in a figure-eight knot. To better explain this concept, let's take a systematic approach to forming increasingly complex knots and see what may be learned.

Take a line or leader, lay the tag end over the bight, and insert the tag end into the resulting loop. You have just made a one-half turn around the line and formed an overhand knot. If, however, you had formed this knot around the standing part of the leader, you would have formed a slipknot. Thus the slipknot is really an overhand knot around the returned standing line. Both of these knots are relatively weak, and neither is particularly useful to the fly fisherman.

Let's proceed a second step. Lay the tag end over the bight, wrap one turn completely around the leader, and insert the tag end into the loop. You have formed a figure-eight knot (Figure 5-4a). By itself, this is not a strong knot because it can cut itself, but when formed over a parallel strand of line or leader, it has multiple uses, such as attaching a fly or joining the end of the fly line to a leader loop. If the figure-eight knot is improved by throwing an extra half-hitch into the returned tag end, as shown in

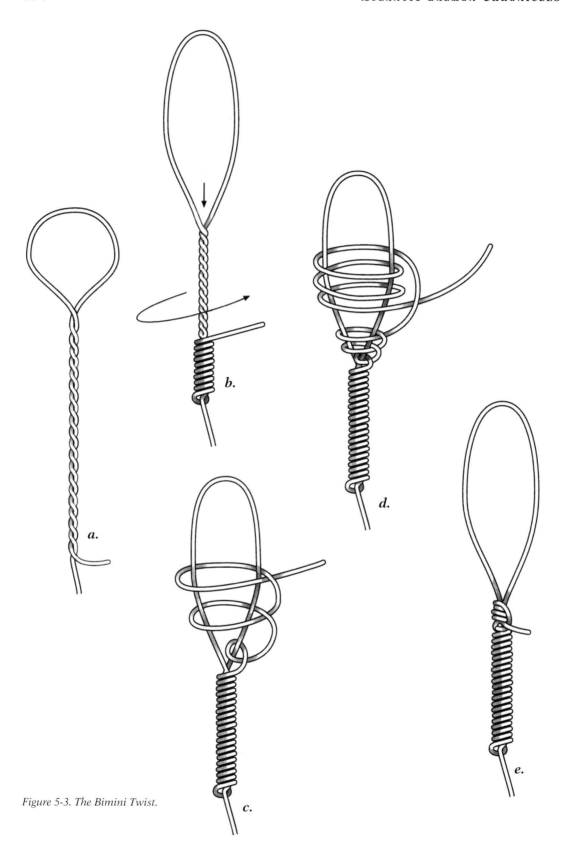

*Figure 5-3. The Bimini Twist.*

Figure 5-4b, you have the recently developed Orvis loop knot, which exhibits about 95-percent breaking strength. Strong and relatively easy to tighten, the Orvis loop is particularly useful for attaching flies to your leader tippet.

Many knots such as the Orvis, the Duncan, and the surgeons knots may be adapted for joining leader segments as well as for attaching flies. In such cases, we shall identify the knot as a loop knot (e.g., Orvis loop knot) when the knot is intended for attaching flies or preparing loops, even if the commonly recognized name does not incorporate the word *loop*. Connections for joining leader or line segments are simply knots.

For the third step, wrap the tag end 1 1/2 times around the bight and then insert the tag end into the loop. Now you have what some incorrectly call a stevedore knot (Figure 5-4c). It's really a pseudo-stevedore with no recognized use. If however you form this knot around a returned standing line, you have a Crawford or Maxima knot (Figure 5-4d). The Crawford knot is recommended for tying flies to leaders and is usually rated at around 90-percent breaking strength.

For the fourth step, wrap the tag end around the bight two full turns and insert the tag into the loop. You have formed a true stevedore knot (Figure 5-4e). Oddly, there is no recognized fishing knot with the stevedore knot tied around the returned standing line.

**SIXTEEN-TWENTY LOOP KNOT.** In the fifth step, when the tag end is wrapped around the bight 2 1/2 times and then inserted into the loop, you create what we may call a 2 1/2-turn stevedore knot (Figure 5-4g). When this knot is formed around a returned standing line, you form a knot with most unusual properties (Figure 5-4h). Note that this knot is similar to the Crawford knot except that it has one extra turn around the standing line. I developed this knot in 1991 in an attempt to make a near-100-percent knot that was easy to tie. I named it in honor of the Sixteen-Twenty Club when I became a member in 1995. This knot should be tightened by first pulling on the

## FIGURE 5-4. SYSTEMATIC DEVELOPMENT OF KNOTS

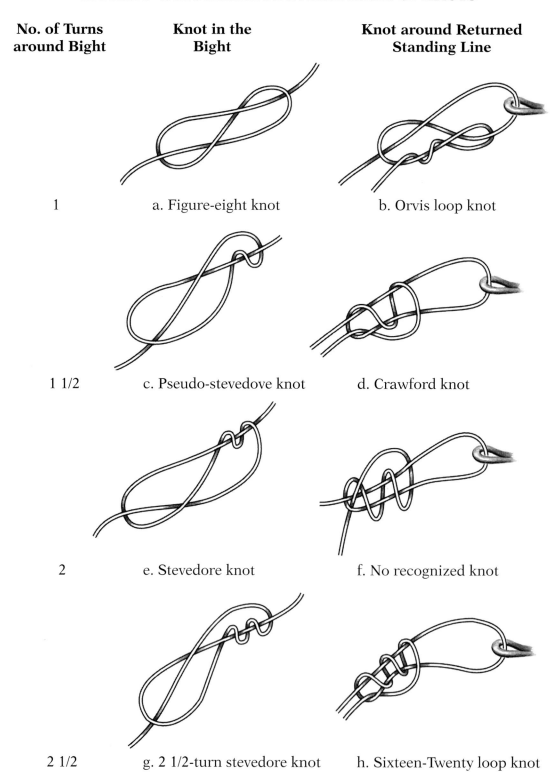

| No. of Turns around Bight | Knot in the Bight | Knot around Returned Standing Line |
|:---:|:---:|:---:|
| 1 | a. Figure-eight knot | b. Orvis loop knot |
| 1 1/2 | c. Pseudo-stevedove knot | d. Crawford knot |
| 2 | e. Stevedore knot | f. No recognized knot |
| 2 1/2 | g. 2 1/2-turn stevedore knot | h. Sixteen-Twenty loop knot |

tag end to close the knot firmly around the returned standing part. Then pull hard on the standing line to draw the knot very tight against the eye of the hook.

Figure 5-5a shows a photomicrograph of the Sixteen-Twenty loop incompletely tightened, while Figure 5-5b shows the same knot after tightening properly. You will note that in Figure 5-5a there is a gap between the wraps or coils of an apparently secure knot. Under tension, the gap disappears as the knot tightens. Figure 5-5b shows the coils tightly adjacent and secured by the overlapping coil (see arrow).

During the development of this knot, I observed that, as the knot was firmly tightened against the eye of the hook, I would feel a slight catch or set. Invariably when I felt such a set, the knot would seldom break before the standing leader did. Eventually I came to realize that it was the set that protected the knot and gave the knot its strength. The set results in the outermost coil or wrap sliding over the inner wraps. It is this feature that gives both the Sixteen-Twenty and the Pitzen loop knots (see below) their strength. When properly tightened, the Sixteen-Twenty loop knot is a virtual 100-percent knot. It does not have the resilience of the Bimini, but it is the strongest knot I have ever tested.

Several years ago, Edgar Pitzenbauer of Regensburg, Germany, independently discovered that the three-turn stevedore knot when tied over a returned standing line resulted in a very strong knot with the same properties as the Sixteen-Twenty knot. Upon tightening, you will feel the Pitzen loop knot take a set or hitch indicating it is at maximum strength. In fact, when you're tying either the Sixteen-Twenty or Pitzen knot, if you do not feel the set, you should cut the knot and retie it. The Pitzen knot is excellent for light trout tippets. When formed in small diameter nylon, the knot is easily closed with the three-turn wrap. It is not as satisfactory in the heavier leaders used for salmon because the tag end exits the knot perpendicular to the standing line. This makes the Pitzen Loop more difficult to tighten properly than the Sixteen-

*Figure 5-5. The Sixteen-Twenty loop knot: (a) an incompletely tightened knot with gap between the wraps; (b) a properly tightened knot secured by the overwrapping coil.*

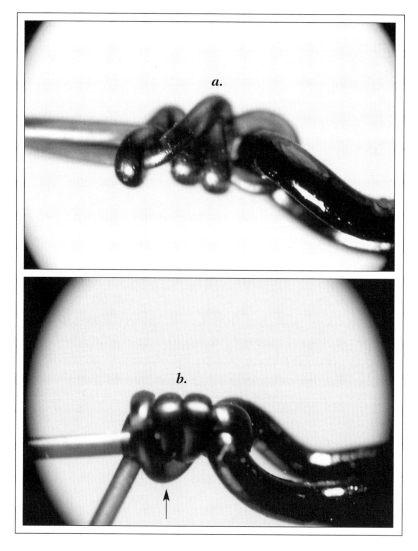

Twenty loop, where the tag exits the knot parallel to the standing line.

By now the reader should recognize that 4-, 5-, and 6-turn stevedore knots tied through the eye of a hook are what we call 4-, 5-, and 6-turn clinch knots. However, as will be discussed subsequently, not all clinch knots are easy to tighten securely in the heavier tippets used for salmon.

**MONO LOOP.** This excellent knot is derived from an older configuration and was perfected by Lefty Kreh, who calls it the *nonslip mono loop*. It's easy to form and has largely displaced the perfection knot for loops in

leaders primarily because it provides a smaller, oval loop
more suitable for joining loops. Oddly, the knot starts out
as a slipknot and ends up like a stevedore or clinch knot
(Figure 5-6). First, form an overhand knot around the
returned standing line (that is, form a slipknot). Keep
both the overhand knot and the loop very small, about
1/4 inch in diameter, since the loop enlarges when
tightened. Now wrap the tag end of the standing line
above the overhand knot with three turns if you're using
15- to 40-pound leader or five turns if you're using 6- to
12-pound leader. Insert the tag end back up through the
overhand knot. Close the coils by pulling on the tag end.
Then insert a smooth object into the loop and pull to
tighten the entire knot. The finished loop should be 3/8 to
1/2 inch in diameter.

When properly formed, this deceptively simple knot
is very strong, testing at about 96-percent breaking
strength. It may be used for forming the loop in the butt
of a leader or in the tippet end when you're using looped
tippets (see Chapter 6), or for loosely attaching flies when
freedom of movement is desired. However, this knot must
be closed very carefully so the turns do not overlap and
weaken the knot. The knot appears so simple that there is
a tendency to tighten it hurriedly and imperfectly. I once
lost a salmon estimated at 25 pounds to a broken mono
loop tied in 17-pound Maxima. You may be assured that I
now close all mono loops very carefully.

**THE TOURNAMENT LOOP.** The mono loop knot is
an excellent knot for preparing loops, but it has one
shortcoming: it was not intended and is not adaptable for
securing flies to your leader. Recognizing the outstanding
properties of that knot, I kept asking myself if there was

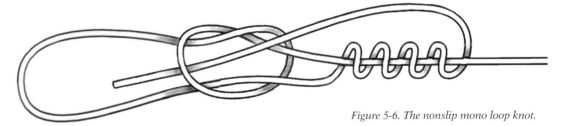

*Figure 5-6. The nonslip mono loop knot.*

any way it could be so adapted. Perhaps a bowline type of knot? Eventually I remembered an old knot called the Homer's loop knot which is the mirror image of the mono loop knot. That is, it is constructed similarly except that the overhand knot is in the tag end and encircles the standing leader. This permits the knot to slip down the standing leader and tighten securely against the eye of the hook—just the type of construction I was seeking.

After fiddling with Homer's loop for a while, I recognized that if the wrappings, as formed in the mono loop and Homer's loop, were reversed (as shown in Figure 5-7) and their number increased, the strength of the knot was enhanced. This is readily perceived in testing the knot. As the tension increases, the coils or wraps around the standing leader first separate ever so slightly and then slide back together, after which the leader breaks. It appears that a degree of resilience is introduced as the stressed coils slip adjacent to one another. This assists in protecting the knot from further stressing, and the leader breaks preferentially.

The tournament loop and the Bimini are the only two knots I know that exhibit such resilience. In forming the reversed wraps in the tournament knot, it helps to place your thumb and forefinger over the wraps and pull gently on the tag end to tighten the coils without overlapping. Seven wraps or turns around the running line are appropriate for 0.009 inch and 0.010 inch tippets (6- to 11-pound test). That's a sufficient number of turns to form a secure knot but not so many that it cannot be easily tightened. This new knot has not been tested in tippets heavier than 0.010 inch.

While I was discussing my passion for knots with a friend one day, he asked what knot I would choose if I were in a fly-fishing tournament where every detail counted. Unhesitatingly, I described this knot. Hence the name "tournament loop." It requires care to form the coils above the overhand knot, but, once formed, it is the most secure knot I know.

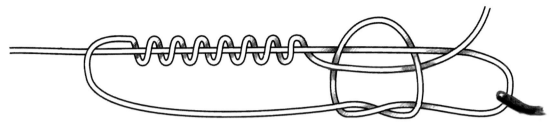

*Figure 5-7. The tournament loop.*

**DOUBLE SURGEONS LOOP**. This knot is frequently used to form loops in heavy leader segments as well as to form a small doubled loop in the Bimini. Take the doubled strands (Figure 5-8), form a small loop about 1 inch long, and tie a double overhand knot. Tighten this double surgeons loop by pulling on the loop. Trim the surplus tag end. The double surgeons loop is popular because it is so easy to tie, but it is not particularly strong, rating only about 80-percent breaking strength.

On a trip to Iceland in 1995, I fished the Laxá í Adaldal River in northeastern Iceland. The Big Laxá, as it's called, is best known for its large salmon and relatively few grilse. In the third week of July, the water was a bit high but very cold, about 41°F. There were plenty of fish in the river but few takers. After determining that we needed to sink our flies near the bottom of this very rocky river, I began fishing tube flies tied on aluminum tubes rigged with an extra-heavy double hook. Hang-ups on the slab rock on the bottom of the river were all too frequent. Five times during the course of the week, my hooks

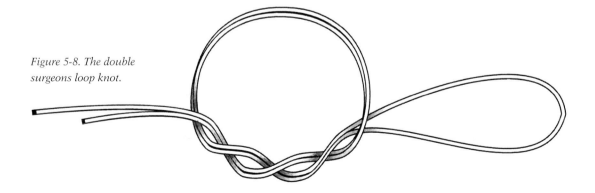

*Figure 5-8. The double surgeons loop knot.*

caught the bottom in such a manner they could not be freed. The only option was to break the leader. My terminal tackle was a 4-foot section of 15-pound Maxima leader looped to the leader butt with the double surgeons loop. The hook in all cases was tied with the Sixteen-Twenty loop knot. In all five instances, the leader broke at the double surgeons loop, not at the hook or in the standing leader itself. Clearly, the double surgeons loop was the weak link in my leader.

**CLINCH KNOT AND IMPROVED CLINCH KNOT**. No discussion of loop hitches is complete without considering the controversial question of whether the clinch knot or the improved clinch knot is better. A number of years ago I lost a very big rainbow trout on the South Branch of the Raritan River when my clinch knot unraveled as the fish ran upstream away from me. At that point I lost confidence in my, or anyone's, ability to properly tighten each and every clinch knot, and until I rewrote this chapter, I refused to use it.

After this chapter had been completed, or so I thought, I had the opportunity to fish the Big Manistee River for spring steelhead with Bob Nicholson of Baldwin, Michigan. Bob is an exceptionally articulate guide who studiously researches his quarry. I noticed that Bob was securing his flies with a seven-turn clinch knot, and our conversation immediately turned to knots as I explained my concern with the clinch knot. Bob explained that he too had been anti-clinch until he found the correct formula. He said that you must use the regular, not the improved, clinch knot; use at least seven turns and do not tighten the knot by pulling on the tag end.

As a result of testing the two knots, I learned that a very secure clinch knot can be tied in 0.009- and 0.010-inch Maxima if one uses at least seven turns and if one closes the knot without pulling on the tag end. After wrapping the turns, you may pull on the tag end to shape the coils, but only if you do not shorten the knot to less than 5/8 inch. Then lubricate the coils well and close the knot by pulling very firmly on the standing leader only.

Pull as hard as you can without breaking the leader. When formed in the manner described, the seven-turn clinch knot may also be used to secure the new gel-spun polyethylene (GSP) materials. At long last I can recommend a properly tied clinch knot.

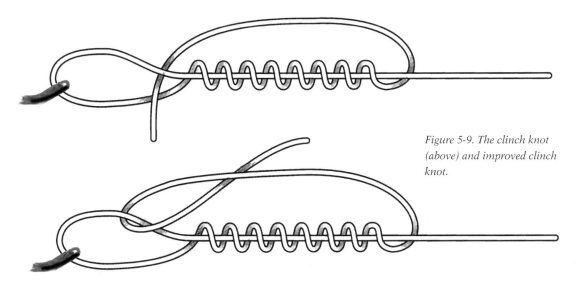

*Figure 5-9. The clinch knot (above) and improved clinch knot.*

But I still cannot recommend the improved clinch knot. Many people use the improved clinch knot on the premise that it will protect a clinch knot from slipping. As the tests on page 174 show, the improved clinch knot is actually weaker than a well-tied clinch knot.

## BENDS

Bends are knots that join or secure the ends of two lines. For the fisherman, their most common use is in forming tapered leaders. While a number of knots such as the figure-eight knot and the barrel knot may be used to join leader segments, the most common knots for this purpose are the blood knot and the double or triple surgeons knot (not the surgeons loop).

**BLOOD KNOT**. There are at least a dozen so-called blood knots. Only three of these need concern the fly-fishing angler. The regular or conventional blood knot is the most common, but not the simplest, of all bends for joining leader segments. It is also the one most despised by fishermen because it is perceived as difficult to form. If you try to tie it with short tags, it can be difficult. If your ends are sufficiently long, it really is easy. Most guides tie this knot quickly and easily because they work with long tag ends.

Until you become proficient with this knot, start by crossing the lighter segment of your leader over the heavier segment with 4-inch ends overlapping (Figure 5-10). Grasp the intersection with your thumb and forefinger and wrap the lighter segment five times around the heavier segment. Return the tag end through the intersection of the segments. Now wrap the heavier segment five times around the lighter segment and insert the tag end through the intersection in the opposite direction.

Lubricate the knot and pull gently on the tag ends to form and tighten the coils. Now grasp the standing lines

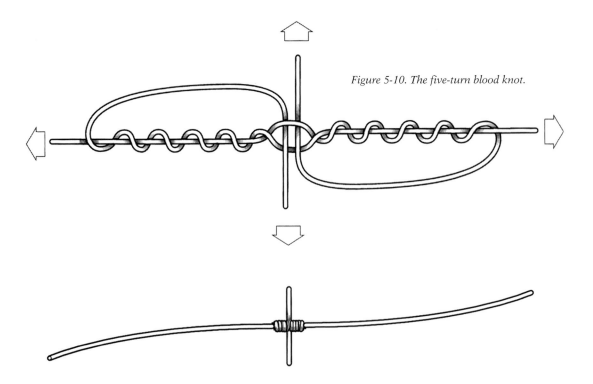

*Figure 5-10. The five-turn blood knot.*

with each hand and pull firmly and rather quickly, but without jerking, to tighten the knot. This knot generates a considerable amount of heat as the coils are tightened, so you must form the knot on the first pull. Subsequent pulls will not tighten a loose knot properly.

The exact number of turns required to form a secure blood knot, or any knot, depends on the diameter and flexibility of the monofilament used. For light segments varying in diameter by not more than 0.002 or 0.003 inch, five turns in each segment is a good starting point. As the difference in diameters increases, you may wish to try five turns in the heavier segment and six or seven turns in the lighter segment, depending on the specific leader material. Under tension, the lighter leader segment slips and closes more easily and may require extra turns to compensate. For heavy leader segments, four- and five-turn or four- and six-turn knots may be appropriate. The strength of the blood knot varies widely because most fishermen do not compensate for differing diameters of their tippets. A well-tied blood knot will test at about 85- to 90-percent breaking strength.

If you use the blood knot, learn to tie it properly. Practice for at least a couple of evenings before you head for the river. Do not put your faith in any of those knot-tying tools. They are gimmicks that require as much practice as does your learning to tie the knot itself.

The improved blood knot (also called the Stu Apte improved blood knot) is used to join two leader segments that differ greatly in diameter. This knot is formed by doubling the smaller of the two strands and then tying a regular blood knot using a single strand of the heavier segment and the doubled strand of the lighter segment. In my opinion, this knot has limited value because looped leader segments are a better solution when you're using tippets that are much weaker than the leader butts.

**BLOODY QUICK KNOT**. This knot is usually called the *quick blood knot* but it also is known as the *simple blood knot*. Confusing, isn't it? The knot is simple to tie, but it is

*Figure 5-11. The bloody quick knot.*

not in any way a blood knot because the tag ends exit from the ends of the knot instead of from the center, as in the blood and barrel knots. When I first showed this knot to an English friend of mine, he exclaimed, "That's bloody quick." This whimsical name has stuck with me, since it clearly distinguishes this knot from other so-called blood knots. I urge others to adopt the name to end the confusion.

To form this knot, overlap the ends by 5 to 6 inches, as shown in Figure 5-11, with the heavier strand over the lighter one. Now wrap seven or eight turns of the heavier strand around the lighter strand. Then cross the heavier strand behind the lighter one and wrap seven or eight turns of the lighter strand around the heavier strand. Pull first on the tag end to partially tighten the knot. Now pull on the standing lines to further tighten. Repeat the procedure until the knot is 1/4 to 3/8 inch long and the tag ends stand at a right angle to the knot. Lubricate the knot well, grasp the two ends of the leader segment, and pull quickly and firmly to tighten the knot. You only have one chance. The knot seizes on the first pull, and subsequent pulls will not improve the knot. If in doubt, cut it out and retie the knot.

This odd-looking knot is the strongest bend and one of the strongest knots I have ever tested. Testing at virtually 100-percent breaking strength, it is stronger than the triple surgeons knot and decidedly stronger than the blood knot.

**ORVIS KNOT**. In addition to being used as a loop hitch, this knot may be adapted as a bend to join line or leader segments. As has already been demonstrated, the Orvis knot is simply a figure-eight knot with an extra half-hitch. When used as a bend, the extra hitch is introduced in the manner shown in Figure 5-12. This is an exceedingly simple and strong (near 100 percent) knot, which I highly recommend.

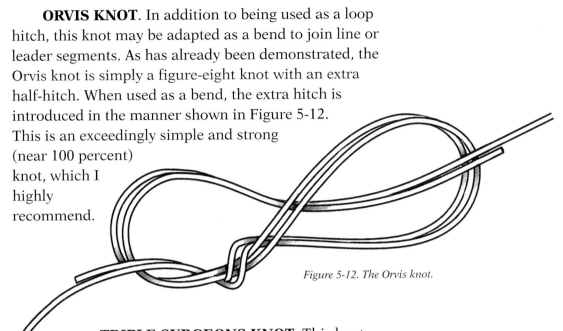

*Figure 5-12. The Orvis knot.*

**TRIPLE SURGEONS KNOT**. This knot consists of a triple overhand knot in the double leader strand. It is one of the simplest knots to form properly, and it is also one of the strongest bends, testing third only to the bloody quick knot and the Orvis knot. As shown in Figure 5-13, it is formed by overlapping the two leader strands to form a coil and then inserting one pair of the strands three times through the coiled loop. The knot is strongest when both pairs of strands at either end of the knot are pulled simultaneously. It may then be tightened by pulling first on the tag ends and finally on the running strands themselves.

If properly formed this knot is not excessively bulky and is significantly stronger than the double surgeons knot, which is not recommended. Having been tested over

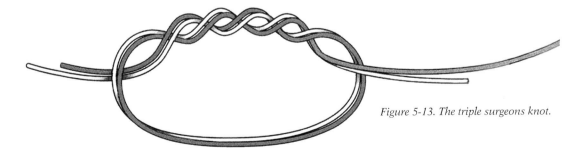

*Figure 5-13. The triple surgeons knot.*

a wide range of leader materials and strengths, the triple surgeons knot is rated at about 95 percent.

**DUNCAN KNOT**. Another bend that is popular for joining leader and line segments is the Duncan knot, or more properly two Duncan loops formed around adjacent leader segments. In Europe, this knot is known as the double Grinner knot. In recent years, DuPont has promoted this knot as an all-purpose connector under the name Uni-knot. A form of the clinch knot, the Duncan knot—as used for leaders only—tests at about 85 percent. It is not as strong as the bloody quick or Orvis knots and cannot be recommended in their stead. The single Duncan loop, testing at about 93 percent, is satisfactory for attaching flies in most cases.

## THE TESTING OF KNOTS

The strength of a knot is a function of the material used, the diameter and physical properties of that material, the manner in which the knot is formed, and how the knot is tested. Important physical properties of the material include tensile strength, elongation (stretch), flexibility, and compressibility. Test parameters should consider the moisture content, the method by which the knot is affixed or suspended, and the rate at which the load is applied. Given all these variables you sometimes wonder how comparable test results can ever be achieved.

Comparable results are, in fact, seldom reported. Many writers blithely quote breaking strengths based on generalities and unsubstantiated by adequate testing, failing to detail important parameters such as the leader material.

The two most meaningful considerations for the fisherman are the leader material itself and the manner in which the knot is formed. Many knots are material specific. Certain materials will not hold a given knot. Certain knots may test near 100 percent with one material and weaker with another. These are the things that leader manufacturers never tell you. Many fail to provide adequate information concerning the materials or performance of their products.

Over a period of some 30 months prior to and during the preparation of this chapter, I extensively tested knots that were known to be useful and reputed to be strong. Some deserved more extensive examination; many did not. Because of my special interest in Atlantic salmon, the final tests of some 15 different types of knots (over 500 individual knots) were conducted primarily with chameleon Maxima monofilament. Maxima, in one of its five types and colors, is used worldwide for salmon and sea trout. It is very popular in New Zealand for brown trout. It presents a good balance between stiffness and abrasion resistance for fish that are not excessively leader-shy. The chameleon is the hardest of the Maxima products, and many anglers believe that its color is advantageous for fishing the tannic waters of North American and European rivers. None of the other Maxima products were tested in this study to prevent conflicting results due to different strengths and flexibilities. In the discussion that follows, keep in mind that these conclusions will not necessarily apply to all of the newer high-tensile polymer and co-polymer leader materials.

For a given leader material, the basic parameter is tensile strength, expressed in pounds per square inch. For selective and leader-shy trout, high tensile strength is often desirable, since it permits a smaller diameter leader for a given knot-and-leader strength. For salmon and saltwater species that are not leader shy, other considerations such as stiffness and abrasion resistance prevail.

Table 5-1 compares the nominal (advertised) and measured parameters for a number of virgin, unstressed leader materials useful to the salmon fisherman. The several classes of nylon monofilaments are listed by type in order of increasing tensile strength. You may note that, in general, tensile strength increases slightly with decreasing diameter of the material. Abrasion resistance is primarily a function of diameter and only indirectly of hardness. Large-diameter materials exhibit the better abrasion resistance.

However, for a given test weight, the lower-tensile-strength leader materials, such as Mason, tend to be harder and less flexible than the higher-tensile co-polymer materials.

The values shown in Table 5-1 for the three polyvinylidene fluoride monofilament materials, the so-called fluorocarbon materials, indicate similar variations. The Stren fluorocarbon product may be classified as being of medium-low tensile strength similar to Maxima. The Fin-Nor fluorocarbon is a stiffer product of intermediate tensile strength. The Orvis fluorocarbon product exhibits a still higher tensile strength. You may note that neither of the Fin-Nor products is within the stated IGFA line class, while one of the Stren samples was significantly weaker than rated. It is not unusual for leader sizes and strengths to be understated by the manufacturer. Nor is it unusual for IGFA-rated materials to exceed the rated class. Extensive testing of 76 different light monofilaments reported in the April 1996 issue of *Sport Fishing* magazine confirmed a wide range of variability, even among products by the same manufacturer.

Since fluorocarbon materials have a lower refractive index in water than nylon and are therefore somewhat less visible, you may wish to consider using the largest diameter material for a given breaking strength (i.e., lowest tensile strength) in order to avail yourself of the best abrasion resistance. Referring to Table 5-1, both the 6-pound Orvis and the 8-pound Stren fluorocarbon qualify as 3-kilogram IGFA tippets, but the larger 8-pound Stren will offer better abrasion resistance. Similarly, the 8-pound Fin-Nor and the 12-pound Stren qualify as 6-kilogram tippets, but the much larger 12-pound Stren will certainly exhibit better abrasion resistance.

You never know these factors unless you test your leader materials. When attempting to set new IGFA records, the prudent angler always should test his leader material ahead of time to ascertain that it meets the required class standards. For a nominal fee, IGFA will test and certify both leader materials and portable scales for individual anglers.

## TABLE 5-1
## PARAMETERS OF UNSTRESSED LEADER MATERIALS

|  | Nominal Diameter (in.) | Measured Diameter (in.) | Measured Break (lbs.) | Tensile Strength (lbs./sq. in.) |
|---|---|---|---|---|
| **A. Nylon Types**[2] |  |  |  |  |
| 8-lb. Mason | -.-- | 0.0137 | 9.00 | 61,100 |
| 8-lb. Ande | -.-- | 0.0106 | 9.42 | 106,700 |
| 20-lb. Maxima | 0.017 | 0.0183 | 23.16 | 88,100 |
| 15- lb. " | 0.015 | 0.0161 | 18.75 | 92,300 |
| 12-lb. " | 0.013 | 0.0153 | 16.90 | 91,900 |
| 10-lb. " | 0.012 | 0.0143 | 14.48 | 90,200 |
| 8-lb. " | 0.010 | 0.0122 | 11.31 | 96,700 |
| 6-lb. " | 0.009 | 0.0098 | 8.17 | 108,700 |
| 8.5-lb. Orvis Super Strong | 0.008 | 0.0085 | 8.17 | 141,000 |
|  |  |  |  |  |
| **B. Fluorocarbon Types** |  |  |  |  |
| 12-lb. Stren | 0.013 | 0.0122 | 11.52 | 98,400 |
| 8-lb. Stren | 0.009 | 0.0090 | 6.60 | 103,700 |
| 12-lb. (6-kg) Fin-Nor* | -.-- | 0.0131 | 15.76 | 116,900 |
| 8-lb. (4-kg) Fin-Nor* | 0.009 | 0.0100 | 10.47 | 103,700 |
| 8-lb. (4-kg) Orvis* | 0.009 | 0.0090 | 8.49 | 133,500 |
| 6-lb. (3-kg) Orvis* | 0.008 | 0.0075 | 6.06 | 137,200 |

* Rated for IGFA Class

---

2. Throughout this book, the nominal or manufacturer's listed strength of leader material will be designated as 6, 8, 12, etc., pounds. As shown in Table 5-1, except for Stren fluorocarbon, the measured strength of standard leader material is always greater than the nominal strength. Conversely, the measured strength of IGFA material should be less than the nominal rating. The two Fin-Nor products were unacceptably strong, testing significantly stronger than their ratings of 13.2 and 8.8 pounds (6 and 4 kilograms) respectively.

In this study, the breaking strengths of the knots were determined with a precision of 0.05 pound using a Berkeley portable test gauge. To obtain truly comparable results among all knots and materials, all knots were tied dry and tested dry (i.e., without saturating the leader and knot with water). Most anglers do not know that nylon-type materials weaken as they absorb water; fluorocarbon products do not. Fortunately for the salmon angler, Maxima products are weakened less by water than are most nylon monofilaments. The decrease in breaking strength for virgin, unknotted Maxima after soaking in water for one hour varies from about 4 percent for 15-pound material to 10 percent for the 6-pound Maxima.

For testing bends, a 32-inch length of leader material with the knot to be tested was suspended between the two cams of the test gauge, and the material was stretched with a constant torque motor at the relatively slow rate of 0.45 inch per second (11.4 mm/sec.) until the knot or leader broke. Loop hitches were tied to the eye of a size 6 Mustad No. 36890 hook, which was fastened to one of the cams. In either case, the results obtained represent near-static or tug-of-war type breaks. If the knots had been tested at a much faster rate of loading, somewhat different results may have been obtained, those representing jerk-type breaks. A minimum of 15 individual knots (and as many as 50 or more) were tested for each knot type or configuration, from which the average breaking strength and average deviation were calculated. For each knot-and-leader combination, the average knot-break strength (kBS) was divided by the average break strength for the unstressed leader (lBS) to define what I have defined as the confidence factor (CF = kBS/lBS). Expressed as a decimal fraction, the confidence factor measures the average strength of the knot relative to that for unstressed leader material, just as it is unwrapped from your leader coil.

## THE TEST RESULTS

**THE PREFERRED KNOTS**. The results of testing 16 significant knot types (10 loop hitches and six bends), listed in order of decreasing confidence factor, are shown in Table 5-2. Leader size, the fundamental parameter, is quoted in inches. Even though we often speak of salmon leaders in terms of nominal breaking strength, such reference is improper because the nominal breaking strengths are unrelated to actual strengths, and they do not provide a meaningful comparison between the different leaders materials.

Before discussing these results, a qualification is in order. The Bimini Twist hitch is often regarded as the strongest of all knots in monofilament. My tests on Biminis tied in various leader materials showed that no Bimini is as strong as the virgin, unstressed leader material, irrespective of how the leader, in which the Bimini is tied, breaks upon testing. In other words, whenever you tie a knot, you stress and weaken the leader material, which lowers the subsequent breaking strength. This is readily demonstrated by stretching a section of virgin leader and then testing its breaking strength. Inevitably, the stressed leader is weaker. In the discussion to follow, the nominal diameter of the leader material is that listed by the manufacturer, but it should be recognized that manufacturers generally underrate both the diameter of leader material and its breaking strength.

As described in part A of Table 5-2, the strongest loop hitches—each with a confidence factor of 0.99 or 0.98— are the Sixteen-Twenty loop, the tournament loop, and the Bimini Twist. I consider the Sixteen-Twenty loop to be somewhat the superior because it is much easier to tie securely than are the other two knots. In 0.010-inch Maxima, the Sixteen-Twenty knot developed a confidence factor of 0.99 with a very low average deviation of 1.1 percent. In my tests, the leader broke 47 percent of the time; the knot, 53 percent of the time. In 0.009-inch Maxima, the confidence factor of the knot is marginally lower for reasons I do not understand.

However, there seems to be a trend for knots tied in 0.010-inch to 0.013-inch leader material to test relatively stronger than for smaller (weaker) or larger (stronger)

**TABLE 5-2**
**COMPARISON OF KNOT STRENGTHS**

| Knot | Leader Size (in.) | Avg. Break Strength (lbs.) | Confidence Factor | Average Deviation (percent) | Leader Break (percent) |
|---|---|---|---|---|---|
| **A. Loop Hitches— in Maxima Nylon Monofilament** | | | | | |
| Sixteen-Twenty loop | 0.010 | 11.20 | *0.99* | 1.1 | 47 |
| | 0.009 | 7.76 | 0.95 | 2.1 | 40 |
| Tournament loop | 0.010 | 11.14 | *0.99* | 2.3 | *87.5* |
| Bimini Twist | 0.010 | 11.10 | *0.98* | 1.1 | *100* |
| Mono loop | 0.010 | 10.84 | 0.96 | 4.6 | 30 |
| Clinch—7 turns | 0.010 | 0.95 to 0.97 | (see text) | | |
| Improved clinch—7 turns | 0.010 | 0.91 average | (see text) | | |
| Orvis loop | 0.010 | 10.70 | 0.95 | 3.0 | *82* |
| Duncan loop—5 turns | 0.010 | 10.52 | 0.93 | 5.5 | 36 |
| Pitsen loop | 0.010 | 9.98 | 0.88 | 3.4 | 36 |
| Double surgeons loop | | | | | |
| without adhesive | 0.010 | 9.06 | 0.80 | 6.4 | 0 |
| with adhesive | 0.010 | 10.07 | 0.89 | 1.7 | 0 |
| **B. Bends— in Maxima Nylon Monofilament** | | | | | |
| Bloody quick | | | | | |
| 7 turns | .010/.013 | 11.09 | *0.98* | 2.3 | *82* |
| 7 turns | .009/.010 | 7.51 | 0.92 | 6.6 | 50 |
| 8 turns | .009/.010 | 7.79 | 0.95 | 3.3 | 55 |
| Orvis | .010/.013 | 11.03 | *0.975* | 2.0 | 50 |
| Triple surgeons | .009/.010 | 7.75 | 0.95 | 3.8 | 52 |
| Blood—5 turns | .010/.013 | 10.31 | 0.91 | 4.0 | 20 |
| Duncan—5 turns | .010/.013 | 9.74 | 0.86 | 6.1 | 20 |
| Double surgeons | .010/.013 | 9.13 | 0.81 | 8.6 | 0 |
| **C. Miscellaneous Knots— in Maxima Nylon Monofilament** | | | | | |
| Riffling hitch | 0.010 | 10.65 | 0.94 | 0.6 | *70* |
| Overhand knot | 0.010 | 8.30 | 0.73 | 7.2 | 0 |
| **D. Loop Hitches— in Stren Fluorocarbon Monofilament** | | | | | |
| Mono loop | 0.009 | 6.17 | 0.95 | 2.7 | 60 |
| Sixteen-Twenty loop | 0.009 | 6.10 | 0.94 | 0.8 | 20 |
| Tournament loop | 0.009 | 6.04 | 0.93 | 1.3 | *100* |

materials. This may be related to how knots are tightened. In very light tippets, we know we can overpower the material so we tend not to tighten the knot fully lest we break it. Intermediate tippets such as 0.010-inch Maxima (11.3-pound breaking strength) are easily tightened to maximum strength. For heavy tippets, such as 0.013-inch Maxima (which actually tests close to 17 pounds), it is virtually impossible to fully tighten a knot with your bare hands. For any material testing over about 15 pounds, you must use gloves or pliers to properly secure the knot. For instance, the Sixteen-Twenty loop in 0.013-inch Maxima is a 100-percent knot when well tied. However, it was so difficult to close completely in the 17-pound material that a comparable confidence factor was not achieved.

When well tied, the tournament knot and the Bimini Twist are somewhat more secure than the Sixteen-Twenty knot. When the tournament knot was tied in 0.010-inch Maxima, the leader broke 87.5 percent of the time. It exhibited the second highest confidence factor of all loop hitches. The advantage of the Bimini Twist is that unless the wrappings are abraded, the knot never breaks; the leader breaks 100 percent of the time. We generally assume that this is the best you may expect from any knot, recognizing that the leader material is stressed in forming the knot.

So what do people mean when they say a knot tests near 100 percent? It should mean that the knot is as strong as any knot you can tie in that leader material irrespective of its relative tensile strength, stretch, or anything else. Alternatively, it may mean that the knot is as strong as a Bimini with a confidence factor of 0.98. From my point of view and considering the deviations found in knot strengths, any knot with a confidence factor greater than 0.97 and an average deviation of less than 2 1/2 percent is for all practical purposes a full-strength (near 100-percent) knot. The confidence factors for the five knots that fulfill this criterion are highlighted in bold italics in Table 5-2. Even though I have listed the knots in the order of confidence factors as determined in these studies, this may not be irrevocably the order of absolute strength for all diameters of all materials. To my knowledge there has never been a study of the variation of relative knot strengths for a single leader material in different diameters.

The fourth-best-testing loop hitch was the nonslip mono loop, which Lefty Kreh has long proclaimed as one of the strongest of knots. This knot is simple to form but requires careful closing to develop maximum strength, as evidenced by the unusually high average deviation that indicates that some of the knots were imperfectly formed.

Using the criteria discussed above, the three full-strength loop hitches and the mono loop constitute an ample selection for most applications. I have labeled these as "the preferred knots" because they combine absolute knot strength with knot security.

As shown in part B of table 5-2, the bend with the highest confidence factor was the 7-turn bloody quick knot. When tied in 0.010-inch and 0.013-inch Maxima, it developed a confidence factor of 0.98 with 82 percent leader breakage, only 18-percent knot breakage! The same 7-turn knot in 0.009-inch and 0.010-inch Maxima showed a confidence factor of 0.92, but if one extra turn was added, the confidence factor for the 8-turn knot was increased to 0.95 and the average deviation was cut in half. That is very significant. To my knowledge this is the first time that tests on this knot ever have been reported. It is as such an "odd duck" knot that no one has bothered with it. Obviously it deserves respect and use.

The second-highest-testing bend was the Orvis knot used to join leader segments. With a confidence factor of 0.975, 2.0-percent average deviation, and 50-percent leader breaks, this is a very good knot because it is so easy to form.

These two bends I have also labeled *preferred knots*. For practical purposes, they are full-strength knots and among the easiest of all bends to form properly.

**OTHER KNOTS**. The Orvis loop knot (for attaching

flies, not as used for joining leader segments) exhibits a very high percentage of leader breaks and relatively few knot breaks. In fact, the Orvis loop knot was one of only four knots, including the Bimini, for which the leader breakage consistently exceeded 75 percent. This indicates that the knot is relatively easily tied in such a manner as to develop maximum knot strength.

The triple surgeons knot, like the bloody quick knot, is excellent for joining leader segments. It has a confidence factor of 0.95 and average deviation of 3.3 percent, and the leader was observed to break prior to the triple surgeons knot more than half the time. For joining 0.009-inch and 0.010-inch leader segments, the Orvis and the triple surgeons knots are equivalent.

The Duncan loop and Duncan knot are popular because they are easy to tie. The Duncan loop, as used for attaching flies, tested fairly well—a confidence factor of 0.93 with 36-percent leader breaks. However, the Duncan knot is considerably weaker (confidence factor of 0.86, 20-percent leader breaks) because the leader cuts itself if the coils are not very tightly drawn.

The five-turn blood knot exhibited a confidence factor of 0.91 with 20-percent leader breaks. This is in line with other tests of this knot in Maxima. The blood knot is recognized as holding better in Maxima, and its confidence factor is somewhat higher than when formed in other nylon polymer and co-polymer monofilaments.

While similar in construction to the Sixteen-Twenty loop, the Pitzen knot is significantly more difficult to tighten properly than is the Sixteen-Twenty knot and exhibits a much greater average deviation; a few weak knots lowered the average test strength of the Pitzen knot. It is, however, an excellent knot for light trout tippets, 3X through 8X.

Knowing that the double surgeons loop was a weak knot, I had long believed that the double surgeons knot was also weak. Just as this book was readied for printing, I read a new book by a well-respected author that reported the double surgeons knot as a 95-percent knot. Back I went to the testing laboratory. My second set of tests do confirm that the double surgeons knot is quite weak: a confidence factor of only 0.81 with no leader breaks, 100-percent knot breaks. Moreover, this knot has the highest average deviation of any knot I've ever tested, 8.6 percent, which attests to the fact that it is not easy to secure. If you like the surgeons knot, add the extra turn and form the secure triple surgeons.

At the request of a friend, I tried what many of us do when tying knots at home: securing the knot with a drop of CA glue. When the double surgeons loop was "improved" with a drop of the adhesive, the confidence factor increased from 0.80 to 0.89 with a 73-percent reduction in the average deviation. For this knot, the adhesive greatly improved the reliability (average deviation), but it did not result in an exceptionally strong knot (no leader breaks). CA glue should never be used on knots subject to great flexing, such as those that join your shooting head and running line. The adhesive introduces a hard spot in your rigging that will break under continuous flexing. Shooting heads so constructed have been known to fly away.

One conclusion that I have drawn from these studies is that any knot that routinely exhibits more than 30-percent leader breaks (less than 70-percent knot breaks) has significant potential as a secure and dependable knot. Weak knots never exhibit leader breaks.

Because of my interest in fishing very small flies, which require light tippets (2X or 3X, 8- or 6-pound test), I tested the strengths of three important loop hitches with the fluorocarbon monofilament. This material has been incorrectly advertised as offering exceptional knot strength. My studies confirm what others have observed—that the material presents decent but by no means exceptional knot strength, perhaps because of the slickness or low coefficient of friction of this polymer surface and its very low (4-percent) stretch. The three knots tested are all useful with leader tippets (see Chapter 6): the mono loop, the Sixteen-Twenty loop, and the new tournament loop. All three knots exhibit similar confidence factors, 0.93 to 0.95, which appears to be the best you can expect in fluorocarbon monofilament.

## LAST CASTS

One of the tactics for inducing salmon to strike is to fish a wet fly, and occasionally a dry fly, using the Portland Creek or riffling hitch. The hitch is prepared by first attaching your fly to the leader in the usual manner and then throwing two half-hitches around the shank of the hook just behind the eye. This enables you to riffle your fly on the surface of the water with a small wake. The obvious question is, "How secure is this hitch?"

The test results for the riffling hitch using 0.010-inch Maxima are shown in part C of Table 5-2. Note a confidence factor of 0.94, the unusually low average deviation of 0.6 percent—the lowest for any knot tested— accompanied by more than 70-percent line breaks. It's a very secure knot when properly tightened so that it cannot slip forward over the eye of the hook. This knot may be tied in two configurations: with two identical half-hitches (clove hitch configuration) and with the half-hitches reversed or of opposite hand (girth hitch configuration). I had expected the girth hitch configuration to be the weaker because it is more susceptible to cutting itself. It is not weaker; both configurations are of equal strength. The security of the Portland Creek hitch is not dependent upon which knot is used to form the hitch.

The nemesis of the salmon angler, particularly under windy conditions, is the formation of knots in your leader. Usually these are simple overhand knots, euphemistically called *wind knots*. They should be called *bad casting knots*, for they are caused by tailing loops in your cast. They are the weakest link in your tackle. Your leader and also the point of your hook should be checked frequently for spurious knots and broken hook points. Ted Williams always recommended checking every 40 to 50 casts. It's surprising what you'll find.

The test results for the simple overhand knot are also shown in part C of Table 5-2. For these tests, the knots were formed with less than 2 pounds of force and were then tightened by the knot-testing machine, similar to the manner in which a salmon might pull against and tighten a wind knot. With a confidence factor as low as 0.62, an average confidence factor of only 0.73, and a very high average deviation, wind knots represent a disaster waiting to happen.

The testing of the clinch and improved clinch knots yielded some surprising results. Initially I tied 10 clinch knots and tested them. The results were good as shown below, but I recognized that the last half of the knots tested much better than the first half. So I tied another 10 clinch knots, each with seven turns as Bob Nicholson had prescribed. The results using 0.010-inch Maxima are as follows.

|                | Avg. Break Strength (lbs.) | Confidence Factor | Average Deviation (%) | Leader Breaks (%) |
|----------------|----------------------------|-------------------|-----------------------|-------------------|
| First 10 knots | 10.74                      | 0.95              | 3.9                   | 60                |
| Second 10 knots| 10.94                      | 0.97              | 1.7                   | 80                |

These results clearly indicate a phenomenon that I define as the *intelligent hands syndrome*: the more knots you tie, the better you become at forming strong knots. This particular example also demonstrates the need to close a knot properly to achieve maximum strength.

In testing knots, you might expect that a knot-break would give a significantly lower test strength than a leader-break. Strangely, the only knot in which this was clearly observed was the improved clinch knot where the distinction is very clear. My testing of the improved clinch knot, using seven turns in 0.010-inch Maxima, demonstrated 55-percent knot breaks and 45-percent leader breaks. Consider the following data.

| | Avg. Break Strength (lbs.) | Confidence Factor | Average Deviation (%) | Leader Breaks (%) |
|---|---|---|---|---|
| When the knot broke | 10.02 | 0.885 | 1.8 | (0) |
| When the leader broke | 10.72 | 0.95 | 0.9 | (100) |
| Average of all knots | 10.34 | 0.91 | 3.4 | 45 |

As many have observed, the improved clinch knot is not easy to tighten. The returned tag end overlaps and interferes with the coils and does not allow them to slide easily into place. You can see it and feel it as you tighten the knot. High-speed motion photography has demonstrated that when coils or wraps are crossed, the monofilament most frequently breaks at that spot. The problem with the improved clinch knot is that you cannot be certain when or if the knot is well formed and tight. If you need to use your fingernail to slide the coils into position, you may be assured that the knot is not secure. As the above data indicate, a well-formed improved clinch is no better than a mediocre clinch knot. A poorly formed improved clinch knot (which results in knot breakage) is measurably weaker than the regular clinch knot. Statistically, the odds clearly favor the regular clinch knot because it is much easier to tighten properly.

Lefty Kreh offered me a tip about closing clinch knots that may help you with any clinch-type knot with coils or wraps around the running leader: "Once you have formed the knot and it is ready to be closed, be sure that you pull on the tag end(s) until the tag end(s) lies flush against the spirals or twists (i.e., coils) that are around the main line. Once it lies flush, wet it and pull the knot to close" (30).

The importance of properly tightened knots was emphasized to me again just last year in what at first seemed an obscure incident. We were fishing the Renous River, a tributary of the Miramichi, following a heavy rain that had raised the river 18 inches. I was using my 11-foot two-handed rod with size 4 streamers tied on heavy-wire hooks. Three times during the morning I lost my fly, apparently snapping it off. Each time, we noted that it was the knot that broke, not the leader. My guide first questioned the leader material; it was the same material I had used all season. Then he wondered if the 1-foot lead head was the problem; it was the same rigging I had used without incident in Norway just two weeks prior. Fascinated by this paradox, I asked my guide to tie on another fly just as he had the first three, using the same double turle knot. After securing the knot as firmly as he could around the hook shank, I placed my forceps on the leader under the eye immediately ahead of the knot and rolled the forceps against the hook eye to further tighten the knot. In doing so, we observed that the knot tightened by about 3/32 inch. (As discussed previously, knots around the hook shank are extremely difficult to tighten properly.) It appears that the incompletely tightened turle knot had slipped enough to break. In any event, switching to a well-tightened Sixteen-Twenty knot solved the problem, not just because it is a stronger knot but because it didn't slip.

This appears to be the first published study that reports the average deviations of the tests and the percentage of leader or knot breaks. Average deviation is an indication of the relative ease with which a knot is formed. If the knot is not easy to form, a few bad knots will greatly increase the average deviation. The security of a knot is indicated by the percentage of leader breaks compared to knot breaks. *A high percentage of leader breaks indicates that the knot has been formed to near maximum strength.* A high percentage of knot breaks indicates that the knot construction is faulty. I believe that the confidence factor is the ideal way in which to express the strength of a knot, particularly if the average deviation is also reported. Certainly it avoids the ambiguous statement that a knot has a certain percentage breaking strength. I encourage other writers to adopt a similar convention so that the relative strength of a knot may be more meaningfully described.

Throughout this chapter I have recommended six knots—four loop hitches and two bends—which fulfill all the functions required by the fly fisherman. These recommendations are based on testing and evaluating close to 800 individual knots of some 25 different types. Everyone eventually adopts his own favorite set of knots. My aim here has been to present important, secure knots in the expectation that they will assist you in understanding how to form knots and in adapting those knots that fulfill your needs.

I have learned that there are good knots and there are bad knots. I have also learned that the typical qualitative statements concerning knot strengths are worthless without substantiating data. The most important thing that I learned, and by far the most significant conclusion that I can offer, is to carefully form your knot and close it properly and precisely. A WEAK KNOT WELL TIED IS FAR SUPERIOR TO A STRONG KNOT POORLY FORMED.

*A Rise in the Slick*
Watercolor
11 x 16 1/2 inches
Private Collection

*Fishing is the least important thing about fishing.*

Arnold Gingrich

# Chapter 6

# Rigging Your Line, Leader, and Backing

Knots and splices are the means by which the fly fisherman assembles his rigging. There may be as many as five elements in the rigging, one end of which you secure to your reel spool and the other end to your fly:

a.   the backing
b.   a running line, if you're using one
c.   the fly line
d.   a sinking tip, if you're using one
e.   the leader, in one or more sections

Let us examine each of these elements to determine which knots or splices are appropriate for each connection.

## SECURING THE BACKING

Many writers recommend attaching the end of your backing to the reel spool with a slip knot, the tag end of which is further secured by a simple overhand knot. I am of the opinion that any connection that must be "secured" with an overhand knot is worthless to begin with. My recommendation is to use the Sixteen-Twenty loop. It is simple to tie and is very secure with all backings, including the new super-slick polyethylene backings discussed below. The Orvis loop knot is a good alternative.

## THE BACKING

There are two main types of backing available to the fly fisherman today: braided multifilament polyester, best known as Dacron or Micron; and the relatively new gel-spun polyethylene (GSP), best known under the manufacturers' trademarks Spectra and Certran. A similar product, Dyneema, is produced by D.S.M. using a different process. Another new product, Kevlar, made of aramid fibers, is also available but less widely used due to its abrasive properties.

Dacron or Micron polyester backing is available in several strengths 12-, 20-, and 30-pound test strengths (hereinafter "pound" or "test") being the most common. Its advantages include a reasonable amount of stretch and negligible water absorption. Unless you are using a very light outfit with a small reel, the 30-pound test should be selected for anadromous fish and saltwater use. While 20-pound backing may be acceptable for light salmon fishing, you never know when you will hook a large, hard-running salmon in fast water, any one of which conditions warrants the use of heavier backing. Dacron has a soft feel, should you need to grasp it. The main disadvantage to Dacron is its relatively large diameter, which limits the capacity of many reels to less than the desired minimum of 150 yards for salmon and bonefish.

In the last few years, GSP backing, sold under a confusing variety of individual trademarks, has replaced Dacron for many applications because it is much smaller in diameter. For instance, 35-pound GSP is the same diameter as 10-pound nylon monofilament, and reels will hold about 75 percent more GSP than comparable strength Dacron. Reels that may hold only 100 yards of

Dacron will hold 175 yards of comparable strength GSP. GSP has only about 3-percent stretch, and the small diameter offers much less resistance in the water to a running fish. Thus the increase in drag as a strong fish carries out line is much less than with Dacron. For this reason alone, GSP has virtually taken over as the backing of choice for billfish and bluewater fly fishing. GSP is very abrasion resistant and absorbs no water.

The chief disadvantage of GSP is also a result of its small diameter. If you happen to grab this backing while a strong fish is running, you can easily burn or cut your hand. Yes, I know you shouldn't grab the backing, but in times of battle, accidents do happen.

Another disadvantage of GSP is that the slickness of its surface makes it difficult to knot, at least with some of the conventional knots. When this material first became available in 1994, many suppliers were unprepared to recommend appropriate knots. Some suppliers developed new untested knots, while others recommended securing the knot with CA glue. Fortunately, we now know that such drastic measures are not necessary.

Surf fishermen who cast to strong-running striped bass sometimes complain that the abrasion-resistant GSP tends to groove their steel-tip guides. Actually, any of the backing materials will groove ordinary stainless-steel guides sooner or later. As was discussed in Chapter 2, the answer to this problem is to replace the factory tip with a hardened tip-guide, preferably of titanium nitride. When you are fighting a fish that has taken you well into your backing, it is best to layer the backing onto the reel spool in a criss-cross pattern as it is retrieved. If loosely wound, the fine-diameter GSP may dig into loosely coiled backing and create a bird's nest. Overall, the advantages of GSP greatly outweigh the modest care required in its use.

I have long believed, and numerous experts now agree, that the best system for assembling your rigging is a series of interlocking loops. Loops make possible the rapid assembly, change, and disassembly of your rigging. For saltwater fishermen this can be critical; even for

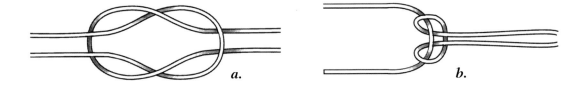

*Figure 6-1. The correct
method for joining loops: (a)
proper square-knot
configuration; (b) improper
girth-hitch configuration.*

salmon fishermen, it may be important when they're
casting to a showing fish.

Loops should always be joined in a "square knot"
configuration as shown above. Connecting loops should
never be allowed to slip into a "girth hitch" configuration
because the girth hitch may cut the mating loop.

The loop at the forward end of your backing is best
constructed with a Bimini Twist. It must be large enough
to encompass the spool on which your line or shooting
head and line are stored. For most purposes, a loop 6
inches long (12 inches in circumference) will suffice.
When GSP was first introduced as backing, there was
some concern that a GSP loop might cut into or through
the fly line or running line to which it was looped, much
in the same manner that braided monofilament loops on
running lines have been known to cut through the loops
of the softer Dacron backing. The simplest way to protect
against such a possibility is to sheath the GSP (or Dacron)
loop with a 2-inch section of squidding or other braided
line or with a similar piece of Larva Lace or other plastic
tubing. However, such a precaution is not necessary when
using 35-pound or stronger GSP backing.

Alternatives to the Bimini include the spider hitch,
the mono loop, and even the triple surgeons loop, subject
to the limitations discussed in Chapter 5. None of these
knots will slip using GSP. The spider hitch is as strong as
the Bimini but does not have the same resilience. The
spider hitch, like the double surgeons loop, will break
when jerked. Don't be seduced; use the Bimini.

Never coat a Bimini with any adhesive; to do so
destroys the resilience built into this knot. Coat any other
knot in the forward end of your backing with a thin
coating of a resilient adhesive, such as Pliobond or

Aquaseal. This prevents the knot from catching on your rod guide and also reduces wear on the knot as it passes through the guides. (Bluewater fly fishermen sometimes add a micro-drop of CA glue to the lock hitches of the Bimini. Be exceedingly careful if you try it.)

Some anglers recommend attaching backing to your line with a blind splice or other permanent connection. Be cautious if you select this option. Unless you do the splicing yourself, you are dependent on your local fly shop or someone else to assist you every time you wish to change the splice. Even if you carry extra reel spools, permanent connections still limit your flexibility in rigging.

## RUNNING LINE

For steelhead and saltwater use, the usual fly line is frequently replaced with a shooting head or a section of heavy fly line 25 to 40 feet long, which is attached to a light, flexible running line, which, in turn, is attached to the backing. Because it is shorter than a standard fly line, the shooting head is often one or more weights heavier to provide the proper head weight for casting. Generally, the

*Figure 6-2. Loop construction: (a) 6-inch spliced loop in braided monofilament backing; (b) one-half spliced loop in braided monofilament backing; (c) 6-inch Bimini-twist loop in GSP backing sheathed with 35-pound braided monofilament backing.*

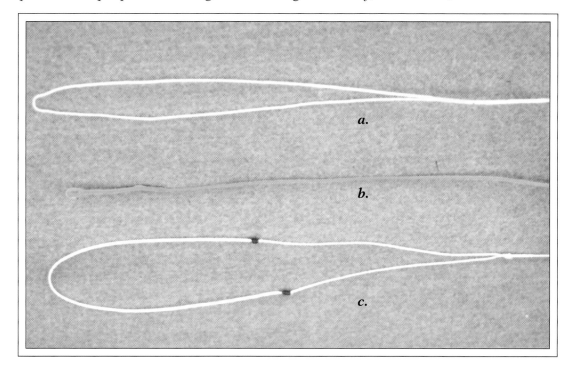

running line is either extruded monofilament nylon or braided-monofilament nylon. The braided variety is much preferred because it is easier to handle, does not have memory, and will not take a set as does the extruded product. Furthermore, braided monofilament, such as Cortland's Braided Mono Running Line or Gudebrod's No. 570 Braided Butt Leader, is soft and flexible and may be coiled at your feet without tangling. Shooting heads and running lines are not frequently employed for salmon fishing with single-handed rods, although they do find considerable use for overhead casting with two-handed rods, especially in Europe.

The running line should be joined both to the backing and to the shooting head or fly line with spliced loops. Use a small loop about 3/8- to 1/2-inch long at the rear of the running line, where it joins the backing. Use a large loop, about 6 inches long, at the forward end, which you loop onto the fly line. As with the backing, the forward loop must be large enough to slip over the reel on which your line is stored.

**SPLICES**. Braided monofilament is best joined with eye splices. No knot presents as smooth or trouble-free a connection as does the splice. That's the reason that many people attach braided loops to the ends of their fly line. Contrary to some perceptions, splices are easy to make using either a bobbin threader or a splicing needle, available at most fly tackle shops.

As shown in Figure 6-3a, slip your needle or threader into the core of the braided monofilament about 2 1/2 inches from the end of the line, and out of the braid about 1 3/4 inches from the end. Grasp the end of the braid with the splicing needle or threader (Figure 6-3b) and pull the end of the braid into the core of the monofilament and back out, leaving a loop not more than 1/2 inch long (Figure 6-3c). Remove the end of the braid from the needle or bobbin. Reinsert the needle or bobbin into the core of the braid about 1 inch from the previous point of insertion and exit 1/4 inch from the tag end (Figure 6-3d).

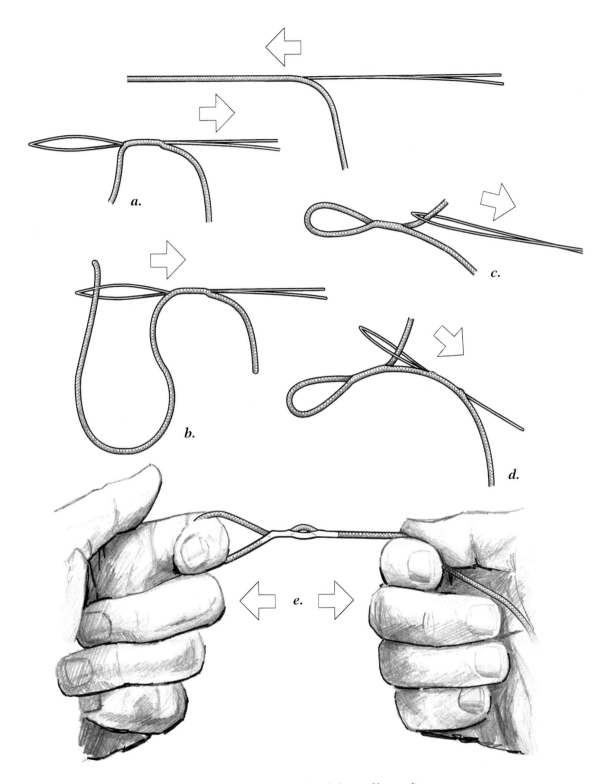

Figure 6-3. Preparing eye splices in braided monofilament line.

Now grasp the tag with the needle or bobbin and pull it into and back out the center of the braid. Clip the tag very close to the running braid and carefully work the tag end back inside the braid (Figure 6-3e). It is not necessary to secure this splice with adhesive. Prepare spliced eyes in both ends of your braided monofilament, and your running line is ready for use.

## THE FLY LINE

Both the front and rear ends of your fly line should be equipped with small loops. You do not need a large loop in the forward end of the fly line because it will only connect to sinking tips and leader loops. There are several good ways to form loops in the ends of your fly lines.

The simplest manner is to fold about 1 inch of the flyline back on itself and whip a small loop. Use red Kevlar thread for whipping. Use red because it will help you to see the tip of your line and Kevlar because it is by far the strongest thread available. Coat the finished whipping with Pliobond or Aquaseal and you are ready to fish. The only objection to this approach is that the whipped loop is significantly larger than the backing to which it is attached. This poses no problem as the line is played out when the fish runs. However, when you retrieve line, the hump of the larger line occasionally may snag in the guides.

One solution to avoiding the hump is to soften about 1 inch of the line tip with nail-polish remover or other solvent and then strip the PVC coating off the inner braid of your line. Double the braid back over the unstripped portion of the line and whip the loop as described above.

Many lines now come from the manufacturer with loops already in place. Most fly shops will install braided loops when you purchase the line. If you wish, you may purchase such braided loops and install them yourself.

The best overall system for attaching braided loops was shown to me by Matt Grobert, a fly-fishing consultant from Mountain Lakes, New Jersey. You start by forming eye splices in two 6-inch lengths of 35-pound braided monofilament backing, as shown in Figure 6-3. Next, strip about 1/2 inch of the coating from each end of the fly line. Coat each stripped section with CA glue and allow it to dry. This stiffens the 1/2-inch tips so they are easier to handle. Now trim the ends of the tips to a needlepoint and insert them into the braided eye splices as far as they will go. Then pull the remaining portion of the braided eye splice onto the fly line and whip the end with flat thread so the braid cannot unravel. Finally, coat the entire braided section up to the loop, but not the loop itself, with Aquaseal or other flexible cement. The result is a smooth and very appealing connection. It has all the advantages of other methods and none of the problems.

Braided loops are fine for trout, light salmon, and saltwater use, say for fish under 15 pounds. However, the braided monofilament fibers are subject to considerable flexing, which eventually weakens the loop. Furthermore, braided loops are often the weak link when you pull on your line to free a fly snagged on a heavy leader. I have had more than one braided loop give way while trying to retrieve a cantankerous rock. When expecting fish more than 15 pounds, I no longer use braided loops, only whipped loops.

## SINKING TIPS AND LEAD HEADS

Most Atlantic salmon fishing is done with floating lines. Fishing the wet fly with a floating line usually results in the fly's swimming 2 to 10 inches below the surface of the water. Under conditions of high or very cold water, it sometimes is necessary to sink the fly into the water column from 2 to 5 feet.

One method of fishing the sunken fly is to use fly lines with sinking tips. The tips are weighted, generally with tungsten powder, and vary in length from 5 to 30 feet, with 10 and 13 feet being the most common. Most manufacturers offer five or six different sink rates, which vary, with line size, from 1 1/4 to 7 inches per second. The disadvantage of using sinking tip lines is that the tips are usually too long and the entire line must be changed in order to change the sink rate. Casting lines with long sinking tips is a chore that no one enjoys.

A better and more flexible system is to employ short sinking tips made of lead-core line, often called "lead heads," looped to the forward end of your floating fly line. Using Cortland's LC-13 lead-core line—which has a sink rate of 8 3/4 inches per second—it is a simple matter to prepare (or buy) short sections of sinking tips 1 to 5 feet long, which may be looped to the forward end of your fly line. If fitted with loops, preferably the whipped ones, such sections may easily be added or removed from your rigging without changing the flyline itself.

It is much easier to retrieve and cast short sinking tips than to struggle with the long tips on sinking lines. The fly rides better in the water because the heavy tip quickly seeks its underwater level, depending on the velocity of the river current, and the fly swings more freely on the end of the leader.

In strong currents, a short 1-foot lead head also may be used to advantage without sinking the fly unduly. Relatively fast currents over shallow, boulder-strewn runs often result in very choppy water with small standing waves. A short lead head helps to prevent the tip of your line from bobbing in the waves (unless, of course, you want the fly to bob, hoping to attract a salmon). I frequently employ a 1-foot lead head to ensure that the fly will not skim the surface in a quirky current.

## LEADERS

For 40 years, the leader material of choice has been nylon, which is a polyamide polymer. Today the generic name "nylon" means any of the polymers or co-polymers used to produce nylon-type monofilament materials. The development of nylon co-polymers has led to a wide and bewildering variety of leader materials with widely varying properties, as illustrated by the extensive selection of materials available to the trout fisherman. With limited exceptions, Maxima nylon, either clear or

chameleon color, is the material of choice for salmon
fishermen worldwide because it incorporates appropriate
stiffness with good abrasion resistance.

The chief advantages of nylon are its high tensile
strength compared to other leader materials, its elasticity,
and its relatively low price. Typical nylons absorb 8- to
10-weight percent of water, which generally lowers the
tensile strength of the material and may weaken the
knots tied therein.

Whichever leader material you choose, your first step
is to construct your leader. Many people do not like to tie
their own leaders. There is a common misconception that
salmon leaders require six or eight segments, as do many
trout leaders. I agree that it is a pain to contemplate such
a task. As recently as July 1995, an outstanding rod
builder published an article on leaders in *Fly Fisherman*
magazine and concluded the article with the oft-repeated
seven-segment formula for salmon leaders first published,
to my knowledge, in the late 1970s. To add insult, that
leader formula provides an insufficiently large butt
section, only 0.021 inch diameter. All this is nonsense.

Have you ever watched a guide urgently retie a leader
so you may repeat your cast to a known salmon lie as
quickly as possible? Frequently, they will strip 3 or 5 feet
of 8- or 12-pound Maxima from a 600-yard spool and tie it
to the existing butt of your leader. Or if you need a
completely new leader, they will cut off the old leader and
replace it with a single length of whatever strength
Maxima is in vogue that day. The reason this works is that
when fishing the wet fly, the river current straightens the
cast and carries the fly. You do not need a finely tapered
leader for fish that are not leader-shy.

There are two compelling reasons for rolling your
own. First, made of heavier, stiffer materials than are used
for trout leaders, the salmon leader is much easier to tie
than most anglers realize. Second, most commercially tied
leaders do not have sufficiently heavy butts, and
consequently the leader may not roll over properly when
cast. Well-tied knots do not impede the flow of momentum

down the leader, nor do looped segments. Charles Ritz, in
fact, documented that knotless leaders are to be avoided.[1]
Knotless, tapered leaders may be satisfactory until, having
changed flies a half-dozen times, you find that your leader
must either be replaced or the tippet extended with a knot.
The only salmon river I know where knotless leaders may
be an advantage is the Laxá í Adaldal in northeastern
Iceland. The flow of this river is controlled by a dam
across the outlet of Lake Myvatn from which the river
flows. A relatively warm and constant temperature in the
summertime leads to considerable weed growth, and a
knotless leader relieves the tedium of constantly removing
weeds from your leader.

If you do prefer to purchase ready-tied leaders, either
have them tied to order or ascertain that they are fresh
merchandise. Never purchase last year's leaders nor buy
them at a midwinter sale. You can never be assured that old
stock has not deteriorated from sunlight or excessive heat.

The butt of a salmon leader should be heavy but
sufficiently flexible so that the monofilament will unfurl in
a tight loop. That's why Maxima and materials of similar
flexibility are so desirable. Having worked my way through
the problems of knotted leaders some years ago, I finally
decided that, for most wet-fly fishing, the proper system
for me was to build a leader 9 feet long using a butt section
about 6 feet long with loops in both ends and with as few
knotted sections as possible. Nowadays those loops are
mono loops, and the tippet is looped to the end of the butt
section. A number of fishing authorities, including Lefty
Kreh, now recommend this system even for trout.

There is no magic in selecting leader length. Nine feet
is a good compromise for wet flies fished within a foot of
the water's surface. However, if you are using a sinking
line or a lead head to sink your fly two or more feet into
the water column, you should shorten your leader to no
more than 6 feet by removing the mid-portion of the
leader. Steelhead anglers frequently use a tippet only 2 1/2

---

1. "The main mistake fly fishers make is to use knotless leaders instead of trying the heavy butt leader. Also
these (knotted) leaders provide an almost perfect turnover. Knotless leaders are like snakes" (46).

feet long when fishing deep. If the tippet is much longer, the fly will not reach the level of the lead head but will tend to rise toward the surface. On the other hand, when fishing in the very low water of late summer you may wish to lengthen your leader to 12 or even 14 feet, particularly when fishing very small flies.

The main reason for using a tapered leader is to provide good energy transfer to turn over small flies. Otherwise, a single length of 0.013-inch or larger Maxima suffices for size 4 and larger flies. For many years, I employed two different leader butts for salmon, depending on the tippet strengths employed. More recently, after considerable experimentation, I have concluded that I need only one leader butt for use with tippet strengths between 6 and 17 pounds. The butt is constructed of 4 feet of 0.024-inch Maxima followed by 2 feet of 0.017-inch material. With a mono loop in each end, I have a 6-foot butt section composed of 40- and 20-pound Maxima segments, the latter of which tests about 23 pounds dry. To this butt section I loop, using the mono loop knot, a 3-foot tippet section of either 0.013 or 0.010-inch Maxima, testing about

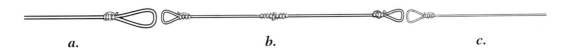

*a.*                              *b.*                              *c.*

17 and 11 pounds respectively. My favorite leader is the 0.010-inch (8-pound) tippet because it readily accommodates size 6, 8, 10, and 12 flies. Unless I am fishing very heavy, rough water, as in the George River, I rarely use a tippet heavier than 0.013 inch in North American waters. Other than pleasing your guide, there is really no reason to carry 15-pound Maxima since it only tests 2 pounds heavier than the 12-pound Maxima.

Interestingly, more than 40 years ago in *A Fly Fisher's Life* Charles Ritz (46) recommended a similar leader system for pursuing very large salmon, a situation in which the first run of the fish must be snubbed or the fish is lost. Between the end of the fly line and the leader

*Figure 6-4. Two-piece leader butt with looped ends for use with looped tippets: (a) fly line; (b) leader butt; (c) leader tippet. Note that these leaders require only one blood knot.*

tippet, Ritz inserted a short, 1-foot midsection of 0.024-inch leader material with loops on both ends. Ritz's system was designed for holding monstrous fish on fast rivers, such as the Alta or the Årøy, and differs from mine in that his tippet consisted of a single 6-foot length of 0.017-inch or heavier nylon fastened to the midsection with a figure-eight knot, a very popular connection in those days. But the intent was the same as mine—to facilitate the quick change of the tippet. Used in this manner with 0.017-inch Maxima, both the figure-eight and Orvis knots (which have confidence factors of 0.80 to 0.85) provide breaking strengths of around 19 pounds.

When fishing size 16 flies, I lengthen the butt section by adding 1 foot of 0.013-inch material (12-pound) material. To this 7-foot butt, I loop 2 to 2 1/2 feet of 0.010-inch or 0.009-inch material, depending on whether I wish to fish an 8-pound or 6-pound tippet.

It should be noted that looped tippets are particularly useful in alleviating wind knots, which usually form in the tippet 1 1/2 to 2 feet above the fly. If the wind knot cannot be untied, it's a simple procedure to unloop the tippet, replace it with a new one, and retie the fly.

Conventional wisdom regarding the construction of tapered leaders dictates that, in order to properly transmit the casting energy down the leader, successive leader segments should be half as short as the heavier preceding segment. I've never had any faith in that concept, although I do consider a heavy and relatively long butt section (0.024-inch minimum diameter) important in transmitting energy from the fly line to the leader. The length of the tippet section, which you loop to the leader butt, is not critical. In general your tippets will be between 30 and 36 inches.

Shortly after the first draft of this chapter was completed, I read parts of Gary Borger's book *Presentation* (09), in which he challenges the conventional wisdom that segments of trout leaders must be graduated in increments of

RIGGING YOUR LINE, LEADER, AND BACKING
not more than 0.002 or 0.003 inch. Salmon fishermen have known for years that's an outmoded concept. Borger proposes a 65-percent rule, which states that adequate leader turnover may be obtained so long as the diameter of the lighter of two adjacent segments is not less than 0.65, the diameter of the heavier. I like his rule; using my formula, the ratios for the adjacent butt segments of my leaders vary from 0.71 to 0.76.

Most salmon anglers use tippets that are much too heavy, especially in view of the fact that the most common sizes of flies in North America are 4 through 10. One recent book on this subject recommended 15-pound leaders for the Moisie, Restigouche, and Grand Cascapedia Rivers. I have caught a number of 20-pound fish on the Moisie and have never used Maxima heavier than 12 pound. Most often I use 8 pound. Lighter leaders allow the fly to work with better action. Most fishermen would do better by tying their knots securely, playing their fish more aggressively (see Chapter 9), and fretting less about unnecessarily strong leaders.

Throughout this book, I have focused on chameleon Maxima leader material because it is universally accepted by salmon anglers. Those who prefer other brands of tippet material should use care when knotting differing brands of material. It is not true than you may not mix differing brands of materials in a leader, but it is true that you must use care in knotting thinner, more flexible tippet material with the larger, stiffer Maxima. That's another reason I prefer looped leader tippets.

## FLUOROCARBON LEADER TIPPETS

In 1993, a new polymer material was introduced into the fishing marketplace—polyvinylidene fluoride, which has come to be called "fluorocarbon" by the fishing fraternity. Table 6-1 compares some of the basic properties of nylon and fluorocarbon monofilaments with polyester (Dacron) and GSP materials. The new fluorocarbon materials possess some unique advantages, especially for the salmon and saltwater-flats fisherman.

**TABLE 6-1**
**TYPICAL PROPERTIES OF LEADER AND BACKING MATERIALS**

| Property | Monofilament | | Braided Polyester | Gel-Spun Polyethylene |
| | Nylon | Fluorocarbon | | |
|---|---|---|---|---|
| Specific gravity | 1.14 | 1.78 | 1.38 | 0.97 |
| Relative sink speed, sec. | 40 | 15 | 32 | (floats) |
| Tensile strength, psi | 60–140,000 | 100–140,000 | 100,000 | 435,000 |
| Elongation to break (percent) | 25–35 | ~25 | 10–15 | 3 |
| Water absorption (percent) | 8–9 | nil | nil | nil |
| Refractive index (water = 1.33) | 1.55 | 1.42 | 1.64 | --- |
| UV susceptibility, percent break strength retained @ 1,000 hrs. | 62 | 100 | --- | --- |

Foremost among these is the fact that fluorocarbon materials do not absorb water and are not subject to ultraviolet degradation, as is nylon. Fluorocarbon retains its integrity indefinitely in the sunlight. In one set of tests, fluorocarbon leader material retained 100-percent breaking strength after 1,000 hours of exposure to ultraviolet light at 74°F, while nylon lost 38 percent of its strength under the same conditions. Fluorocarbon exhibits much better abrasion resistance than does nylon. For wet-fly or saltwater-flats fishermen, particularly those fishing very small flies, the high specific gravity of fluorocarbon (1.78 versus 1.14 for nylon) helps to sink the fly. In addition, the lower refractive index of fluorocarbon makes the leader material less visible, but by no means invisible, in water.

For all these reasons, fluorocarbon is an ideal choice for leader tippets in the 4- to 8-pound class. The only disadvantage is the price, which is three to five times that of nylon.

If I wish to fish 6-pound tippets with very small flies, such as the size 16 flies described in Chapter 10, I loop the tippet to the butt of my leader as usual, but I do take extra care with the loop knot and the tippet knot. If I'm daring to chase an IGFA record, I generally choose the Bimini Twist for the tippet loop, not for its strength but for its added resilience. Otherwise, I will use the mono loop because it is a bit quicker to tie. The tippet knot is always the Sixteen-Twenty knot because it is very strong, and I have complete confidence in my ability to secure it properly.

## ASSEMBLING YOUR RIGGING

For salmon and saltwater-flats fishing, I rig two or three reels—usually two All-Mode reels and one direct drive, each with a different weight of line—although I seldom take but two of these onto the water with me. (With the advent of the Bringsén reel, I rarely use a conventional anti-reverse reel anymore.) If I anticipate using my two-handed rod, I'll also carry my direct drive "Spey" reel. For 7-weight and heavier lines, I use the same rigging system on all reels. The backing is 150 yards of 30- or 35-pound GSP. On top of this I add 15 yards of 35-pound braided-monofilament running line. I prefer blaze orange over the white because it is easier to see on the water. Next comes the fly line (30 yards) or a shooting head (25 to 40 feet). Thus I have 23 to 45 yards of fly line plus the soft braided-monofilament running line to work with before I ever get into the GSP backing. In actuality, only large fish take out more than 45 yards of line, so only infrequently do I have to play fish with much of the GSP backing in the water. But it's there when I do need it. With this system, I need change only the fly line or shooting head as the occasion requires, regardless of whether I'm fishing for salmon or bonefish or in the surf.

Not many of us can cast a full 30-yard fly line using a single-handed rod, especially in a wind. It is much easier to cast a shooting head. For this reason, I usually shorten the rear end of my weight-forward fly line to about 70 feet, that being the limit of my ability to pick up and cast line. In those rare circumstances where I need to cast farther, I use the fly line as a 70-foot shooting head ahead of the braided monofilament running line. It is not exactly neat, but it is better than pausing to change to a shooting head for an occasional cast. The shortened fly line has little or no effect on my ability to mend the line, since using a single-handed rod I cannot mend 70 feet of line with any degree of accomplishment.

For wade-fishing with the two-handed rod, I mark my fly line at end of the head (i.e., at the end at the rear taper) and again 10 feet farther back. With my Spey line, the marks are at 52 and 62 feet respectively. Unless conditions dictate otherwise, I strip in line to the 52-foot mark, make my cast, and shoot 10 feet of line; thus my cast is 62 feet plus a 10-foot leader for a total cast of about 72 feet. That's long enough to cover most water without being excessively tiring even in a strong wind, and it makes for a very convenient cast-and-step-down sequence, as described in Chapter 9.

If you cannot easily pick up 52 feet of line, don't fret. Cut back the head of your line to whatever length you can easily handle, say 45 or 40 feet, and reattach the running line. The point is that you want to shoot only the smaller running line, not the weighty portion of the head. Design your casting head to accommodate your ability.

I do not like sinking-tip fly lines and avoid them whenever possible. Most tips are too long, and you never seem to have the correct tip density. Changing a whole line is a pain. To avoid these problems, I long ago switched to interchangeable sinking tips constructed from Cortland's LC-13 lead core line as described previously. The lead line weighs

13 grains per foot and is available in 30-foot coils. The sink rate is 8 3/4 inches per second, which compares favorably with a rate of 6 1/4 to 7 inches per second for lines with ultra-fast sinking tips. I carry sinking tips 1, 3, and 5 feet long, constructed with whipped loops on each end. Obviously, they can be looped together if other lengths are required, which they seldom are. Make certain that the whipped loops are large enough to slip over your fly, so you can add or remove a lead head without cutting and retying your fly. It's a neat system and sure beats carrying all those extra lines.

Sinking tips are useful in rivers with ledge or slab rock, such as the Laxá í Adaldal in Iceland. In the example cited in Chapter 5, I was using an aluminum tube fly to reach the fish at the bottom of the river and as a result lost several flies on the rock ledges. A better system would have been to use a standard wet fly or plastic tube fly with a 2- or 3-foot lead head between the fly line and the leader. The sinking tip would then drift the fly near the bottom of the river, but the lighter, free-swinging fly would have been much less susceptible to snags. Short sinking tips are also the ideal manner with which to combat the tendency for heavily dressed, integral-body flies and plastic tube flies to skim or wake on the surface.

If you must fish very deep (as do steelhead anglers), a trick to consider is inserting a 3- or 5-foot lead head between the butt of your leader and the tippet (or delete the leader butt completely). The leader butt cuts through the surface currents and allows the long lead head, tippet, and fly to sink rapidly. The tippet must be short enough so that it is not pushed to the surface by the current. Not being leader-shy, salmon will not veer away from a fly on the end of the 3-foot tippet.

Sinking-tip lines and perhaps the lead-head tips themselves are not without their problems, however. In recent years on certain rivers in Canada, the use of sinking lines has become quite controversial because some people have used large hooks on very short leaders to snag salmon. This is particularly true in low water or in late fall, when the fish are approaching the spawn. I have never seen nor heard of salmon being snagged with short-lead heads, probably for the same reason that I use them. The short sinking tip gets the fly down into the water column but permits it to swing freely on the long leader. Such action is not conducive to snagging. Nevertheless, it represents a concern and a situation that must be avoided.

The knots that I use to assemble leaders vary according to the size of leader material and the intended use. For joining 0.012-inch butt sections and larger, I use the blood knot because the triple surgeons knot yields a knot larger than I like. The Orvis knot is a good alternative. If I intend to knot smaller-sized tippets, say those testing at 10 pounds or less, I generally use the bloody quick knot because it has a very small profile and is very secure. However, for most purposes, including trout fishing, I usually loop the tippet sections onto the leader butt through mono loops.

I pre-tie all my leader butts and secure the knots with a drop of CA glue. In a leisurely evening, you can tie five or six leader butts, which should last you for an entire season. I also pre-tie a number of 8- and 12-pound leader tippets so they are instantly available when I need them. If you prefer to purchase your leaders, I suggest you cut off the tippet, leaving a 6-foot butt to which you add a nonslip mono loop. You are thus prepared to add looped tippets as desired. It's a neat system that serves all purposes.

It is of great advantage for the salmon angler to adopt one system of rigging for all his equipment. The various components become readily interchangeable. You don't have to cut this line or that backing nor add a loop here and a knot there. The greatest advantage is that you do not have to remember how each rod is rigged and what components, if any, are interchangeable. It's enough to remember which reel contains what line.

## LAST CASTS

It need not be re-emphasized that proper rigging is fundamental to successful angling. But the proper rigging of your fly entails more than just attaching it to the eye of your hook with a secure Sixteen-Twenty knot. Before fishing, always ascertain that your fly rides properly submerged in the current. While fishing on the Matapedia one year, I showed Gilles, my guide, the Sixteen-Twenty knot and suggested he try it. "It won't work here," he informed me and handed me a heavily dressed size 2 Green Highlander with which to demonstrate the knot. Warily, knowing that I was being set up, I attached the leader to the eye, made a few casts, and observed that in the fast current the fly did indeed skim the surface just as he had predicted.

Heavily dressed flies, flies with large heads, and double hooks with large up-turned eyes are prone to ride up and skim the surface, particularly in strong currents. Most anglers know that a bare hook sinks rapidly, but few recognize that all those feathers, fur, and thread you tie to the hook impede its sinking. As discussed in Chapter 4, even double-hook buck bugs will hydroplane. Several years ago, I asked a friend to tie me some large Kola Rats without specifying the wing hair. He chose Australian opossum. It was a huge mistake. The kinky hair tended to clump, and even his size 1/0 double-hook Kola Rats rode to the surface. That's another reason to favor slender flies with small heads in fast water. If you wish or need to use heavily dressed flies in fast water, you may want to pass the leader tippet through the eye and tie it around the hook shank at the head of the fly. Many guides do this routinely, even when it's unnecessary, to avoid the possibility of flies skimming the surface.

Hydroplaning is not a function of the knot used. It depends on how the fly is dressed and how the leader is attached to the hook. But beware—knots tied around the hook shank are harder, sometimes much harder, to tighten than when tied on the eye because the head is not hard or perfectly round as is the eye. Use extra care in tightening such knots; be certain they cannot slip—and break.

*A Beached Salmon*
Watercolor
9 3/8 x 14 inches
Private Collection

# Chapter 7

# Equipment, Clothing, and Physical Conditioning

Rod, reel, line, leader, and a box of flies. What more do you need on the river? If you look into your tackle bag or fishing vest, or read the advertisements, it seems that quite a variety of other equipment is required to fulfill the role of the well-dressed angler. The problem, even for experienced fishermen, is to determine what gadgets are best left at home.

Somewhat arbitrarily, I have divided this world of gear and preparation into three categories: equipment, clothing, and physical conditioning.

## EQUIPMENT

**WADERS**. The wise choice for the salmon angler is the stocking-foot neoprene wader. No other wader is as versatile in both hot and cold climes nor will sustain the abuse that neoprene will. When worn with proper undergarments, either 3mm or 4mm thickness will protect you from the chill of late October fishing and yet not be uncomfortable in the heat of summer. For years I used the same pair of waders year round, although I have recently switched to waist-high waders for summer fishing, not because of the heat but because I seldom wade over thigh-deep in the summer.

Stocking-foot waders are not the easiest garments to put on or take off, but their comfort in the water is unsurpassed. Being relatively close fitting, they offer much less resistance to rushing water than do other types, a significant advantage when you're wading fast streams in high water. If you have a choice, avoid waders with seams in the crotch. That's where they most often pull apart and begin to leak. Nothing can spoil a day astream more quickly than leaking waders. Always keep at hand a tube of liquid adhesive with which to repair leaks—at least overnight. I prefer Liquid Nails for Small Projects because it's useful for a myriad of purposes, much better than most sportsman's goops I've tried. It air-hardens sufficiently in 30 minutes and does not harden in the tube as do many of the goops.

Stocking-foot waders require separate wading shoes. For all but the coldest waters, this is a significant advantage over boot-foot waders. Wading shoes may be laced as tightly as you desire and provide much more ankle support than any boot foot. You can, if required, lace your shoes tightly and hike overland in stocking-foot waders, something you wouldn't even consider with boot-foot waders. On the other hand, boot-foot waders worn with heavy wool socks may insulate your feet better in very cold water, such as is encountered in winter steelhead fishing.

Unless you are under 35 years of age and nimble as a goat, I strongly recommend either shoes with carbide-tipped studs or rubber wading sandals called Korkers. Properly studded, such shoes offer unbelievable traction on slippery rocks. Unless you have tried them, you cannot understand how much better they are than felt soles alone.

If you don't like studded soles permanently affixed on your boots, there is an alternative. The first couple of years that I fished in Iceland I used Korkers, the bottoms of which were fitted with carbide-tipped studs. These sandals fit over a normal wading shoe, and while somewhat bulky, they provide better traction than do studded shoes. Korkers are the ultimate in wading traction, but for casual use they may not be worth the extra hassle to carry or wear.

Be very cautious in your choice of soles. In late summer, the rocks in many such rivers as the Miramichi and those in Iceland are covered with a 1/8-inch layer of slime. Good traction is mandatory. When first introduced a decade ago, the studded soles offered by Weinbrenner and later by several other companies contained studs that extended some 2mm beyond the felt sole. They provided excellent traction in fast water and on the mossy and grassy rocks. Over eight or nine years, I wore out two pairs of studded soles and in 1996 ordered a new pair of these boots. Surprise! The new boots contained studs that barely extended through the felt sole and would not grip the rocks or penetrate the moss and slime as did the original soles. After a three-day trial, which included wading the shale ledges of the upper Miramichi River, I found the new boots totally unsatisfactory and returned them to the manufacturer. It turns out that the manufacturer decided to use both a thicker felt sole and shorter studs. When queried on the change, the designer of the boots replied that the shorter studs were desirable to prevent anglers from skating "on the long studs across the bottom of fiberglass drift boats!" In my opinion, soles with the shorter studs are unsafe, cannot be recommended, and should not be worn. At this writing, Bare Sportswear, L.L. Bean, Danner, and Simms all offer boots with the longer studs. The Russell Moccasin Company will furnish them upon request, and Korkers, Inc. will provide felt or rubber soles with almost any length studs you require. Regrettably, Orvis recently switched to the unacceptably short studs.

Within the last year, L.L. Bean has introduced wading shoes with sticky-rubber Aqua Stealth soles, with or without studs, that may presage the boot of the future.

Built like a hiking boot, these shoes utilize the sticky-rubber technology developed for rock-climbing equipment. Friends who first used them reported that these boots offered much better traction than felt on slippery rocks, on wet grass, and in the mud. Based on those reports, I obtained a studded pair for evaluation. Although mine have yet to be used a full season, they offer excellent traction and are unquestionably the most comfortable wading shoes I have ever worn. However, not everyone is yet convinced that Aqua Stealth soles without studs are equivalent to felt under all conditions, specifically on wet grass. Time will tell.

While the synthetic leather used in wading shoes today seems to last forever, felt soles wear and eventually need replacement. Whoever does the repairs, make certain that only the bottom felt containing the studs is removed. Do not remove the midsole. It has been attached with a hot-melt adhesive whose adhesion cannot be duplicated outside the factory. Apply only a thin layer of contact cement to the midsole and replacement felt. Korkers recommends Barge cement, which is included in their felt-sole replacement kits. Depending on your particular shoe, you may need to cut off the heel section from a one-piece sole and cement it on top of a heel block.

Always wear a wading belt fastened securely around your waist. It makes your waders more comfortable and prevents any significant amount of water from spilling into your waders when you eventually take that fateful fall. Frequently, when fishing in the summer with full-length, bib-type waders, I fold them down at the waist, but always with the wading belt securely fastened underneath. The new 4 1/2-inch-wide belt offered by Hodgman is outstanding. I especially like its Velcro closure, which is instantly adjustable. If drawn tightly, these belts provide support in the lumbar regions over the kidneys, which greatly reduces back strain. These belts are particularly useful when you're casting from a canoe. You should try one of these belts if you have any back problems.

A final word about waders. For a number of years,

many of the brands were made by the same manufacturers in Taiwan. Only the embellishments and the
names were changed. Despite all my fancy fishing tackle, I
have yet to spend $100 for a pair of waders. Waders
receive hard wear, but the neoprene fabrics are much the
same in all brands. I would much prefer to replace my $85
waders every few years than to fret about caring for a
$300 pair.

For the canoeing angler who may exit the canoe only
to land a fish, waders are cumbersome to wear all day. A
better solution is to wear lightweight rubber boots or
Wellies, 10 or 12 inches high. You can step from the canoe
without worrying about wet feet. If you anticipate the need
for waders at some point during the day, carry them with
you in the canoe. On the other hand, if the weather is cold
and blustery, waders will keep you warm and comfortable.

Much as I dislike carrying additional pieces of luggage,
the only satisfactory way to carry waders and shoes on
airlines is in a separate wader bag. Mine is about 17 by 10
by 9 inches, is made of thin nylon, and holds my waders,
wading shoes, wading belt, Gator socks (see page 225), and
inflatable wading suspenders. Newer bags are generally of
nylon mesh, so the contents may dry more quickly. Even so,
the separate bag is desirable if you must pack your
equipment before the waders are thoroughly dry.

**WADING STAFF**. A wading staff is often looked on
with disdain, mostly by people who haven't tried one.
Years ago, I tore the ligaments in my ankle, so I started
using a staff at an earlier age than many people. I actually
like fishing with a staff; I find it to be of great assistance,
even for trout fishing. A staff serves as a third foot to
improve your balance, which makes wading boulder-
strewn rivers much easier. However, a staff should *never*
be used to wade into water that is deeper or faster than
you would normally wade in. If in doubt, wade without
using your staff. When the going gets too rough, quit. You
still have your staff for balance. You should wade in swift
currents with your body parallel to the current. Always

wade such currents with a side step, never by crossing one foot ahead of the other.

One-piece wooden staffs are ideal, if the handle is wrapped with cord to provide a secure grip and if the tip is weighed slightly so the handle floats out of the water. The main disadvantage to one-piece staffs is their length. Many automobiles do not accommodate them easily. Since most of my salmon trips require air travel, I have settled on multipiece staffs, which can be collapsed and carried along with my four-piece rods in a travel case. Some of my friends use those folding staffs that are connected by an elastic cord. I do not like them because they are insufficiently stout.

Several years ago, I discovered what may be the best of all staffs. It is the Tracks hiking staff made by Cascade Design of Seattle, Washington (103). I first used this staff on the Routeburn Trek in New Zealand, a three-day hike over some very difficult terrain, and have used it for all my salmon fishing ever since. It is available in two versions, a two-piece Sherlock Walking Staff, which collapses to 34 inches, and a three-piece Sherlock Travel Staff, which collapses to 22 inches. The lengths of both models adjust with a push-button detent through the 3/4-inch outer tubing. This outer tubing is covered with a soft foam, which is easy to grip and makes the staff float with the top of the handle out of the water. The handle is fitted with a round wooden knob, which can be removed to reveal a camera stud to which you may fasten a small tripod head. The tip of the staff is fitted with large rubber crutch tip that prevents any noise on the rocks as you wade or drag it. The staff tip may be unscrewed to access a metal point useful for hiking over hard terrain. The only deficiency in the staff is the tendency for the rubber tip to be sucked off in a mucky bank. You should secure the crutch tip to the staff with a good adhesive.

Cascade Design now also offers a five-piece Fish Stick designed specifically for the fisherman. The sections are connected by an internal elastic cord. However, as with other makes of this design, this staff is not nearly as sturdy as the Sherlock Staffs.

I have made only one modification to my Sherlock Treks staff. I removed the wrist strap and replaced it with a 1/8-inch tether cord about 3 1/2 feet long, with a snap swivel at the end, which I fasten to a "D" ring on my wading belt. In the tether, at about 5-inch increments, I form four or five overhand loops some 3/4 inch in diameter. Thus, if I need to shorten the tether, I need only to pass the snap swivel through the "D" ring and snap it into another of the loops. Resting on the ground, the wading staff should extend to your armpit.

The proper length of a tether cord is best determined by throwing the staff over your off shoulder and letting it hang down your backside without quite touching the river bottom. To set the length, stand on level ground with the staff over your shoulder and adjust the tether so the staff hangs 2 to 4 inches off the ground. Many people actually fish with the staff in this position. More often, I just let the staff float downstream of me. The Treks staff floats with its tip under the surface and its handle an inch or so above the surface, easily within my reach. You can increase the angle at which the staff floats by filling the lower section of the staff with water. This is one piece of equipment that is a delight to use and a pleasure to recommend.

**FISHING VEST**. Every stylish trout fisherman wears a fishing vest. Experienced salmon anglers do not, because the tackle requirements are much different. Wading in the river, the salmon angler seldom changes leaders and may not change tippets unless a fly is lost. So the wading angler needs, at most, a coil of tippet material and relatively few flies, which he may change should conditions require. I carry in my shirt pocket a small floating fly box that contains the various flies I may wish to try as I wade the river. On occasion, I may find myself missing a desirable pattern, but then salmon are not all that selective anyway. For all these reasons the fishing vest is of little use to the salmon fisherman. If you really desire a vest, consider a fleece vest, which will provide comfort in cool weather yet has sufficient pockets for your needs.

*Figure 7-1. An assortment of fly boxes. Left to right, front row: author-designed tube fly box, Nubby Tack box. Second row: Wheatley No. 1632 fly box, Scientific Anglers box circa 1970, all-foam Morrell box.*

**TACKLE BAG.** A tackle bag, on the other hand, is essential. In a bag approximately 13 by 10 by 6 inches, you can carry two or three reels, eight or ten boxes of flies sorted by color or size, leaders and coils of leader material, insect repellent, sunscreen, pliers, a camera, a scale, and other miscellany. The good news is that most nonresidents fishing in Canada will have a guide to carry the bag, and he should never be more than a few hundred feet away. If you are fishing from a canoe, you have everything you need at your fingertips.

Before leaving on a salmon trip, I pack my one tackle bag with all my fishing tackle except the rods. With the possible exception of a quality camera, which I hand carry, all this tackle goes aboard the airplane with me and is never out of sight. If I cannot get everything into the one tackle bag, I am carrying too much. My biggest problem is the large "Spey" reel for my two-handed rod, which usually goes into the luggage with my clothing.

However you pack, never allow yourself to be in the position that if equipment stowed in your luggage doesn't get there, you don't fish.

**FLY BOXES**. Salmon flies are expensive and warrant proper care. By far the best boxes for single-hook flies are the Wheatley aluminum boxes fitted with No. 5 and No. 7 clips. Some of these boxes are available with a center leaf and hold 80 to 140 flies each. The No. 1632 box holds 110 flies and is particularly suited for an assortment of single-hook flies. The Perrine Nos. 95 and 96 boxes are similar to the Wheatleys but are less sophisticated and less expensive.

Boxes with foam pads should be used with caution. The foam holds moisture and hastens the rusting of your hooks. Not many of us have the discipline to dry out such boxes after every dunking or rain shower. Furthermore, many foam boxes do not hold large flies securely. The flies wiggle, work holes in the foam, and may fall out. If you avoid the rust problem, foam boxes are satisfactory for flies size 6 and smaller and are ideal for flies size 10 and smaller. But choose your foam carefully. It should be dense and firm, neither brittle nor porous. The new all-foam boxes with magnetic closures by Morrell are satisfactory for small flies and inexpensive enough that you may treat them as throwaways. The best of the lot seems to be the polypropylene boxes with self-hinges offered by Sue Burgess from the United Kingdom. Available in different colors and quite inexpensive, they may be found in most Canadian tackle shops but are difficult to obtain in the United States.

What salmon anglers need is a well-designed box for large double-hook flies. The Wheatley No. 1642-1 1/2 holds 70 flies and does an adequate job, but I would prefer a box that holds my doubles upright and is available in different colors so you may code the contents. The plastic boxes with slotted inserts offered by Scientific Anglers in the 1970s were not perfect but better than many of today's boxes. I still try to buy all those old boxes I can find.

The new Nubby Tack boxes by Limited Seasons Company (112) show considerable promise for securing double-hook flies. The fly pads contain tough plastic knobs 1/8 inch in diameter. The hook barbs are pressed between the knobs. Hooks size 2 through 12 hold quite well in the upright position. While these boxes have not yet passed the test of time, they appear to be the best fly boxes developed since the incomparable Wheatleys.

Appropriate boxes for long tube flies are virtually impossible to obtain in the United States. L.L. Bean and others offer a five-compartment saltwater fly box with lengthwise compartments. It's a good compromise but thicker than necessary and does not have small compartments to hold your hooks. A fly box I designed specifically for long tube flies with three compartments for hooks is shown in Figure 7-1. A similar box, DeWitt No. 1043C, with six compartments positioned cross-wise, is perfect for tubes less than 3 inches long.

**NETS AND OTHER LANDING DEVICES**. There are at least six methods for landing salmon. Beaching and hand-tailing require no equipment, and these methods are discussed in Chapter 11. Nets, the tailer, the new BogaGrip, and gaffs offer you choices you didn't know you had.

Short of hand-tailing, a large black landing net 32 inches in diameter and at least 36 inches deep is the best and most humane way to land a salmon, particularly a large one. Some of the newer nets offer collapsible handles; soft, knotless netting that does not roughen the fish nor catch its gills or mouth; and even built-in scales for weighing the fish. If you are fishing without a guide or he is up in the bushes asleep, it is not particularly difficult to net your own fish, if you can find the net. When fishing with a guide, insist that he retain the net. Too often the net is stuck in the bushes a quarter-mile upstream.

The tailer is an ingenious device that consists of a loop of wire affixed to a handle in such a way that when slipped over a salmon's caudal peduncle (tail), the loop

*Figure 7-2. An assortment of landing and release devices. Left to right: antique canoe gaff, House of Hardy tailer, Abu No. 35 hand gaff, Model 130 BogaGrip, Ketchum release, H.L. Leonard Co. priest, and Normark 50-pound Weigh-In scale.*

may be instantly tightened to hold the salmon. However, if applied crudely, the wire loop may damage the salmon's skin severely or even break it, causing infection and eventual death. Tailed fish should be grasped by the tail with your hand, and the tailer should be removed as quickly as possible. Take your photograph and gently release the fish to fight another day.

The BogaGrip is a new device that operates much

like a pair of pliers to grasp the fish by the lower jaw. The fish cannot escape because the more it pulls, the tighter the grip. It's a great device for toothy creatures, such as barracuda, but obviously you must be within arm's length of the fish to grasp it. The BogaGrip is advertised as an ideal way to suspend fish for weighing. It is well suited for such species as black bass that, because of their neck structure, should be handled by the lip, but its suitability for large salmon remains to be determined. Both the 30- and 60-pound models of the BogaGrip have built-in scales that may be certified by the IGFA, even though the scales are only graduated in half-pound increments.

The gaff is an archaic and cruel instrument, which is banned in most salmon jurisdictions. 'Nuff said.

**LANYARD**. Fishermen go wild over gadgets of all varieties. Problems arise when you have to decide which gadgets to carry and which to leave home. Then you have to remember where you stored all that stuff. One gadget that I have come to appreciate is the lanyard or necklace. When I first saw one, I thought it was an affectation, but having used mine for more than eight years, I am convinced.

My necklace is homemade of 1/8-inch braided nylon cord with three snap swivels whipped onto the cord. It is 33 inches in diameter and slips inside my shirt or jacket when not in use. Commercial lanyards such as the Sportsman Elastic Necklace offered by Dr. Slick or the Flyfish Lanyard by May Fly contain five clips or snaps that, if you use all of them, make the lanyard cumbersome and much too heavy around your neck. Don't try to attach more than two or three tools.

Originally, I started with just the mandatory nipper and a 4 1/2-inch pair of pliers with which to tighten knots. Later, I added a small diamond hook file for touching up the points on small flies. I find this a near-perfect set of tools. If you are seeking new pliers or forceps, I recommend you look at a 5 1/2-inch combination tool, such as the SNH55B forceps offered by Dr. Slick. It serves as both pliers and scissors and also has a point with which to clean out the eye of your hooks or open split shot. You might also consider a pair of mitten clamps, which have excellent holding power, although not all of them possess a cutting edge.

**INSECT REPELLENT**. The scourge of salmon fishing in the north country during June and early July is the hordes of mosquitoes and black flies seeking to trade some very irritating proteins for a drop of your blood. For some of us, those insect proteins can be very irritating, even hazardous to our health. One of my friends is so allergic to black flies that even a single bite near the eye will cause it to swell shut. He avoids the torment during the height of the bug season by encasing himself in a bug-proof mesh jacket and head net complete with lightweight gloves.

For most of us, the repeated application of a suitable insect repellent suffices. By far the most effective repellent for mosquitoes is diethyl-meta-toluamide, better known as DEET. The only problem is that some people are allergic to pure DEET, and young children should not use formulations containing more than 10 percent DEET. Ethyl hexanediol (as found in 6-12) is somewhat more effective than DEET for black flies but is much less effective for mosquitoes. Skin So Soft, developed and sold by Avon Products as a bath oil, has become a popular alternative to DEET, even though Avon disclaims its efficacy as a repellent. Recently an unidentified source has recommended a mixture of equal parts DEET, Skin So Soft, and water. The mixture is as effective as pure DEET, smells much better, and is gentle on the skin. It's the only repellent I need any more. If you prefer a grease, a friend of mine strongly recommends Vick's VapoRub.

## CLOTHING

The selection of clothing is largely a matter of personal preference, but certain fundamentals do pertain. The fisherman must be able to protect himself from the elements of nature: rain, heat, cold, and insects are the major concerns. I do not include snow because we seldom encounter it while fishing for Atlantic salmon.

**RAIN GEAR**. The fundamental and most essential piece of clothing is a quality, hip-length, waterproof rain jacket. The jacket must, above all, be waterproof, not just water repellent. It is no fun to fish all day in the rain only to find that your jacket leaks a little—or a lot. Nothing ruins your day more quickly.

The technology of rain-gear manufacture has changed rapidly in recent years. The trend has been toward gear made of waterproof-and-breathable fabrics that are lightweight and somewhat porous to water vapor. There are two main types of waterproof-and-breathable materials available: those that utilize the absorbent-film principle— many of which are based on Entrant, an elastic polyurethane coating—and those that work on the microporosity principle, such as the well-known Gore-Tex films. The newer three-layer Gore-Tex material utilizes both principles, which makes it totally waterproof, unlike the original two-layer Gore-Tex. However, do not believe the extravagant claims made for breathable rainwear or the new "breathable" waders. The truth is that the permeability of any of these materials is insufficient to transfer large quantities of perspiration vapor. While I still question the extent to which breathable waders "breathe" underwater, the product-development manager of a large private retailer, whose judgment I respect, assures me that Gore-Tex waders do breathe somewhat below the water level, even if most of the perspiration escapes through the top of your waders as the air is pumped by your leg movement.

My personal rain-gear preference is a lightweight, compact, and totally waterproof rain jacket, such as Patagonia's Triolet or Storm Jacket. The newer Triolet jacket employs three-layer Gore-Tex construction, while the proven Storm Jacket uses two-layer ripstop nylon fabric coated with a proprietary waterproof-and-breathable coating. I used a Patagonia Storm Jacket with complete satisfaction on all my trips through Iceland,

Europe, New Zealand, and Australia, in hot weather and in cold, for more than nine years until the waterproof coating eventually wore thin. Well-designed jackets such as these come with adjustable hoods and cuffs, Velcro closures over the zipper, numerous pockets with zipper closures, and Houdini drawcords for the waist and hem. The Climb Very Light and Mountain jackets offered by The North Face are also very appealing. Your choice may depend upon whether you prefer a soft or somewhat crinkly feel to the jacket material. Unfortunately, all such jackets are very expensive.

I strongly prefer a hip-length jacket for two reasons. First of all, salmon fishermen do not generally need to wade deeply, as do steelhead fishermen, and therefore are not concerned about jackets trailing in the river. In addition, the hip length offers more protection on those numerous occasions when you wear it without waders, as in a canoe or in the woods. My extra-large jacket measures 32 inches from neck seam to the hem, but the hem drawcord allows it to be shortened if I need to wade deeply. Several manufacturers offer "shorty" or waist-length models that are stylish with waders, but they have limited usefulness off the stream. For this very reason, Patagonia lengthened its original SST Fishing Jacket by 3 inches.

A number of other manufacturers now offer similar jackets, including L.L. Bean, Cabela's, Campmor, Columbia, Helly-Hansen, Recreational Equipment Inc. (REI), and Simms. Choose a forest green or medium-light blue or sage color if you have a choice. Some fish are wary of unusual backgrounds. The better you blend with the background, the closer you may approach such fish.

If you are not sure about a certain jacket construction, ask your salesman for the details. If he doesn't know, shop elsewhere. This is another situation where you can learn much by reading manufacturers' catalogs, especially informative ones like those from Patagonia or The North Face. Not infrequently, the style, size, or color you prefer may not be available locally, and not all merchants are willing to enter special orders to accommodate you. In such cases, call the manufacturer. If it does not offer direct mail-order service, most will refer you to an affiliated shopping service that can provide any of the manufacturers' products almost overnight.

Be cautious if you are tempted by waxed-cotton products, such as the well-known Barbour rain jackets. Waxed cotton looks very stylish on the stream the first year, but it is unnecessarily heavy, and as it wears it needs rewaxing all too frequently to retain its water repellency.

**LAYERING FOR COLD WEATHER**. Everyone has by now heard of the layering principle. Choose your clothing so that you may put on or remove layers as the weather and temperature dictate. However, this principle requires you to choose clothing for its ability to layer with proper mobility as well as for warmth. In general, thin garments layer best. Synthetics wearing against wool or cotton help reduce the friction between layers, which enhances mobility and prevents your clothing from binding.

The coldest, most uncomfortable fishing I have ever experienced was in northeastern Iceland a few years ago on the Laxá í Adaldal River. It had been a very cold and late spring, and there had been virtually no summer. On this particular July 19, the wind was out of the north, blowing straight upstream at velocities in excess of 25 knots. The air temperature was 39°F, and the water temperature was 41°F. It was the kind of day when you constantly asked yourself if you were having fun yet. If I had not traveled 2,500 miles to fish, I certainly would have stayed inside and read a book.

I really had not gone to Iceland prepared for such cold, yet thanks to neoprene waders and layers of clothing, I was quite comfortable—except for the tips of the fingers on my right hand, which I have since learned how to protect.

Below my waist, my layers always start with cotton briefs because I like the support they provide. In cold weather I need not fret about excessive perspiration with cotton briefs, although a wide variety of synthetic briefs are now available should you prefer them. Next come a pair of knee-length polypropylene hose such as the Gobi-Plus by Wigwam. I like the longer-length hose because if my feet and legs are warm, so generally am I. For many years, until I adopted the vapor barrier concept (see page 224), in cold weather I would then add a pair of tapered fleece pants made of Polartec 200 or a similar polyester material. Several companies offer these, some with instep straps, which I do not recommend. Finally, I put on a pair of the heaviest wool socks I could find. I emphasize heavy, not for warmth, but for comfort underfoot. You might also consider one of the specialty climbing or trekking socks by Thorlo or the new vapor barrier socks (see page 225). All this tucked into my neoprene waders guaranteed my comfort in the water, even while fishing from a boat in 25°F weather. Nowadays, vapor-barrier socks replace the heavy wool socks; they provide greater warmth and are much easier to put on and take off.

A word of caution regarding fleece pants. Under a protective layer, they are soft and quite warm. Without a protective layer, they are useless. Wind will whip through them, and you will feel as if you are standing naked.

Above the waist, I use the same layering principles in a different combination. First, I put on a lightweight, long-sleeve polypropylene or polyester undershirt. My preference here is Patagonia's lightweight Capilene, a treated polyester. As underwear, it is unexcelled and is recommended by numerous mountaineering authorities. Next comes one of my secret weapons against the cold: a sleeveless wool sweater. Sleeveless sweaters or vests are particularly useful in keeping the core of your body warm, which in turn causes excess blood to be circulated to your extremities, thus warming your fingers and toes. Then I add a very lightweight shirt, such as one of Viyella or the new polyester microfleece. Next to last comes a heavyweight wool sweater, tightly woven to trap the heat. Nowadays, more people are substituting a synthetic fleece or pile jacket for wool because it is lighter and dries faster. Others still prefer a lightweight down jacket in place of the sweater, but if it gets wet, down becomes useless. I have no doubts that eventually I'll switch to the synthetic fleece. The last layer is, of course, my waterproof rain jacket, even if it is not raining. It makes a superb windbreaker, and if it happens to rain, I'm ready.

You will note that this system involves five layers above the waist and four layers below the knees. The components can be rearranged to suit the changing weather. If it warms up, at best I have to remove and carry either the rain jacket or the sweater.

**THE VAPOR BARRIER CONCEPT**. During the last decade, a number of scientific studies have investigated the mechanisms by which the body is cooled and warmed. These studies have extended our understanding well beyond the traditional concept of dead-space insulation illustrated by the layering of clothing described above. The most significant finding has been the role that the skin's moisture layer plays in cooling and warming the body.

The body loses heat by radiation, conduction, convection, and evaporation. Clothing significantly reduces heat loss by radiation, leaving convection and evaporation as the main methods of heat loss. Respiration and perspiration are, of course, the chief sources of evaporative heat loss. The body prefers an average skin temperature of about 75°F and a relative humidity between 70 and 90 percent, which serves to maintain a layer of warm, moist air on the skin. If the environment differs significantly from those ideal conditions, the body strives to maintain its temperature and will, for instance, react to heat by inducing perspiration or to cold by initiating shivering. In severe cold, the core or trunk shuts down blood flow to the extremities, and the fingers and toes are the first to feel the effects. The trick is to maintain the layer of warm, moist air on the skin undisturbed by convective or conductive losses. In cold weather, that's what the insulation of your clothing attempts to do.

The best method of maintaining that warm, moist

layer is with a vapor barrier. A vapor barrier is simply a waterproof film or fabric worn close to the skin to retain the body moisture instead of allowing it to escape through convection or otherwise. No, it does not result in sweaty feet. Worn close to the skin, the vapor barrier protects the moist layer about the skin and maintains optimal humidity at its surface. The consequence is that the skin reduces its production of insensible perspiration by as much as 85 percent and thus stops almost all evaporative heat loss. Excellent descriptions of the vapor-barrier principle are presented in *Cold Comfort* by Glenn Randall (44) and *Pleasure Packing* by Robert Wood (54). The vapor barrier principle is best applied in very cold climes, such as for winter mountaineering, but it also has application wherever evaporative or convective chilling is of concern, such as that day on the Laxá í Adaldal with a wind-chill temperature of 11°F.

**SOCKS**. The simplest application of the vapor-barrier principle for your feet is to wrap each in a sheet of thin plastic film or insert them into polyethylene booties, over which you wear a layer or two of insulating socks. Stuffed inside your neoprene waders, your feet will be warm and cozy. If you question this concept, wrap one foot with plastic and leave the other unwrapped; then let your feet decide for you. Some people object to the feel of the plastic film next to their skin, as do I. You may, if you wish, wear thin polypropylene socks under the plastic film, which will wick away insensible perspiration without destroying the vapor barrier, but do not wear heavier socks. If you do, the vapor barrier is destroyed, and your feet will start to perspire and become clammy and cold.

A more realistic application of the principle is to wear specially designed vapor-barrier socks, such as the neoprene socks offered by Gator (107) or Seirus. Made of 1mm neoprene with a fleece liner, these socks slide easily into your waders and are extremely comfortable with or without a wicking sock underneath, although I much prefer the feel of the wicking sock. If you need additional warmth, add a pair of wool socks over the Gators, and you will have licked the cold-foot syndrome. As long as the water temperature is above 40°F, I find no need for wool socks over the Gators.

Gator socks have an additional advantage in that they are designed for use with hiking boots, not just waders. I have not tried hiking long distances in waders while wearing vapor barrier socks. I suspect that in all but the coldest weather your feet might perspire sufficiently to require you to remove your waders. Gator socks are one of the few items I recommend specifically and enthusiastically.

A word of caution concerning the large number of elastomeric insulating socks being offered these days: it simply is not true that coated fabrics make you sweat or that breathable fabrics keep you dry. It all depends on how you use them. Insulating socks, such as those made by Polartec, provide warmth but cannot serve as a vapor barrier. Neoprene wading socks do provide the requisite vapor layer, but such 3- or 4-millimeter socks are suitable only for wading. Gore-Tex socks, particularly those lined with Thinsulate, are reported to work well, although I have not personally tested them.

**GLOVES.** Fingers are the hardest part of your body to keep warm, particularly if you try to keep some uncovered to retain your sense of touch. For all but the coldest weather, say wind-chill temperatures above 40°F, I like fingerless wool or fleece gloves. If you like the feel of wool, get heavy Ragg gloves with long cuffs. They are very comfortable and dry quickly. If you like the synthetic fleece gloves, consider the variety of offerings by camping specialists such as Campmor and REI, or try Patagonia's Bunting, Simm's Windstopper, or Wind River's Windblock gloves. With the exception of quality rain gear, which many fishing stores sell, I find that the best selections of such specialized outdoor clothing as socks, vests, and jackets are to be found in well-equipped camping and mountaineering stores, many of which issue excellent catalogs. If you wish to see and feel the products and do not live close to a large metropolitan area, such stores are a staple of most any university town.

Most of us will go to great lengths not to cover our fingertips so as to retain a sense of feel. However, I have observed that an acute sense of touch is not necessary for fly fishing. It is the annoyance at the loss of touch to which we react. With a little practice, flies are easily threaded onto leaders with thinly gloved fingers, and knots can be tightened with forceps or small pliers. The biggest problem in changing flies with gloves on is the proclivity of those small hooks to jump into knitted gloves. If you use looped leaders, it's a snap to change leaders and tippets. Learn to fish with gloved fingers. It's much better than cold or frostbitten fingers.

In colder weather, some people use neoprene gloves not unlike those worn by football players. Such gloves are usually 2mm or 3mm thick, stiff, and very difficult to work in, although some of the newer 1mm gloves, such as those by Thunderwear or Swan Enterprises, show considerable promise. I much prefer to wear lightweight polypropylene glove liners on one or both of my hands under fingerless wool or fleece gloves. The polypropylene liners occupy more space than you might imagine, so make certain that your outer glove is large enough not to restrict any circulation in your fingers. The two gloves together provide decent protection for all but the most severe conditions.

In the coldest weather, the vapor-barrier principle may be applied to the unique advantage of the fisherman. If you wear a thin vinyl, polypropylene, or latex rubber glove under the polypropylene liner, you will retain a modicum of the moisture layer (and hence heat) at your fingertips. The reduced evaporation from your fingers is enough to take the sting out of cold fingers. Oddly, this combination, especially with vinyl liners, actually improves your sense of feel because your fingers do not slide against the polypropylene liners. Vinyl gloves are extremely inexpensive and may be purchased from grocery stores or any laboratory supply house (111). Thin latex gloves are available at most drugstores.

Better gloves, like rainwear, are constantly being developed for specialty uses, such as kayaking and canoeing. Check out camping and canoeing suppliers from time to time. Such outfitters are usually well ahead of fishing stores in offering the newest products.

**SUN GLOVES**. Just as you protect yourself from the cold, you must protect your hands, head, and eyes from the sun. Hands are all too often neglected and frequently become sunburned, rough, and scaly. Don't neglect your wrists either. I always wear long-sleeved shirts while fishing, regardless of the temperature, as protection from whatever is lurking out there. Recently on a jaunt to our local trout stream, I rolled up my sleeves and fished for less than three hours in mixed sun and shade. That evening I noticed that my upper wrists were very red and quite tender under the hot shower.

Several years ago, a new product called Sun Gloves was introduced to minimize sunburned hands. Made of thin nylon, these gloves protect the backs of your hands but very little of your fingers. More recently a similar but better glove, called Sun-Checkers, has become available. Sun-Checkers are about 8 1/2 inches long from knuckle to cuff and protect the wrists, as well as half the finger joints. The major deficiency in both of these commercial sun gloves is that the palms are not treated to help you grip the fish.

Well over 10 years ago, I made my own sun gloves by cutting off the fingers from a pair of thin-cotton welder's gloves whose palms had a rubberized coating. Such gloves are now available with rubber dots on the palms and are much better at holding fish than are Sun Gloves. In addition, such cotton gloves do not curl or gather under your fingers as do sun gloves made from a thin nylon or Lycra. The major disadvantage of the homemade model is that the cut-off fingers must be coated with Pliobond or rubber cement to prevent them from unraveling.

Sun gloves have other uses. One is to provide a modicum of warmth when cool waters or the chill of evening numbs the fingers. Such gloves are particularly appreciated in situations where unusual casting positions may cause the heel of your casting hand to chafe against the cork grip.

**HATS**. Hats are such a personal item that advice should be given and received with caution. The choice of a hat depends on your sensitivity to sun and sunburn and your tolerance for cold, to say nothing of everyone's desire to express his individuality.

Under ideal conditions, nothing beats the wide-brimmed western or cowboy hat—ventilated straw for the summer, felt for the spring and fall. But my 40-year-old Stetson is useless in the wind and a hassle to carry on an airplane.

For warm-weather fishing, I like a cap with a very long brim, a full 5 inches long. If you pull down the brim to cut out all the reflections from the sky, your vision of the water is greatly improved, particularly when you're wearing polarized sunglasses. The long brim helps to provide a glare-free view of the water without your having to lower your head and strain your neck muscles. My personal favorite is the Hemingway cap with a leather brim sold by the reorganized J. Peterman company of New York (114).

Fishing all day in the sun, whether on the river, tidal flats, or open ocean, calls for a brimmed hat, preferably one that offers generous neck protection, with a wide neck. Don't take chances with severe sunburn. Being of fair complexion, I have to hide from the sun, although on a recent bonefish trip to the Bahamas I found a way to achieve some relief. I discovered that if I coated my ears and neck well with SPF 30 index sunblock lotion, I could fish all day without burning. But you must cover all the skin well, even the crevice between your ear and your hair. Remember that ultraviolet radiation readily penetrates the clouds and can cause severe sunburn even on overcast days.

You know the old saying, "If your feet are cold, put on your hat." If you keep your head warm, your body can survive a lot of chilling. For fall fishing I like the Filson Style 6 Mackinaw hat. It is warm, and if I pull the hood of my rain jacket about it, my eyeglasses are well protected and the hat will not blow off in any wind. For late-fall or winter fishing, when warmth is most important, I choose a Dacron or other non-itching synthetic stocking cap with a small built-in bill, which shields my eyes. If it gets really cold, I can fold the stocking cap down around my neck.

**COMFORT KIT**. Many of us participate in a number of outdoor activities in which the weather is always our silent partner . . . and sometimes not all that silent. Over the years, I have learned that it is difficult to always have exactly the right clothing for all weather conditions, particularly when the weather changes from fair to stormy, from hot to cold. To combat unseasonable conditions I carry a "comfort kit" consisting of a spare bandanna, either polypropylene glove liners or fingerless wool gloves, vinyl gloves, and spare wool socks, all of which fold neatly into a thin Dacron watch cap that slips into the inner pocket of my rain jacket. Sometimes I add a thin sleeveless sweater, which folds into one of the outer pockets. Here wool is better than pile because it is much more compact. Thus I am prepared for most unexpected changes in a day's weather.

**SUNGLASSES**. Every fisherman should have a pair of brown or amber polarized glasses with which to view his surroundings. Only the brownish tints with 12-to-20 percent transmitted light are satisfactory for penetrating the water's surface through a strong reflective glare. For early morning or late afternoon, you may wish to consider a light tan polarized glass with about 30-percent visible light transmission. Polarized glasses greatly reduce eye strain, especially when you concentrate on casting to a known lie.

If you do not wear prescription glasses, the choices are relatively simple and are mostly a matter of style. If you do wear prescription lenses, the choices are anything but obvious, particularly if you are tempted by the photochromic option. Some years ago I ordered a pair of polarized, photochromic bifocals from a reputable

*Figure 7-3. Salmon angler's toys. Courtesy of Paul Schmookler.*

supplier. It was one of my great outfitting mistakes, for such spectacles are available only with glass lenses. The glasses were too heavy for any use except driving. I also found, to my dismay, that the photochromic option was of limited value for fishing.

Unlike flats fishing, where you are likely to need polarized glasses all day long, the salmon and trout angler occasionally finds himself in the shade or under a cloud, where dark glasses may be a hindrance. How do you compromise without having to change glasses constantly? The best solution I have found is to use those inexpensive clip-on glasses with flip-up plastic lenses. They scratch rather easily, so I buy several pairs at a time. These flip-up glasses are the near perfect answer to my needs—with one exception. In a strong wind, as when you are traveling by motorboat, they may flip up, and they can flip off.

Ed Jaworowski, the fly-casting authority and professor of classical studies at Villanova University, gave me a tip that solved my flip-up problem and also provided the solution to a problem I didn't know I had. To avoid having his glasses covered with sea spray while traveling in an open boat, Ed uses a pair of polarized wraparound glasses called Solar Shield, which fit over his regular glasses. Made of plastic, they are inexpensive and won't blow off. When he reaches his destination, he removes the Solar Shield and begins casting using his regular fishing glasses.

On very dull days, most polarized glasses are of little assistance and may even be a hindrance. I first used the Solar Shield on a gray, overcast day in Greater Exuma in the Bahamas. When I put the shields on over my regular polarized glasses, the sky lit up as if the sun was shining brightly. It was an amazing and eerie experience. When a second pair of polarized glasses is placed over the first, virtually all of the shorter wavelength blue light is absorbed and even a dark, dreary day appears bright. If you try the Solar Shield or any similar product, be certain that the plane of light polarization of the two pairs of glasses is of the same orientation. If the planes of light are perpendicular to one another, it will appear as dark as night to you.

**LUGGAGE**. How best to pack your clothes and miscellaneous equipment? We have already discussed the rod case (Chapter 2), the wader bag, and the tackle bag. Everything else should be packed in one piece of very sturdy luggage. Those elephants tromping on airline baggage can be rough. For a number of years, I carried a piece of commercial soft-sided luggage with many pockets. Being well organized, I liked the convenience of the many pockets. Gradually, I came to realize that the convenience of pockets did not compensate for the lack of large clothing compartments or space for large or irregularly shaped items. So I opted for a leather-trimmed duffel bag made to withstand the rigor of the elephants. Make certain your bag has a full leather bottom with a covering flap that buckles over the zipper. Bags such as this are made by a number of companies, including L.L. Bean, the Duluth Tent and Awning Co., and Orvis. The sizes vary by manufacturer. The large size, typically about 29 x 14 x 13 inches (5,300 cubic inches), is your best bet because you always seem to find need for one more piece of something. The extra-large sizes (7,000 cubic inches) offered by some companies are tempting, particularly since many of them are now equipped with wheels so you can pull them through the airport. However, they are really too large for a week's fishing trip. If filled to capacity, they are too heavy to manage easily.

I find that I do not miss all those pockets in my former luggage because I have found a neat way to compensate. Several companies, including Eagle Creek, Lowe Alpine, Outdoor Research, and SierraWest, offer a wide variety of organizers or portable pockets that consist of layers of nylon stitched together in a variety of shapes, each pocket being secured by its own zipper. Such organizers vary in size from small wallets designed to hold your passport to pockets 10 x 14 inches or larger into which you may stuff socks, handkerchiefs, writing material, a small calculator, and other notions. Several of these organizers will hold all your small clothing, toiletries, and gadgets neatly segregated.

Top off your luggage organization with several nylon-mesh ditty bags. They are particularly useful for small flashlights, an alarm clock, replacement batteries and film, and spare fishing accessories, such as the wader repair kit, shoelaces, extra cord, and the like. You may wish to segregate such items by use so that you take along only those bags you may need on a particular trip. One manufacturer offers such bags in different colors to help you codify the contents.

You'll need at least one totally waterproof bag in which to carry your camera and other sensitive gear. Some bags even float while loaded, but such bags tend to be rather bulky. Recently a new waterproof, humidity-proof bag, which you may find indispensable, has come onto the market. It promises to revolutionize your ability to carry cameras and telephones (heaven forbid) completely protected from the elements. It's even odorproof and therefore presumably safe from bears and raccoons. The

*Figure 7-4. A variety of organizers. Note the waterproof bag for the camera.*

bags, developed by Watersafe (118), are reported waterproof to depths of 200 feet, but they do not float.

The last thing I pack in my duffel bag is a canvas or nylon tote bag about 15 inches square. Its uses are limitless. You can tote your lunch and spare equipment to and from the river, carry small fish, stuff it with dirty clothes, or loan it to a friend in need. Perhaps its most precious use is to hold the gifts you purchase for your spouse and children before you return home.

## PHYSICAL CONDITIONING

Most salmon fishermen (and women) are more than 50 years of age. Most men over 50 are out of shape. The corollary is that many salmon anglers are not sufficiently fit to wade the rivers or even to cast all day from a canoe.

Wading a river is exhilarating and can easily become strenuous exercise for your legs and thighs. It took me years to convince my wife of that fact, and she only truly understood after she read the details in one of her medical journals. How many times have we seen one of our fishing partners spend his first eight hours of the year on a salmon stream only to collapse over his drink before dinner? Or watch a roommate retire early from near exhaustion and 30 minutes later, after he has relaxed in bed, suddenly scream in anguish from the cramps in his legs or the charley horse in his thigh? Such situations may not jeopardize your health, but they certainly do dampen your enthusiasm and ruin your disposition. They are like a very bad case of black flies. The difference is that you can do something about the conditioning of your legs.

Years ago when I traveled extensively on business and fished only intermittently, I experienced the agony of leg cramps every spring on the evening following the opening of trout season. Eventually I came to my senses and decided that if I was going to wade the rivers until I am 85 years of age, as I have pledged to do, I should undertake some exercise program that would provide a reasonable degree of fitness, particularly during the winter season when my fishing trips slow to a crawl. But what program?

One's exercise routine is every bit as personal as one's choice of clothing. Like the choice of clothing, certain principles prevail. The exercise program must provide a sufficient degree of conditioning, and it must be easy enough to perform so that you will participate on a regular basis. If it's too boring or requires too much effort to accomplish, that rowing machine will merely gather dust in the corner. I know; my rowing machine does.

Exercise programs that can be performed at home are, in my opinion, much better because of the convenience. You don't have to drive to the YMCA or health club. My son emphatically disagrees with that view, for he loves the health club. The point is that everyone has his own preference. Do what is easiest for you and that which you can accomplish on a regular basis.

After several false starts, including that abandoned rowing machine, my own program is based on a stationary bicycle and a treadmill, which just happen to be adjacent to my fly-tying corner. Three times a week, I mount the bicycle and read a book or stare at the television for 25 or 30 minutes while pedaling merrily through a routine that causes me to ride at 12 to 15 miles per hour while expending 105 to 125 watts of energy. It's the near-perfect exercise for the calf muscles, the hamstring muscles of the back thigh, and the hip and groin. In recent years, I have added a routine with 5-pound dumbbells that I perform while pedaling. This has greatly benefited my arms and shoulders, specifically the deltoid muscles, and helps to relieve the stress of casting all day on the river. Occasionally, mostly for a change of scenery, I tromp at 3 to 3 1/2 miles per hour on my wife's treadmill, which most experts agree is the best overall exercise for people of all ages. However, I find that the bicycle-and-dumbbell routine is of such great benefit in conditioning my legs, arms, and shoulders (as well as my heart) that I have no need for additional equipment. Following this program, I no longer get leg cramps.

Whatever exercise program you choose, even a simple walking program, remember the KISS principle— Keep It Simple, Stupid—and you will succeed.

## LAST CASTS

This chapter might well be entitled "Preparation." That's what we are talking about: how to select your equipment and your clothing and prepare yourself to better enjoy your adventure. It's not easy in this frenetic world in which we live. Few of us take enough time to prepare appropriately.

What equipment do I actually take with me to river? Aside from my rod and reel (usually two rods and reels if I am fishing from a canoe), my tackle bag contains eight to ten fly boxes; a leader pack with extra pre-tied butt sections; spools of 6-, 8-, and 12-pound tippet material (testing 7, 11, and 17 pounds respectively); a thermometer, a tape measure, an IGFA-certified scale, insect repellent and a head net; and a pair of Sargent side cutters (for cutting hooks and for use as a fly vise). I also carry a flat metal box containing small screwdrivers, wrenches, round and flat files, and Pliobond and CA glue. Depending on the river, I may throw in a BogaGrip for landing fish. In addition, I carry a 13 x 16 x 6-inch tote bag with top zipper, which holds my rain pants, rain jacket, gloves, a small thermos, and camera with extra film stored in an inner pocket. Long years of experience have taught me that it is better to be slightly overloaded than to arrive at the river unprepared.

The Boy Scouts have a good motto: Be prepared!

*West Falls Pool*
Oil on Board
17 7/8 x 25 inches
Private Collection

*The earth does not belong to us. We belong to the earth.*

Chief Seattle, 1854

*The wildlife of today is not ours to dispose of as we please; we each and every one of us hold it in trust for those who come after.*

King George VI, ca. 1948

# Chapter 8

# Conserving Our Endangered Salmon

The Atlantic salmon is one of God's noblest creatures. That it is loved and revered is unquestioned. Why then is the fate of *Salmo* left to those who would destroy it? Lumber and timber interests deforest the woodlands and scour the headwaters. Grazing interests despoil the meadows and foul the spawning gravels. Agricultural operations pollute the waters with unnecessary runoff. Power companies dam the rivers with woefully inadequate plans for fish ladders and none for the downstream passage of the smolts. Fishermen claim the right to net the species to protect their livelihood. The native peoples claim historical priority over all the other interests. Who then has the greater right, the preferential claim? Can these different economic interests and divergent political philosophies ever be resolved? Must every scarce resource be threatened with extinction before we collectively awaken to the danger? How are the conflicting demands for subsistence, employment, resource utilization, and recreation to be apportioned in a

world of declining resources? Does recreational use even
have a claim to the resource?

It is ironic that in the last three decades our technical
knowledge has increased exponentially while our ability
to resolve, or even to reach a meaningful consensus on the
need to resolve, conservation issues has collapsed. We
each fight for our piece of the salmon pie unmindful that
unless our appetites are curbed, there will soon be no pie.

To conserve a species, you must first honor it. I have
always been impressed that the true sportsman honors his
prey, whatever its fate. As a young lad, I first observed this
in the grain fields of southern Illinois where my father's
friends idolized the coveys of the Bob White quail they
pursued. Later I recognized that the honor accorded the
quarry often was proportional to the difficulty of the
pursuit, sometimes hinging on the mental agility or
physical ability of the prey to avoid capture. This seems
particularly true of the salmon and may be the reason we
accord it such an honored place in our hearts. Obviously,
the fisherman has one distinct advantage over the hunter:
the successful angler can release his prey to fight another
day. It's as Lee Wulff first said 60 years ago: "Game fish
are too valuable to be caught only once" (57).

In today's world, we fish and hunt for pleasure—for
sport, we say—certainly not for subsistence. While an
occasional repast may be the reward for a successful
outing, fishermen have long since recognized that modern
tackle and advanced techniques can decimate a fish
population, even that of the Atlantic salmon, which
admittedly is among the most difficult of all fish to entice
to the hook. Thus conservation of the species becomes
every bit as important as the pursuit. Increasingly, a
successful catch is followed by an immediate and
satisfactory release. This is but one facet of the sporting
angler's commitment to conservation. In this chapter, we
shall explore recent studies by fish biologists of the man-
induced stressing of the salmon and the consequences
thereof. Our expectation is that this new insight will teach
us how to better protect the species and preserve our sport.

## A NEW LOOK AT THE LIFE CYCLE

The life cycle of the salmon is well known, but meaningful specifics are not. Those specifics can, and increasingly do, make the difference between a resource wasted by ignorance and indifference on the one hand and enlightened conservation and meaningful utilization on the other.

**BIRTH**. The life of the salmon begins with the birth of the alevin, that tiny 3/4-inch creature that emerges from the eggs deposited and fertilized in late October or early November of the previous fall. The time required for incubation depends on the water temperature and the number of degree days—the number of days by which the water temperature exceeds 32°F. At 45°F, the incubation requires seven weeks (84 days), whereas at 37°F the eggs require approximately 20 to 21 weeks to hatch. In much of Canada, incubation requires approximately 110 days, after which the alevin hatches as a tiny translucent minnow with black eyes and a yolk sack attached to its belly. The alevin remains in the gravel for several weeks until the yolk sac is absorbed, at which time the alevin emerges from the gravel as an inch-long fry ready to feed, mostly at night, on the microscopic insect life about it.

Fry grow slowly until they reach a length of about 1 1/2 inches, at which time they develop the black parr marks on their sides. The young parr feed ravenously during their first summer and fall, reaching an average length of 3 to 3 1/2 inches by their first winter in North America waters. Those who have hooked parr on a size 4 fly know just how aggressive these young fish can be. Parr growth is greatly affected by the availability of food and the water temperature. In Ireland and France, where most of the fisheries are sustained by hatchery fish, eggs hatched in December may grow into 6-inch parr by the following September. These young fingerlings will be ready to migrate to the sea as age 1+ (read: age one year plus) smolt in their second spring. Some precocious parr develop very rapidly, reaching sexual maturity by their second summer (age 1+).

Parr in rivers cease feeding when the temperature falls below about 50°F because their immature muscles are impaired by the cold and become incapable of holding them in the feeding currents. In colder climes, where rivers cool early in the fall, their only option is to dig into the gravel and wait out the long winter.

Parr in southern Canada typically will stay in the river between two and five years (and up to seven years in the far northern rivers). The average is three and a half years. In the spring of their seaward year, at an age determined primarily by size, the parr undergo a physiological, hormonal change not unlike adolescence in humans. Triggered by the increasing photoluminescence of spring, in the short period of six to eight weeks the parr lose their dark markings. Their tails become more deeply forked, and their bodies assume a silvery hue typical of the smolt stage. As the rivers swell with the spring floods and the waters warm, 5 1/2- to 7-inch smolts assemble in large schools, and between early May and July they begin their hazardous run to the sea. Smolts move downstream mostly at night, although late-running July smolt are occasionally seen during the daytime. In normal currents the smolts drift down tailfirst; in very slow water they swim headfirst.

As we shall see, genetic diversity is a key concept in the propagation of salmon, and the smolt stage is a good example. A study of the north-shore rivers of Quebec revealed a wide range of ages in any given smolt class, usually from 2 to 5 years of age for wild smolts (6). Whether age 1+ hatchery smolt or age 2+ wild smolt have the same chance as age 5+ smolt for maturing to become adult salmon is unknown. Clearly, the chance that unfavorable ocean conditions will decimate the smolt class of a given year is greatly reduced when only a portion of the parr population of a given river age goes to sea in any particular year. The early years of life are perilous for young salmon. It has been estimated that only about half the fertilized eggs will produce fry. Only 2 percent survive as smolts to enter the ocean, and these survivors are subject to heavy predation by birds and fish.

**GROWTH**. After spending a short time in the estuary becoming acclimated to saltwater, the post-smolts (as they are then known) begin to disperse. (A post-smolt is an immature salmon that has not yet spent one winter in the ocean.) Little is known about the life of the post-smolts immediately following their entry into the sea. It is often said that the post-smolts disappear into a "black box" only to reappear one or more years later as adult salmon.

In 1965, the life of the Atlantic salmon at sea finally began to become clear. That year, the recovery of tagged fish demonstrated that most of the North American MSW salmon congregate to feed in the Davis Strait off the west coast of Greenland. However, the pathways of the one-sea-winter (1SW) fish (grilse), particularly those from the Bay of Fundy, are still not well known. (Recent studies confirm that inner Bay of Fundy salmon do not migrate to the North Atlantic but remain in the vicinity of the bay to feed.) Previously, some had inaccurately assumed that the post-smolts headed south to the Sargasso Sea to feed on small eels, called elvers. More recently, we have learned that some salmon feed in a wide circuitous journey that takes them from North America across the northern Atlantic Ocean to the Faeroe Islands and back. The area north of the Faeroe Islands is also the main feeding ground of the Scottish and Norwegian salmon, although some of them do migrate west to Greenland before returning to their native rivers. A good account of the migration routes may be found in the proceedings of the Fourth International Atlantic Salmon Symposium (39).

The growth history of a salmon may be determined by reading the rings on its scales, similar to determining the age of a tree. The complete life history, including the age at which the smolt first ventured seaward, the time spent in the sea, and the initial and repeat spawning ages

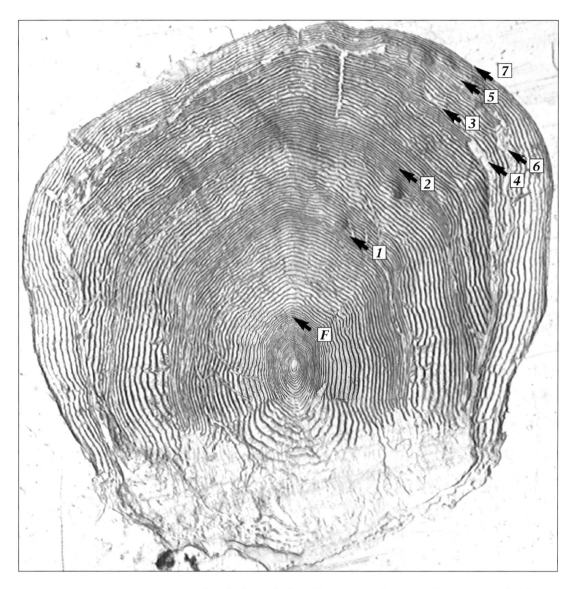

*Figure 8-1. Scale taken from a 37-pound, 47-inch female salmon caught on its third spawning migration in the Teno River, Finland. The arrows indicate the different life stages: F, four years as a parr in the river; 1–3, three years at sea; 4, first spawning run; 5, fourth year at sea; 6, second spawning run; 7, fifth year at sea. Courtesy of the Teno River Fisheries Research Centre.*

may be deduced if sufficient scale samples are available to provide a discernible history. A fish that has spent 1SW in the ocean before returning to the river is called a *grilse* and in North America will weigh between 2 1/2 and 5 pounds. Grilse up to 7 and 8 pounds are found in Ireland and up to 12 pounds in France, where the longer season and milder winters favor more rapid growth. Seven-pound grilse are also found, of all places, in the Alta River of Norway, 300 miles north of the Arctic Circle. The explanation for such large 1SW fish so far north lies in their proximity to excellent feeding grounds.

**THE RETURN**. Salmon that have spent one or more winters in the ocean may return to their natal stream during any month of the year depending on the river-specific strains. In North America, we are familiar with early returns in May, heavy runs from June through September (depending on the river), and very late returns in mid-October on such rivers as the Miramichi and Margaree. In northern Scotland, some strains begin to return as early as January, with various runs continuing into December in the southern rivers. Some Scottish rivers, such as the Tay, have four distinct runs of fish, one in each season of the year. In the Ponoi, the Varzuga, and other rivers on the Kola Peninsula of Russia, certain strains of fish enter the river in September and October but do not spawn until the fall of the following year. If they survive the exhausting rigors of two river-bound winters, such fish will spend about 18 months in the river before returning to the ocean, during which time they will not feed. A similar situation exists in the Serpentine tributary of the St. John River in New Brunswick and the George River in Quebec.

What motivates salmon of any smolt class or year to return to their river of origin at different times is not known. I emphasize "river of origin" as compared to "natal river" because it has been well documented that the river to which salmon return is determined by that in which they became smolts (i.e., smoltification). Wild fry or parr, or even hatchery fry, transported from their natal river to another almost always return to the river from which they went to sea. We do know that there is no direct relation between the age at smoltification and the time spent at sea, although the return is unquestionably influenced by genetic makeup. The exact timing of the return to the river is thought to be determined by genetic and environmental factors, including the length of the migration route combined with a modicum of opportunity.

Parr that go seaward after only one year in the river were once thought to inevitably return the following year as grilse. We now know that young post-smolts, particularly the female fish, may grow slowly in the ocean and return after two or more years as MSW salmon. Once salmon enter the estuary of a river, they usually pause to become acclimated to freshwater before starting their ascent up the river. Concomitant with the salmon's acclimation to the freshwater, its digestive system shuts down, and it will not feed again until it descends the river following spawning. But like all laws of nature, there are exceptions. In August 1993, George and Ernie Curtis were fishing the Miramichi at George's Black Rapids camp near Blackville, New Brunswick. Noting that fish were rising to small black flies on the surface, George switched to a size 12 Preacher and promptly landed a grilse. The following evening the phenomenon repeated itself when Ernie also landed a grilse. When the fish were cleaned, it was observed that the stomachs of both were stuffed with the black flies. Whether this behavior results from incomplete acclimation to freshwater is unknown, but Black Rapids is only three miles above tidewater.

Occasionally, one hears tales of large salmon "feeding" on live insects during their return to the river, but I have been able to find only one reference that confirms the fact. In 1974, Robert Stoddard of Worcester, Massachusetts, reported in the *Atlantic Salmon Journal* (51) both grilse and salmon feeding on budworm moths. He wrote: "We cleaned all our fish and in the majority of grilse and some salmon (of 10 to 12 pounds) we found budworm moths in their stomachs—in some cases in limited quantities and in a few cases completely full. The above experience was unique to me in over 40 years of salmon fishing."

Typically, salmon will move well up the river to spawn. The largest salmon, particularly the female fish, tend to enter the rivers early and push right up the river if the water and weather are favorable. High water in the chutes and rapids may delay the ascent. Hot, sunny days and high water temperatures cause the fish to become lethargic, in which case they may seek deep holes or cool, spring-fed pools, where they will linger for weeks if necessary. Significant salmon migration during the spate that follows a heavy rain is common. If very high or very low water hinders their ascent to the preferred spawning grounds upriver, they will spawn wherever in the river they can find suitable gravel.

For some years, we have known that salmon seek to return to the specific stretch of the river in which they were born or released prior to smolting. Recent studies of micro-tagged smolts on the Rangá River in Iceland have confirmed that the return can be highly specific. Of 50,000 hatchery smolts released into the river for one study, 380 of these fish were recaptured upon their return to the river. Of these, 37 percent were recaptured at or within 1.5 kilometers downstream of the release site; 57 percent were recaptured within 3.5 kilometers below the point of release. Only a few recaptures were observed upriver of the release site. Interestingly, the data suggest that salmon migrating through areas with good fishing sites may be less vulnerable to angling than when the fish are closer to their birth or release site.

In some rivers, there is evidence that the larger fish tend to spawn somewhat lower in the main river than do the smaller salmon, probably due to the availability of larger, more suitable gravel. Grilse frequently spawn in the smaller tributaries. Again this depends greatly on the individual river. In the Alta River in Norway, for instance, many of the large 40- and 50-pound salmon spawn in the vicinity of Toppen, the uppermost pool on the river, just below an impassable falls.

**SPAWNING**. In Canada, the hen salmon seeks out suitable gravel beds on which to spawn in late October or early November. In warmer climates, such as in Ireland, the salmon do not spawn until late December or January. Under favorable conditions, salmon are careful to select quality sites and may prepare several sites before they are satisfied. Several years ago, spawning studies on the upper Moisie River revealed a series of redds that had been abandoned without any egg

*Above and opposite page:*
*Figure 8-2. Salmon returning*
*to the river. Courtesy Atlantic*
*Salmon Federation.*

deposition. (The redd is the area of disturbed gravel that contains one or more nests into which the hen lays her eggs.) It appeared that after preparing the nests, the fish recognized that in low water the eggs would be uncovered, and they abandoned the location for another more favorable one. How the salmon were able to recognize the situation is unknown, although we may speculate that the lower velocity of falling-water levels may have provided the necessary alarm.

Low on the gravel bar, the hen prepares a nest-like depression 6 to 12 inches deep in which to deposit some of her eggs. The gravel is moved by the force of suction as she flaps her tail on the gravel. Some remarkable underwater photographs of salmon spawning in the Utsjoki River have been recorded by the Finnish Game and Fisheries Institute. Figure 8-3 shows a 12-pound hen turned on her side, her tail flapping to rearrange the gravel for the nest. The area of disturbed gravel may be 12 to 18 inches wide; the length depends upon how many nests the redd contains. Once the nest is completed and

*Figure 8-3. Hen salmon cutting a nest. Courtesy Teno River Fisheries Research Centre.*

the hen begins to lay her eggs, the competition among male fish to fertilize the eggs can be fierce. Often the honors go to the largest male, but at times as many as seven cock fish may fertilize the eggs. A 1999 study on the reproduction of wild salmon progeny, conducted by researchers from Laval University, indicates that the occurrence of multiple matings, by both cock and hen fish, is the most significant determinant of the number of offspring produced. Using microsatellite loci to analyze parentage, the data indicate that a greater number of alevins are produced from multiple pairings than from one-on-one mating.

Figure 8-4 shows a cock and hen salmon lying side by side ready to mate. The videotape from which this photograph was taken showed the pair vibrating intensely, as they do just before the eggs and milt are released.

Sexually mature (precocious) parr can and frequently do fertilize a portion of the eggs by slipping in behind the cock salmon, which helps to expand the genetic diversity of the species. One study estimates that as many as one-

*Figure 8-4. Pair of salmon spawning. Courtesy Teno River Fisheries Research Centre.*

third of all eggs are fertilized by precocious parr. Such parr, whose growth energy has been concentrated in developing their gonads, rarely, if ever, survive to see the sea. Contrary to conventional wisdom, there is no evidence that parr beget grilse nor that grilse necessarily beget grilse. This is best confirmed by the ratios of male and female grilse found in most rivers. Most Canadian rivers have fewer than 20 percent female grilse, and many have virtually none—direct evidence that female smolts are predisposed to return as MSW hens. In the prime salmon river of the world, the Alta, the majority of the spawning fish are 3SW hens and 1SW cock grilse. We do not understand why a much larger percentage of males return as grilse than do females, but clearly it is nature's way of ensuring an adequate supply of cock fish for spawning. Very recently, controlled spawning studies have demonstrated that the progeny of precocious parr are, in fact, identical to those of MSW salmon.

After the eggs are fertilized, the hen pushes gravel back into the nest with her tail and mounds the nest slightly. Considering the size of some spawning gravels, this is no small feat. A study of gravel in Ireland showed the preferred size of the gravel to be in the range of 1 1/2 to 4 1/2 inches, with a mean diameter of 3 1/2 inches. Undoubtedly, the preferred gravel (and hence the redd location) is influenced by the size of the hen fish. Hen grilse would have great difficulty moving 4 1/2-inch gravel. Obviously the gravel must not be subject to siltation or so small as to smother the hatching alevins or prevent their emergence.

When the first nest is completed, the hen moves upstream a short distance and prepares a second nest. Frequently some gravel from the second nest washes down upon the first, thus providing additional cover from predators. The location of successive nests depends entirely on the gravel. Some may be virtually adjacent, in which case the all the nests are within a single redd. Others may spread over a length of a hundred yards or more, in which case each nest may be contained within its own redd. Controlled spawning studies of both wild and farmed salmon confirm that a grilse or small salmon will lay 300 to 500 eggs in each nest, while large MSW hens may deposit up to 1,000 eggs per nest. Thus the number of nests prepared by a hen depends on her size and the number of eggs she carries. Typically the spawning process is repeated five to as many as fourteen times over a period of five to eleven days, until the hen is exhausted. More often than not, many of the nests will be fertilized by different cock fish, which further contributes to genetic diversity. Cock fish may remain sexually active throughout the fall spawning season, up to two months or more. The spawning process is traumatic for both cock and hen fish. Both invest approximately the same energy into spawning, but the cock fish expend more energy to somatic or physical activity. Their struggles to fertilize the eggs account for their greater injury and mortality. One study has estimated the mortality for spawning cock fish at 30 percent compared to 4 percent for the spawning hen fish.

After spawning, the hen Atlantic salmon typically rests for a period of days, sometimes much longer, to recover from her spawning trauma. Eventually, weather and river flow permitting, she begins her migration back to the sea. In the northern rivers of both Canada and Europe, especially the longer ones, winter sets in and the rivers ice over before the salmon can complete their descent. They are forced to spend the winter in ponds, holes, or deep bogans along the lower river.

This is a particularly hazardous period for the fish. Physically spent and not feeding, they can only wait out the long winter. If spring and high waters arrive early, a significant fraction of the large salmon, variously estimated from 10 to 20 percent, will survive the long journey back to the sea. In the warmer climes with shorter rivers, such as Ireland or even the Bay of Fundy, the hens usually return to the ocean before winter impedes their downriver migration.

The majority of spawning fish in most Canadian and Northern European rivers are MSW hen salmon and male grilse. Female grilse are rare. Unlike the hens, the cock grilse and MSW cock salmon suffer considerable physical damage in their fights to dominate the matings. Fins are torn and their flanks are scraped and scarred from the arduous spawning exercise. Those badly injured fall prey to the scavaging eels. The surviving male fish usually rest for a period of weeks to recover; they seldom return to the ocean before spring.

Many of the large grilse of Ireland and France, as well as those of northern Norway and Finland, do return to the ocean to spawn again. Except in the shorter rivers of southern Canada, only limited numbers of North American grilse and no sexually mature parr ever survive the spawn. The physical rigors of spawning and the lack of fatty reserves, as well as the hazardous spring descent through rapids and over waterfalls, combine to doom a spawned grilse to the same fate as that of the spent Pacific salmon.

## STRESSES IMPOSED BY NATURE

The life of a young salmon is unquestionably perilous. From the moment the alevin hatches until the adult salmon returns to the relative safety of its natal river, some predator seeks to feed upon it: parr upon fry; birds and small fish upon parr; birds and larger fish upon smolt; seals and killer whales upon the salmon. In addition, there are the forces of nature that constantly threaten. In summer, hot weather warms the water and deprives the salmon of life-giving oxygen. Extreme winter cold fills the sanctuary pools with frazil (slush) ice, which may suffocate the salmon. Springtime floods and prolonged drought, river currents and oceanic tides, disease, and a scarcity of food are also normal dangers.

**PREDATORS**. Of all the perils faced by the wild salmon, perhaps the best example of the natural dangers is the rapidly increasing toll taken by predators. When discussing the predation of salmon, many think first of the seals, dolphins, and killer whales that pursue the salmon in the ocean. While these large saltwater predators, of which the surging populations of the protected gray seals are the worst, wreak their havoc, it is the freshwater life of the young salmon that poses the greatest threat to its survival. Much of this is a direct result of man's tinkering with natural populations.

During the five stages of the salmons' life cycle, they are eaten by more than 50 different predators. By far the most dangerous are the birds that feed on marine life in freshwater: mergansers, cormorants, kingfishers, herons, bitterns, and in Europe goosanders and shags. Small kingfishers may eat three parr per day, 300 per season. A merganser may consume 8 to 60 per day, depending on the size of the parr; that's as many as 5,000 per year. Ten mergansers feeding over 10 or 15 miles of river can devastate a parr population; yet on some rivers we see flocks of 30 or more birds. Goosanders have been observed to capture over 4,500 parr and 1,000 smolts per year. Cormorants are the most destructive, particularly on the smaller rivers when the smolts are moving downstream. They may eat 5 to 20 smolts per day, 125 to 350 during a three-week smolt run to the sea. Cormorants are also very destructive in the winter time. As the larger rivers freeze over, the cormorants move upstream to the tributaries, where they find easy pickings of the young parr.

When the smolt enter the river estuary, they often pause to become acclimated to their new saline environment. At such time, they face a previously unrecognized jeopardy: schools of cod and other marine predators. These fishes gather in the estuary at high tide in search of the alewives (gasperau) and smelt that migrate back to the ocean about the same time as do the smolts. In one instance in the Bay d'Espoir, Newfoundland, sea-ranched rainbow trout that had escaped from their sea pens to feed upon migrating smolts were believed to have decimated that year's class of juvenile salmon. The result was a precipitous decrease of grilse returning to that Newfoundland river the following year.

Mammalian predators competing with the salmon have become a major problem in the waters between Labrador and Newfoundland and in the upper St. Lawrence River. Harp seals do not normally feed on salmon, but their burgeoning populations pose a serious threat when these arctic mammals move southward in May to breed. These seals feed on the same energy-rich capelin as do smolts and MSW salmon. Between 1982 and 1997, the population of harp seals in Canadian waters tripled to more than 6 million, which are now estimated to consume more than 1 million metric tons of capelin each year. One current hypothesis is that, as a result of a sharply reduced food supply, smaller salmon are returning to the Canadian rivers—if as post-smolts they do not die of starvation at sea.

The basic problem is that virtually all of these predators are protected by laws or treaties instigated by

*Figure 8-5. A spring-run male steelhead, with torn dorsal fin and scarred flanks, caught off the spawning bed (at rear of photo) in the Pere Marquette River near Walhalla, Michigan. Note the white milt exuded by the fish in front of the angler's knee.*

well-meaning conservationists, such as Canadian-U.S. treaties protecting American mergansers and Canada geese. We protect only what we can see; we ignore that which we cannot. This is the salmon problem in a nutshell: we have no regard for the fate of an anadromous fish that roams outside territorial waters.

## STRESSES IMPOSED BY MAN

The Atlantic salmon is disappearing from the north Atlantic Ocean. That is a fact. In spite of the conservation measures employed over the past 20 years to stabilize salmon populations, both MSW salmon and grilse are diminishing worldwide. The oceanic population of MSW salmon of North American origin has diminished from 850,000 20 years ago to 197,000 in 1997 and about 80,000 in 1999. That's at least 4,000 fewer fish than are needed to sustain the propagation of the species in all the salmon rivers of North America. During this time, the salmon catch in Ireland has diminished from an average of

600,000 MSW salmon in 1980 to 120,000 in 1997. It is expected to decline still further.

It's when man tinkers with or aggravates the stresses of nature that the troubles arise: the altering of the river structure, whether by silting the spawning gravel or damming or diverting the river flow; the introduction into the river system of non-native species or exotic invaders, which may alter the pelagic food chain; and actions such as the introduction of nonindigenous strains that facilitate the transmission of parasites and infectious disease. Worst of all is the contamination, accidental or otherwise, by agricultural and industrial pollutants that drastically alter the ecology of the river. All contribute directly to the demise of the salmon, even though that demise may be gradual and only belatedly recognized.

In this section, we shall review the causes for the salmon's disappearance, some of which are not fully substantiated, and consider possible solutions toward increasing the salmon escapement. Ironically, escapement is how we measure the return of spawning adult salmon, literally by the number that escape the perils of nature and the malevolence of man to return to the spawning beds. The reader should recognize, however, that this review summarizes only the status of problems, focusing primarily on those subjects of greatest concern to the salmon angler.

The litany of great rivers despoiled by man is long. The Connecticut River was in colonial times one of the greatest salmon rivers in North America. As late as 1790, salmon were ascending the full length of the river. A decade later, a dam was completed at Hadley Falls, and 15 years later salmon in the Connecticut River were extinct. It has been estimated that by 1870, 50 percent of the original productive capacity of all the Atlantic salmon rivers in North America had been destroyed. By 1970, an additional 18 percent of that original capacity had been eliminated. Today less than one-third of the original carrying capacity remains. Just within the last year, research on the impact of aquaculture by Atlantic Salmon Federation scientists has confirmed that the salmon stocks in 33 rivers in the Bay of Fundy are at or very near the point of biological extinction.

The Thames River, the longest in England and a major salmon river in ancient times, had not seen salmon for two centuries until a restocking program was initiated a few years ago. The last wild salmon was taken from the Thames in 1833. The Seine in France; the Rhine, the Elbe, and the Weser in Germany; the Duero on the Iberian Peninsula; the Griden in Denmark; and the Kenii and the Ir in Finland all saw their salmon eliminated by exploitation and wanton pollution. An interesting survey of the history and demise of both the Atlantic and Pacific salmon is presented in Netboy's treatise, *The Salmon: Their Fight for Survival* (42).

Man-made stresses fall into two categories: those overt actions that are taken with the knowledge that they will impact adversely on the welfare and escapement of the salmon, and managed actions that, even though they may be well intentioned, jeopardize or indirectly impact the existence of the wild salmon.

**DAMS**. Three centuries ago, all the great rivers of the northeastern United States and the northern European countries held enormous stocks of salmon. Salmon were so plentiful in southern New England that the contracts of indentured laborers were said to include limits on the frequency with which the fish might be served. Dams blocking the ascent of fish, of which the Connecticut and the Penobscot in Maine are prime examples, are now an old story. The first dams did not provide for fish ladders, and the ladders in the newer dams, particularly the high dams, are often inadequate to accommodate the sizable runs of the various anadromous species that occur in late spring. Even today, most dams do not provide for the downstream passage of smolts. Too often the turbine blades of the electrical generators are efficient fish grinders. Gradually this problem is being rectified. Some

of the newer slow-speed turbines are designed to pass 85
to 90 percent of the smolts without injury.

Fortunately, recent efforts to abolish useless dams are
beginning to bear fruit. In November 1997, the U.S. Federal
Energy Regulatory Commission ordered, for the first time,
the removal of an operating hydropower dam. The
commission found that the economic value of the power
generated by the 160-year-old Edwards Dam on the lower
Kennebec River in Maine was greatly outweighed by the
benefit of a healthy fishery for migrating salmon, striped
bass, sturgeon, shad, and the various baitfish. The Edwards
Dam was breached in July 1999. Two months later, in
September, before the dam had been completely removed,
school-sized striped bass were being caught beneath the
Fort Halifax Dam, 17 miles upriver from the Edwards site.

In addition to the overt damage caused, dams can
also be the source of unintentional or passive damage.
Before the high dam was built on the Alta River in
Norway in 1987, detailed studies found that the dam
would not affect that magnificent fishery, since it would
be located upriver of an impassable falls. The river flow
through the summer was carefully plotted. Since the dam
was completed, the natural flow during the fishing season
has been rigorously maintained. Whatever water flows
into the lake behind the dam is released to flow into the
river. No more, no less, not even during the record low
water of August 1997, when additional water in the river
would have been most welcome.

Between 1981 and 1983, parr (pre-smolts) were
sampled from three sections of the Alta. The population
density of pre-smolts from the upper or Sautso beat was
greater, and they grew faster than those further
downstream. Age 0+ parr were 0.5 to 1 cm longer (a very
significant difference), and age 3+ pre-smolts were 1 to 2
cm longer than those from the lower river. The age at
which parr become smolts is determined by size, not river
age. The faster growth and younger age for smoltification
of parr from the upper Sautso beat were confirmed by the
scale analysis of adult salmon caught in the upper river.

*Figure 8-6. Salmon pens in a Norwegian fjord.*

*Opposite page: Figure 8-7. Satellite rearing tanks on the Restigouche River.*

After the dam was completed, the pre-smolt growth in the river was monitored for the five-year period between 1987 and 1991. No significant change in the growth rate of the pre-smolts was observed. However, there was a 12-percent decrease in the pre-smolt population density throughout the river. An even greater decrease in the pre-smolt density was observed for the upper Sautso section. This change has dire implications for the long-term maintenance of the MSW salmon population. The cause is attributed to the change in the temperature of the water. The water released from the Alta dam during the winter is about 1°F warmer than the natural flow before the dam was built. The slight increase in water temperature has caused the peak hatching of the alevin to occur some 27 days earlier than prior to the dam construction. (As mentioned, the duration of egg incubation is directly related to the water temperature.) In that cold climate, the alevins hatch and consume their egg sacs before their natural food sources are readily available. Significant algae

growth makes it much more difficult for the young fry to obtain adequate food during the late winter, and many fry are starving, hence the reduced parr population. The dam has caused a change in the ecology of the upper river, which is resulting in a diminution of the salmon stocks, at least in the short term.

**NETS**. The netting of salmon is an ancient practice. It has become a serious threat to the oceanic populations only since the development of efficient harvesting methods and the identification of the major migratory feeding grounds in the Davis Strait and off the Faeroe Islands. Drift nets and long lines facilitate salmon harvest on a scale only dreamt about 50 years ago.

Even though some nets have been removed by buyouts, many have not. The nets that remain are primarily those that capture indiscriminately all salmon irrespective of their river of origin or size. Therein lies the problem. Some rivers have sufficient spawning stocks, but many do not. And the oceanic trawlers do not discriminate. To stabilize populations and prevent the harvesting of salmon destined for rivers with inadequate numbers of spawning fish, the interception of mixed salmon stocks by oceanic netting must be abolished. In 1997, commercial fishermen in Greenland, Labrador, and Quebec netted 144 metric tons of wild salmon, equivalent to about 27,000 MSW salmon. That is better than three times the MSW salmon catch in Canada that year. The commercial operators have insisted that they will not reduce their take unless recreational angling is also banned. They know that banning sport fishing is politically unacceptable because the economic value of a recreational fish is 50 times that of a netted fish.

If netting in the open ocean can be controlled by international agreements, then in principle the problem reverts to the territorial waters of each country. If a particular country chooses not to control the netting of its own fish in its own waters, it has no one else to blame for the disappearance of its salmon stocks. Canada presents such an example.

While Americans should be slow to criticize anyone on salmon management, the Canadian experience is a fine example of how not to control netting. As late as 1996, the principal commercial nets remaining in Canadian waters were those in the rich feeding grounds in the Davis Strait off the coast of Labrador and along the lower north shore of Quebec. The Labrador nets, which were removed in 1997, were particularly offensive because they captured mixed river stocks of MSW adult fish. The Quebec-north shore nets, the last of the commercial nets in North America, were finally pulled in 2000. But the nets of the native Canadians—or First Nation peoples as they are known—continue to decimate the indigenous breeding stocks in some of the major estuaries, such as that of the Restigouche. The native netting is frequently unregulated and is widely suspected of capturing more salmon than the law permits. Without question, it harvests the largest, most fecund fish. The native gill nets also maim a large number of fish, many of which escape only to die a week later. Four years ago on the Matapedia, less than two miles upstream from the Restigouche nets, we observed a cock salmon estimated at 25 pounds lying badly wounded in 3 feet of water. It was scarred with net marks and blind in the right eye. The next morning we found the fish dead on a shoal a half mile downstream.

The Canadian situation is compounded by a decree from the Canadian Supreme Court that First Nation peoples do indeed have the first right to the salmon, superseded only by any conservation needs. Translated, this means that if a river is open to salmon fishing, the native peoples have the right to take their share first. Fortunately, the more enlightened tribes now readily cooperate in the conservation of the salmon. For 20 years, the Gesgapegia band of the Mi'kmac nation on the Grand Cascapedia has cooperated with the camp owners in managing that river for the benefit of all parties. More recently, the Eel Ground band on the Northwest Miramichi has begun to restrict its netting and to cooperate in the conservation of the salmon on that important river. For many it's still a question of economic control. Frequently, the real issue is not the value of the salmon per se but that of political leverage and continuing reparations. If economic demands are not met, some bands have been known to resort to outrageous fishing behavior to leverage their demands. But let it be emphasized that Canada is not alone in netting its escapement salmon. Each year an increasing number of rivers around the rim of the North Atlantic fail to meet the required escapement population.

**SALMON FARMING: THE ESCAPEE PROBLEM.** When salmon farming was first introduced in the 1970s, many of us viewed this new industry as the salvation of the wild salmon. The cost of raising salmon in confined pens, we reasoned, was so much less than that of netting salmon on the high seas that it was only a matter of time before the trawlers and their drift nets and long lines would become uneconomical. How wrong, how very wrong we were. Atlantic salmon aquaculture is now a worldwide industry, with Norway as the major producer followed closely by Chile. Atlantic salmon farms are everywhere: in the Baltic Sea; along the coasts of Scotland; in the bays of Ireland; in the waters off the northeastern United States; and even in the estuaries of Washington, Oregon, and British Columbia. Not only has salmon farming not saved the wild salmon, but it is now threatening to destroy the river-specific genetic pools of all wild salmon. It may also be the source of parasites that will decimate future stocks.

Vast quantities of pen-raised salmon escape their confinement only to seek out a nearby river in which to spawn. Not having been imprinted with the waters of any particular river, the escapees roam randomly until the urge to spawn directs them to ascend the nearest river. Interbreeding with native stocks, the farmed fish dilute the gene pool of the native fish introducing, as it were, new strains that are not either physically or genetically adapted to the particular river. In some cases, such as the Vosso River and the once fabled Årøy in Norway (both described in Chapter 11), the foreign strains have overwhelmed the native stocks and destroyed the river-adapted characteristics of the native fish. Most often the result is smaller, weaker fish less able to fend for themselves in the sea and far less capable of replicating the species.

**SALMON FARMING: THE SEA LICE PROBLEM.** In the late 1980s, a second serious problem with salmon farming was recognized, one that has devastated the sea-trout fishing from Norway to Ireland and now threatens all rivers near to salmon farms. Only too late have we recognized that the salmon pens and impoundments in the fjords and estuaries create the ideal environment for the incubation of sea lice.

The infectious stage of the sea louse is the larval form. The larvae attack the sea trout and juvenile salmon and literally suck life out of the fish. One egg-bearing sea louse represents a potential for 400 to 500 larvae. A typical salmon farm holding 300,000 fish, with an average of one-half oviparous louse per fish, could result in the production of 70,000,000 sea-louse larvae! Infections of three lice per fish are common. On a young fish, more than three are detrimental, yet bad infestations may number 10 to 30 or more lice per fish in a normal year. In the Bay of Fundy, 1995 was a particularly bad year because of high water temperatures. One Fundy grower was quoted in *Atlantic Fish Farming* as reporting an average of 60 to 70 lice per fish that year, with individual larval infestations as high as 400 per salmon!

Sea lice are particularly detrimental to sea trout (anadromous brown trout) and have destroyed the sea-trout fisheries in many Norwegian rivers; in most of the west coast rivers of Scotland, England, and Wales; and in essentially all the salmon-farming bays of Ireland. Despite denials of any responsibility by the salmon farms, the evidence is overwhelming. In Ireland, there are 27 recognized sea-trout fisheries with salmon farms in their estuaries; 24 of these have had their fishery devastated by sea lice. Of the 31 sea trout rivers without a salmon farm nearby, none have been affected by sea lice. The statistical probability of this being a chance relationship is $7.08 \times 10^{-12}$.

As a result of the lice infestations, the killing of any sea trout in western Ireland is currently prohibited. But the worst is yet to come. Sea lice do not discriminate between trout and salmon, and more recently the concern has shifted to lice attacking salmon smolts on their way to the sea. Smolts passing through the estuaries, bays, and fjords are infested by the sea-louse larvae, which the smolts readily recognize as an unwelcome parasite. In some instances, the smolts have returned to their natal rivers to rid themselves of the parasites. Do the young smolts possess an innate sense that freshwater is lethal to the lice? More likely, the smolts return to the safety and comfort of freshwater to escape the hostile estuarine environment. The circumstances under which they return to the sea a second time to feed and grow are unknown.

At this writing, a great deal of research effort is being focused on the sea lice problem. Except under very controlled conditions, as in hatcheries, chemical treatments are impractical and not a viable option; many of the chemicals are highly toxic to other forms of marine life and are illegal to use. Very recently, a new dimension has been uncovered. DNA studies at the University of St. Andrews have demonstrated that the lice that attack the farmed salmon and rainbow trout are genetically distinct from those endangering the wild salmon and sea trout. This implies that lice found on farmed fish come from the farmed strains. It has also been demonstrated that individual lice on wild sea trout carry genetic coding that suggests that they may be of farmed origin, probably as a result of the inbreeding of the various strains of lice. What this finding portends for the wild salmon we do not now know.

**SALMON FARMING: CREATING INFERIOR STRAINS**. Of all the problems arising from salmon farming, the most troubling is the fact that farmed fish are not only destroying specific river-adapted strains, but they are creating strains of fish that are physiologically inferior to the wild salmon. They are developing, over time, genetically inferior progeny unable to cope with the rigors of an anadromous life. Of all the species of animals, fish show the most phenotypic variation (i.e., distinguished by visual characteristics). Salmon, for instance, exhibit great adaptation to their freshwater environment. Studies on the River Imsa in Norway have shown that the body shape of hatchery-raised Atlantic salmon can change markedly from that of the wild fish within a single generation. First-generation hatchery parr have smaller heads and fins and narrower caudal peduncles (the so-called wrists) than wild parr from the same river.

Hatchery parr released into the river and allowed to smoltify along with wild parr do not show significant differences in growth until they return to the river. Then the differences become marked. In the River Imsa experiments, both male and female hatchery fish ascended the river later than their wild counterparts, spawned later, and were more likely to stray into other nearby rivers. This is but one piece of evidence that the early river life of wild parr is instrumental in defining their ability later in life to adapt and survive.

It has now been demonstrated that salmon born and raised in farm-like environments are physically and physiologically less capable of reproducing the species than are the wild salmon. In a landmark study led by Ian Fleming at the Norwegian Institute for Nature Research in Trondheim (18), the reproductive behavior of wild and farmed salmon was observed in detail. Four large spawning tanks were erected. As control groups, one tank contained only wild salmon netted from the River Imsa and one tank contained fifth-generation farmed fish of the Sunndalsøra strain, which represents more than 80 percent of the farmed salmon in Norway. Two tanks contained mixed wild and farmed stocks, equal numbers of male and female fish. The spawning behavior of all the fish was observed 24 hours per day for seven weeks during November and December, until only one hen had not spawned.

The fish were identified individually, and all instances of behavior were recorded: aggression, submission, cruising, and breeding. The latter included male quivering and female digging and courting. The greatest differences between wild and farmed salmon were exhibited during breeding and spawning. In comparison with their wild counterparts, farmed females displayed poorer breeding behavior, were courted less often, constructed fewer and poorer nests, spawned less frequently, were less efficient at nest covering, incurred more nest destruction, retained a greater weight of unspawned eggs, and suffered greater egg mortality. Overall, the reproductive success of farmed females was less than one-third that of wild females. A particularly interesting observation was that many of the eggs deposited by farmed females remained unfertilized when wild males were absent. Consequently, the reproductive success of farmed females in the absence of wild males was less than one-tenth of that in the presence of wild males.

Farmed male fish were much less successful than farmed females in breeding. Compared to their wild counterparts, they were much less aggressive, courted less, and participated in fewer spawnings over a greatly shortened period of time. Based on embryo counts from nests fertilized by farmed males, it was estimated that they achieved only one to three percent of the reproductive success of wild males.

Very recent studies of salmon aquaculture in the Bay of Fundy have disclosed that many of the escaped salmon entering nearby rivers are sexually immature and incapable of spawning. This finding both confirms and explains the Norwegian studies on spawning efficiency, but it also raises serious questions about the long-term effects of deviant fish in the river. When a mature salmon enters freshwater, its digestive system shuts down and it does not feed. When a sexually immature salmon returns to fresh water, does its digestive system also shut down, or is this mutant now a predator of its own species? Will it cannibalize both eggs and parr, as do anadromous rainbow trout?

Ecological adaptation, together with genetic diversity among various populations, has resulted over the centuries in the biological diversity of species. Perhaps more than any other analysis of the interactions of farmed and wild salmon, the Norwegian study clearly demonstrates the perils that farmed salmon pose to the wild fish. The greatest danger posed by salmon farms is the diminution of the genetic diversity of the species. The sad part is that the importance of genetic diversity is so poorly understood and appreciated by so few.

## ENHANCING WILD SALMON STOCKS

The most successful programs for enhancing wild salmon populations have been those involving the artificial propagation of wild salmon stocks using brood stocks native to the particular river or tributary. The key word is enhancement. Artificial propagation cannot sustain a population that the river itself is incapable of supporting. Such programs are not without significant problems, particularly those concerning the altering of the genetic pool of the native strains.

Hatchery programs that supplement native wild stocks are virtually always successful in increasing the freshwater survival of parr and smolts. The levels of survival increase directly in proportion to the time spent by the young fish in the hatchery environment. One study lists the average freshwater survival rates for the hatchery release of eyed eggs, fry, parr, and smolts as 2.7, 4.3, 7.5, and 39 percent respectively, compared to less than 2 percent for the smolt survival of eggs hatched in the wild. However the saltwater survival rates are inversely related, with wild-smolt survival rates three to four times that of hatchery-raised fish. There is good evidence that the longer a juvenile salmon stays in the river, as compared to hatchery fish released at smoltification, the better are its chances for survival in the ocean. Perhaps it's a simple example of parr acquiring "river smarts" and survival experience before being tossed to the predators of the sea.

There are many other problems posed by the introduction of hatchery fish into a wild environment. One of the most troublesome is the declining survival of successive generations of river-specific hatchery-raised Atlantic salmon. This has been well documented in the Chinook and coho hatcheries of Oregon, Washington, and British Columbia, where the initially successful return of hatchery-reared salmon declined markedly over a period of years. While not directly comparable because Pacific salmon always die after spawning, it appears that successive generations of hatchery-raised stock do not have the viability to maintain wild populations. There is no explanation for these phenomena at this time.

For those interested in a detailed review of wild salmon enhancement programs and their associated problems, an outstanding summary may be found in a paper entitled *Enhancement of Wild Salmon Populations* (25) presented at an international symposium in Kongsvall, Norway, in 1993 by Bror Jonsson and Ian Fleming.  They summarize hatchery enhancements by emphasizing that "poorly managed hatchery programs thus may alter or even destroy the biological diversity of the species" that they are designed to maintain. Most certainly, such programs must not be used to excuse habitat destruction and other misguided actions that impair the spawning escapement.

**SATELLITE REARING PROGRAM**. The most successful of the artificial rearing programs is that of raising river-specific hatchery fry for four to six months in satellite tanks located along the shores of their natal rivers. The program originated in New Brunswick about 1982, initially as a cooperative venture between the

Canadian Department of Fisheries and Oceans and the
Rocky Brook Salmon Club. In the fall, male and female
MSW salmon are captured, and suitable specimens are
stripped. The eggs are artificially fertilized and incubated
in the hatchery, and the fingerlings are raised to the fry
stage in the hatchery. In late spring, the fry are released
into rearing tanks. Extreme care is taken to ascertain that
each tank contains only fry that are the progeny of cock
and hen fish native to that particular stretch of river.

The first of what have become known as "satellite
rearing tanks" was installed at Rocky Brook on the
Miramichi. The fiberglass rearing tanks are 10 feet in
diameter and hold 5,000 fingerlings. The tanks are fed
with water from small feeder brooks to imprint the parr
(as they smoltify) with native water. The cost of each tank,
materials, and technical advice is $4,000, a modest
amount readily raised by local interests.

The fry are fed daily throughout the summer and
early fall, and in October or early November they are
released into the river as small 0+ parr, 2 3/4 to 4 inches
long, depending on the temperature of the water in which
they are raised and how they are fed. Typically 90-plus
percent of the fry will survive to release, greatly improving
the spawning success as compared to 0+ parr hatched in
the wild. Parr this small usually require two additional
years to reach smolt size, thus providing adequate time
for developing the physical strength and survival skills
necessary when they eventually run to the sea.

The satellite rearing program has been so successful
that, with the assistance of the Miramichi Salmon
Association, by 1996 there was a total of 17 tanks at 13
locations, each holding about 5,000 fry. By actual count,
the adipose fins of 82,022 young parr from the 13
locations were clipped and the fingerlings released into
their natal rivers that fall. That's a remarkable survival
rate of 96.5 percent of the fry throughout their first
summer and far exceeds fry survival in the wild. By 1997
the program had increased to 27 tanks in 19 locations that
released 133,000 parr throughout the Miramichi River

system, with a survival rate of 94.5 percent. With the assistance of the Atlantic Salmon Federation, the program has also been introduced into the Restigouche River and to other provinces of Canada.

In theory, the satellite rearing program resolves many of the problems associated with survival of the alevins through their first year of river life. However this program is not without its hazards. Foremost is the fact that supportive or supplemental breeding may eventually reduce the genetic variability of the very populations it was meant to assist. The milt from hatchery-selected male salmon is seldom used to cross-fertilize the eggs of several hen fish, as frequently occurs in the wild. For a number of years, New Brunswick hatcheries did employ two-on-two mating, in which eggs from two hen fish were divided into two parts and the eggs mixed and fertilized with the mixed milt from two cock salmon. This program was abandoned because the hatcheries resisted the time required to repeatedly cross-fertilize multiple male-female pairs. An additional complication is that the visual or random selection of suitable breeding stock for the hatchery may result in less favorable matings than those between wild fish.

Perhaps the greatest accomplishment of the satellite rearing program is in enhancing the education of the public. It encourages the contribution of both time and money by anglers and camp operators, in a collaborative effort to restore our salmon stocks.

**CATCH-AND-RELEASE**. When I first outlined this chapter, I sought to emphasize the role that all salmon anglers may play in the conservation of our beloved fish. The deeper I delved into the subject, the more I realized that, however complicated the subject, there are two key areas in which we anglers may uniquely contribute. Through our own actions we can preserve MSW salmon by observing the strictest of conservation measures: by not killing any large MSW salmon. By our own words we can preach the urgent need for the political resolution of the internecine salmon wars occurring in virtually every country except Iceland.

Catch-and-release is now a proven conservation measure, but not everyone embraces the concept or accepts the evidence, particularly in those venues where the killing of all landed salmon has long been the practice. Old-time guides are among the fiercest in their opposition. Consider the story of "Oscar," who was employed as a guide at a well-known camp on the Restigouche River. Oscar just could not accept the concept of catch-and-release. He was convinced that released fish could not survive. Even more compelling was his fear that if catch-and-release became law throughout the Province of Quebec, he and other guides might become unemployed as anglers lost interest in fishing only for the sport.

Several years before New Brunswick instituted its no-kill policy for MSW salmon in 1984, the enlightened new owner of this camp, one of the finest on the river, decreed that all large salmon were to be released unharmed unless, for some reason, they were damaged and unlikely to survive. Well sure enough, every fish Oscar and his sports caught that first season was "damaged," and Oscar killed every salmon. Clearly, he could not accept the idea of releasing the fish to spawn and perhaps to fight another day. Needless to say, Oscar never guided at that lodge again.

I have talked to guides who, like Oscar, argue that you cannot always tell if a fish is damaged, so why throw away a fish that may not survive? What they fail to realize is that even if only eight out of ten released salmon do survive, that nevertheless adds a very significant spawn to the river. In most cases, the specious argument against catch-and-release is based entirely on the fear of losing employment.

Old guides, however, can be taught new tricks. There is great emphasis on the Alta River these days on releasing MSW hens to allow them to spawn. Odd Hansen, one of the senior guides on that river, was so concerned for the welfare of his fish that he would not lift my 30-plus-pound hens out of the water for photographs. He insisted that their heads remain under water.

In venues where the killing of all landed fish has long been routine, old habits die slowly. Some vigorously contend that their license or rod fee entitles them to whatever they catch, not realizing that each dead salmon represents many thousands of alevins that will never hatch. Others argue convincingly that catching a fish that you intend to release is immoral and ethically indefensible. That reasoning might carry more weight were it not for recent studies on the mortality of angled fish.

Many years ago, the Province of New Brunswick adopted a spring season for kelts or black salmon, those fish that had spawned the previous fall and were returning to the sea. As they descend the river and encounter alewives and herring migrating upriver to spawn, the blacks feed voraciously and will attack any streamer pattern that even resembles a small fish. Having lost a third of their weight over the winter, the kelts tug and pull on your line but show little of the fight of a bright salmon fresh to the river. Even though it provided action for a few anglers and early season employment along the Miramichi, vigorous arguments erupted concerning what many considered an unethical fishery.

Eventually, action was initiated in 1994 to resolve the controversy and to ameliorate the damage done by the catch-and-release of seaward-bound kelts. While the catch-and-release mortality for MSW salmon had been estimated at 3 and 6 percent along the Miramichi and Restigouche Rivers respectively, there was no information concerning kelt mortality. The most definitive of several related studies was sponsored jointly by the Canadian Department of Fisheries and Oceans and Queens University on the effects of angling on 1SW kelts returning to the ocean as compared to bright grilse that had recently entered freshwater from the ocean. Fresh fish were captured in counting traps and were then fought to exhaustion by experienced anglers, and immediately thereafter metabolites in the fish were analyzed. While the bright grilse were in better condition (larger weight/length factor) and took longer to exercise exhaustively, the consequences of the exhaustive angling were amazing. The white-muscle energy stores of both the bright fish and the kelts decreased following angling but were regenerated more rapidly in the kelts than in the bright fish. Similarly, the build-up of white-muscle lactate and intracellular acidosis (both measures of exhaustion) was much greater in the bright fish and took considerably longer to return to normal levels. Furthermore, 12 percent of the bright fish died within 12 hours following angling. No mortality was observed for the kelts. These studies demonstrated convincingly that angling results in relatively less physiological deterioration and less mortality in kelts than in bright grilse.

A similar question arises regarding late-season angling. Does late-season catch-and-release impair the salmon's spawning ability? In this set of studies, pre-spawning salmon and grilse were fought to exhaustion in October at a water temperature of 6°C (42.8°F). The decrease in energy stores and the increase in white-muscle lactate in both salmon and grilse were similar to those described above for kelts. The physiological disturbance in MSW salmon was less than for grilse. In particular, the increase of the white muscle lactate in grilse was significantly greater than for MSW salmon. The survival of fertilized eggs from those fish that had been fought and those that hadn't was identical, 98 and 97 percent respectively. Clearly, these studies suggest that late-season angling in cold water is not necessarily harmful to the fish or their spawn. What mortality does occur probably results from angler-induced injuries (e.g., lifting by the gills) rather than from physiological debilitation.

As a result of the studies described above, the Province of New Brunswick has now established for the Miramichi River a single season for all salmon, kelts and bright fish alike. The season now begins April 15 and continues until October 15 on the lower main river.

Hot-weather-angling catch-and-release fishing can be very stressful, even fatal. In a third study by the same group of researchers, 1SW grilse were fought to exhaustion during the summer with water temperatures of 20 ± 2°C (68°F). As was observed in the previous studies, the intramuscular energy stores were nearly depleted following angling exhaustion, but unlike the response of fish caught at 6°C (42.8°F) in the fall, there was no energy (glycogen) resynthesis during a four-hour recovery period. The grilse did not regenerate energy. Most importantly, there was a marked postangling mortality; 40 percent of the fish died within 12 hours of being caught. These studies confirm the need to restrict or prevent angling of salmon in the very warm waters of summer. They are now being used by the Atlantic provinces of Canada as guidelines for the temporary closure of rivers during very hot weather. Taken together, this new information may lead to what Bielak envisions as a catch-and-release fishing "window," that portion or portions of the season during which angling may be conducted with negligible mortality (07).

An important aspect of any catch-and-release program is how long the fish is held out of water and how it is handled during that time. There appear to be no published studies on large salmon, but some ancillary information may serve as a guide. A study on small rainbow trout weighing 1/2 to 1 pound conducted by some of the same researchers who participated in the three studies described above demonstrated that exhaustively exercised fish responded poorly to air exposure. (The fish were not fought with rod and reel but were exercised in a circular tank.) Trout exposed to air showed a retention of carbon dioxide in the blood, while the blood oxygen content fell by more than 80 percent. Survival of a control group of unexercised fish was 100 percent after 12 hours versus 88 percent in the exercised group. However, fish held out of water for 30 and 60 seconds immediately following exercise showed 12-hour survival rates of only 62 and 38 percent respectively.

These results confirm the need to minimize air exposure during catch-and-release, but they are misleading in their applicability to larger fish, especially MSW salmon. It is well recognized that the ability of fish to withstand the stress of air exposure is a function of body weight. As discussed in Chapter 11, if properly handled, large salmon can and do survive air exposure for periods up to two minutes or more. This, of course, is demonstrated in every hatchery where salmon are exposed to air for the minute or more required to strip them of their eggs or milt. The survival rate for the stripped fish is very high.

## THE SPECTER OF DISEASE

As if the wild salmon did not have enough problems, in recent years a new specter has re-emerged, that most dreaded by marine biologists and fisheries managers alike: disease. Disease pathogens are very common and always present in the marine environment, but most are well dispersed and dormant. Wild salmon tend to be immune to marine pathogens unless and until the conditions are altered drastically.

When conditions become unfavorable, the outbreak of disease can result in disastrous situations, such as the discovery in the Baltic Sea of a deadly disease, M-74, that attacks only female salmon and that is still uncharacterized; the discovery in 1996 of the fluke *Gyrolactylus salaris* in the Laerdal River of Norway (see Chapter 11); and the outbreak in 1997 of furunculosis, a highly contagious bacterium, in the Miramichi River in New Brunswick.

The most recent devastating outbreak was in 1997 in the Bay of Fundy in which many of the 77 salmon farms in the bay were infected with infectious salmon anemia (ISA), a virus similar to influenza. (There are 110 farm sites in the so-called Quoddy region, which include the 77 farms in the Bay of Fundy and 33 sites in the adjacent Cobscook Bay in Maine.) ISA is an especially virulent disease for which there is no treatment. To what extent the outbreak of the ISA virus is solely attributable to the salmon farms in the bay is yet to be clarified. However, the evidence seems overwhelming that the spread of the disease was directly attributable to the overcrowding of fish in the farms. One overwrought biologist graphically described it as "living pollution." In early 1998, the New Brunswick Department of Fisheries and Aquaculture ordered the slaughter of 850,000 juvenile salmon in the infected farms. By June that year, another 544,000 fish were eradicated, and in August still another 306,000 fish were destroyed. In total, more than 1.7 million of the 1997 class of fish were eliminated at a cost of more than $15 million. The economic loss in jobs, profits, and taxes is incalculable. The real price in terms of infected wild salmon is yet to be determined.

## IN SUMMARY

*Human nature includes the strong tendency to remain in denial until things are undeniably bad. So crisis management of our salmon has begun.*

Carl Safina
*Song for the Blue Ocean*

The factors and forces affecting the survival of wild Atlantic salmon are the most complicated and interwoven set of parameters imaginable. Physical scientists such as myself are unaccustomed to wrestling with the enormous perplexities of biological systems, and I admit to being overwhelmed at times by the vast amount of data and confusing interactions. But out of this comes my summary of the situation today.

Canadian rivers are breeding, on average, about half the fish required to propagate the species. While some river systems, particularly the larger ones, generate adequate numbers of smolts, inadequate numbers of salmon are returning from the ocean, and we do not know why.

Oceanic disappearance of post-smolts is the major

problem. The prevailing hypothesis is that the number of post-smolts surviving the run to the sea is inadequate to escape the gauntlet of oceanic hazards. Commercial catch statistics confirm that salmon in the ocean, both juvenile and adult, travel in schools. If inadequate numbers of post-smolts are available to form or join protective schools, the depredation by the various predators increases greatly. Likewise, the ability of smaller schools to find food is severely diminished.

Many factors must be taken into consideration. Juvenile salmon in the North Atlantic are maturing earlier, perhaps too early for optimal survival. Are younger smolts (age 1+, for example) with less river experience unable to cope in the saltwater environment? What is the effect on young smolts as they migrate through estuaries containing disease-laden salmon farms? Is the disappearance of the post-smolts simply the result of predation by hungry cod or the wasteful by-catch (unintentional catch) of factory ships? Many believe that the latter is woefully underestimated. What are the effects of the recent decrease in the surface temperature of the North Atlantic Ocean? We know it shifts the North Atlantic toward a cold-water ecology, decreases and disperses the winter feeding range of MSW salmon, and results in a lower catch rate than in areas of warm sea-surface temperature. Does it also result in a lessened availability of the small fish and crustaceans on which the smolts and salmon feed? Do oceanic mammals take more mature salmon than we realize? Is the poorly regulated commercial harvesting of capelin in Canadian waters and of the sand launce, the sprat, and the Norway pout in northern European waters robbing the salmon of major food sources? We simply do not know the answers. Undoubtedly, all are contributing to the demise of the wild salmon. The one thing we do know is that a single-issue focus and single-source solutions will not reverse the decline of the wild salmon.

The return of salmon to the rivers presents other problems. After spending less time at sea, smaller salmon

are returning in fewer numbers to spawn. The decrease in average size is not just the result of netting the largest, most fecund fish. Much of it stems from the changes in the river life of the juvenile salmon, some physiological, some phenomenal. The recent impact of salmon farming has been disastrous. Most frightening is convincing evidence that the pathology of aquaculture escapees is increasing with time. We do not know how to repair the damage and deterioration they cause, and we cannot reverse it. We have no means to control the salmon farms, because they represent economic and political forces too powerful to counter.

For all these demonic forces edging the Atlantic salmon ever closer to extinction, the worst may be yet to come: transgenic salmon, the aquaculture of genetically altered salmon bred to be fat, dumb, and happy, and to grow rapidly to gigantic size. Can you envision the havoc that such fish, which inevitably will escape their pens, might impose on the wild salmon stocks of a river? Pleading the case against the aquaculture of transgenic

*Figure 8-9. Salmon trap and counting station on the Ouapetec River. A census of returning salmon is essential to determine the escapement and spawning populations of a river.*

*Opposite page: Figure 8-8. Alta River guide Odd Hansen releasing the author's 34-pound salmon. Odd was so concerned for the fish that he would not lift it from the water for this photo to be taken.*

salmon, Fred Whoriskey, Vice President of Research and Environment for the Atlantic Salmon Federation, explains that our choices are "not wild salmon and ___, but *wild salmon* **or** ___."

## THE VERY LAST CAST

*May we find wells of hope deeper than the shallow pools of optimism in which we sometimes paddle.*
                                                 IONA Community, Scotland
                                                 *Order of Worship for Jubilee*

The Atlantic salmon is disappearing from the North Atlantic Ocean. The precipitous decline in wild salmon stocks is a problem of monumental proportions and inordinate urgency. Can we act in time to save the wild salmon, or is it already too late?

It seems strange that we subsidize the logging of primeval forests, the grazing of pristine prairies, the netting of scarce fishes. Yet we do little to restrict the depletion of irreplaceable virgin resources or the harvesting of endangered or nonregenerative species. Public spending to facilitate the private harvesting of natural resources is accepted, but the use of public monies for conservation of species and the recycling of resources is not, often on the pretense that it hinders private enterprise. Hiding behind excuses such as the lack of international agreements, the need for employment, or aboriginal rights is no longer an acceptable rationalization for the squandering of scarce natural reserves.

The status of the Atlantic salmon is but a reflection of the use and misuse of our once bountiful resources. In the words of Wilfred Carter, President Emeritus of the Atlantic Salmon Federation, "We reap the harvest while raping the habitat" that produces the bounty. Unlike land and forest and fresh water, anadromous fishes are not within the province or purview of any one nation. If we cannot preserve threatened resources within our own boundaries, can we expect other nations to conserve a common resource? The Atlantic salmon crisis is but a small window on the future of our planet.

It's obvious that when it comes to salmon propagation and survival, the simple answer is you can't mess with Mother Nature. For the real world, perhaps Anthony Netboy's conclusion said it all: "Only a deceleration of industrial activity, coupled with something like the Indians' awe and veneration of the wondrous animals who supply us with food [*and sport, I add*], can ultimately save the salmon and other endangered species" (42).

If we do not decelerate salmon killing activities, ours may well be *the very last cast*.

*Canoe and Salmon*
Watercolor
10 1/2 x 16 1/8 inches
Private Collection

# Chapter 9

# Techniques for Fishing the Wet Fly

**DAY ONE, COURSE 101**

We were fishing out of the Black Rapids Lodge on the lower Miramichi River. The camp is operated by George and Jean Curtis, a truly delightful couple who own over a mile of water just below the well-known public water at Gray Rapids. It was Jack's first day on a salmon river. An experienced and accomplished trout fisherman, Jack had always resisted our efforts to ensnare him in salmon, as he put it. He explained his reluctance with the "cocaine theory"—he was afraid to try it for fear he might like it too much.

The top of the Black Rapids water begins with the river spilling over a narrow ledge into a short run with a deep hole called the "Bathtub." When the fish are running, the tub almost always holds a fish or two. As the river flows over the lip at the bottom of the tub, it pours out into a broad, rapid flow some 400 yards long. In low water, almost the entire river flows through this channel.

This flowage was created in 1963 by Ted Williams and George's father, Roy, who was Ted's personal guide for almost 30 years. The bulldozer did a fine job of placing large rocks, behind which the salmon can rest on their journey upstream. It did too good a job of leaving soccer-ball-sized rocks along the river edge. Splendid salmon water, but wading that soccer field can be very difficult.

George was guiding for Jack, Lloyd, and me that day, and, as is our custom, the new kid on the block got first chance at the prime water. As Jack stepped into the water, he was again reminded to keep his rod low and not to strike if a fish showed. He was to let the fish hook itself. With George behind and to his left, Jack began his casting at a 45-degree angle across the current and downstream. Playing out his cast until the fly was dangling directly downstream, he stepped down about 6 feet and began his second cast. This rhythmic process—cast and step down, cast and step down—was repeated under the watchful eye of George, who occasionally admonished Jack to forget the false casts: "You're not trout fishing." The wading was particularly rough in one section, and George suggested that Jack head back toward shore, lengthen his casts, and direct them more directly downstream at about a 30-degree angle to better counter the faster current.

About 20 minutes into this session, Jack completed a long cast and relaxed as the fly glided downstream in the current. Just as it began to slow in the current at the end of the drift, the water boiled under the fly, but Jack felt nothing. "Relax," George advised. "Mark your line, strip in 10 to 12 feet, and wait." Jack stood impatiently waiting for the next direction. After waiting the customary two minutes, George advised Jack to resume casting exactly the same length of line as before the strike. Several more casts failed to raise the fish a second time. Perhaps the fish had moved. Resuming his cast-and-step-down procedure, Jack finished fishing the pool without further action and waded from the water with a grin. "See," he said, "I told you it's easy to not catch a salmon."

"But you are not done," George interrupted. "Go back

and try it again," at which point George started downstream to check with Lloyd on the pool below.

Again starting at the top of the run, but without George's watchful eye, Jack's first few casts were almost perfect. Thinking he saw a fish roll across from him, Jack then proceeded to cast directly across the stream. The current caused the line to form a deep bend, carrying the fly downstream at nearly twice the current's rate. After several baggy casts, Jack resumed stepping downstream following each cast. But now a number of his casts were at a 60-degree angle across the current instead of 30 to 45 degrees. To counteract the faster swing of his fly, Jack now began false casting to straighten his line between casts, which served only to lessen the time his fly was in the water and to lessen his chance of raising a fish.

Pausing to realize his error, Jack corrected his presentation, directed it more downstream, and made a dozen very satisfactory casts as he approached the spot where he had raised the fish on his first pass through the pool. Again there was a boil as the fly passed over the resting salmon. Reacting instinctively as a trout fisherman, Jack struck and pulled the fly right out of the fish's mouth. Instantly he cast again to the same location. Nothing. Five rapid casts in a row, still nothing. Unbeknownst to Jack, George had come back upstream and was sitting high on the bank observing all this, suffering in silence. Jack continued his progress down through the pool, at one point wading over his knees to waist depth and right through one of the best holding sections at the tail of the pool. As he fished out the last glide, he wound in his line and turned ashore. George had seen enough and arose to meet Jack as he trudged back up the path.

"Some bad news," George greeted him. "You have just flunked Salmon Fishing 101."

## A SALMON IS NOT A TROUT

The preceding tale illustrates at least seven types of mistakes made by the beginning salmon fisherman: (1)

fishing a high rod, (2) false casting, (3) casting across the current, (4) failing to rest a rising fish, (5) striking a rising fish, (6) rapidly repeating your casts, and (7) wading too deeply. At least four of these faults are directly attributable to trout fishing.

False casting is a horrendous habit. The aim of the salmon angler fishing the wet fly is to lay down a straight cast so the current may sweep it at the proper speed to entice the salmon. The fly should fish properly from the moment it lands on the water. You have no fly to dry, so why false cast? The only valid reason is to correct a poor cast made to a fish in a known lie. Otherwise, why not mend your cast, let the current straighten the line, fish out the cast, and see what happens?

Rapidly repeated casts are likewise trout induced. But they don't work for salmon, at least not when you're fishing the wet fly. Salmon attack a fly with much more restraint than do trout, and almost never will a salmon instantly return to a fly.

Many trout are not hooked because the angler fails to react to the rise quickly enough to set the hook. Many salmon are not hooked because the angler reacts much too quickly. As a general rule, never strike a salmon. You let the salmon attack the fly, seize it in its mouth, and start to return to its lie, whereupon the fish hooks itself. This is without question the most difficult aspect of salmon fishing for the experienced trout fisherman to master. It is not difficult to exercise restraint when fishing the wet fly, for often the fish has seized the fly and is starting its downward plunge before the fisherman is fully aware. But it takes the patience of Job to see a salmon surge upon a large Bomber floating on the surface, mouth agape, and slowly—ever so slowly—swallow it. Some writers argue about whether or when to strike a salmon. For the beginning salmon angler, it should be a firm rule never to strike, the few exceptions to which we shall discuss later.

For too many anglers, the concept of fly fishing seems to be the image portrayed in Robert Redford's movie *A River Runs Through It*—that of a fisherman standing in the middle of a stream, rod held high, repeatedly false casting over a boulder-strewn stream, followed by the single presentation of a floating fly to an unseen quarry. That's not even a proper image for much trout fishing. It most certainly is not the way to hook and fight large salmon.

We seldom realize how much of our fishing literature and equipment, even our art work, is influenced by dry-fly fishing for trout. Without question, the quick strike is the hardest habit for trout fishermen to overcome. The other trout-induced faults are, with practice, more easily relearned. Recall the comparison I drew between hunting and fishing in the introduction. If you exchange your shotgun for a rifle, instinctively you adopt a different shooting posture and habits. When you exchange your trout rod for salmon, so likewise must you alter your mind-set.

## WHY DO SALMON TAKE THE FLY?

As was noted in Chapter 4, salmon have been known to strike at almost anything, including weeds clinging to a leader knot. Lee Wulff once described a salmon striking a bare leader knot riffling on the surface. Why they do this we simply do not know. Over the centuries, many responses have been ascribed to the salmon, all of which are based on recognized human emotions. I've never been convinced that fish think or respond like mammals or even birds. Nevertheless, it may be instructive to examine salmon behavior with a view to understanding what types of fly presentation may induce the strike.

Based on years of observation, Hugh Falkus divided salmon response into six types of striking motivations or "takes" in *Salmon Fishing: A Practical Guide* (16), which, listed in approximate order of likelihood, I paraphrase as follows:

1. Feeding habit—a deliberate take, frequently ascribed to a reflex action resulting from early river life as a parr.

2.  Aggression—the "crunch" take, a seemingly automatic reaction to intrusion into the salmon's territory.
3.  Inducement—a response or take primarily based on chasing an escaping quarry.
4.  Curiosity—a gentle nontake in which the fish rises to or touches the fly with mouth closed, with no intention of taking the fly.
5.  Irritation—a response, usually aggressive, resulting from prolonged aggravation such as the repeated casting over the fish.
6.  Playfulness—behavior, such as bumping the fly or flipping with its tail, in which the salmon makes no effort to seize the fly with its mouth.

Undoubtedly, salmon do demonstrate a variety of behaviors at one time or another. Whether they can properly be defined in terms of mammalian behavior is debatable. For instance, I have trouble accepting the notion that feeding behavior is simply a reflex response the salmon acquires as a parr in its early river life. Perhaps, but the largest parr foods are insects. Parr never feed on shrimp or elvers or minnows as large as themselves. And what differentiates the irritation response from inducement or aggression? Or playfulness from curiosity?

My concern with the Falkus responses is the tendency to take them too literally and to apply them too broadly. In a controversial book entitled *Atlantic Salmon: Fact and Fancy* (01), Gary Anderson takes the theory of responses one step further by describing the various types of flies that should appeal to the six striking motivations. The problem with such categorization is that is easy to discern the salmon's response to flies fished on the surface but improbably difficult to attribute specific responses to underwater lures. And, finally, even if we recognize a particular "emotion," can we really select a fly to induce that response?

## THE CONVENTIONAL
## FISHING OF THE WET FLY

The salmon angler spends, on average, more than 95 percent of his time fishing wet flies, which accounts for 98 percent of the fish caught. This is due partly to convention and partly to the scarcity of good dry-fly water, much of which is inaccessible to the wading angler.

Fishing the wet fly is the simplest, as well as the most productive, method for salmon. Whether you are wading the shore or fishing from a canoe, the approach is essentially the same. Let's assume you are fishing from a canoe. The guide has just anchored the canoe in a new position and nods for you to begin fishing. You stand up, extend the leader and perhaps 2 feet of fly line beyond your rod tip, and begin casting. Including the leader, you have a 10- or 12-foot cast. No, it's not too short. If your guide has quietly positioned your canoe, you may easily attract a fish at such a distance. Whether you cast to and fish on one or both sides of the canoe depends on your guide's reading of the water. After the cast, immediately lower your rod tip to within 6 inches of the water's surface. Let the line drift dead astern and then slowly sweep it 10 or 15 degrees to the opposite side of the canoe with your rod tip, as shown in Figure 9-1 (page 293). Salmon, just like muskellunge, frequently strike as the fly courses sidewise at the end of the retrieve. As we shall discuss later in this chapter, a low rod is absolutely the best way to fight a large salmon.

Now, cast the same-length line to the other side of the canoe and, as it flows astern, repeat the sweeping motion to the obverse side. One of the great advantages of fishing long two-handed rods is that the sweeping adds an extra 15 feet or so to the cast—an extremely effective 15 feet, which is often productive.

For normal currents, cast downstream at a 45-degree angle to the current. Even in slow water, resist the temptation to increase that angle. In fast currents, you cannot maintain the proper swing of your, fly even at 45

degrees. You may compensate in one of two ways: by
mending your line to straighten it in the current or by
decreasing the angle of your cast to 30, 20, or even 15
degrees. With these smaller angles, your fly spends less
time in the water on each cast, but the speed of the fly
relative to the current remains appropriate.

Having fished out your first two casts, one each on
the right and left sides of the canoe, strip off about 4 feet
of line, and again cast to both sides of the canoe. There is
no science in how much to lengthen your cast each time.
Search the water quickly with 4- to 5-foot extensions of
the line. The time for finesse in your extensions will come
later. Salmon have excellent eyesight, which is limited
only by the cone of vision of their eyes and is thus
dependent on how deeply they lie in the water (50). If a
salmon sees your fly and really wants it, he will charge 25
feet or more to take it.

Each time you strip off line to make another cast,
retain a 3- to 6-foot loop of line between your reel and
your casting hand. During the cast, hold the loop against
the cork grip with your index and middle fingers. The
purpose of this loop is to allow the fish to hook itself.
The size of the loop depends on the current. In slow
water, a 3-foot loop suffices. In very fast water, a 6- or
even 8-foot loop may be desirable.

As illustrated in Figure 9-1, continue to search the
water on either side of the canoe by successively
extending your casts. By lengthening each succeeding
pair of casts, you cover an ever-increasing fan-shaped
expanse of water downstream of the canoe until you
have reached the limit of your casting range. Hopefully,
this will be at least 50 feet, but if it isn't, don't fret. The
importance of one's ability to cast great distances is
greatly overemphasized. Most salmon are hooked at
between 25 and 45 feet. Long casts (say 60 feet or more)
are advantageous primarily in that you can cover much
more water with one placement of the canoe, which
saves precious time and results in more fishing time.
However, using a single-handed rod, casts so long that

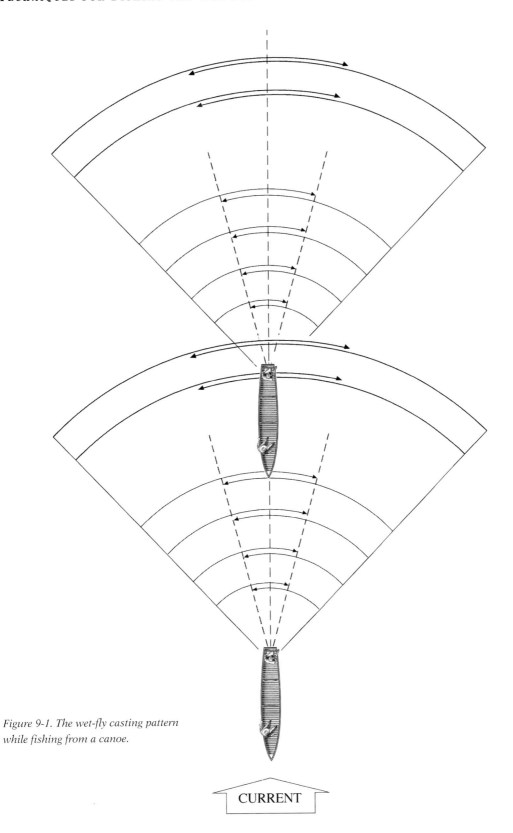

*Figure 9-1. The wet-fly casting pattern while fishing from a canoe.*

CURRENT

they require stripping in line and perhaps a false cast to extend line are a waste of time. It would be much better to move the canoe (or wade deeper). The best advice is to not attempt casts that you cannot easily pick up without stripping in line.

After covering as much water as is practical, the angler usually nods to the guide and sits down while the guide quietly repositions the canoe 60 or so feet downriver. Once the canoe is again anchored, the angler commences casting as before. In the course of an hour, your casting pattern will be that shown in Figure 9-1.

For anglers wading along the shore of a river, the technique is much the same as from a canoe. When you first step into the water, wade cautiously to knee depth, but do not go deeper unless your guide so advises. Salmon frequently lie in shallow water and very often run upriver near the shore. Pinet's Pool on the upper Moisie is so shallow that it looks like a spawning bed, which it is. Large salmon frequently rest in those shallows before they tackle Big Bend pool and the long rapids below Camp Joseph.

Since you will not be as close to a salmon as when fishing from a canoe, begin your casting with 10 feet of line extending from the rod. After each cast is played out, lengthen your line another 4 or 5 feet and repeat the cast. Resist the temptation to cast more than 45 degrees across the current. One of the fundamental principles of fly casting for salmon is to maintain a straight line on the water because it ensures proper fly speed, keeps the fly at an appealing angle to the fish, and promises good hooking at the strike. As you continue to lengthen each succeeding cast, place great emphasis on one good cast. Train yourself to avoid false casting at all costs. If you find you must limit your cast to 45 feet, do so. Don't get entangled in stripping and shooting line or competing with yourself for long casts that you cannot control. The proper presentation of your line and fly is the single most important aspect of salmon fishing. Forty years ago, in *Lee Wulff's Handbook of Freshwater Fishing* (57) Wulff wrote, "The placement and movement of the fly are at

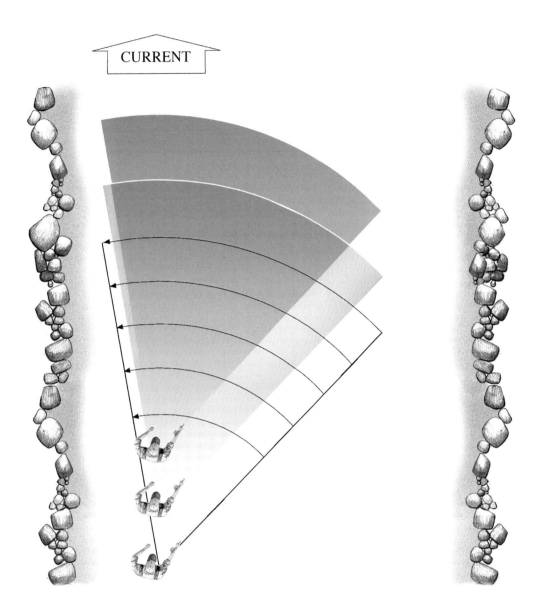

*Figure 9-2. The wet-fly casting pattern while wading.*

least three times as important as the [fly] pattern." In today's hard-fished waters, that advice carries greater wisdom than ever.

Proper presentation is the secret to enticing *Salar* to the hook. When fishing from a canoe, I often alternate two rods, each with a different fly. Usually I fish a single-handed rod first, followed immediately over the same water with a two-handed rod. In the last several years, I have noticed that I hook approximately three times as many fish with the longer second rod. It is clear to me that my ability to place and control the fly with the two-handed rod is so much better. The salmon react accordingly.

Once you have reached a convenient casting limit (which I term *the limit cast*), you now begin the cast-and-step-down procedure. Move downstream two to three steps (4 to 6 feet), depending on the clarity of the water, and repeat your limit cast. The distance you move each time you step down is the subject of great controversy. On many public waters, such as the Miramichi River in New Brunswick where anglers fish down the river sequentially in a "daisy chain," it is customary to move only 3 or 4 feet. But that is not based on the salmon. It is determined primarily by the desire of each angler to spend as much time as possible on the beat before rotating off the river. The shorter the distance you move, the longer you get to fish. Experienced salmon anglers, particularly those fishing private waters, know that it is better to cover a given stretch rather quickly before repeating your pass through the pool. The second time through you may slow your progress to fish particular portions of the pool as conditions warrant.

When the fly has swept through its arc and is hanging directly downstream of your rod tip (at what the British call the "dangle"), slowly strip in 2 or 3 feet of line before you step down to repeat your limit cast. Many salmon attack the fly near or at the end of the cast. The stripping is an attempt to induce the salmon to take your fly before it escapes upstream. This slow strip takes but a few seconds; the results can be surprising. It even works with dry flies. Until I fished Norway, the largest salmon I had ever landed was taken out of the junction pool where the Ouapetec River joins the Moisie. That fish had shown to a wet fly fished in the conventional manner, but after two rises refused to come again. So I switched to a size 2 Bomber, which I floated over the fish a mere 20 feet away. On the third cast, instead of lifting the fly in the usual manner, I slowly stripped in about 6 inches of line. On the

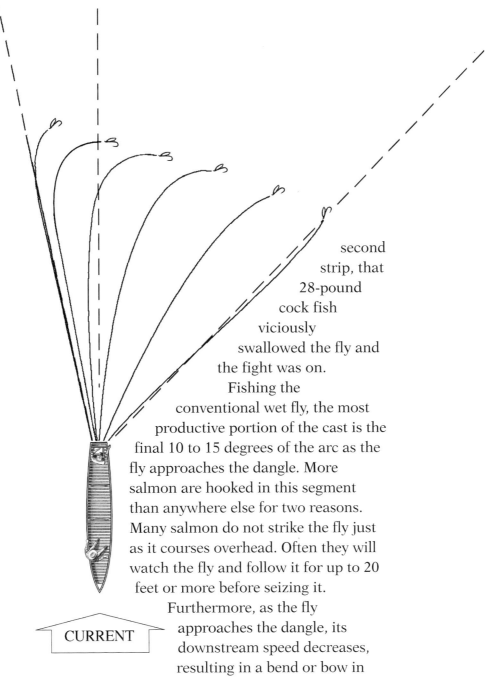

CURRENT

second
strip, that
28-pound
cock fish
viciously
swallowed the fly and
the fight was on.
Fishing the
conventional wet fly, the most
productive portion of the cast is the
final 10 to 15 degrees of the arc as the
fly approaches the dangle. More
salmon are hooked in this segment
than anywhere else for two reasons.
Many salmon do not strike the fly just
as it courses overhead. Often they will
watch the fly and follow it for up to 20
feet or more before seizing it.
Furthermore, as the fly
approaches the dangle, its
downstream speed decreases,
resulting in a bend or bow in
the end of the line. That bend is the single most attractive
spot for the salmon to take the fly. Wulff described it this
way in *The Atlantic Salmon* (58): "As the fly nears the end
of its swing, it makes a quick turn into the current and
then moves rather slowly in regard to the stream bed,
although its speed through the water continues to hold up.

*Figure 9-3. The j-bend, the
hot spot in the wet-fly
presentation. Note that the j-
bend is accentuated by
sweeping the fly 10 to 15
degrees beyond the dangle.*

It is at this point that salmon have a strong tendency to take a fly. Many fishermen look for their strikes at this 'bend' of the retrieve." When I first read Wulff's writings 40 years ago, I wrote in the margin of my book, "I'd call it the 'j.'" I still do. The j-shaped bend is the hot spot in wet fly fishing for salmon, although I have never seen any writer but Wulff describe it.

**MENDING YOUR LINE.** Using the conventional presentation, every angler should strive to cast a straight line and to make sure that the line remains straight throughout the drift. Frequently it's not all that easy. The river current is usually fastest in the middle. If you are casting from the shore toward the middle, it's often easy to maintain a straight line. But if you are casting across the current into slower water, as frequently happens when fishing from a canoe, the current will push the line downstream faster than the fly, and the line will form a deep curve, or "bag," as shown in Figure 9-4. A simple trigonometric calculation will demonstrate that the speed of the fly may be increased by 50 percent as it sweeps across the river, in which case the fly will appear so unnatural that it will be refused by the salmon.

The solution to a baggy line is to mend your line. Mending is accomplished by lifting the baggy line off the water and repositioning it upstream to eliminate the bag, preferably without disturbing the fly. Hold your rod horizontally, lift your rod, and rotate your wrist in a semicircular motion in the direction you wish to move the body of the line. Some describe it as a half-moon wrist-flip, usually upstream. In a 1996 article entitled "Steelhead on a Greased Line" in *Wild Steelhead and Salmon magazine* (52), Jim Vincent appears to have been the first to point out that that if you push your hand forward about 18 inches in front of you as you start the mend, the mend "will start on the line from the tip of the rod" where the slack is, not from further down the line. Most of us subconsciously do push our hand forward slightly; a purposeful 18-inch push makes quite a difference in the ease of mending. A long rod and an upstream wind greatly facilitate mending. That's why long rods are so popular with steelhead fishermen.

An experienced angler can reposition all of the line and the butt of the leader with very little movement of the fly, but don't expect to become that proficient in your first year. Sometimes it is easiest to attempt two or three short mends,

lifting and straightening only a portion of the line on each flip. Try to keep the fly movement short and slow in keeping with the natural movement of a small drifting creature. If you do end up moving the fly on your last mend, don't worry abut it. Unless the fly moves at the moment a fish is attacking the fly, it doesn't matter at all. But remember that salmon will ignore or turn away from a fly that is violently mended just as it comes into their cone of vision.

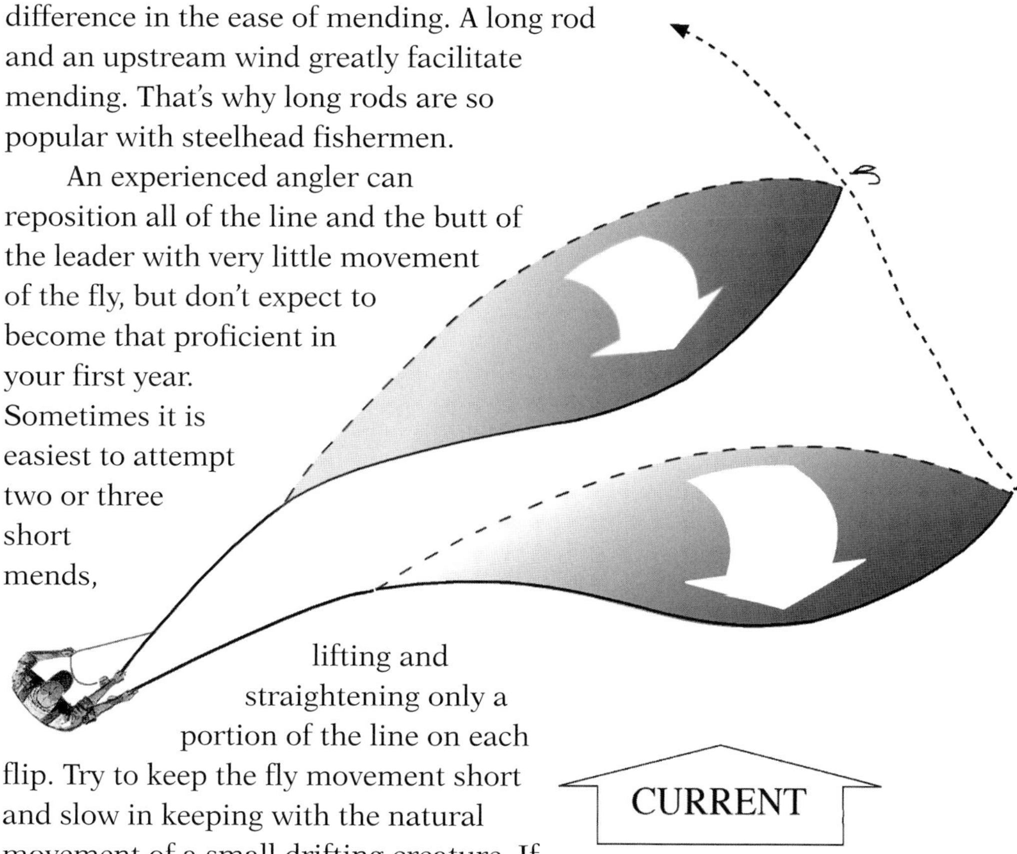

Downstream mending is sometimes desirable when you are fishing very slow currents. A downstream mend intentionally creates a bag in the line whose very purpose is to increase the speed of the fly. Such a mend must be used judiciously so as not to impart too much velocity to the fly, but it can be very useful when fishing slow currents or in guiding flies around obstructions in the river. Mending should be performed cautiously on flat, glassy water or in very shallow pools where the slap of the line may alarm the fish.

It is not necessary or even desirable to mend on each and every cast. Thorpe McKenzie, one of the most

*Figure 9-4. Mending the line.*

accomplished salmon anglers I've known, says he mends less than 10 percent of the time, but Thorpe is also an excellent caster. Vincent Swazey, a very experienced guide and outfitter from Boiestown, New Brunswick, points out that salmon behave erratically and will occasionally ignore a well-mended cast only to attack a speedy, unmended one. It never hurts to experiment.

Having mastered the basic presentation of the wet fly, you are now ready to consider many other factors that affect your success. These include speed of the fly in the water, the depth at which it moves, the action (if any) imparted to the fly, and unusual presentations that may be required in difficult waters or to entice stale fish.

**TO STRIKE OR NOT TO STRIKE**. Previously, I have cautioned against striking a rising salmon. For most wet-fly presentations, this should be the rule. Unlike trout, salmon do not instantly eject a fly, and if given the opportunity a salmon will hold a fly in its mouth until it has returned to its lie. The angler should pay close attention to his fly as it drifts downstream in the current. The instant you see or feel any evidence of a strike, you should relax your grip on the loop of line held under your index and middle fingers and allow the fish and current to gently pull away the line. If you drop a large loop, you give too much slack to the salmon. After taking the fly in its mouth, a salmon either surges back toward the bottom of the river or turns away, right or left. In either case, the fly will be drawn toward the back of the mouth, which usually results in solid hooking. Ideally, the hook will lodge in the corner of the jaw, in what we call the "scissors."

The nonstrike rule also applies to those situations in which a fish strikes at a fly but is not pricked by the hook. In such cases, fish out the cast; occasionally the fish will circle and return instantly to the fly. A fish pricked by a hook never does.

You never can be certain if a fish that struck and missed will return on subsequent casts. Usually they do, and occasionally you hear stories about a salmon rising a dozen or more times to a fly, sometimes eventually taking, sometimes disappearing forever. Several years ago on the Ouapetec River, I experienced a weird combination of behaviors. As my size 6 hairwing fly approached the dangle, I felt a very sharp pull. Had the fish felt the hook? I was inclined to think so because it was such a strong tug. In any event, I relaxed for two minutes, waiting for the salmon to settle back in its lie. There is no set rule as to how long you wait before repeating your cast to a rising fish. Some anglers say 15 seconds, which I feel is much too short a time. Most agree on one to two minutes. I've used two minutes for years, probably because an early mentor recommended it. But I have had good success with this relatively long wait, and I recommend it.

On my second cast to the fish, there was a giant swirl, but I felt nothing. So I waited another two minutes. On the third cast, there was another large swirl but no hit. After waiting another two minutes, I made a fourth cast but there was no swirl, only a very soft underwater take. The fourth time, the fish clearly wanted the fly, and shortly thereafter I landed a bright 22-pound hen.

If a fish has struck and missed the fly, instantly mark your line, preferably by locking it with your fingers against the rod grip. If you were casting with a loose line and are unsure of the length, shorten your line by about 2 feet while you're waiting the customary minute or two. If your second and third casts to that fish do not provoke any further response, shorten your line by 4 feet and repeat the cast. Then lengthen each of your next four casts by 1 foot until you have thoroughly covered the area where the fish was resting. An alternative approach to a fish whose location is well marked is to cast a slightly longer line past the fish and then pull the fly over the fish.

If a fish has touched the fly only lightly, it usually pays to wait for 45 to 90 seconds and then cast back directly to the fish, so that the salmon has no opportunity to observe the fly leisurely as it floats toward him. The fish must decide instantaneously to strike or to reject the fly. Ernie Long, a well-known guide on the Miramichi, strongly recommends shortening the waiting time when you're fishing the Butterfly. Wait only 15 seconds, he advises, and then cast directly to the known lie.

There are several other tricks you may try to provoke a return strike. The most common is to change flies, usually to a smaller size, first of the same pattern and then of a different pattern. Another way is to insert a stack mend (aerial mend) into your cast so that the fly falls slightly upstream of the fish. The stack mend adds slack to the cast and slows the fly, much as with the Patent method discussed later in this chapter. The salmon will often attack this slowly drifting, helpless "insect."

Frequently, a fish will move after missing a strike. Typically, it will go back downstream 12 feet or more. Some years ago, I experienced such a fish at Camp Joseph on the upper Moisie. After two showy strikes, the fish disappeared. I fished out the area, and we then proceeded to make one canoe drop downstream. Thirty feet into that next drop, the fish hit with avengement. With salmon, you just never know.

There are exceptions to the no-strike rule. When a salmon seizes a fly directly downstream of the angler, it frequently holds the fly in the front of its mouth, where there is little mouth surface that the hook can penetrate. Often the angler will feel a short tug or pull followed by a slackening of the line as the salmon turns away. It's extremely difficult to hook such a fish; the only chance is with an instantaneous strip of the line with your rod held low. The usual striking movement of the rod tip does not work because the tip will not respond quickly enough to set the hook.

A second exception to the no-strike rule, which constitutes a must-strike situation, is when fishing the Patent method to be described later.

**SPEED OF THE FLY**. If only we knew what range of fly speeds was most appealing to the salmon, we might save ourselves much aggravation. It seems generally accepted that a speed of 1 1/2 to 3 miles per hour is the

most enticing, but obviously this depends upon the
current, the size of the fly, and its dressing. If the fly
moves too slowly or too rapidly relative to the current, it
appears unnatural to the fish. A 1-inch fly, lightly dressed
on a light hook, may fish fine in a very slack current,
while a similar fly on a 1-inch brass or aluminum tube
may require twice the current speed to fish enticingly.
This is particularly true for flies with long tails, such as
the various shrimp patterns that must have sufficient
current to prevent the tail from drooping. Flies with
drooping tails are a sure put-off, as was noted in the
example of the drooping Green Machine in Chapter 4.[1]
Undoubtedly, the best way to determine the proper speed
is with the riffled fly as described in the following section,
but few of us have the patience to riffle a fly just to test
the speed of the current.

Fortunately, a properly fished wet fly will ride the
current at an appropriate speed if there is no drag, as from
a bagging line. This is true even when the fish is resting in
a whitewater rapid. Many rapids have pockets in which the
fish may hide from the sun, as well as from their enemies.
I can recall a number of instances in which a properly
drifted wet fly attracted strikes in very fast whitewater.
Grilse, in particular, like to rest in such currents.

Occasionally, a large salmon will rest in almost dead
water at the edge of a slow current. I once observed a 30-
pounder porpoising in virtually dead water at the edge of
an island in the Moisie. The only way to fish it was to cast
slightly upstream and strip the fly back toward the canoe
in midstream. We succeeded in attracting the fish, but
that's all; one giant swirl at the fly and we never saw the
fish again. In hindsight, this would have been an ideal
situation in which to fish by "backing up" the canoe as
discussed on page 316.

---

1. It is my opinion that this may explain why long-tail flies are popular in Scandinavia but not in North
America. The faster rivers in much of Scandinavia enable a long fly to fish properly without drooping. A 6-inch
Sun Ray Shadow or long-tailed shrimp pattern will droop badly in many of the slower Canadian rivers, such as
the Miramichi. It may also explain why long Waddington shanks are not popular in North America.

**BRIGHT FISH, STALE FISH**. Most discussions of salmon fishing implicitly assume that you are angling for silver-bright salmon fresh from the sea. During their first 10 to 14 days in the river, bright fish usually distribute themselves throughout the lower river and generally take a fly well and fight very aggressively. They represent the epitome of salmon fishing.

However, you should assume that even bright fish will distribute themselves irregularly and disproportionately throughout their range. Some pools or beats will hold many willing salmon, while other pools will hold few or none. On any given day, the preferred lies will vary, primarily with the water level as it influences the water currents, but also with the wind, sun, and shadows. For this very reason, private camps always rotate their beat assignments so that each angler has an equal opportunity at the better pools, for both morning and evening sessions. The most disproportionate distribution of salmon I have ever seen was on the Laxá í Adaldal in mid-July 1999. For whatever reason, Beat Lower 3 was the hot spot at that time. Between July 11 and 25, the eight beats on this section of the river yielded 52 salmon. Twenty-four of these (46 percent) were caught in Lower 3—14 during the morning sessions and 10 during the evening periods. There is no explanation for such a concentration of taking fish. Three weeks later, Lower 3 was barren.

After the salmon have spent three weeks or so in the river, the physiological changes associated with spawning slowly begin to emerge. Salmon lose their silver sheen and begin to turn dark. Salmon that have been in the river a month are decidedly colored, and by the time of the fall spawn they will be black on top, with rose-colored sides. These changes are evidence that the salmon's metabolism is shifting toward a reproductive mode in which they begin to lose interest in chasing those colorful flies swimming about their pools. Such fish we term *stale*.[2]

---

2. To avoid confusion, I make a distinction between *stale* and *dour*. The Scottish term *dour*, to me, means a fish (often a fresh fish) that is temporarily put off by weather conditions, bad light, or commotion. *Stale* I consider a long-term condition related to time spent in the river. But favorable water conditions can invigorate stale fish, in which case they may fight well.

Unfavorable river conditions are a major contribution to a salmon's lack of interest in your fly. High water temperatures (especially those over 65°F), which threaten the salmon's metabolism, and very low water levels, which threaten their safety, are particularly effective at putting fish down. In the low-water conditions of a hot or dry summer, salmon seek safety and comfort in deep pools or spring-fed runs, where they may rest immobile for weeks, if necessary. Jean-Paul Dubé, a well-known Gaspé angler, has suggested that the problem "may not be in the fish, but in their lies," that "sulkiness is caused more by light or unusual conditions than by the fish's mood" (05). A strong summer sun almost always puts down the salmon, especially if it is shining into the fish's eyes. I've long contended that fishing rivers flowing southward—such as the Moisie, Matapedia, and the Grand Cascapedia—is advantageous in this respect, since those fish do not frequently face directly into the sun. In *Fly Fishing for Salmon* (22), Neil Graesser said it differently: " . . . it makes sense to cover as much of your beat as you can before the sun's rays are shining directly downriver."

Stale fish are difficult to motivate or attract, often impossibly so. For example, MSW salmon begin to enter the Alta River in early June, and by midsummer's day the run is in full swing. (Grilse normally enter the river in July.) Between June 24 and 30, 1998, six rods fishing out of the Stengelsen lodge on the lower river caught 42 salmon, each weighing 18 to 38 pounds, and only one grilse. Four rods fishing out of that same camp eight weeks later caught nine salmon weighing 15 to 26 pounds and 15 grilse. There were lots of MSW salmon in the river in August, but they were stale; most had been in the river for more than two months.

When you do hook a stale fish, you may be disappointed by its fighting ability. My first two 30-pounders, caught within 45 minutes of each other during the last week of August some years ago, were, in retrospect, a huge disappointment. I had expected a really tough battle; instead I engaged in a determined but unspirited tug-of-war. Later, I compared my adversary to an overaged heavyweight boxer shuffling about the pool. Stale fish simply do not fight with the gusto of a fish fresh from the sea. That's why experienced salmon anglers insist on being on the river in June and July when fresh fish begin to run the river.

The behavior of rising fish is frequently an indication of freshness or staleness. As a general rule, rolling or porpoising fish, or those that show with just their fins and tails out of the water, are considered resting or "taking" fish, which sooner or later may be induced to strike. Jumping fish are most frequently running fish not inclined to hold in the pool for any length of time and decidedly uninterested in your fly. But this generalization is just that—a rule that works about half the time.

When the usual fishing techniques fail to move fish, uncommon tactics are necessary. The most common of these tactics include changing the size and style of your fly and altering the manner of its presentation. Very small flies, sizes 12 and 14, are often required for late summer fishing. In Iceland and Scotland, small tubes with size 14 treble hooks are common. The Irish love their small shrimp patterns, often tied on size 14 Esmond Drury treble hooks. Small single-hook nymph patterns are frequently employed on the Miramichi. You can sometimes attract a stale fish by altering the depth and speed of your fly. While the low-water conditions of late summer would seem to call for flies fished slowly at or near the surface, just the opposite can be productive. Small flies fished 2 or more feet deep on long, light leaders may move otherwise quiescent salmon. The best time to attract stale fish is during the spate that immediately follows a rainstorm. Experienced anglers know that a rise of even a centimeter in water level can often be enough to trigger a response in salmon.

Late-season salmon are often particularly difficult to move. Several years ago, the fishing on the upper Miramichi during the first week of October was

outstanding. The following week, the last of the season, you couldn't buy a strike. Only by fishing large bright flies deeply along the seams of the current could we move the odd fish to tug at our fly. We never did find the formula for enticing those fish.

The simple truth is that there are no rules for attracting stale fish. You should try all the tricks you can think of, and they don't have to be reasonable. Certainly, you should not worry about whether or not your guide approves. If no one is catching fish, a new approach is clearly required. It might as well be yours. For just about the time you have exhausted your repertoire and are abandoning the beat, some neophyte will come along, drag a size 2 Bomber across the surface, and hook the largest salmon in the pool.

*Figure 9-5. Nervous water, caused by a boulder-strewn bottom, frequently indicates an excellent holding area for salmon.*

## ALTERNATIVE TECHNIQUES FOR PRESENTING THE FLY

**THE GREASED-LINE TECHNIQUE.** The conventional method of fishing the wet fly causes the fly to course under tension in a 45-degree arc across and down the river. If your fly line is straight, the fly swims under tension at a speed determined by the river current. Using modern lines and techniques, you can control the depth of the fly by the density of the fly line, the use of lead heads or sinking leaders, and the size and style of the fly. The fish's view of the fly varies from a broadside view when cast directly across the current to an end-on view as the fly nears the dangle. Some feel the end-on view is less enticing to the salmon, although catch statistics certainly do not support that view. Most takes occur near the dangle as the path of the fly changes from broadside to end-on (37b).

Enter Arthur H.E. Wood, father of the greased-line technique. In the early 1900s, Wood recognized that a fly drifting just under the surface of the water, free of line drag, was very effective for attracting salmon, and he developed a unique method for presenting the fly, which he called the *greased-line method*. The silk fly lines in use during that time were not easy to float, and it was common practice to fish the wet fly on an ungreased, sinking line at some uncontrolled depth. By greasing all of his silk line up to the leader, Wood was able to keep his fly swimming just under the surface during much of the drift. Modern PVC fly lines accomplish the same effect without dressing. A novel feature of this technique is that it also presents the fly broadside to the salmon during much of the drift, thus providing a better and presumably more enticing view to the fish. Wood kept copious notes and records regarding his method, and between 1927 and 1933 discussed at length a proposed book with Donald G.H. Rudd. A year after Wood's death in 1934, Rudd, writing under the pen name Jock Scott, compiled Wood's papers in an excellent little book entitled *Greased Line Fishing for Salmon*. This book has been reprinted several times, most recently in 1982 with an introduction added by Bill McMillan that discusses the applicability of the technique to steelhead (48).

Using modern floating fly lines, which do not require greasing, the greased-line technique is simply a method for controlling your cast with a series of mends. Usually the cast is made across the current, 90 degrees more or less, and immediately a mend is thrown upstream so that the fly leads the line downstream. Drifting ahead of the line, the fly is tethered but not under the tension of the conventional wet fly cast. As the varying currents move the fly and line, repeated mends are usually necessary to keep the fly swimming ahead of the line as shown in Figure 9-6.

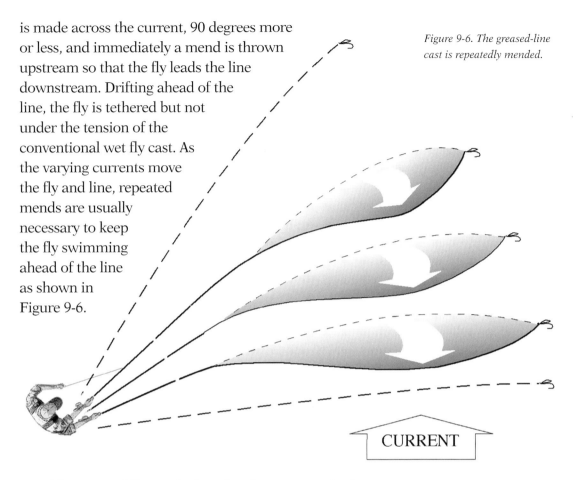

*Figure 9-6. The greased-line cast is repeatedly mended.*

CURRENT

The greased-line technique is advantageous in that, with repeated mends, you can lead your fly downstream for much of the drift while maintaining the broadside presentation. As shown in Figure 9-7, the path of the conventional wet fly is the arc a–g. Repeated slack mends at points b, c, d, etc., allow the fly to float downstream more than would otherwise be permitted on a taut line. The path of the fly, arc a–e, is somewhere between the downstream drift of a dry fly cast on a slack line and the tethered arc of the conventional wet fly. A slight downstream curve or bow in the line just prior to mending, in the words of Jock Scott, "helps to present the fly broadside to the fish; but it must not be allowed to develop into drag." As the fly starts its swing and nears the dangle, the fly necessarily must turn in line with the fly line as in the conventional presentation. Wood's view was that the greased-line portion of the drift

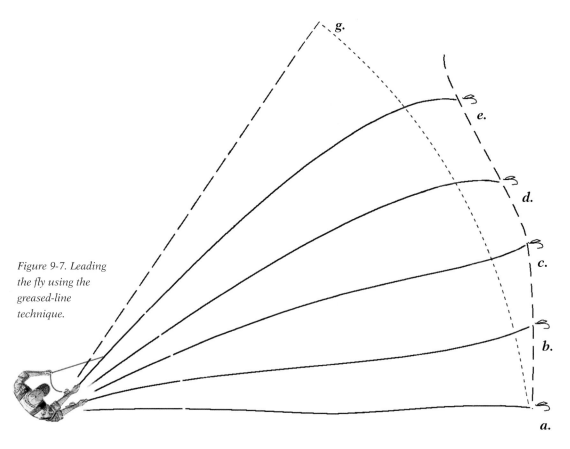

*Figure 9-7. Leading
the fly using the
greased-line
technique.*

was completed at
that point.
    Unlike the
conventional
tethered wet fly, the greased-line fly floats ahead of and
*somewhat* free of the leader. It is restrained but not towed
by the leader. If it were not restrained, it would sink to the
bottom. The key to a successful greased-line cast is to
present a fly that moves at the same speed as the current.
This may be accomplished by mending the line,
manipulating the fly, and selecting the proper fly size and
dressing. Mending plays such an important role in greased-
line fishing that long rods are desirable for optimal
manipulation of the line. Wood used a 12-foot single-
handed rod; many anglers use a long two-handed rod.
    The type of fly most desirable for greased-line fishing
has been the subject of much debate. Many anglers have

assumed that single-hook flies, particularly those dressed as low-water flies on lightweight hooks, are most appropriate. That assumption seems to be based on logic rather than on technique. A skilled angler can manipulate a greased-line fly, even a bulky one, to float with the current, come to a dead stop, or swim faster than the current. Anthony Crossley, an early and skillful proponent of the technique, greatly favored double-hook flies because of their better hooking capability. He demonstrated, as have others since, that double-hook flies, such as a Muddler Minnow, may be properly presented if greased lightly to prevent the fly from sinking too deeply.

In addition to a desirable presentation, an important advantage of the greased-line technique is its hooking ability. Flies, even double-hook ones, are seized and held in the mouth of the salmon as it returns to its lie. Unlike trout, salmon sense no urgency to expel a fly immediately. Jock Scott strongly emphasized the need to feed slack line freely to the fish, to let the bagging line pull the fly into the corner of the mouth where the fish hooks itself. The amount of slack depends upon the current: 2 to 3 feet in a slow current, 4 to 6 feet in a stronger current. There is seldom, if ever, a need to strike a salmon using this technique. The salmon hooks itself.

Of all the methods for fishing salmon, the greased-line technique is the least understood by the average angler and the most misunderstood by many writers, probably because it is so seldom practiced properly. In addition to the original interpretation by Jock Scott, lucid descriptions of the method have been presented by Lee Wulff in *The Atlantic Salmon* (58) and Hugh Falkus in *Salmon Fishing: A Practical Guide* (16). Unquestionably, the best review and most comprehensive discussion of the technique is Jim Vincent's "Steelhead on a Greased Line" article mentioned previously (52). The article covers not only the basic technique but also discusses such important parameters as presentation; drag; mending; flies; hooking; and the different types, temperatures, and colors of water. Vincent's article is that rare combination of technique, analysis, and critique by a perceptive angler.

**FISHING THE PATENT**. A method for drifting wet flies freely with the current was developed (discovered is a more appropriate word) by Col. Lewis S. Thompson in 1928 on the Restigouche River. It is called Thompson's Patent or simply the Patent method. A wet fly is cast on a slack line like a dry fly. Instead of floating freely on the surface as would the dry fly, the wet fly sinks and drifts with the current. The method was developed with the very large hairflies in use in those times, flies as large as 5/0. When used today, it may be employed with flies as small as size 6. Rather than appearing as an insect swimming with the current, the hair and feathers with which the fly is dressed pulse and quiver and thus present the appearance of life within the fly itself.

A brief history of the Patent is given in Bates' book, *Atlantic Salmon Flies and Fishing* (03), including a lengthy excerpt from Thompson's article in the March 1934 issue of *The Sportsman* that includes the following: "The method is simplicity itself. Throw it up- or downstream, at any angle, or straight across. Instead of having the line out straight, the rod will be stopped about 45 degrees and the line pulled up before the fly hits the water. The hair fly instead of having its hair all in a line as it would be on the end of a taut line is spread out in an A-shape, and it looks like no other fly on earth or in the water. You can use it on a dry (sinking) or a greased (floating) line."

Fishing the Patent is analogous to dry-fly fishing and has been described just that way: "dry fly fishing with a wet fly." The fly is cast with a slack line and sinks slowly depending on its size and the river currents. Because of the slack line, it is essential that the fly be visible, so that the angler may observe the take and know when to strike. The primary use of this method is to entice fish that have previously risen to a different fly or are resting in a known lie. Like the dry-fly drift, the Patent cast covers only a limited amount of water. It is not useful for searching the water.

**BACKING UP**. There are some situations in which you would like to surprise a fish with a first or fresh look at a fly without having the fish exposed to several successively approaching casts, as in the conventional downstream approach. Heavily fished waters, an insufficient current, jaded or dour fish, or the Hamlet fish, which first shows and then refuses to return, are typical examples. "Backing up" is just such a technique, most frequently employed after the water has been fished downstream in the conventional manner.

The basic concept for the wading angler is simple. Instead of fishing out a cast and then stepping down, as in the conventional wet-fly approach, cast directly across the stream (Figure 9–8a), and immediately begin to walk or back upstream (Figure 9–8b, c, d) to draw the fly more or

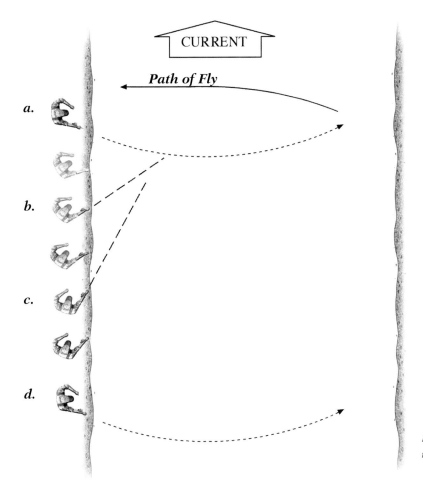

*Figure 9-8. Conventional method of backing up.*

less directly across the river toward the bank from which
you are casting. The rate at which you back up is
determined by the river current and the distance between
subsequent casts. As the river carries the fly downstream,
walk upstream at such a rate that the path of the fly is that
shown in Figure 9-8. This technique is similar to the
conventional wet-fly method in that it embodies guiding the
fly, mending as necessary, across the river as the current
carries it downstream. Properly executed, it draws the fly
across the vision of a resting salmon. The salmon sees the
fly approach from the side or even from behind and then
recede from its vision as the fly crosses the river. It does not
drift with the current as would an insect. The salmon is
often inclined to strike before the fly escapes from its vision.

However, if you intend to make a number of casts
while backing up, the proper path of the angler is not as
shown in Figure 9-8, for obvious reasons. If the angler
makes a 40-foot cast from point **a** and then backs
upstream without stripping in any line, he would be 40
feet upstream (Figure 9-8d) from where he started when
the fly reaches the dangle near point **a**. That's fine for one
cast, but a subsequent cast at point **d** leaves a 40-foot
interval between casts, which is obviously much too great.

To fish a stretch of water properly while backing up,
you must first decide approximately how close together
you want your casts. Clearly, you want them spaced
farther apart than in the conventional downriver
approach, but not as far apart as 40 feet. Technically, the
proper spacing depends on the depth and clarity of the
water in which the fish are resting. Fish are nearsighted
and in most rivers cannot clearly discern objects at
distances greater than 15 to 20 feet. Since we want our
salmon to get one unobstructed look at the fly, let's
assume that casts spaced 14 feet apart are appropriate,
recognizing that we may miss covering an occasional fish.

With the cast spacing in mind, the proper cast would
be much like that shown in Figure 9-9, where the first
cast is made from point **f** across the stream, with a
decided upriver mend so that a bagging line will not

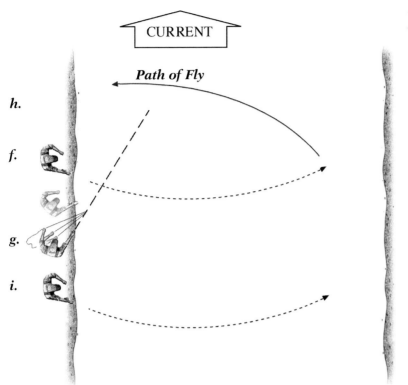

*Figure 9-9. Improved method of backing up.*

carry the fly across the current at too great a speed. The angler now backs 14 feet upstream toward point **i** while stripping in about 18 feet of line (Figure 9-9g). This produces a cross-current drift, with the fly approaching the dangle at point **h**, 22 feet downstream of the angler; it still provides the essential cross-river drift to the fly. If the angler did not strip in line, his fly would course downstream as a conventional wet-fly drift and would not provide the desired cross-river path. Now a second cast is made across the river from point **i**. The drift of the second cast will be approximately 14 feet upriver from the previous cast. This allows you to space your casts an appropriate distance, but not so widely that you fail to cover most of the water.

The backing-up technique is little known in North America. Most American salmon books do not even discuss it (as European books do not recognize the Patent method). This omission is undoubtedly due to the fact that backing up is generally done from shore, as along well-manicured paths in Scotland or Ireland. Backing up may be done by wading upstream in shallow water if conditions permit, but the shores of most Canadian rivers do not facilitate such wading. The technique is particularly useful in broad, smooth glides; in slack or low-water conditions; and where a strong upriver wind makes downstream casting impossible. The presentation is also said to be particularly effective at night for sea trout (anadromous brown trout). I have never used the technique on a long run or pool, but it's quite useful to cover short stretches of known lies or where a fish has jumped behind you.

A major advantage of the backing-up technique is the high proportion of hooked fish that are landed—much higher than for the downstream method. Not infrequently you will move several fish of which you were unaware when fishing down the run. As you approach the top of a pool or run, be sure to back further upstream so your fly covers all the water at the very top of the pool. An excellent discussion of backing up may be found in *Fly Fishing for Salmon* by Neil Graesser (22).

Backing up by canoe is unknown in North America, primarily because Canadian guides position their canoes in the river with an anchor and do not maintain canoe position by continuous rowing, as in Norway. Thorpe McKenzie declares emphatically that "backing up by boat is, by far, the most effective [method] with an experienced gillie on the rope or oars" (37b). It enables you to quietly position your canoe for the perfect cross-river cast.

**INDUCED COMMOTION.** In Chapter 4, I briefly discussed commotion flies, such as the Butterfly and Sili-leg Bomber, which, in and of themselves, create commotion as they are fished. There is also what I term *induced commotion*, in which action is imparted to the fly by the angler. The best-known induced commotion is that caused by the riffling hitch. Other induced commotion involves twitching or jigging the fly and the stripping retrieve.

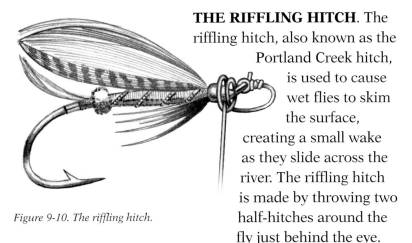

*Figure 9-10. The riffling hitch.*

**THE RIFFLING HITCH**. The riffling hitch, also known as the Portland Creek hitch, is used to cause wet flies to skim the surface, creating a small wake as they slide across the river. The riffling hitch is made by throwing two half-hitches around the fly just behind the eye. As discussed in Chapter 5, the exact configuration of the hitches is not important, as long as the knot is configured such that the leader pulls from the underside of the fly and leads from the fly on the side nearest the angler, as shown in Figure 9-10. When you are fishing from the left bank of a river (the bank is always determined by facing downriver), the hitch should be attached to the near or right side of the fly as the fly floats down the river. Most anglers just push or shift the hitch to the near side before casting. For double-hook flies, the leader should leave the knot on the bottom of the fly so that the leader will provide some lift to the fly as it rides the current.

A hitched fly should be fished on a tight leader so that it produces a noticeable wake on the surface of the water. If the fly sprays water, it is moving too fast. If you relax tension on the leader, the fly will sink.

Fishing the riffling hitch is an extremely effective technique for two reasons. It is always useful as a change of pace, particularly for stale fish. Frequently, a salmon that has seen every wet fly in the book and ignores dry flies will attack a hitched fly with gusto. If aggression is a salmon emotion, the hitched fly may well provoke it. Even more important is the perception that a fly riffling in the current presents the ideal speed at which to attract a salmon. Lee Wulff went so far as to state that "the most perfect speed is that at which a hitched fly riffles best." The riffling hitch should be part of every angler's arsenal. The technique is discussed in detail in a recent book by Art Lee, *Tying and Fishing the Riffling Hitch* (34).

Dry flies can also be caused to skim the surface without using a hitch. In the proper current, dry flies may be skimmed by raising your rod and drawing the line tight. As the fly rises on the surface, gently lead it across the stream at the slowest rate at which it will riffle on the surface. Don't lead too fast, or the fly will throw a spray of water.

**JIGGING**. Jigging or twitching is another method of imparting action to the swimming fly. As the fly courses through the water, the angler gently pumps the rod in a short jigging motion. The action must be short and sharp, usually once every two or three seconds, just enough to twitch the fly as if it were a nymph or drowning insect. Some anglers find jigging effective; most do not find it worth the effort. The first year our group fished the upper camp of the Riviere St. Jean on Quebec's north shore, the guides insisted we jig. I was perplexed because it's so unusual to find guides with such a dogmatic opinion on this subject. Only at the end of the week did we learn that this idea had been impressed upon the guides by the same would-be advisor who told them that dry flies didn't work on the St. Jean.

**STRIPPING**. Stripping in line to impart action as the fly courses downstream is a European technique that has been very slow to cross the Atlantic. Depending on the water, the strips may be 2, 6, or up to 15 inches in length. Generally, the shorter strips are quick and sharp, while the longer strips are slow and easy, but again there are no fixed rules. Try whatever proves effective for you. You should not strip in very fast water. In very slow water, long, slow strips may be the only means by which you can impart action to attract a fish. While fishing Lough Furnace in Ireland, my gillie recommended short 2- and 4-inch strips for my two-fly cast. In Norway, 8- to 14-inch strips are commonplace. My experience with stripping has been primarily on fast rivers such as the Alta and the

Laerdal where it is a proven technique with the long tube flies popular in those waters. It is especially useful in preventing fly "droop" as the fly enters slack water at the end of a cast.

Match your strips to the current. Use short strips for slow currents and placid waters. Long strips are best for the faster currents. How fast to strip is a question of judgment. Forty to fifty per minute is considered fast. However, one of the most accomplished salmon anglers I know, Lilla Rowcliffe of Surrey, England, does it differently. She uses a long two-handed rod, casts far, and strips very rapidly. On the Big Laxá in Iceland, I timed her stripping. Many times it was 90 to 100 per minute. Needless to say, stripping that rapidly, she covers a lot of water in the course of a morning. Is it productive? During the third week of July 1999, she caught 11 of the 25 salmon landed that week. All but three were over 14 pounds.

## FIGHTING THE SALMON

Once your fish is hooked, the fun begins. Most anglers handle themselves well until the salmon has taken the hook and is headed back to its lie. Then they tend to lose composure because, I'm convinced, of an improper mindset. All sporting endeavors have an element of mind games, and salmon angling is no exception. Fighting any salmon, we all worry during the first few minutes about whether the hook will pull out or the fish will throw the fly. Large jumping grilse used to be my nemesis because I did not treat them with the same respect as I do MSW salmon.

Four simple rules may help you to maintain composure:

**RULE 1**. Focus your attention on the fly or the tip of your line from the time your cast hits the water until the line dangles downstream of you. The instant you see a fish attack your fly, loosen your grip on the loop of line carried under the rod handle and allow the fish to take the fly and surge back toward its lie—if it wants to. As the line draws tight, the fish will hook itself. If the fish does not surge away, slowly raise your rod tip and firmly set the hook. The advantage of such concentration is that you are unlikely to be surprised by a rising fish and less likely to instinctively strike the fish like a trout fisherman. The late Father Elmer Smith of Prince William, New Brunswick— creator of the all-white Priest fly—is quoted in *Fishing Atlantic Salmon: The Flies and the Patterns* by Joseph Bates Jr. and Pamela Richards Bates (05) as saying that "the secret of success that often works is to pay more attention to fly movement than to fly speed."

**RULE 2**. Do not use a heavy drag during the first few minutes of the fight. I set my initial drag at about 3 ounces, just enough to prevent spool overrun, and then, unless it's an extremely large fish (30-pounds-plus), I tighten the drag only after the fish has made its first long run, which Wulff called "the surge." To quote Lee from *Leaping Silver* (59): "With that first surge of power spent, the salmon will be much easier to handle. Then he'll be like a man who has just sprinted a hundred yards, out of breath although still possessed of his strength." As will be described in the next chapter, I learned more about fighting salmon while landing my first Sixteen-Twenty fish than I did in the previous 20 years. That fish ran something over 100 yards against a 3-ounce drag, but I was always in complete control. I have long recommended that beginning salmon anglers set their drag at a measured 8 ounces and leave it there. Anglers are often afraid a large salmon will run away from them because they have heard too many tales about 200- and 250-yard runs. That's utter nonsense. Those stories are gross fabrications. A 150-yard run is deathly tiring to any but a monstrous 40-pound fish. Besides, most salmon are reluctant to leave their immediate pool. Only if you have hooked a fish immediately above a very long rapids need you fear a fish running away.

**RULE 3**. Give slack line to a jumping fish. Everyone knows the age-old adage: Bow to the jumping salmon.

Literally, dip your rod tip or thrust your rod toward the salmon to create a slack line so that the fish cannot snap your leader during its jump. Salmon cannot easily throw a hook as do trout and tarpon. Unless the fish is very poorly hooked, in which case there is nothing you can do about it, a jumping salmon is unlikely to throw the hook if you give it slack. It is very hard for trout fishermen, or most any of us, to overcome the tendency to hold the line tight during a jump. One of the most gratifying feelings is to tighten up on the salmon after a jump and find that it is still on your line.

**RULE 4**. After the initial run, fight your fish forcefully with the midportion of your rod, not the rod tip. If you keep your rod tip near the surface of the water, you will be forced to fight the fish with a lateral pull. It is preferable, if possible, to fight the fish from the side on which it is hooked. If you hooked the fish so that the hook is in its right jaw, try to fight the fish from that (near) side. If you must fight a fish hooked on the "far" side of its mouth, fight a bit less forcefully, since the far hooking is somewhat more likely to pull out.

Try to keep the fish off balance. As the position of the fish permits, pull first ahead of the fish (say, to your right) and then behind the fish (to your left). That's absolutely the best way to tire a salmon. This is where the 8-ounce drag rule is helpful. It's enough drag to tire most fish but not so much that the hook will pull out or the fish will break the leader. Note that I have used the term *fight*. You fight a fish forcefully; you don't "play" a salmon, particularly if you intend to release it. Too often, playing less than forcefully results in a salmon so exhausted that it cannot survive. I once watched in horror as a friend "played" a 22-pound fish for 75 minutes! Literally, he nursed it to death. The rule of thumb (attributed to Lee Wulff) for the time required by the average angler to land a large salmon is a minute per pound. That's a good median, although there may be exceptions for grilse. I've landed some in less than a minute, but then a bouncing 6 1/2-pound fresh grilse once took me almost 12 minutes on light tackle.

You can exert much more control over a salmon than you realize. You can even lead them upstream away from a rapids or downstream toward a convenient beaching area. Twenty-odd years ago, on my first trip to the Grímsá River in Iceland, I was fishing Svartistokkur, a narrow run about 250 yards long with 20-foot rock cliffs on either side. Casting from the high bank, I succeeded in hooking a 16-pound hen lying at the head of the run, but there was no way I could land her there. Remembering Lee Wulff's advice, I gently tightened the line and walked the fish downstream 200 yards to a convenient beaching point. If you lead the fish steadily, without any waiver or quiver in your line, most will follow like a gentle collie on a leash. But the lead must be a steady, firm pull. If your line pulses or vibrates, as when reeling, the fish will become alarmed and will always react vigorously. Trout, incidentally, can also be led away from an obstruction or to the top of a pool in the same manner. Anglers tend to play a fish warily because they are afraid they will lose it. If you fight too gingerly, you will. The best advice is retain your composure, use a light drag, bow to a jumping fish, and hang tough.

When a fish is reeled in close to shore, watch its head. Attempt to maintain control; try not to let the fish run far. If possible, keep your rod more or less perpendicular to the line so the tip will absorb any sudden moves by the salmon. Keep your fish parallel to, in line with, the leader. It may shake its head but so positioned it cannot roll up onto the leader and break it. If possible, force it to back up so as to deprive it of oxygen. Once you get the fish into slack water and it is deprived of oxygen, it will give up. In this new era of salmon conservation, that's the secret for gently landing your fish quickly so that it may be released to continue its spawning journey.

Few anglers realize that a salmon can be defeated "psychologically." Think about it. Why can we land a 20- or 30-pound salmon on a 6- or 8-pound tippet? Because the fish gives up. If tired fish went limp, became a dead weight, and sulked on the bottom of the river, we might never retrieve them. But they don't. Once their energy is exhausted, they can be led as if on a leash. Then you only need worry about a sudden roll on the leader or the thrashing that inevitably occurs as the fish approaches the shore.

## LAST CASTS

None of us knows enough about the enigmatic salmon or fishing the wet fly under ever-changing conditions. The best salmon anglers are those who repeatedly fish a given stretch of river and know virtually every rock and rapid. But that knowledge transcends to another river only in principle. Every pool of every river is as different as are the strains of fish themselves. What works in one pool or river is not necessarily successful in another.

Before composing this chapter, I reviewed a number of major works. Some authors emphasize technique; others prefer anecdotes. Some write in a cursory manner; others compose more skillfully. Collectively, they just about say it all. With great reluctance I finally determined not to include some advanced subjects in this book, among them run timing, reading the water, taking behaviors and notes on the best taking times, which are between 10:00 A.M. and noon, and 6:30 and 8:30 P.M. in most of Canada and Scotland. (Did you know that virtually no salmon are caught between 1:00 and 4:00 P.M.? That's nap time for the angler.) These are subjects that are properly assimilated under the tutelage of a skilled guide or mentor. For those so inclined to pursue these matters, the most complete reference is *Salmon Fishing: A Practical Guide* by the late Hugh Falkus (16), which is the only thorough presentation of all these subjects. I think so highly of Falkus' work that is easy to forgive his last 80 pages on fishing with bait.

Sometimes I summarize salmon fishing as preparation, presentation, and pugnacity. And the greatest of these is presentation. Properly presenting the fly is an art—the indefinable essence for successfully fishing the wet fly.

*A Big Salmon*
Watercolor
9 3/4 x 14 1/4 inches
Author's Collection

# Chapter 10

# Fishing Very Small Flies

### LITTLE FLY, BIG FISH

We were beginning our third drop of the evening. Jim, my guide, had just let the canoe drift down another 60 feet and was setting the anchor in Pool Number 4. I again checked the drag on my McNeese reel, an anti-reverse reel with one of the smoothest drags ever devised. It was almost filled with a TT8F line and 300 yards of 35-pound Spectra backing—the new multifilament gel-spun polyethylene backing that has replaced braided Dacron for many purposes. Of course, no one needs 300 yards of backing for salmon, but it came in one continuous length, and I had been reluctant to cut it back to the more usual 200 yards. The drag on the reel was unusually light, about 3 ounces, just enough to prevent an overrun. My rod that evening was a 9 1/2-foot for an 8-weight line, made of second-generation graphite. It was slightly soft in the tip, a property that was highly desirable for the task at hand.

As I ran the leader through my fingers, I checked

**325**

carefully for wind knots, particularly in the 24-inch tippet section that had been cut from 6-pound IGFA fluorocarbon material. I had deliberately chosen the fluorocarbon product because of its enhanced abrasion resistance, a lower refractive index that makes it somewhat less visible, and especially for its specific gravity that would help my tiny size 16, single-hook flies to sink. I had observed that unless the fly bodies were properly proportioned and made of nonsynthetic materials, these 16s might easily float or wake on the surface.

Changing flies, I carefully knotted another no-name creation with a Sixteen-Twenty loop knot. If properly tightened, this knot is every bit as strong as the leader material itself. In all my salmon fishing, I tighten my knots with a small pair of pliers until the knot barely slips on itself. Then I place the bend of the hook between the leaves of my nippers and carefully but firmly secure the knot against the eye of the hook as tightly as I can without breaking the leader. Of course, with 12-pound or stronger leaders, you can pull with considerable strength.

Jim secured the anchor and nodded that I should begin fishing. This time we were on the left side of the current, so I stripped out about 8 feet of line, stood up in the canoe, and began casting to my right. Three times I floated out the cast. Stripping out an additional 4 feet of line, I made a fourth cast. The fly floated about 20 feet, suddenly the line tightened, and immediately the fly and line tip sank into 5 feet of water. As I sat down in the canoe, Jim looked up and asked what was the matter.

"Fish on," I replied.

"Trout?" Jim asked.

"No," I said. "It's not dancing. It's just sitting on the bottom. Lift the anchor."

Still somewhat puzzled, Jim carefully lifted the anchor and began to row the canoe downstream of the fish while I maintained a very light tension on the line. Now some 70 feet below the fish, I started ever so gently to tighten the line. There was no slack.

The fish began to stir and moved out into the main

current. As it did, I slackened the line so the fish could move easily and begin to tire itself without a mad rush and jump for freedom. After mildly agitating the fish for perhaps two minutes, I again began to tighten the line. The fish began its first run of perhaps 90 feet, culminating in a straight-up leap. As it cleared the water, we realized it was a good fish, definitely larger than 15 pounds. Now the fish was moving downstream faster than I could recapture line. Pumping the rod was of no avail against the light drag.

Meanwhile, Jim was rowing the canoe downstream toward a sandy beach 500 yards below us. As we crossed out of the main current of the Moisie and crossed into the Ouapetec current where it joins the Moisie, the fish came alive. Suddenly, it was making its long dash for freedom. As something over 80 yards of backing disappeared, I began to think seriously of tightening the drag. I hesitated, knowing that the tension of that much line in the water was already increasing the drag. At about 100 yards, just as I reached for the drag knob, the fish exploded straight up in a tremendous jump. With my rod pointed low, almost in the water, I instantly thrust the rod toward the fish to create as much slack as possible. With such a small hook, my greatest concern was that the fish would fall back on the leader and tear out the hook.

With that jump behind us it was, as Lee Wulff used to say, just a matter of hanging on. I made about three turns of the reel handle when suddenly the line went slack. I reeled furiously but felt nothing. I was sick. Had the hook pulled out? For what seemed like an eternity, in reality not more than about 50 seconds, I retrieved slack line—some 75 yards of it. Suddenly, the line tightened ever so slightly. The fish was still on. In retrospect, it is obvious that the drag of the line pulling downstream on the fish caused it to swim upstream directly toward me to escape the drag. (Trout as well as salmon react in this manner; it's a very useful tactic when you want to move a fish upstream of you.)

Now the end of the fly line was back on the reel. As the fish felt the line tightening, it made one more half-hearted jump. Obviously, it was tiring. Our only worry then was that the hook might not hold, particularly as we tried to net the fish. I stepped from the canoe and asked Jim to enter the water some 30 feet downstream. He waded to knee depth, lowered his net into the river, and waited motionless. As the fish approached Jim, I tightened the drag a bit and then backed slowly up the sloping bank away from the water, lifting the rod tip sufficiently to raise the salmon's head. On the first pass, the fish veered away from Jim, so I gently gave enough line for the fish to back downstream some 20 feet. Again, I lifted the rod tip and took several steps backward to bring the fish in toward Jim. One lift of the net and the salmon was ours. The entire fight took 24 minutes.

The rest of the experience was as nerve-wracking as the fight. Immediately after the capture, we took the fish to camp and weighed it on a very old Chatillon spring scale: 19 pounds, 4 ounces—12 ounces shy of qualifying for the Sixteen-Twenty Club. My elation turned to despair. Was I, like others before me, to be denied by a few ounces? Very dejected, I told Jim not to clean the fish but to ice it thoroughly. I have no idea why I gave such instructions. It was as if a premonition was guiding me.

Before dinner that evening I commented to Jim that I was puzzled because a salmon 38 inches long should weigh about 22 pounds. Nothing more was said until breakfast the next morning when Jim announced that a supply plane would be in about noon, and he would send the fish down to Sept Isles. Unbeknownst to me, the plan was to reweigh the fish in town. I heard nothing more until Lucien Rolland and Marc Prefontaine flew into camp the following Saturday.

"Congratulations, Mr. Nightingale," they said.

"What did I do?" I asked.

"You are in the club," they answered, "the Sixteen-Twenty Club."

It turns out that on a certified scale some 22 hours after its capture, the fish weighed 9.19 kilograms (20.26 pounds). Thus, I became the fifth person to have landed a 20-plus-pound salmon on a size 16 single-hook fly.

Four months later, in November 1995, this fish was recognized by the IGFA as the world record for the 3-kilogram (6.6-pound) leader class.

## SMALL FLY TACTICS

Almost every fish we catch can teach us something if only we pause long enough to observe. The experience described above was one of the most enlightening of my entire fishing career. It has added an entirely new dimension to my fishing, a transition from the mechanics of "catching" to the appreciation of artful angling. It also taught me that fishing very small flies is an art unlike any other salmon angling.

Few among us have ever had a large salmon sip a fly at the surface without either showing itself or at least creating a wake or swirl. It is so unusual that my guide could not believe that I had hooked a salmon. It's not unusual for a large salmon to take the fly and return to its lie. However, we generally do not give the fish sufficient slack in the line to do so. On a tight line, the fish is instantly alarmed and begins a flight for freedom. That's why Jim hesitated to lift the anchor. Never before had he experienced an unseen salmon take the fly and settle back on the bottom of the river for more than two minutes.

Many times I have been asked what it takes to land a large salmon on a very small hook. Always my answer is preparation, perseverance, and providence. First you must have a large fish attack your fly. But it's careful preparation that lands the fish. The one word that best describes the preparation is *resilience*. My rod was long (9 1/2 feet) and relatively limber. The anti-reverse reel provided assurance against my clutching the reel handle an instant too long. My leader tippet was connected through a Bimini Twist, which provided additional resilience in the leader.

When I decided to pursue the Sixteen-Twenty goal, I spent several months that first winter testing hooks. I knew that the hook had to be a true trout-size 16 with a gape of about 1/8 inch. An oversized hook, such as the Partridge Wilson series, would not qualify. Obviously, the most important quality would be the strength of the hook. Other features such as the body length, hook lead, and wire size were of secondary consideration. The results of testing a number of standard hooks were appalling, for the hooks from several well-known manufacturers straightened at 3 to 3 1/2 pounds of pull. When the Gaelic Supreme wet-fly and nymph hooks by Sprite of Reddich were brought to my attention, I knew I had the answer. The Gaelic nymph hook has a round bend, 3x-long body, and half-upturned eye, and is well tempered. It will not deform at less than 6 pounds. Furthermore, recent experience with this hook has been outstanding. It seemingly never fails to set in the fish's jaw. Once set, that small hook never pulls out. If the fish is lost, it's because the leader broke.

Once I settled on the hook, it was a simple matter to tie flies with various sizes of bodies. In addition to standard patterns, such as the Green Butt and Silver and Rusty Rats, I tied a number of no-name specials using very fine materials that fit the scale of the hook. Varying styles of size 16 flies are shown in Figure 10-2 (see page 335).

The actual Lady Mary fly on which I landed my qualifying fish is shown in the center of Figure 10-2. It turns out that with an overall length of 0.8 inch, this is the smallest fly on which a qualifying fish has ever been landed. Prior to tying my size 16s, I had not seen samples of the larger flies used by my predecessors. The dressing for the Lady Mary, named after the fact in honor of my wife, is given in Chapter 6.

One way of preparing larger flies is to first snell your hook with the appropriate leader and then tie whatever body, hackle, and wing you wish forward past the eye of the hook using the leader as part of the fly body. A Lady Joan fly of more typical size (1.2 inches) with the body and hackle tied out onto the leader is shown at the top of Figure 10-2. Such flies may easily be tied up to 1 1/2 inches or more in length, the equivalent length (but not the bulk) of a standard size 4 wet fly.

Relatively large dry flies are easily constructed, providing that the underside of the fly body is clipped away so as not to impair the gape of the hook. The Prefontaine dry fly shown in Figure 10-2, with an overall length of 2.4 inches, is tied in such a manner.

The Mickey Finn is a streamer fly in which the wing extends well behind the barb of the hook. Some feel, erroneously I believe, that such hook placement on large flies increases the chance that the odd salmon will nip at the tail of the fly and not be hooked. Such concern is of no consequence with these small flies, although a fly tied on a 1/2- or 1-inch tube (similar to the Green Butt shown in Figure 10-2 on page 335) does assist in placing the hook toward the rear of the fly. All things considered, tubes such as these are the best way to prepare these very small flies, both wet and dry. Because the eyes of these small hooks are smaller than the inside diameter of the tubes, it is necessary to wrap or build up the hook shank just behind the eye to prevent the hook from slipping into the tube. More recently I have developed a better alternative. Cement a small brass bead onto the hook just behind the eye (see Figure 4-1 on pages 105–106). The diameter of the bead is chosen to slip tightly into the tube body. It's a simple, foolproof way of fitting hooks into tubes. Alternatively, you may insert a short section of 1/16-inch tubing into the rear of the tube, into which you then push the hook itself.

It is difficult to force size 16 wet flies to sink properly, especially if they are tied with synthetic materials or on plastic tubes. It helps to use tinsel or floss and natural, not synthetic, hair. The use of denser fluorocarbon leaders or tippets is also desirable, particularly in slow water. In faster water you may wish to insert a 1-foot lead head (see Chapter 6) between your line and your leader to assist the fly in riding at the proper depth.

For use in Iceland and Europe, where weighted flies are permissible, I prefer tube flies tied on 1/2-inch aluminum tubes. The weight of the tube eliminates any problems with small flies floating or waking on the surface.

With only limited experience in hooking salmon of 20

or even 16 pounds on very small hooks, it is difficult to determine where fly patterns matter at all. It is my opinion that the shape and configuration of very small flies are most important. You should strive to create a significant profile. Bright flies and dark flies have their usual significance, depending on the sky, but details of coloration seem less significant than with larger flies.

The actual playing of a salmon on a size 16 single hook is determined by the manner in which the salmon reacts. Mine largely spent itself on its long run, so I did not face a protracted downriver fight. That is exactly what Lee Wulff recommended almost 30 years ago: let the fish expend its energy with a long run or two. It is surprising how tiring a very long run is to a fish tethered to your line. Edward Hewitt is quoted as remarking that he never saw a salmon swim 200 yards without giving up. It's so tiring that the fish will frequently turn upstream to seek additional oxygen from the current. A fish's blood constitutes only about 2 1/2 percent of its body weight, and its oxygen-carrying capacity is much less than for mammals, whose blood is typically eight percent of the body weight. If the fish sulks behind a boulder or in a deep hole, it regains oxygen and you face a protracted fight that always favors the fish. That's what makes landing 27- and 30-pound fish on small hooks so very difficult. You are constrained by how much pressure you can put on the fish, yet if you do not force the fight, the fish will wait you out. The critical point comes when you reel in the fish for landing. That's the time that the hook is most likely to pull free. Were you fishing a size 16 treble, you could be assured that one of the barbs would be secure. With a single hook, you never know until it's over.

A very light drag is absolutely essential for hooking and playing large salmon on small hooks. I recommend a drag of not more than 3 ounces to start. Once the fish is hooked, let it make at least one long run to tire itself and then tighten your drag to about 1/2 pound and commence the fight. Don't be afraid to force the fight. Those small size 16 hooks do not pull out easily. Most of us hook so few large fish that we invariably overreact when a fish is hooked. We strike too hard, use too much drag on the reel, and we may even add additional drag by fingering the line. Salmon, unlike trout, cannot easily throw a small hook. But they sure can break a taut leader.

My second Sixteen-Twenty fish was more exciting than the first because I could anticipate the action as it unfolded. The fish, estimated at 23 to 26 pounds, took my Green Butt tube fly at the end of the chute where the Ouapetec River spills into the Moisie. Instantly the fish surged 20 yards up into the rapids, where it made a tremendous leap, and then slid back into the quieter water below. I stepped into the canoe and John E., my guide, cautiously worked the canoe below the fish, where after two minutes of relative inactivity I gradually tightened on the salmon. The fish made a short 30-yard run downstream, then turned upstream, and we began a tug of war. I reeled; it ran. I reeled harder; it ran farther.

This time I was using my Bringsén reel, which is ideally suited for this kind of fight since both reel and drag control are in the handle (see Chapter 3). After reeling in line, I instantly reversed the handle to minimize the drag. If I needed additional drag to snub the fish's surge, I placed my thumb on the revolving spool. When the fish stopped, I reeled. At one point I began to question whether my 6-pound leader could outlast this very strong fish. Then I noticed than the runs were shorter, the tug on the line weaker; I began to regain line. With less than 60 feet of line out, I reeled in the fish for netting.

And then disaster struck. Aware that most fish are lost at the net, I carefully instructed John to wade out knee deep, immerse his net in the water, and remain motionless until I led the fish over the net. Unfortunately, it did not work that way. When the fish was about 2 feet from the net, John reached out and touched the fish with the net, whereupon the fish rolled on the leader and in an instant was gone. The leader broke about halfway up the tippet, suggesting that it may have been frayed on a submerged rock. That's one fishing experience I never

*Opposite page, top:
Figure 10-1. The author with
his first Sixteen-Twenty
salmon.*

*Opposite page, bottom: Figure
10-2. A variety of size 16
single-hook flies, clockwise
from top: Lady Joan tied
forward onto the leader
(courtesy of Lucien Rolland),
Black Bear-Green Butt (by the
author), Elver (by the
author), Mickey Finn (by the
author), Prefontaine
(courtesy of Lucien Rolland);
and center: Lady Mary (by the
author).*

wish to duplicate. The action was exhilarating; the result was devastating.

Even that experience taught me something that has since been very helpful in landing other fish. When you reel in a fish, ideally you want the fish's body to be in line with your fly line and leader. The in-line configuration prevents the fish from rolling up the leader. The fish can only shake its head, a condition far less likely to free the fish than a roll. As I reeled in this second fish for landing, I remember noticing that the fish's body was at a 50-degree angle to the line. Before I could correct the situation, John reached out, the fish rolled, and it was free.

## THE SIXTEEN-TWENTY CLUB

The Sixteen-Twenty Club has been called the "world's most exclusive angler's club" because membership is by accomplishment only, an admittedly difficult feat. The idea for the club was conceived in 1964 by Lee Wulff and five friends at the Moisie-Ouapetec Camp, owned by the Prefontaine family. Lee was preaching the joy of using light tackle, and the discussion turned to how big a fish you could land on a very small hook. Eventually, membership in the club was based on catching a salmon of over 20 pounds on a size 16 single hook, which was considered the minimum practical size.

Alain Prefontaine became the founding member of the club on July 11, l964, with a fish of 20 1/2 pounds. Four days later, on July 15, 1964, Lee Wulff landed a 23 1/2-pound fish and thus became the second member. Four years passed before Lucien Rolland became the third member with a 23-pounder on July 14, 1968. Numerous others vied for membership over the years, but always they were thwarted. Finally on July 9, 1984, Marc Prefontaine joined the club with a fine salmon of 23 1/2 pounds. Eleven years would pass before I became the fifth member with a hen fish of 20 1/4 pounds on July 6, 1995.

On August 27, 1998, Karin Caine of Montreal, Quebec, became the sixth member of the club with a 45-

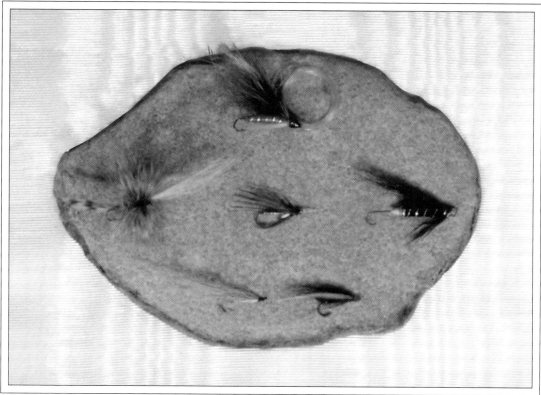

Top: Figure 10-3. Lucien
Rolland with Marc
Prefontaine (left) awarding the
Sixteen-Twenty pin to the
author.

Bottom: Figure 10-4. Karin
Caine (second from right)
receiving congratulations from
Joan Wulff with (left to right)
John Houghton, Chairman,
ASF (Canada); the author; and
Katharine Mott, Vice-
Chairman, ASF (Canada).
Photo courtesy of Bill Caine.

inch hen fish (estimated at 32 pounds) caught out of Club
de Peche au Saumon le Canadien, Inc. on the
Bonaventure River. The fish took a green and black
Karin's Ecstasy tied on the same Sprite hook I use, and it
was landed in 25 minutes. Her success was well deserved.
During the previous three years, Karin had landed at least
12 grilse and four salmon on size 16 hooks, not including
one likely qualifier that was lost in a rapids. The real
significance of her accomplishment is that she has
become the first angler to break the magical 30-pound
mark on a size 16 single hook.

Except for Lee Wulff, repeat performances have not
come easily. Lee caught a total of 11 qualifying salmon,
his largest being 27 pounds. As he wrote on several
occasions, one of his great disappointments was never
achieving the 30-pound mark. One person did succeed in
landing a 30-pounder some years ago, but the fish was
disqualified because it had been hooked by the guide. As
this is written, Lucien Rolland has caught three qualifying
fish over 20 pounds, including one on a Gray Wulff dry fly
on the Grand Cascapedia on August 13, 1978. So far, the
author has been limited to one fish landed and one
"released by the net."

## LAST CASTS

Membership in the Sixteen-Twenty Club holds special
significance for me. It took me a year to fully realize what
I had done, to appreciate the skill of the accomplishment
and the luck that got me there. Like so many things in life,
it's the joy of skillful achievement that remains after the
accolades have ceased.

Nothing is more exciting than fighting a large salmon
on very light tackle. On light tackle, you come close to
seeing the fish in its own environment, to meeting the fish
on its own terms. All of a sudden, landing the fish
becomes secondary. Keeping the fish is inconsequential.
Of such is the true joy of angling.

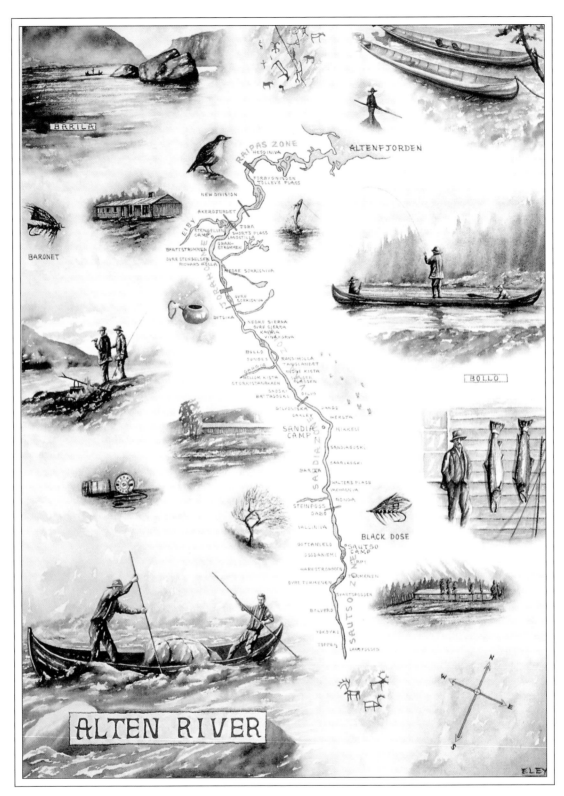

*The Alta River Map by David Eley*
Watercolor
Author's Collection

# Chapter 11

# Sacred Rivers of the Salmon

## IN THE SHADOW OF THE GREAT STEEPLECHASE

There I was, the cool, collected technician standing in the midst of the "Platform of Despair," so nervous I could scarcely keep my balance let alone cast a mean line into that frothy, fury boiling under me. For once in my 50-year fishing career, I was overwhelmed by the river that surrounded me. I could sense the spirit of Charles Ritz guiding me, reminding me that, yes, I might hook a salmon but, no, I would not land it in that maelstrom.

By a fluke of the weather and the overwhelming generosity of my hosts, I was fishing the Årøy, one of the most legendary rivers in all salmondom. A sheet of white foam flowing toward the Sognefjord at three times the velocity of the Restigouche or the Moisie, the Årøy carries a physical ferocity, a historic aura, and the largest salmon in Norway, if not in all the world. It's not the most beautiful of rivers; there are many more glamorous in

339

*Figure 11-1. The nervous author fishing from the "Platform of Despair," the Årøy River in Norway.*

Norway or Canada. It's certainly not the most fishable, rivaling the upper gorge of the Alta as the most unfishable. That's why Charles Ritz labeled it "the great steeplechase course" in his book *A Fly Fisher's Life* (46). But I was enjoying what many only dream about, the opportunity to at least hook a 40-plus-pound salmon.

I was experiencing what others have written with poetic lyricism—that fishing Atlantic salmon is not just about catching salmon on a fly. It's about the romance of rivers and one's encounter with the noblest of God's creatures. It's about the craft of the angler, skillfully searching and artfully attacking an unseen quarry. It's about man being engulfed by the spirit of the river and, win or lose, reliving the encounter in his dreams forever.

Salmon fishermen are very possessive of their favorite river. They guard its reputation and are quick to take offense at those who would besmirch its honor or deprecate its prestige. Normally, this is not a concern for the beginning salmon angler, except to the extent that it may affect the venue you select for your induction into the bondage of rivers.

# CANADA

The most difficult question facing the neophyte angler is where to start. Salmon fishing in the United States is virtually nonexistent since January 1, 2000, when the Maine rivers were closed for all migratory Atlantic salmon angling. Canada is the place to start, but where? Salmon fishing is not inexpensive. If you value your time, even at wage rates, the trade-off between time and money is problematical. In general there are three levels at which one may pursue the salmon: (a) the itinerant or auto-camper who arranges his own accommodations and fishes public, lottery, or ticketed waters, often without a guide where permitted; (b) the public salmon camps, which offer differing levels of accommodations for fishing both public and private waters; and (c) the private camps with full accommodations offering guided fishing on private waters, usually for six days or a week.

For those with a friend to guide them, fishing public waters may be the most adventurous. It enables you to explore the different waters and to readily sample various locations, but it requires time, often a great deal of time. In my younger trout-fishing days, I often opted for that type of experience. In later years, with limited vacation time, I could never afford the time to explore new salmon venues. A summary of these types of opportunities for New Brunswick and the Gaspé Peninsula of Quebec may be found in Paul Marriner's *Atlantic Salmon: A Fly Fishing Primer* (37).

**THE MIRAMICHI RIVER**. Nowhere is the concept of public salmon camps utilizing both public and private waters better exemplified than along the Miramichi River in New Brunswick. The Miramichi River, along with its tributaries, is the largest and most productive salmon river in North America. Now that extensive netting of

*Figure 11-2. Map of the Miramichi River by Erin M. Hunt. Courtesy of Larry Hunt.*

MSW fish in the estuary and on the Northwest Miramichi has been controlled, the Miramichi system is beginning to recover some of its former fame. The annual run of fish averages more than 100,000 salmon and grilse. This run now is estimated to contain one-third of all the MSW salmon returning to North American rivers, up from the historical level of 11 percent. This significant increase reflects the serious decline in MSW salmon in other rivers, as well as the renewed vitality of the Miramichi system. While MSW salmon constitute only about 25

*Figure 11-3. The upper Miramichi River near McNamee, New Brunswick.*

percent of the run and are greatly outnumbered by grilse, increasing numbers of 30-pound salmon are seen or caught in the system each year.

The Miramichi offers a long season for the salmon angler, the longest in North America. When anglers speak of the Miramichi, unless otherwise indicated, they mean the main Southwest Miramichi River, where the season opens April 15 for kelts while the black salmon are still in the river and, with exceptions, continues through October 15. The portion of the main river above Burntland Brook closes September 30, the portion above Juniper Forks closes September 15, and the entire upper river above Rocky Brook closes August 31. These restrictions protect those fish that have reached the prime spawning grounds. The first run of large salmon begins in early July and continues into August, when large numbers of grilse appear. The fall run of salmon on the main Southwest Miramichi and its Cains tributary is larger than the

*Figure 11-4. The lower
Miramichi River near
Blackville, New Brunswick.*

summer run, although the fall fish tend to move upriver
rather quickly. If you can fish the main river about the
time of the full moon in September or early October, the
fishing can be outstanding.

A slow-flowing river, in most places the Miramichi is
easy to wade, which also makes it easier to land fish. By
convention, canoes are not employed on the river except
during the kelt season in April and May, when very high
water prevents wading. Salmon anglers on the Miramichi
typically employ 9- or 9 1/2-foot rods with an 8- or a 9-
weight line. Single-hook flies are the more popular,
approximately twice as popular as are double hooks, a
preference that I personally do not share. In addition to
the four wet fly patterns discussed in Chapter 4, three
local patterns are in vogue: the ubiquitous Green
Machine, the Butterfly, and, for fall fishing, the Chief
Needahbeh. All are discussed in Chapter 4.

The Miramichi is the ideal starting point for the
beginning salmon angler to fish both public and private
waters under the tutelage of an experienced camp operator

assisted by competent guides. Open to all fishermen, these public camps provide the optimum experience for limited budgets. Along the Main Southwest Miramichi, there are numerous well-known and dependable public camps, beginning above the village of Renous and continuing upstream to Boiestown. A number of such camps are advertised in each issue of the *Atlantic Salmon Journal*.

By virtue of the sheer number of fish and the opportunity to catch 20- and 30-pound salmon, the Miramichi is a world-class river. For the American angler, the Miramichi offers proximity, availability, and excellent grilse fishing, as well as the possibility for large salmon. That combination is hard to match.

**THE MOISIE, THE RESTIGOUCHE, AND THE GRAND CASCAPEDIA.** Large rivers tend to produce large salmon, and these three rivers and their tributaries stand above all others for one reason: they are the big-fish rivers of Canada. Each year fish weighing 30, 40, and—on rare occasions—even 50 pounds are landed on one or more of these rivers. Most of the water on these three rivers is privately owned or held on long-term leases from the Canadian provinces where, except for the Grand Cascapedia, public access to the better waters is very limited. Nevertheless, each of these rivers has well-equipped private camps that do accept guests and provide generous accommodations. Sometimes it seems the prices charged for a week on these rivers is anything but modest. However, if you consider that all camp costs must be amortized over a six- to eight-week season, the prices are far from exorbitant.

The Moisie and the Restigouche are comparable rivers but differ in meaningful respects. The Moisie is the longer and larger river with three significant tributaries, two of which hold very large salmon. The Restigouche, together with its four major tributaries, is more heavily fished and yields more fish over 30 pounds. In the last six years, two fish over 60 pounds have been landed in the Restigouche. Fifty- and reportedly 60-pound fish have been hooked in the Moisie, but, aided by strong river currents, none has been landed. Over the years, the catch of MSW on each river has been similar, although since 1989 the Moisie has yielded somewhat more MSW salmon than has the Restigouche.

The Restigouche has a much larger population of grilse than either the Moisie or the Grand Cascapedia. Table 11-1 compares the average annual catch of MSW salmon for the three rivers for the nine-year period between 1988 and 1996, together with average percentage of grilse in the catch. You will note that more than 50 percent of the catch on the Restigouche is 1SW fish. Grilse on the Grand Cascapedia make up about 8 percent of the catch, while on average only 2 percent of the fish in the Moisie are grilse.

The Restigouche and its principal tributaries—the Matapedia, Upsalquitch, Patapedia, and Kedgwick— appeal to many anglers because the large grilse population promises success while the presence of large salmon proposes excitement. Between the estuary at Campbellton and the Kedgwick Lodge on the Little Main Restigouche above Kedgwick, New Brunswick, there are some 18

**TABLE 11-1**
**CATCH OF MULTI-SEA-WINTER SALMON ON THREE RIVERS**
**1988–1996**

| River | MSW Salmon 9-Yr. Total No. | MSW Salmon Range No./Yr. | MSW Salmon Average No./Yr. | 1SW Grilse Range No./Yr. | 1SW Grilse Avg. % of Total |
|---|---|---|---|---|---|
| Grand Cascapedia | 8,888 | 826–1,127 | 988 | 38–129 | 8.0 |
| Moisie | 14,297 | 717–2,262 | 1,588 | 14–52 | 2.1 |
| Restigouche* | 14,576 | 678–3,312 | 1,822 | 790–3,942 | 52.9 |

* 8 years, 1988–1995

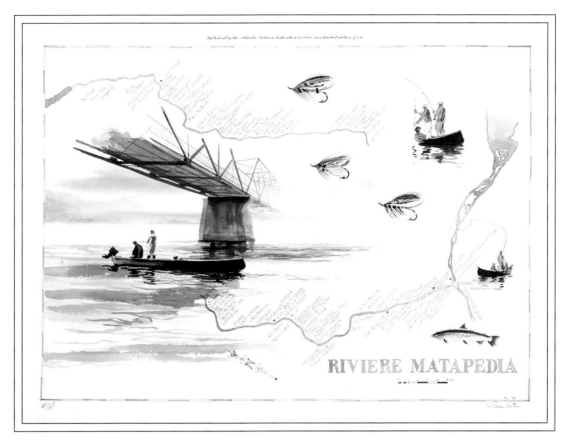

Figure 11-5. Map of the Matapedia River by Pierre Lutz. Reprinted by permission of the Atlantic Salmon Federation.

camps, at least four of which are open to the public. They are Pinkham's Lodge at Tide Head, New Brunswick; Grog Island located three miles above Matapedia, Quebec (for spring and early summer fishing); Red Pine Mountain Lodge near St. Jean Baptiste, New Brunswick; and the Kedgwick Lodge. Larry's Gulch, upriver from Kedgwick, is operated by the Department of Natural Resources and Energy of the Province of New Brunswick and occasionally is available for booking, particularly during the catch-and-release season beginning September 1.

The tackle used on the Restigouche and Matapedia Rivers is identical to that for the Miramichi except for local preferences in fly patterns. Green, yellow, or gold flies— such as the Green Highlander, the various Cossebooms, and the Colburns—are popular on the Restigouche system and the clear water rivers of the Gaspé Peninsula.

The Grand Cascapedia, located on the Gaspé Peninsula, empties into the Bay of Chaleur 60 miles east

of Matapedia, Quebec. Much smaller than the
Restigouche, it is a magnificent river, swift and dangerous
with alternating rapids and deep pools. It's a perfect
example of Alex Bielak's dissertation hypothesis that the
geomorphology and harshness of a river determine the
ultimate size of the fish in the river (06). Rising in the
Chic Choc Mountains on the north side of the Gaspé, the
Grand Cascapedia offers 60 miles of fishable water.
Historically, six private camps controlled most of the
river: Horse Island, Lorne Cottage, New Derreen, Middle
Camp, Tracadie, and Three Islands. In 1982, the private
camps joined with local native and non-native residents to
form the *Société de Gestion du saumon de la rivière
Cascapédia inc.*, one of the most interesting affiliations of
diverse fishing interests found anywhere. Formed in place
of a *zone d'exploitation controlée* (ZEC) found elsewhere
on the Gaspé, the society controls the fishing on the entire
river. It leases back to the six lodges those sections of the

*Above: Figure 11-7. The lower
Matapedia River, two miles
upstream from the junction
with the Restigouche.*

*Opposite page: Figure 11-6.
The Restigouche River at
Brandy Brook, Quebec.*

*Above: Figure 11-8. Map of the Grand Cascapedia River by Pierre Lutz. Reprinted by permission of the Atlantic Salmon Society.*

*Opposite page: Figure 11-9. Pool 47, Big Jonathan, on the Grand Cascapedia River, Quebec.*

river that the lodges had traditionally held. The society then arranges daily fishing by permit on the entire river. Half of the society's board of directors is composed of native or First Nation residents. The other half of the board is non-native residents, many of who traditionally operated the camps and guided on the river. The private camps, in addition to providing most of the employment in the river valley, share their pools with public anglers on strictly rationed allotments that prevent overfishing. One pool per camp, usually the home pool in front of the lodge, is reserved for camp use only. During its 17 years of operation, the society has become the model for managing Canadian salmon waters for the benefit of all.

Nine-foot single-handed rods and short two-handed rods are standard on the Grand Cascapedia. Fly patterns are similar to those used on the Restigouche, with one exception. There is a local preference for stonefly patterns

of all colors, including the "toothpick" models that incorporate toothpicks into the body of the fly to help this abomination to float. I like the stonefly fished wet, but I much prefer to fish tube flies or Bombers on the surface than to cope with a damp, barely floating stonefly.

An interesting account of the major sporting camps on the rivers of Quebec, including the Restigouche, the Matapedia, and those of the Gaspé and the Quebec north shore, is presented in Sylvain Gingras' book, *A Century of Sport* (20).

For me and for many, the Moisie is the queen of the Canadian rivers. Its recorded history began in 1535, when Jacques Cartier discovered what he thought briefly to be the legendary Northwest Passage to the Orient. An excellent summary of the history of the Moisie from 1858 through 1970 is given in *The Moisie Salmon Club*, a book by Edward Weeks on the history of the Moisie Salmon Club (53).

The Moisie rises in northern Quebec and flows south 240 miles through the Laurentian Plateau, entering the Gulf of St. Lawrence 11 miles east of Sept Iles, Quebec. The Moisie is a rapidly flowing river somewhat larger than the Restigouche, and its fishable portion flows 91 miles from the Katchapahun Pass (also known as the Obstruction) to the St. Lawrence. Its passage is impeded only by small rapids above and below Camp Joseph, the infamous chute of the Cran Serré and the "twelve mile" rapids above the Moisie Salmon Club. The first seven miles of the lower river is public water open to anyone on a daily fee basis. Immediately above the public water is that of the Moisie Salmon Club, the first of six camps on the main river. The second camp is located upriver at mile 28, at the junction of the west and east (Nipissis) branches of the river and is operated by Moisie Nipissis Outfitters, which also maintains a satellite camp near the railroad bridge at mile 13 1/2. Camp Dorée at mile 39 is located at the mouth of the Dorée River. Camp Ouapetec at mile 60 is at the junction of the Moisie and Ouapetec Rivers, and Camp Joseph is located at about mile 70 near the mouth of the Joseph River. Both are operated by Moisie Ouapetec

*Opposite page: Figure 11-10. The Katchapahun Pass, 91 miles upriver from the St. Lawrence Seaway, was the upper limit of salmon migration prior to the installation of a fish ladder in 1966.*

Outfitters. The uppermost, or Haute Moisie Camp, is located at about mile 90, a mile below the Katchapahun Pass, or great falls. Before the installation of a fish ladder in 1966, these falls prevented the migration of the salmon farther upstream. In addition, there is a camp, operated on a casual basis by the Montagnais Indians, on the Nipissis River about 12 miles up from the fork with the Moisie. The Forks, Dorée, Joseph, Haute Moisie, and Nipissis camps all accept guests, but availability is limited due to the great demand for all of these venues.

As is true of all great rivers, the Moisie has several distinct strains of salmon. The fish ascending the East Branch or Nipissis River are more slender, with a lower condition factor (weight-to-length ratio) than those of the main river. Bielak has analyzed the historical catch data for the two branches (06). He suggests this may be one of a few well-defined cases where the fish have genetically adapted themselves to develop the physical profile required to negotiate the "Chute" rapids of the Nipissis two miles upriver from the forks. Fish bound for the Nipissis branch arrive at the mile 28 junction some 10 days later than those ascending the main branch. East-branch fish must wait until the heavy June water flow through the chutes subsides before attempting to ascend the Nipissis.

The salmon ascending the west branch of the Moisie are, for a given length, heavier, with broader tails and a higher condition factor than those of the east branch. West- or main-branch female salmon weighing 20.5 pounds are, on average, 2.5 centimeters (1 inch) shorter than their east-branch counterparts. Before ascending the Ouapetec, many very large fish rest at the junction pool at mile 60 where the Ouapetec enters the Moisie. In 1995, I observed in the counting trap two miles up the Ouapetec River two hen salmon, one weighing 36 pounds and the other something more than 40—it was so large it could not be weighed accurately. Anecdotal evidence suggests that a few super salmon weighing more than 50 pounds enter the river very early each year and rapidly ascend the main river to the Katchapahun Pass and beyond.

*Figure 11-11. The Moisie River at the junction with the Ouapetec River.*

The tackle used on the Moisie is similar to that for the Restigouche or Miramichi except that two-handed rods and 10-weight single-handed rods are more common on the lower river during the high water of early June. Flies for the Moisie are unique in that, along with the usual patterns recommended in Chapter 4, small black flies, sizes 8 and 10, are very popular. Local patterns include the Black Moisie, the Monroe Killer, and the Undertaker. I particularly like the Kola Rat described in Chapter 4.

Because of its mountains and rugged gorges, its tempestuous waters and large salmon, the Moisie is the epitome of the perfect salmon river. Many honor it as the greatest of our North American salmon rivers. It was so suggested to Edward Weeks, who relates how a member of the Moisie Salmon Club requested that he name his book "The Sacred River." Weeks rejected that title (in favor of *The Moisie Salmon Club* [53]) on the basis that, however honored, "no river is sacred in America." I am not so confident about that. For this piscator, the Moisie is my sacred river.

# ICELAND

Iceland, like Ireland, is a delightful place to fish. The weather is mild and the people friendly. The majority of the younger folk speak fluent English. The principal advantage of Iceland is that by any measure the fishing can be outstanding. Iceland has more than 100 salmon rivers, of which one knowledgeable writer rates 20 as world class. That's an exaggeration in as much as few rivers in Iceland yield salmon more than 20 pounds, but there is an excellent variety of productive rivers from which to choose: from the tiny Ellidaár running through the center of the capital, Reykjavik, to the mighty Laxá í Adaldal in northeastern Iceland.

The Icelandic rivers are the best-managed salmon rivers in the world. No salmon are harvested in any of the waters surrounding Iceland. In 1932, the government banned all ocean fishing and coastal netting, except for a few estuary nets that have since been removed. The last six were removed in 1997 thanks to the efforts of Orri Vigfusson and the North Atlantic Salmon Fund. All rivers are carefully managed for maximum productivity and are well maintained by river associations composed of the farmers who own the surrounding land and the fishing rights. The enviable result is that there is virtually no poaching. Fishing is permitted for 12 hours per day between 7:00 A.M. and 10:00 P.M. with a compulsory midday break. Generally, the schedule provides fishing from 7:00 A.M. until 1:00 P.M., and then again from 4:00 P.M. until 10:00 P.M. For the dedicated angler, it's the perfect way to accumulate a significant sleep deficit. A summary of Icelandic fishing is given in Philip Lee's book, *Home Pool: The Fight to Save the Atlantic Salmon* (35).

**THE GRÍMSÁ**. On my first visit to Iceland in 1977, I fished the Grímsá, which is located about two hours north of Reykjavik. A modest-sized river, the Grímsá, along with the Thverá and the more famous Nordurá, empties into the Hvitá River, a milky glacial river originating in the

*Figure 11-12. The Grímsá River upstream from the Laxfoss.*

Langjökull glacier to the east. Usually the Grímsá fishes 10 rods on five beats with 67 named pools on the main river and 21 more on the small Tunguá tributary. Not all the pools are fished regularly, and in August the Tunguá is closed to all fishing to protect the spawning grounds.

Two decades ago, you could catch—or at least hook—record numbers of fish in the Grímsá, not unlike the situation today with the Ponoi River on the Kola Peninsula of Russia. My first week on the Grímsá, I landed 23 fish and lost 24 more. Not bad for a neophyte. The Grímsá remains today an excellent river for those seeking the all-around experience. An attractive lodge sitting on the edge of the Laxfoss (falls) was built in 1973; it is well maintained and offers excellent food. Some of the pools are easy to reach by paths from the lodge, but an automobile is required to reach the majority of the upriver pools.

**THE LAXÁ Á ÁSUM.** The Laxá á Ásum River, located on the north coast of Iceland just below the town of

Blonduós, has until recent years been the most prolific salmon river in the world. To those fishing only two rods, the river typically yielded an incredible average of seven fish per rod per day throughout the 90-day season. In high season, 20 fish days were common. It seems inconceivable that a two-rod river could yield 1,200 to 1,400 fish per season. A "millionaire's river," the Laxá á Ásum is the most expensive salmon river in the world. Yet because it is so prolific, it is fully booked for a year or more in advance.

This short, easily waded river rises in the outflow of Lake Laxávatn and flows 15 kilometers through rolling farmland to the Húnavatn estuary, which it shares with the famous Vatnsdalsá. These two rivers, in turn, join the well-known Vididalsá at the neck of the Húna fjord to form what may be the greatest concentration of world-class rivers found anywhere.

Proving the axiom that small rivers produce small fish, the Ásum salmon are small, running 6 to 10 pounds, with a surfeit of grilse. In the last three years, the rod catch on the Laxá á Ásum has diminished for unexplained reasons. Whether this is related to the general disappearance of smolts at sea is unknown. Certainly, the future for this once-fabled river is unclear at this writing.

**THE LAXÁ Í ADALDAL**. The Laxá í Adaldal River, near the northeastern town of Húsavik, is arguably the best salmon river in Iceland. One of the two largest salmon rivers in the country, with a nominal flow rate of 45 to 50 cubic meters per second (cms), the Laxá í Adaldal is only marginally smaller than the Miramichi (with a midsummer mean monthly flow of about 54 cms). It contains the largest salmon in Iceland. Each year the "Big Laxá," as it's known, yields fish up to 30 pounds. In any other Icelandic river a 20-pound fish is considered unusually large. The Laxá truly is a world-class river.

The fishable portion of the river is approximately 30 kilometers. The river is fed by the outflow from Lake Myvatn, which aids in maintaining a constant flow and a somewhat constant water temperature. However, the

*Opposite page: Figure 11-13. The lower Laxá á Ásum River near Blonduós.*

weather in this part of Iceland is influenced primarily by the polar breezes off the Greenland Sea to the north, and the air temperature during a week may vary widely from the mid-40s to 80°F.

The upper portion of the lower river, known as the Arnes beats, is controlled by the Steingrimsdottir family, who operate the Veidiheimilid Lodge and provide guide services for eight rods. The very comfortable lodge contains two single and five double rooms with bath *en suite*, plus two single rooms with adjacent bath. The food is outstanding, often prepared by vacationing chefs from Reykjavik. Relatively expensive bookings are generally available not more than a year in advance.

A two-handed 10-weight rod at least 14 feet long is desirable in fighting the northerly upriver winds on the Big Laxá. Shorter rods are fine for windless days, but a single-handed rod is almost useless on this river. Traditional North American flies are widely used in Iceland. In addition, a number of local fly patterns that are particularly effective have been developed. Blue flies such as the Blue Charm, the Hairy Mary, and the Laxá Blue are particularly desirable. On bright days and in late summer, green patterns such as the Green Highlander, the Cosseboom, the Green Pearl, and even black-and-green stoneflies are very productive, presumably because they reflect the colors of the hillside vegetation and the weed-strewn river. Other unique patterns include the Sweep, Black Sheep, and Collie Dog. The latter two may be tied on double hooks or Esmond Drury trebles or as tube flies. Tube flies are very popular in Iceland, with hook sizes ranging from size 4 down to size 14, or even size 16 trebles for the tiny microflies popularized in recent years. As in Norway, and unlike in North America, long tubes are also frequently employed. It continues to puzzle me why the Norwegians and Icelanders can catch salmon on 5- and 6-inch-long flies, but we in North America have been taught that salmon will only nip at the tails of such lures. Clearly, this is one subject on which Lee Wulff's teachings need to be revisited.

*Opposite page: Figure 11-14. Fossbrún or Falls pool on Arnes beat number 7, Laxá í Adaldal River.*

# NORWAY

Norway is a storied land of Vikings and the Sami people, of the nisser[1] and the trolls, of millennia-old *stavkyrkje* (stave churches) and ultramodern bridges, of fjords and rivers and their salmon. The fabled salmon rivers of Norway, once sullied by netting, poaching, and lawless overfishing, are struggling to regain their fame. A few have remained unspoiled, but the future of many lies in a tenuous balance between restoration and depredation.

Fly fishing for salmon as we know it today was introduced to Norway during the mid-19th century by the British nobility, who leased and developed the best rivers. Such rivers became known as the "Lords' Rivers" and included the Alta, the Årøy, the Diva, the Laerdal, the Mals, the Namsen, the Rauma, the Stjørdal, the Tana, and the Vosso. Many of these remain among the best rivers today, but not all.

**THE VOSSO**. For many years the Vosso River northeast of Bergen produced the heaviest average fish in all of Norway and was surpassed only by the Årøy for the largest individual fish. Cyril Mowbray Wells, a housemaster at Eton College, fished the Vosso from 1920 until 1950, during which time he caught 1,496 salmon weighing 40,896 pounds. That's an average of 50 fish per season with an average weight of 27 pounds, totally inconceivable in today's world. Thanks to several decades of trawler overfishing off the Bergen Coast, the unregulated netting and lawless exploitation in the Bergen fjord and the estuaries, and incredible poaching in the river, increasingly few of the genetically programmed large salmon reached the spawning grounds. By 1992, natural spawning in the river had collapsed. The annual run of salmon in the Vosso had diminished so drastically that the river was closed to all fishing for six years in hopes of restoring the once-mystic run of large salmon. In

---

1. Small Christmas people.

the interim, another man-induced disaster has dashed hope for an early return to greatness: pen-raised escapees.

The fjords around Bergen are the home to salmon farming on a scale so immense that is difficult to believe. Acres and acres of fish may be seen happily frolicking about their pens as you tour the fjords or travel by rail from Bergen to Voss. As you might expect, not all those fish stay in their pens. Seals frequently rip and storms break apart the pens from which these fish, with indiscriminate pedigrees and of unknown gene pools, flee to the nearest river in response to the spawning urge. The Norwegian Fishery Board estimated that along the Norwegian coast in 1996 there were two to three times more escaped farmed salmon than wild salmon. Many of the escapees have adopted the Vosso and other valued rivers as their "natal" stream with the obvious consequences. They are cross-breeding with the indigenous Vosso strains. Incredible as it may seem, at a NASCO Conference in Bath, England, in April 1997, farm spokesmen admitted that many salmon had been deliberately released into the fjords, and they even argued that the inevitable crossbreeding was not detrimental. The reason for this devious act was that Norwegian farmed salmon were flooding the European Union market. Under pressure from the European Union, of which Norway is not a member, the Norwegian government reduced the subsidies to the salmon farms. The farm owners responded by dumping their surplus fish.

What the resulting salmon stocks will be in the Vosso and other rivers is subject to conjecture, but the consequences seem dire. A survey of the Vosso redds in 1996 indicated that 60 to 80 percent of the spawning fish were farm escapees. Of 148 fish captured for the hatchery, 112 (81 percent) were farmed salmon. It seems likely that the tough, heavy-bodied fish for which the Vosso was famous are on the verge of extinction. The anticipated reopening of the river in 2000 should provide much-needed information on the effect of undesirable interbreeding.

**THE LAERDAL**. Long proclaimed as the queen of Norwegian rivers and the river of kings, the Laerdal is an aristocrat among salmon rivers. More kings and celebrities have trod its shores than those of any other river. Rising in the mountains southeast of Borlaug, the river flows swiftly through the Laerdal Valley into the Sognefjord at the town of Laerdal. One authority rates the valley as one of the three most beautiful in all of Norway.

The fishable portion of the Laerdal River between the fjord and the Sjurhaug waterfall is 13 miles. Historically, the Laerdal was the most prolific river in Norway. In the years immediately following World War II, the Laerdal yielded twice as many rod-caught salmon as the Alta and three to four times as many as the Tana/Teno, the boundary river with Finland.

Like too many Norwegian rivers, the Laerdal was devastated between 1960 and 1988 by an indiscriminate long-line fishery in the sea and by Norwegian drift netting along the coast and in the fjords. The nettings also destroyed the fabulous prewar runs of sea trout for which the river was famous. The long lines were eliminated in 1972, but the drift netting was not banned until August 1988. Slowly, the Laerdal was beginning to regain its reputation. In 1996, the Laerdal yielded 344 salmon, with an average weight of 15.8 pounds, which was the largest average in all of Norway because the river contains so few grilse.

This remarkable recovery terminated abruptly in the fall of 1996 when the fluke *Gyrodactylus salaris* was discovered in the river. This parasite was first observed in Norwegian rivers in the early 1970s, and it eventually spread to 39 rivers (and 38 hatcheries). The fluke kills salmon parr by attacking their fins and skin. It may be eliminated with treatments of Rotenone, which suffocates gilled species, but such treatments must be scaled to kill all the fish life to deprive the parasite of the host needed to propagate in the river. Less severe treatments may not eliminate the parasite. The first Rotenone treatment of the Laerdal was made in April 1997 and a second that August. As a result, the river is expected to be closed to all fishing until the year 2002. For leaseholders and the anglers to whom the river is so beloved, the prospects for the next decade are not encouraging.

As salmon rivers go, the Laerdal is of modest size, about one-third the width of the lower Miramichi but with a velocity two to three times that of the Miramichi and similar woodland rivers of North America. In 1996, the Laerdal suffered a severe drought resulting from the lack of snow pack in the southern mountains. During August of that year, the river flow fell to an unfishable low of 17 cms, comparable to the near-record low of 18.3 cms in the Miramichi during the drought of August 1995. A month later, the Laerdal flow was down to 8 cms. (A flow of 8 cms is about 2,500 gallons per second, the volume contained in a modest backyard swimming pool.) Under normal conditions, if the flow drops below 20 cms for five consecutive days, the river owners can demand the release of additional water, up to 12 million cubic meters per season, from the power dams in the mountains. One of the ironies of the 1996 drought was the inability of the dams to release water to maintain the flow in the Laerdal. In 1996, there was none available. Many of the mountain reservoirs were virtually dry.

A crystal river flowing so fast you dare not wade, the Laerdal offers both challenge and opportunity. All Laerdal fishing is from the river bank or from wooden walkways or platforms hung along the rocky walls of the canyon. The manner in which you fish such water is similar to our normal wet-fly tactics except that the fly moves much faster in the water and you must adapt accordingly. On my first trip to the Laerdal, I was hypnotized watching the movement of my fly in the transparent waters, something that usually goes unnoticed in the tannic waters of the North American forests. It was also educational in that I could observe how best to manipulate my fly with the two-handed rod.

An experienced master of the river, Børge Hansen recommended a stripping tactic that is widely used in European rivers but infrequently encountered in North

America. As the fly swept through the limpid water, Børge retrieved line in short 6- to 14-inch strips, hoping the salmon would be enticed by an escaping quarry. He summarized his technique with the surprising statement that he rarely caught a salmon unless the fly was being stripped forward as it drifted downstream in the usual arc from river center toward the near shore. Many anglers believe that salmon will not chase an elusive quarry. I have since wondered if this stripping technique was developed to keep the heavier aluminum and copper tube flies used in high water nearer to the river's surface. In any event, it's widely used throughout Europe, and it works.

Børge advised me that in low water, under a bright August sun, I should not expect to find fish lying in open water, no matter how deep the pool. These are smart fish; they know to hide from the sun. Instead of lying at the tail of the pool or deep in the middle, the fish were found under the oxygen-rich whitewater at the head of the pool. Thus protected from the sun's rays, they were also well-shielded from the angler's barbs. The only fish caught that particular week was lured by a large fly that was allowed to drift downstream from the pool above.

As are many accomplished anglers, Børge is also a bit of a philosopher. The proper salmon fly, Børge insists, must have "a little black, a little blue, a little silver, and much luck." How could it be said better?

By North American standards, many Norwegian lures are outrageously long. The swift, rocky rivers demand a fly that is easily seen by the fish. Flies, especially tubes 4 to 6 inches long with treble hooks, are commonplace. None of the dainty 10s and 12s we use on the Moisie. Fishing tube flies in the crystal-clear waters of the Laerdal was an interesting experience. It was exciting to follow the gyrations of a Sun Ray Shadow as it swirled in the quirky currents of this tumultuous river. Who said that underwater flies cannot create commotion?

The Laerdal is a very intimate river, one you want to embrace and never leave. Its salmon pools are among the finest found anywhere. The Bjorkum pool is one of the

*Opposite page: Figure 11-15. The Laerdal River downstream of the famous Bjorkum pool.*

most magnificent salmon pools on earth. It ranks with the Malangfoss on the Mals, the Niedre Sierra on the Alta, and the Million Dollar Pool on the Restigouche as the best of the best. Seductive is an understatement. The scenery and the people make fishing the Laerdal a memorable experience even if you never land a fish.

**THE ÅRØY**. If ever there was a private river, the Årøy is it. Flowing from Lake Hofslo on the northern side of the Sognefjord, the Årøy was once home to the largest salmon in the world. The river has been controlled since the mid-1920s for all but six years by only two lessees. From the 1920s until 1965, Nicolas Denissoff, one-time finance minister to Czar Nicholas II of Russia, leased the river and subleased portions of it. He bought out netting rights in the fjord, stocked the river from his private hatchery, and pursued every opportunity to preserve the heavy-bodied fish for which the river was famous. One of the most memorable pictures from the Denissoff period is that of the cardboard outlines of four salmon weighing 53, 54, 54, and 58 pounds respectively, all caught in the same year. The world record for the largest fly-caught salmon is an Årøy fish of 76 pounds landed by Denissoff in August 1921.

The aging Denissoff relinquished his lease in 1965, and through 1971 the Årøy lease was shared by the Brooks family and four other parties. Since 1971, the Årøy has been leased by Jacques Bemberg, who reserves it for the private use of family and friends throughout the short season.

Less than three-quarters of a mile long, a third of which is unfishable rapids, the Årøy is one of the shortest salmon rivers in the world. It is fairly deep, but only 25 to 45 yards wide. The river no longer begins with the impassable Helvedesfoss waterfall below Lake Hofslo, but flows from a tunnel cut into the mountainside, the exit flume from the power-generating station above. Fishing the Årøy is an experience unlike any other. Because the heavy currents flow right to the bank, there is no wading. You cast from the shore or from fishing platforms built on piles driven into the river bottom.

*Figure 11-16. The Årøy River—notice the weir, in the right-front of the picture, beneath which the salmon may rest.*

These are affectionately and respectfully known as the "Platforms of Despair." One such platform, that shown in Figure 11-1 (page 340), actually crosses the river.

At strategic points throughout the upper river are plank weirs also mounted on piles. The weirs slope downstream at a 45-degree angle and are constructed of 2-inch by 6-inch boards on 8-inch centers. The 2-inch gap between boards allows water to surge through the weir, creating a quiescent area immediately downstream in which the salmon may rest. I am convinced that the real reason for those gaps is a fiendish plot to snag your flies as they wash through the weir.

The tackle used on the Årøy is best described as monstrous: heavy two-handed rods and sturdy reels with 300 yards of backing. In Denissoff's day, anglers used 17-foot split-cane rods specially constructed in Reddich, England. Today, the rods are heavy graphite. Today's leaders are short lengths of 45- or 50-pound nylon.

*Figure 11-17. John Nesset, third-generation river keeper on the Årøy River, displaying the cutouts of four 50-pound salmon in Charles Ritz's book,* A Fly Fisher's Life.

Denissoff's leaders consisted of three strands of 25-pound gut (later nylon) twisted together to form a 75-pound leader. The purpose of such heavy tackle was to snub any fish hooked upstream of the Great Rapids. If a fish reaches the rapids, there is no return.

**THE ALTA**. The Alta is unquestionably the best salmon river in the world today. While not as prolific as the Laxá á Ásum or the Ponoi in Russia, the Alta is extremely well managed to produce quantities of very large salmon. It rivals the Laxá á Ásum as one of the most expensive of salmon rivers. Even so, only occasionally are rods available to the non-native angler.

The river originates high in the Finmark Plateau south of Kautokeino and collects behind a 360-foot-high dam located in the Alta Canyon a mile upriver of the impassable Longfossen Rapids. Water from the head pool flows through a mile-long tunnel, some 15 feet in diameter, to

enter the river at Toppen, the uppermost salmon pool on
the river. Downriver of Toppen, the Alta Canyon is the
deepest and longest in northern Europe. The river flows
swiftly northward for 27 miles to the fjord at the town of
Alta. The river proper is owned by the state, but the fishing
rights are controlled by the Alta Laksefiskeri
Interessentskup, an association of 220 landowners from a
special district within the Alta Kommune. All Alta residents
are entitled to fish the river without charge until
Midsummer Day (June 24), but only with flies. From June
24 through July 11, the river is leased for successive six-day
periods to three syndicates composed largely of Americans,
for whom catch-and-release is strongly encouraged.

From July 12 through August 16, local residents are
offered the opportunity for prime fishing with flies only
by participating in a lottery held each March. Typically
3,000 entries seek 400 cards, each valid for 18 hours of
fishing a specific beat on a given day. As in many such
lotteries, the best 200 cards go quickly; the remaining,
lesser openings are often slow to fill. Prime tickets are
often resold by the lottery winners for substantial sums.
The last two weeks of August are again leased, one week
to each of two international syndicates.

Fishing during the June/July lease period is divided
into five beats of two rods each. Except for the Sautso or
upper zone, where some wading is productive, all fishing
takes place from narrow river boats, each with two guides
or boatmen. For reasons that are lost in tradition, fishing
begins at 8:00 P.M. and continues until 4:00 A.M., with a
lunch break at midnight. In the land of the midnight sun,
this schedule has the obvious advantage of fishing in low
light rather than in the bright sun of midday. Because the
river normally flows so swiftly, the high-prow Sami-style
river boats are used exclusively. The boats are 28 feet long,
4 feet wide, and 18 inches deep, and they provide a very
stable platform from which to cast. The boats are not
anchored but are maintained in position by the bow
oarsman, who rows at a constant cadence of 60 strokes
per minute. The stern boatman deftly slides the boat back

ATLANTIC SALMON CHRONICLES

*Above: Figure 11-18. A downriver view of Toppen Pool and the Alta River from the tunnel portal.*

*Opposite page: Figure 11-19. The upper Alta River near Sautso.*

and forth across the river with his 11-inch-wide stern paddle. Operating in unison, the boatmen skillfully cover the productive water downstream of the boat with virtually no false casting and a minimum of mending. It's quite an experience to fish a long run with the boatmen for 30 or 40 minutes without anyone speaking a word.

In August, the fishing is condensed into four beats of two rods each. August fishing hours are from 12:00 or 1:00 P.M. until 8:00 or 9:00 P.M. with a lunch break at about 4:00 P.M. During the low water of August, several pools on the upper Sautso and Sandia beats are wadable. The beats for both the June/July and August periods are rotated so that everyone fishes all the water. Typically three nights are spent at the lower Stengelsen lodge and three at the Sandia and Sautso lodges on the upper river.

The Alta is a large river, and large rivers require long rods. While there are a number of runs and pools where the single-handed rod may be used satisfactorily, a 12- to

*Figure 11-20. The lower Alta River near Stengelsen.*

*Figure 11-21. The Borgund Stavkyrkje in the Laerdal Valley.*

16-foot two-handed rod with a suitably fast action for overhead casting is preferred for the Alta. The long rod is advantageous in reaching the seams of currents where large fish often lie, such as the Nedre Sierra Pool on the Vina beat. In that pool, the boat is walked down the shoreline by the bow boatman while the angler casts 50 feet across a slow current to reach the seam of the faster current along which the large fish lie. This is also one of the few pools on the river where, because of a brushy shoreline, a true Spey rod with a soft action is advantageous for roll casting. Several beats, including the Nedre Sierra Pool, are also fished by roping. One of the guides holds the boat with a 50-foot length of rope, while the other guide manipulates the boat just off shore with either a pole or oars. This technique is particularly appropriate where a strong current runs along a brush- or tree-lined shore that prevents backcasts across the current.

Flies of every description are used on the Alta, including large doubles, Waddington shanks, and Esmond Drury trebles. Tube flies dominate the selection for midsummer fishing, in part because the fly size can be selected independently of the hook. Size 6 and 8 treble hooks are the most popular for all tubes. In high water, aluminum and copper tubes are used to sink the fly to the level at which the fish are holding. Waddington shanks are very popular for both midsummer and August fishing. Popular patterns include the Sun Ray Shadow and the Red and Black; goat hair flies such as the all-black Alta Ghost, the Alta Red, and the Alta Blue Charm; various shrimp patterns such as Ally's Shrimp; and, best of all, the Willie Gunn in any configuration.

The quality of Alta fishing has been maintained over the years by the consortium of river owners, who, like their Icelandic brethren, recognize that quality sport fishing yields a financial return far exceeding that of any agricultural or aquacultural endeavor. Thirty-pound salmon are very common, and a half-dozen or more 40-pounders are caught each year. The 50-pound fish is no longer a summertime routine, although five between 50 and 54 pounds were taken in the 1990s. The average weight of the 743 MSW salmon caught in 1996 was 22.4 pounds, an average boosted by the fact that there are virtually no salmon between 10 and 20 pounds (2SW fish). Recent studies have disclosed that the bulk of spawning fish in the river are 3SW hens and 1SW cock grilse. Unlike in the Canadian rivers, many of the robust 6- and 7-pound grilse return to the sea after spawning and return two years later as 3SW repeat spawners. Most of the truly large salmon, over 40 pounds, are MSW repeat-spawning cock fish that do not survive to spawn again.

In spite of its very large salmon, the average weight of all fly-caught fish in the Alta was a very modest 8.4 pounds in 1996 and 9.9 pounds in 1997 because of the large number of grilse in the river. Before 1989, the drift nets in the sea off the Norwegian coast captured large numbers of grilse. When the netting was eliminated in 1989, the grilse catch immediately jumped from 500 to 600 per year to its present level of 1,600 to 2,000. For those of us who feel we have caught one too many grilse, those Alta fish provide a totally new dimension. A 7-pound Alta grilse is one terrific acrobat.

Anyone fishing in Norway should allow a week for sightseeing. Rich in Nordic culture and breathless scenery, Norway offers a new adventure around every curve in the road. Some of the mandatory sights are the stave churches dating from the Middle Ages. As of 1995, there were 32 of these magnificent structures still standing, although several have since been torched by vandals. The oldest, the Heddal church in Telemark, was consecrated on October 25, 1147. The Borgund columnar church, located 25 kilometers upriver from Laerdal, was built in the first half of the 13th century and is the only *stavekyrkje* not to have undergone significant renovation.

For those interested in native cultures, I particularly recommend a visit to Karasjok and Kautokeino in Finnmark, the center of the Sami (Lapp) culture. Even if you do not fish, a visit to Alta is worthwhile just to view and explore the rock carvings of the Komsa culture.

Dating from the late Stone Age, 4200 to 500 B.C., the carvings present a fascinating written history of the Stone-Age culture of this region.

## FINLAND

The boundary between Finland and Norway is marked for more than 200 miles by one of the great river systems of the salmon world. Yet this magnificent river is virtually unknown to most North American anglers. The Finns call the main river the Teno (Tenojoki); the Norwegians know it as the Tana (Tanaelva). Rising in the Finnmark Plateau of northern Finland and northeastern Norway, the river drains an enormous area bounded on the east by Lake Inari on the Finnish-Russian border and on the west by the Alta River watershed.

The Teno/Tana River is huge by any standard, larger than any other salmon river in Norway and much larger than any Atlantic salmon river in Canada outside the Ungava region. The lower 40 miles of the river flow northward entirely within Norway. The river enters the Tana fjord some 60 miles west of Kirkenes and 75 miles east-southeast of the North Cape, Europe's northernmost land mass. One hundred and forty miles upriver from the fjord—between Karasjok, Norway, and Karigasniemi, Finland—the river divides, with the Karasjokka branch flowing to the west and south into Norway. The boundary branch, now called the Inari (Inarinjoki), continues southward for another hundred miles, where it culminates in numerous small lakes in the Upper Anarjokka National Park of Norway and the Lemmenjoen National Park of Finland.

Salmon begin to arrive in the Teno/Tana in early June, immediately following the ice breakup. By the end of the month, mixed stocks of 1SW grilse up to the 4SW- and 5SW monster salmon for which the river is famous are coursing upstream toward the spawning grounds. Highway E6 from Alta and Lakselv to Kirkenes crosses the river at Tana Bru, and below that point fishing this

*Opposite page: Figure 11-22. Komsa-era rock carvings at the Alta fjord.*

very wide river is primarily with spoons, always from a boat. Bait of any kind is prohibited throughout the length of the river.

The bulk of the salmon fishing by both the Finns and the Norwegians in the Teno River is by "harling." Two to four spoons, wooden plugs (called wobblers), or large flies are trolled behind a boat that is rowed back and forth across the river. It's a very effective method for attracting large fish, especially those lying in holes up to 20 feet deep. Each year, dozens of salmon between 35 and 50 pounds are caught, virtually all by harling. In July 1998, a fish weighing 70 pounds was reportedly caught on a fly near Tana Bru, but no photographs of the fish have emerged. Boat fishing is permitted along the entire length of the river, but motors may not be used while fishing and the boat may not be anchored. The latter restriction is designed to prevent the snagging of fish in the deep holes.

Fly fishing from the bank (that is, by wading) is permitted along the entire length of the Teno/Tana River, and guides are not required. A daily license costs about $18. Halfway between Tana Bru and Karasjok, Norway, on the eastern bank lies the Finnish town of Utsjoki, where a major tributary by that name enters from Finland. Depending on the water and the weather, the fly fishing 30 miles either upriver or down from Utsjoki can be outstanding. A special fly-fishing section has been established in the Boratbocka area below the Alakongas Rapids, about 20 miles downstream from Utsjoki. From June 20 to July 20, 35 permits for this section are issued daily, each of which must be purchased on site; none are sold in advance. Each permit is valid for fly fishing in the restricted area from 7:00 P.M. until 7:00 A.M. the following morning.

Fly fishing in late June and early July can be very productive, but the situation changes in August, when the Teno typically runs low. As the river drops, wide boulder-strewn shores are exposed, which makes wading extremely difficult and can make casting a fly to holding areas offshore an exhaustive exercise.

Oddly, there is relatively little fly casting from boats,

primarily it seems because of limited demand. Having watched fishermen harling on several evenings, I could discern no reason that a dedicated fly fisherman could not enjoy very productive angling from a boat rowed, just as is done on the Alta. Later I learned that is just what determined fly fishermen do.

While the opportunity to catch very large fish is appealing, other factors limit the resource to visiting anglers. No salmon fishing is permitted for area nonresidents, either domestic or foreign, in most of the Finnish or Norwegian tributaries of the Teno/Tana. This is a major restriction for visiting fishermen, since many of the best fishing venues, particularly those most accessible to fly fishermen, are off-limits. Even so, 6,000 to 7,000 nonresident fishermen, mainly from southern Finland, purchase some 20,000 day licenses to fish the Teno mainstream each year.

The Finnish Game and Fisheries Research Institute maintains a fisheries research station in Utsjoki specifically to study Atlantic salmon in the Teno and its adjoining tributaries. Many of their findings parallel those observed elsewhere but with river-specific differences. About half of the fish caught in the Teno are MSW salmon, and half are grilse. The age for smoltification in the Teno River system is between three and seven years, with an average age of four years. Recent studies point toward a lower smolt age for the large 3SW and 4SW females and a higher smolt age for female grilse. The seven-year smolts develop primarily in the small upstream tributaries, from which it may be deduced that the preponderance of grilse mature. The studies strongly suggest that the larger MSW salmon develop from three- and four-year smolts spawned not in the upriver tributaries but in the main river. These studies bring into question the long-held axiom that there is no correlation between age of smoltification and salmon size. The data, in fact, suggest a reverse correlation for this river.

The most surprising observation resulting from the institute's studies is the size of Teno River grilse: the

*Figure 11-23. The Teno River near Utsjoki, Finland, in August. In early June, this river would be 10 feet higher.*

majority are between 2 and 4 pounds, the preponderance of which spawn in the smaller tributaries. Some larger grilse, up to 6 1/2 pounds, do breed in the main river. Why Teno grilse should be decidedly smaller than Alta grilse, only 50 miles to the west, is unknown. It's another example of river-specific genetics.

## IRELAND

When I first outlined this chapter, my intent was to survey some of the world-class rivers of the world. By my definition, a world-class river contains a significant percentage of 20-pound salmon, reasonable numbers of 30-pounders, with the opportunity for even larger fish, and without a surfeit of grilse. By that restrictive standard, Ireland does not possess world-class rivers, even though a salmon weighing 47 pounds, 13 ounces was netted in Galway Bay in June 1997. However, Ireland is such a delightful place to fish that it should not be overlooked. The weather is mild, if windy, and the rivers and lakes are very accessible. Except for a few private rivers, virtually the entire island is open to visitors for fishing. The people are among the friendliest I have met on any river.

**THE RIVERS**. The geology of Ireland has created a plethora of rivers and river systems. Many of these are short and populated primarily with grilse; a few are large with salmon up to 16 pounds. A 20-pound salmon in any Irish river is a very large fish. A truly outstanding summary of the trout and salmon rivers of Ireland is presented in Peter O'Reilly's book, *Trout and Salmon Rivers of Ireland* (43). It discusses in detail, with maps, all the significant streams of the two fishery districts of Northern Ireland and the seven fishery regions of the Republic.

Knowledgeable fishery authorities agree that the best rivers in Ireland include the Corrib, the Delphi, the Erriff, the Feale, the Moy, the Munster Blackwater near Cork, and the Shannon; in Northern Ireland the Bann and the Bush are best. "Best" in this case is determined by dependable quantities of fish, which for Irish rivers include copious quantities of grilse. For MSW salmon, the Corrib, the Delphi, and the Moy (Ridge pool) in western Ireland, as well as the Munster Blackwater and the Shannon (at Castleconnell), are usually cited as among the more dependable, particularly during April and May, when the MSW salmon run in Ireland. Two private fisheries north of Newport should also be mentioned, the Owenduff and the Owenmore. Public access to the Owenmore is extremely limited, but a week's fishing is occasionally available at one of the three lodges on the Owenduff.

Fishing Irish streams is genteel compared to angling the rivers of Norway, Canada, or even Iceland. Over the centuries, the river banks from which most fishing takes place have been manicured. Some have been developed to the point that stone casting piers, from which you can reach every conceivable salmon lie, have been installed at strategic points along the banks. The Ballynahinch Castle Fishery, located in the beautiful Connemara region west of Galway, is an excellent example. Built upon the site of a 14th-century castle—once the fortress of Grace O'Malley, the pirate queen of Connaught—the Ballynahinch manor was erected as an inn in the early 18th century by the Martin family. The facility passed through several owners before being purchased in 1924 by Maharaja Jam Sahib of Nawanagar (better known as Ranji, Prince of Cricketers), who developed the property into a quality fishery. Ranji erected the fishing piers and huts along the river and spared no expense to improve the salmon and sea-trout fishery.

One of the most upscale accommodations in Ireland, on a par with the fine manor houses of Scotland, the Ballynahinch Castle Fishery consists of 2 1/2 miles of river plus the Lower Ballnahinch Lake. The salmon fishery on the river consists of seven beats, each of which the tenant for the day may share with one guest. One-handed or short two-handed rods are the norm. Flies are primarily Irish counterparts of our standard hairwing flies. The most popular are the Ballynahinch Badger (a hairwing Blue Charm tied with a badger wing) and any of the several shrimp patterns, usually in sizes 6 through 12. Mike Conneely, fishery manager at Ballynahinch, insists that the somewhat stiffer European badger hair is much preferred over the gray squirrel or woodchuck hair often used for the Blue Charm wing.

While the accommodations at Ballynahinch are expensive, the fishing is quite reasonable ($90 per beat per day in 1997), in keeping with the modest quality of the fishery. In 1997, 120 salmon were caught at Ballynahinch. You can take your spouse on a fine fishing vacation there, at considerably less expense than at one of the prime fishing camps in Canada.

**LAKE FISHING FOR SALMON**. The geology of Scotland, northern England, and Ireland gives rise to a fishery unknown in Canada and the United States: lake fishing for migratory (sea-run) salmon. Many of the short

Irish rivers flow from series of lakes in the highlands, and the salmon often move right through the rivers to spawn in the lakes or in the headwater streams. With so much water for the salmon to roam, lake fishing (*loch* in Scotland, *lough* in Ireland) can be very frustrating, unless the topography of the lake aids in concentrating the fish in known lies.

One of the more interesting Irish lake fisheries is the Burrishoole Fishery in County Mayo, operated by the Salmon Research Agency of Ireland. The fishery consists of two lakes, Lough Furnace and Lough Feagh. Lough Furnace is a saline estuarine lake subject to very high oceanic tides that twice a day replenish the salinity of the fresh water flowing from Lough Feagh above. As a result, the salmon find Lough Furnace the ideal habitat in which to rest before ascending through either the Salmon Leap or the Millrace to Lough Feagh, in which they spawn.

As a teenager, I was fortunate to fish the small lakes of the Nipigon country of western Ontario for brook trout. Lake fishing for salmon is very similar. The difference is that for brook trout you paddle a canoe; for salmon you drift your boat with the wind. Your gillie, if you have one, maintains the boat perpendicular to the wind, and you fish ahead of the boat as it drifts downwind. Without a gillie, the knowledgeable angler employs a small electric motor to maintain position. A 10- or 11-foot, single-handed rod assists in making long casts, thus enabling you to cover more water with a single cast. Typically your leader—or "cast" as the British call it—consists of a 6-foot length of 8-pound leader to which is joined another 6-foot length of 6-pound tippet. An 8-inch stub of material is left at the intersection of the two pieces, to which is attached an upper or "bob" fly. Except for early-season fishing, the bob fly is generally a dark size 10 or 12 single-hook trout fly. The tippet or point fly is most frequently one of the shrimp patterns for which Ireland is famous, in sizes 8 through 12. Casting is easy since it is always downwind. After each cast is made, action is imparted to the fly, just as in brook-trout fishing, generally by the slow stripping of the line, 2 to 10 inches at a time. A modest wind is of

*Figure 11-24. Beat number 2 at the Ballynahinch Hotel Fishery near Clifden, County Galway.*

decided benefit, since it riffles the surface and imparts additional action to the bob fly.

Lough salmon, I learned, usually do not strike with the ferocity of river fish, and hooking lough salmon is much more akin to trout fishing in that the fish tend to sip the fly. When the salmon strikes, you must instantly set the hook. You cannot depend on the fish to hook itself when it turns away, as you can in river fishing.

Lake fishing is relaxing and offers a delightful change of pace, but it will never replace the romance of the river.

## OTHER VENUES:
## RUSSIA AND SCOTLAND

**RUSSIA.** The new frontiers for salmon fishing today are the rivers of the Kola Peninsula in northwestern Russia. Except perhaps for the Laxá á Ásum in Iceland, the Ponoi River is the most prolific river in the world today.

*Figure 11-25. The famous Ridge Pool on the Moy River in downtown Ballina, County Mayo.*

The annual rod catch is now more then 9,000 fish, of which the vast majority are released. The 1997 catch was 9,269 fish, including 2,773 grilse, yielding a salmon-to-grilse ratio of 3.3 to 1. Under careful management, the increase in productivity of this river in the past few years has been remarkable. The catch during the 17-week season in 1997 averaged 6.5 fish per rod-day. In June 1997, Hadley Ford, a director of the Atlantic Salmon Federation (U.S.), landed 120 fish and Mollie Fitzgerald landed 105 during their six days of fishing. Clearly, the Ponoi is a great place to experience that joy of catching so many fish you don't care if the next one is lost. However, fishing the Ponoi is unlike anything seen at the private camps on the major Canadian rivers. In high season, as many as 22 fishermen are in camp together. While there is plenty of water and salmon to accommodate 22 rods, the congeniality of the intimate fishing camp is lost in this setting.

East of Murmansk, on the north shore of the Kola

Peninsula, are several large, tempestuous rivers flowing into the Barents Sea, all of which contain very large salmon, many over 30 pounds. The best-known of these are the Kharlovka and the Yokonga. Others include the Rynda, the Eastern Litsa, and the Varzina; portions of these rivers have still not been fully explored. The struggle for control of these rivers in the last few years has been fierce. In 1995, several parties were forcibly removed from the Kharlovka River by armed security forces employed by a competing outfitter in collusion with unscrupulous regional officials.

Fortunately, it appears that many of these problems have finally been resolved. In 1998, the operating rights on the Kharlovka, Yokonga, Eastern Litsa, and Rynda were purchased by Peter C. Power, an experienced businessman from the United Kingdom. Currently, he is developing the Yokonga River, where he has erected a magnificent log lodge imported from Canada. Perhaps at last these fine rivers are in the hands of reliable management.

**SCOTLAND**. No discussion of the classic salmon rivers is complete without acknowledging the rivers of Scotland. Fishing for Atlantic salmon with artificial flies was born in Scotland and northern England, and the prime rivers of Scotland have traditionally been our prototypes. Sadly, the great rivers of Scotland are no longer the epitome of quality salmon fishing. Few, if any, can meet my definition of "world class" today. Too many years of relentless poaching and unfettered netting, particularly along the northeast coast of England (not subject to Scottish law) and the Faeroe Islands, have impaired the carrying capacity of these once-famous rivers.

What netting started, the outbreak of the disease ulcerative dermal necrosis (UDN) all but finished in the 1960s. More recently, another villain has emerged to take its toll—the intense agricultural cultivation throughout Great Britain. As in Ireland and parts of Atlantic Canada, such agricultural practices resulted in trampled stream banks, unbridled erosion, compacted gravel, and fouled spawning beds, as well as providing deleterious nutrient enrichment from chemical fertilizers. A few rivers remain worthwhile, if you can obtain access during prime season or immediately following a spate. Like the big-fish rivers of Canada, virtually all of the salmon waters in Scotland are privately held, and access is not assured. For the casual visitor to Scotland, the easiest and best access is through the hotels and guest manors that maintain beats on the better rivers.

Historically, the four great Scottish salmon rivers—the Tweed, Tay, Aberdeen Dee, and Spey—were world renowned for their spring runs of large salmon. In the last three decades these spring runs have declined precipitously for reasons that are not understood. The larger runs on these rivers are now the fall runs, some of which continue into November. Two fish per rod per week is now the norm on these rivers.

Remarkable insight into the current status of salmon fishing in Scotland may be found in a delightful little book entitled *Six Months in Scotland* by Syl Nemes (41b). He describes in considerable detail the decline of the Scottish salmon over the past 30 years. Nemes suggests that the problem originated with the historical Scottish laws. "From the earliest times the right of fishing for salmon has been regarded as one of the *reglia minora* vested in the Crown," solely for the patrimonial benefit of the Crown and its lieges. Over the centuries, the salmon rights in Scotland have been awarded, divided, and reassembled until today there are 62 salmon-fishing districts. All are privately owned and controlled.

The Scottish salmon laws were most recently revised in 1986. They permit unlimited fishing 197 days per year, a day shy of 33 weeks, but never on Sunday. The season for each river is determined individually to accommodate the variations in the arrival of the salmon. The Scottish season is more than twice as long as the 90-day seasons in Quebec and Iceland. It's 64-percent greater than the effective season (excluding black salmon) of 120 days on the Miramichi. The proof is in the pudding, as my

Scottish ancestors might say. The salmon catch (read: kill) by all methods—fixed engine (i.e., stake nets), net, coble (i.e., rowboat), and rod and line—has declined from some 600,000 in 1965 to 123,900 in 1996. The catch in 1997 was 86,842, a decrease of 30 percent from the previous year. The latter is the lowest annual kill since the records began in 1952. Interestingly, the annual rod-and-line catch has remained relatively constant at 50,000 to 60,000 since 1952. The take by fixed engines and net-and-coble has declined to a meager 37,065 fish, a decrease of 89 percent since 1952! By comparison, in 1994 the Miramichi River system alone yielded half as many fish as the rod catch for all of Scotland: 8,400 bright MSW salmon, all of which were released, and nearly 20,000 grilse. This seeming paradox in the constancy of Scottish salmon taken by rod and line during the period may be explained in part by the huge increase in the number of anglers (and concomitant decrease in the number of fish caught per rod-day). Also, as Nemes points out, salmon farm escapees undoubtedly have greatly bolstered the catch statistics in recent years.

Derek Mills and Neil Graesser present detailed reports and maps for each river in the excellent book *The Salmon Rivers of Scotland* (40). Similar to O'Reilly's later work on the Irish rivers (*Trout and Salmon Rivers of Ireland*), Mills and Graesser's presents detailed reports and maps for each river, its beats, advantages, and disadvantages, with adequate information on availability and booking. It's required reading for anyone fishing in Scotland. Nemes' book contains a good discussion, with booking details, of the rivers in and about Aberdeenshire, including the Dee, Don, North Esk, and Beauly.

Very recently, in Finland a newsletter called *The Atlantic Salmon Review* (27) has begun publication that presents "inside news for the Atlantic Salmon fisherman." Published four times a year, the *Review* publishes detailed information, including catch statistics and booking information, about the major salmon rivers of the world. For instance, the Summer 1997 (Volume 2) newsletter devoted eight pages to the beats on the Tweed, one of

Scotland's largest and best-managed rivers. The addresses
for booking agents in Scotland are given in that review.
More recent issues have focused on the rivers of Norway
and Iceland.

## "AND MILES TO GO BEFORE I SLEEP"

The poet Robert Frost didn't have the Atlantic salmon
in mind when he penned that famous line, but somehow
it seems so very appropriate when discussing salmon
rivers. So many rivers, so little time.

Salmon fishing means many things to many people.
To the neophyte, it's about catching strong fish in
freshwater rivers. Three grilse make for a very exciting day.
For those more advanced, the attraction may be the
opportunity to catch very big fish on small flies or light
rods. Your first 20-pounder and 30-pounder are milestones
you never forget. For the seasoned salmon angler, it's the
total experience that you savor, much like a cup of fine
coffee or your favorite single malt. You've tasted it a
hundred times before, but each day, each river yields
unexpected experiences, newfound friends and memories.
Often I have mused that perchance we don't truly angle for
the fish. Perhaps we really cast for memories.

Friends accompany me to each new river, but some
decline to return a second time. Their idea of adventure is
to seek the new and the different. Mine is to revisit known
pools and re-explore familiar haunts. In my later years, I
have been fortunate to search for memories in Canada,
Iceland, Ireland, Finland, Norway, and Sweden. I am
always reminded that nothing can compare with the
outdoor experience. Much is made of man's need to
commune with nature. It is real! I realized that 50 years ago
on my first solo canoe trip through the wilds of Quetico
Provincial Park. I relearn it every day—on the river.

*Guide and Canoe*
Watercolor
9 3/4 x 14 1/4 inches
Private Collection

# Chapter 12

# Guides: Joy and Tribulation

## GOOD GUIDE, BAD GUIDE

Fall on the Miramichi is a fisherman's delight. The weather is good—warm days and cool nights, usually without rain. Typically, there is a large run of MSW fish beginning about the time of September's full moon, and the fishing on the lower river is almost always dependable. Because the lodge owner was ill, the reservations that Lloyd and I had made a month earlier were canceled the day before we were to leave for Blackville. We were left without a place on the Miramichi to fish during that last week in September. Near panic set in. I was like an addict in need of a fix. After several calls, someone mentioned a new lodge at Black Rapids run by George and Jean Curtis, where there was space available.

I remember nothing about the fishing on the afternoon of our arrival, but the next day was an adventure I'll never forget. There had been lots of rain, and the rivers were high, so George suggested that we fish the Cains, a major tributary of the Miramichi. We waded across the Cains and hiked downstream a half-mile to a long bend in the river. In late morning, just as I was finishing my first pass through the designated water, I hooked a fine hen

393

fish, which, after a short fight, began to tire in the fast water. Having watched my casting and playing of the fish, George still knew nothing about my ability to land the fish. So George picked up his black landing net, walked downstream about 40 feet, waded into the river knee deep, immersed his net in the water, held it motionless, and said, "There's the net. Bring the fish to me." Instantly, I knew I had found a knowledgeable guide. The keys were knee deep, motionless, and "bring it to me."

That fish, incidentally, was a 14-pounder caught on a size 6, Chief Needahbeh fly. T'was a good morning. I was introduced to the Cains, the Chief, and a new friend all on the same day.

Not all adventures end as well as the one with George Curtis. Several years later, we were fishing out of the upper camp on the Riviere St. Jean on Quebec's north shore, about 150 miles northeast of Sept Iles. This river had been for many years privately held as one of the secret gems of salmon-dom. When the Province of Quebec took over the management of the river, it installed a local river authority whose principal interest was in providing employment to people from the neighboring village. Little, if any, thought was given to how to run the camps, nor was any effort made to develop the guides, who were literally untrained in their craft. Problems developed because the local guides would not recognize that theirs was a service economy, dependent upon visiting anglers.

The upper camp on the St. Jean is some 25 miles upriver from the St. Lawrence Seaway and a mile below the falls of the St. Jean chasm. Several hundred yards below the falls, the chasm empties out into three of the finest salmon pools you will ever see anywhere in the world: classic deep pools, the epitome of a salmon river, with large boulders to break the rush of water. Each pool has a well-defined lip, above which the salmon lie. Only the tendency for hooked fish to go over the lips of the pools and down the rapids spoils what would otherwise be salmon heaven. That and the guides.

The first year we fished the St. Jean, my guide was

*Opposite page: Figure 12-1. Guide George Curtis on the Miramichi River. Courtesy of George Curtis.*

Dan, a likable but obviously inexperienced young man. Having tired of wet flies, I decided to try a Bomber. Dan nearly had a fit. "Bombers don't work here," he announced with great indignation, as if any dolt knew that. The second year, I again fished with Dan, and it was obvious that he had learned something the previous year. About the third day, when the fishing was slow, Dan very politely suggested that I try a Bomber. "But you told me last year that Bombers don't work here," I objected equally politely. Dan smiled quietly, and I attached a Bomber.

After two seasons on the St. Jean, we were uncertain about returning. We knew that the food was mediocre and the guides were inexperienced, usually indifferent and sometimes insolent. But the water was beautiful and productive. Eventually we decided to try our luck once more. By that third year, Dan had gone off to Sept Isles for training as an underwater welder, and my guide was Leo, the head guide for the upper camp. As usual, we were fishing four in a 22-foot canoe. The guide's helper was in the bow, the two sports in the middle sharing the rod, and the guide in the stern. Late one morning while standing behind Leo, I hooked a 12-pound hen fish at the lip of Basin Pool. Instinctively, the fish went over the lip and headed down the rapids for Long Beach Pool, a half-mile downstream. Usually, the guide would immediately start the motor, the assistant would weigh anchor, and we would follow the fish downstream. But this morning, nothing moved except the fish. In desperation, I reached forward, tapped Leo on the shoulder, waking him from a sound sleep, and asked with all the sarcasm I could muster if he would mind starting the motor so we could follow the fish.

We never returned to the Riviere St. Jean.

## GUIDES ARE PEOPLE, TOO

Tales about bad guides are legendary; stories about good guides seem much less noteworthy. Three factors contribute to the differing views and attitudes about guides: culture, experience, and expectations. I am convinced that, of these, culture is by far the most important because it provides the clearest demarcation between peoples. If you can bridge the culture gap, you can communicate. If you can communicate, you should be able to work together. I have had excellent guides in Canada, Iceland, Ireland, Finland, and Norway despite the different languages.

The experience factor cuts both ways. A very experienced guide is usually willing to provide all the assistance and advice that an inexperienced angler can absorb, if the angler is in an absorbing mood. If he isn't, he should not be on the river in the first place. Remember, it's to your guide's advantage to have you do well. A good guide prides himself on having his clients among the most successful on the river.

The greatest conflicts come when experienced anglers are inflicted with inexperienced or unknowledgeable guides. Almost by definition, a hired guide is expected to be knowledgeable. Many aren't, and they know it. That's the basis for conflict, particularly if the guide becomes defensive. Some will try to bluff and intimidate you or become very demanding, particularly about fly patterns and sizes. When your guide demands a Night Hawk when you only have Black Hawks or Black Rats, or when he wants a size 10 single, not your size 8 double, watch out. It is almost better if such guides go hide in the woods. The greatest conflicts between experienced anglers and inexperienced guides come when you're fishing from a canoe because neither of you can walk away. Under such conditions, when all else fails, politely inform the guide that you like to experiment and prefer to try some new ideas. Then do it your way with authority. If the guide sulks, so be it.

Guides who are hired by and work for a single camp or outfitter for the entire season are usually more experienced and more dependable than those who work by the day. For that reason, it is to your advantage to book your fishing trip with a camp that operates on a specific schedule, requiring three-, six-, or seven-day bookings.

*Figure 12-2. Guide Ernie
Long on the Miramichi River.*

Confirmed bookings require a predetermined number of
guides, which, in turn, leads to commitments by the camp
to the more-experienced guides.

There are a number of what I call room-and-board
lodges, particularly in New Brunswick and Nova Scotia,
that accept per diem bookings. Usually these lodges have
two or three good guides committed and readily available.
However, if their bookings suddenly increase, the quality
of the guides available may be questionable. In such
cases, it is best to inquire before you commit yourself.

The main difference between good guides and bad
guides is one of expectation. But then we can say that
about almost every person we hire or every position we
accept. The onus for bridging the "expectations gap" lies
clearly with the angler. You may expect to be shown where
fish should be found, assisted in fishing there and in
landing any fish. The guide expects you to be somewhat
knowledgeable, of good humor, and understanding of the

vagaries of the salmon. Throughout North America, the average catch is about one-half fish per rod-day. You cannot expect three or more fish per day any more than you can demand fair weather or the absence of insects.

The bond that forms between knowledgeable guides and experienced anglers is one of the great joys of salmon fishing. You assist each other with your knowledge and experience, and each of you learns from the other. I enjoy and actually prefer tying my own flies to the leader. But so does Jim, my guide on the Moisie. My compromise is to let Jim assist me with all but critical knotting. I insist on tying my own knots when I'm fishing size 16 flies or searching for an IGFA record. If my tackle fails under such conditions, I want no one to blame but myself. Often I let Jim take the lead in suggesting what flies to try. He knows that I prefer small, double-hook patterns, so we start out with whatever colors strike his fancy, most often black. Shortly, we are both conferring on colors, and if I feel so inclined I am free to choose my own colors. It is a give-and-take proposition, which helps to bond the angling experience.

A guide is a friend, companion, assistant, and instructor, as well as an employee. He may be helpful, useless, friendly, distant, congenial, or arrogant, sometimes almost simultaneously. You are his employer but an intruder into his private wilderness.

## ONE GUIDE'S PERSPECTIVE

Legendary guides do exist, but they are few and far between and always fully booked. Just try to book a week or even a day with one of the premier bonefish guides in the Florida Keys. Outstanding guides are in great demand, not just because they can show you where the fish are, but also because they are proficient instructors of casting, catching, and the nature that surrounds you. Regrettably, such guides rarely take the time or have the inclination to write or speak about their subject. When they do, you listen.

Ernie Long of McNamee, New Brunswick, is such a guide. A full-time guide on the Miramichi River since

1972, Ernie was named to the Miramichi Salmon Museum Hall of Fame in 1995. Ernie is somewhat unusual in that he enjoys talking about his craft and is good at it. He suggests six attributes of a good guide, which I paraphrase as follows:

1.  Personality
2.  Communication skills
3.  Guiding skills
4.  Canoe-handling skills
5.  Salmon-netting skills
6.  Follow-up

Ernie's perspective begins with personality because he believes that it is the guide's responsibility to go to the camp or cabin and meet the guests. The guide should get acquainted and answer any questions the guests may have concerning the schedule or equipment. His goal is to resolve any concerns early and quickly. Too often, the first time the guests meet the guides is when all gather at the camp or dock after breakfast, at which time there is a very brief introduction, while the anglers are jockeying for the selection of guides and the guides for their preference of guests.

As we have already discussed, the importance of communication cannot be overstated. Ernie suggests that the guide must be prepared and willing to give clear and concise directions, particularly with regard to canoeing, wading the river, and similar matters largely within the guide's purview. He feels that it is his responsibility to provide whatever direction is required for a successful day on the river.

Under "guiding skills," Ernie includes knot-tying skills; the ability to read the water; the ability to discern between running fish and those likely to take a fly; matters of river courtesy (such as the priority of anglers, the rate at which one fishes down a beat, and encroachments); and, lastly, availability. The guide should assist you when and where you need it, not at his convenience. Availability may be the most underrated of all the attributes, for it connotes awareness, one of the most precious of all guiding skills.

It is interesting to me that Ernie lists canoe handling and fish netting as separate skills, for I would be inclined to group them under general guiding skills. This reflects the importance Ernie assigns to these two functions. Regrettably, the skillful handling of a canoe can no longer be taken for granted. Canoe handling takes practice, lots of practice, for which many guides no longer have the time or the inclination. The ubiquitous outboard motor has seen to that. Outboards are fine for traveling up and down the river, but they are very noisy and greatly disrupt the fishing. For that very reason, on the section of the Moisie where we fish, outboards are banned except for upriver travel. Canoe poling is a lost art for all but the most senior of guides, and paddling is admittedly an inefficient mode for most purposes. That leaves only rowing, which is really quite an efficient manner to move about the river. It's quiet and gives the guide complete control of his beat.

Everyone agrees that netting is a principal skill for a guide. My observations suggest that it is the skill most lacking in the majority of guides. How many times have you seen a guide stab at a fish two or three or four times in order to net it? Or perhaps you have watched a guide follow a fish up or down the bank hoping to intercept it? Or attempt to net the fish tail first? I will acknowledge that many guides are equipped with insufficiently large nets, but whose fault is that?

Perhaps the most impressive of Ernie's list of qualities is "follow-up," for it again indicates an unique degree of awareness on his part. Many of us routinely correspond with our guides during the off-season with a picture or two in the fall, a Christmas card, and perhaps a note of anticipation in the spring. But Ernie suggests that a good guide should do likewise. "Write your guests; let them know you are thinking of them," he suggests. "It may be just the encouragement they need to book a return trip next summer." Smart guide, that Ernie.

Fishing with Ernie is one of those rare experiences you never forget. He is by far the most observant guide I have known. Ernie notices everything: the flow of the river and how the currents may affect your presentation and the fish's lie, the wind and how it affects your cast, the sun and the clouds and how the shadows determine in which portion of the pool the fish will rest. Ernie is also very observant of the angler: how he casts, how much he false casts, how and where he wades, how his fly rides in the water, and especially how he reads the water.

After fishing with Ernie for a day and a half, I asked for his view on how large a loop of line I should carry between my casting hand and the reel. He answered that he had been noticing my 2-foot loop, which he felt was about right for the slow currents, but for fast currents he would recommend a somewhat larger loop. If the spring floods have not altered the river, Ernie knows the bottom like the back of his hand. While we were fishing the Stanley Pool at Wilson's, he advised me that the bottom was fine gravel for the first 100 yards, after which there was a small hole on the left where the bottom changed to small boulders. Sure enough, at 90-plus yards, I encountered the hole and moved shoreward to avoid the boulders.

In discussing guides and how they interact with the angler, Ernie believes that the ability to read the water and ascertain where the salmon lie is the most important skill. Assisting the angler with presentation of the fly is second in importance, and the choice of flies a distant third. Most guides are too critical, he claims. Anglers fish for fun, and they do not like to be hassled about skills they have not mastered. His approach is to observe the angler for an hour or so to detect what faults need correction. Then he picks the most important problem and politely suggests to the angler the means for improvement. He works with the angler until that deficiency is no longer limiting and then moves on to the second problem. If a guide tries to correct two or three problems at the same time, Ernie believes that the fisherman becomes so confused that he often corrects none.

The one thing that Ernie will not tolerate is a guide's fishing or even handling a sport's rod. Guides are there to assist the client, he asserts. You cannot assist if you are fishing or even thinking about fishing. A guide should never touch the angler's rod without permission.

As you might surmise, Ernie is a also a great story-teller, which is not at all a bad quality for a guide. Certainly, it helps to relieve the boredom on those days when the fish are sulking. My favorite Ernie story illustrates his wry sense of humor. It seems that Ernie was guiding a lady on the first day she had ever fished for salmon. A pleasant but somewhat reticent person, she demonstrated adequate fishing skills and late in the morning hooked her first salmon, a cock fish of about 14 pounds. Suddenly, this shy, reticent lady became invigorated by the action. As the time approached to land the fish, Ernie lifted his net and entered the water. She obtained her first good look at the fish and screamed, "That's a big fish, a very big fish. How big is it?" Ernie directed her to stop reeling in line and to walk slowly back up the bank away from the water. This she dutifully did again screaming, "That's a big fish. How big is it?" While Ernie netted the fish, again she yelled, "How big is it?" As Ernie brought the fish to shore, he glanced up and down the river and noticed that there was nobody else in sight. Softly he said, "Ma'am, there is nobody here but you and me. How big do you want it to be?"

## WADING GUIDES AND CANOE GUIDES

For many anglers salmon fishing means wade-fishing, but not to all. In fact, salmon anglers are sharply divided as to their preference for wading or canoeing. Often the decision is made for you. On big or fast rivers, you must canoe; on smaller or more placid waters, wading is frequently the mode of choice. I love to wade small rivers provided the bank is not so heavily overgrown as to prevent a decent backcast. Wading gives me a sense of control, since I can cover most of the water in any manner I wish. The main advantage of the canoe is that you can cover much more water, and you are free to range upstream or down as the fishing dictates. Canoe fishing is also much less demanding of aging legs.

It should come as no surprise that few guides are equally accomplished both on shore and on the water. The basic skills required are different. Guiding the wading angler requires greater skill because the guide must constantly monitor the angler, his line, the river currents, the wind, and the weather, as well as be on the lookout for showing or striking fish. Regrettably, many guides—dare I say most younger ones?—are not up to such a challenge. Too often, the guide will position you in the river and stand by, letting you fish as best you are able and waiting to net a fish. The problem I have with such guides is that they want to talk when they should be observing, or they wander away just when you need some assistance. And many want to fish whenever you lay down your rod. One of the best guides I know on the upper Miramichi, a very accomplished angler, seems never to resist that temptation. My view is that when I am paying for the privilege, only I fish. Rested water is just as valuable as unfished water. A guide fishing behind me just might hook the fish that I could have hooked on my next pass through the pool.

Aside from exercising the necessary canoeing skills, the first responsibility of canoeing guides is to position your canoe in areas where the fish are likely holding. Then their task is to observe your fly throughout the cast, constantly checking for wind knots, broken hooks, tangled casts, shifting currents, as well as always being on the alert for showing fish or a strike. Concentration is their byword. You will likely learn more techniques much more quickly from the canoe guide, since there is no place to which he can wander. But best of all is the camaraderie that you develop with an accomplished canoe guide. The three days I spent on the upper Alta with Agnar Johnson, a guide with whom I had never fished before, were the most enjoyable of my entire fishing career. Agnar is that accomplished!

Recognizing the differing attributes of wading guides

and canoe guides may not influence your choice of rivers, but it should alert you to the skills you may reasonably expect from your guide and how you may react in unfamiliar circumstances.

## LANDING FISH

One of the principal duties of a guide is to assist you in landing your fish. I say "assist" because the guide cannot do a proper job without your cooperation. Furthermore, many anglers prefer to land their own fish. We shall consider several methods of landing fish, in reverse order of your proximity to the fish.

**BEACHING**. Beaching is one of the easiest methods of landing salmon. It does not require you to be close to the fish, but it does require a sloping shoreline, preferably not in fast water. When the fish is about ready to be beached, walk back from the shoreline 20 or more feet, so you are not forced to work with a short line. Next, loosen the drag on your reel, so you aren't tempted to pull the fish ashore. Point your rod at a 30-degree angle to the river, preferably upstream, so as to flex the midportion of the rod, not the tip. That way, any sudden movements by the fish will not cause a broken tip. I prefer to keep my rod low, with the tip only a foot or two above the ground, so I am not tempted to lift the rod tip high. The light drag on your reel also will guard against a sudden dash for freedom by the salmon. If the fish veers away or makes a short run, so be it. It is very unlikely to escape, unless it thrashes on the beach and breaks the leader. Unless the fish is very tired and well spent, it is likely to make at least one attempt to veer aside and avoid the beach. The trick is to gently slide the fish onto solid ground, not necessarily completely out of water. Once grounded, the fish is helpless. It can only flop about and thrash forward. At that point, you should lower your rod, walk behind the fish, grasp it by the tail and lift it out of the water. Don't slide it onto the sand unless it's a keeper. Keep your rod in your off hand all the while, so that if the fish does flop back into the water, it is still secured to your leader. Grilse you intend to keep are easily landed by placing your hand under the belly and flipping the beached fish onto the shore.

**NETTING**. Netting a large fish is much simpler than most people realize. All it takes is good form, which many, even some experienced, guides never bother to learn. Almost everyone can net a bass or crappie easily, but there is skill required in netting a 20-pound salmon. The three essential factors were mentioned in the opening paragraphs of this chapter. If your guide is netting the fish, he must wade knee-deep into the water. At that depth, the fish is not unduly alarmed and will often swim or be guided easily over the net. Too often guides will wear ankle high boots and expect to net your fish from the shore. Not my fish; I'll land my own first.

The guide should immerse his large, preferably black, net 18 to 24 inches into the water and remain motionless. Black nets blend with most river bottoms and generally do not scare the fish. Knotless cotton nets are preferred to minimize damage to the fish's skin. Once the guide is motionless, it is your turn. You should now be upriver of the guide, generally 25 to 40 feet. Either by reeling in the fish or by backing up the river bank, you now lead the fish over the net. If the fish shies away, try again. When the fish is over the net, the guide lifts the net over the nose of the fish and swiftly encircles the fish. Usually, the fish will be headed upstream so that the netting requires a downstream stroke of the net by the guide. At the same instant, you should lower your rod to provide slack in the line and leader. Should the fish escape the net, it can easily break a taught leader while flopping on the ground. Many fish are lost that way. I prefer to back up the shoreline while landing the fish. If you reel in the fish, there is the danger of shortening your line and allowing the fish too much leverage.

You can net your own fish easily by following the above guidelines. Whenever possible, wade into the

*Opposite page: Figure 12-3. Guide Jim Lynch on the Moisie River.*

*Figure 12-4. Guide John Edwards on the Moisie River.*

river at least knee-deep to allow yourself maximum flexibility, for you never know which way the fish will head. Don't forget to loosen the drag on your reel. Then reel or pull the fish toward you. Net the fish head first. Once the fish is netted, lower your rod, lift the net, and carry the fish ashore.

**THE TAILER.** A tailer comprises a handle, about 30 inches long, to which is attached a 40-inch loop of flexible wire cable. When the loop is slipped over the fish's tail and is tightened, the loop instantly encircles the tail much like the noose of a snare.

The tailer is used much in the same manner as the net, except the handle is shorter, which means that you must be closer to the fish. Generally, you slide the tailer over the tail of the fish with an upriver sweep of the tailer (if the fish is heading into the current). Once the fish is tailed, pull it toward you, lower your rod, and grasp the tail of the fish firmly with your hand so you can release the tailer immediately. The tailer can easily damage the fish's skin and should only be used if other methods are not practical. Never drag the fish ashore with the tailer unless you intend to kill it. The tailer does not work well with grilse because the tail structure is immature and not sufficiently stiff for the tailer to obtain a secure hold.

Because so many fish are damaged by the improper use of the tailer, some jurisdictions, including the Province of New Brunswick, no longer permit the use of tailers. If you feel it necessary to use a tailer, check the regulations first.

**HAND-TAILING**. The most artful manner of landing grilse and even large salmon is by hand-tailing, literally grasping the fish with your hand around the tail end of the body—the so-called waist or caudal peduncle—just ahead of the tail or caudal fin. Guides in a number of areas, notably Iceland, pride themselves on their ability to hand-tail fish. Hand-tailing is similar to using a tailer except that you must be somewhat closer to the fish. If survival of the salmon is your main concern, and increasingly it is becoming everyone's concern, hand-tailing is second only to netting as the most humane manner in which to land a fish.

In my experience, hand-tailing by the angler is best accomplished by wading a little deeper, which is less threatening to the fish. Allow the fish to swim upstream of you a few feet and then gradually pull the fish back downstream to you. The fish seems not to know just how close your hand is, and you will be able to grab the tail with your off hand held just at the surface of the water. Once tailed, the fish remains as if paralyzed, virtually motionless, and is easily removed to the shore.

## RELEASING FISH

In 1996, the new Norwegian Wild Salmon Centre and Aquarium was opened in the village of Laerdal, where the Laerdal River enters the Sognefjord. To supplement the aquarium display and to preserve hen fish for spawning, Børge Hansen personally delivered to the centre during the season 25 MSW salmon he had caught in the river. I witnessed one such capture. Some 15 miles upriver from the centre, a hen salmon of about 16 pounds was beached, and the hook was removed. Securely held by the tail, the salmon was allowed to recover for several minutes. Børge then lifted the fish from the water, supported its belly with his other hand, and walked upriver as rapidly as the rough terrain would permit to a small brook in which the salmon could be penned. During the transfer, the salmon was out of the water for 94 seconds. Leaving me to guard the fish,

*Above: Figure 12-6. Fish ladder at the Norwegian Wild Salmon Centre in Laerdal, Norway.*

*Opposite page: Figure 12-5. Guide Volund Hermodsson on the Laxá í Adaldal River.*

Børge drove downriver several miles and returned an hour later with a fish trailer in which to transport the salmon. The salmon was placed head first into a clear plastic bag, which was filled with water. The fish and water bag were hand carried to the nearby road, and the fish was placed in the trailer and trucked to the centre. At the centre, the fish was removed from the trailer, hand-carried up a series of flumes that served as a fish ladder for the centre, and deposited into the top of the aquarium pool. During this second transfer, the fish was out of water for 64 seconds. Less than three minutes later, I observed this fish swimming with the others in the aquarium. Whatever conditioning might have been required after such an ordeal, four days later that salmon was fully adapted to its new environment.

The scenario described above should not be considered exemplary, but it does reveal that mature salmon can survive considerable stress if handled very carefully. A fish to be released should be landed gently and minimally. Do not remove the fish from the water. Both the angler and the guide should participate in the release; it's much easier with four hands, since one of you can grasp the fish by the tail and steady the fish while the other swiftly removes the hook. Hooks are best removed with forceps, a hemostat, or long nose pliers. Grasp the hook and remove it with a quick twist of the wrist. If both barbs of a double hook are imbedded, don't even think about recovering the hook. Cut the leader as close to the hook as possible and set the fish free. The lost fly is your contribution to salmon conservation.

After the hook has been removed, hold the fish by the tail and support it with your other hand under its belly. Try not to disturb the mucous film on the fish's skin any more than is absolutely necessary. This film protects the fish from infections. Head the fish into a moderate flow of water so that water flows over its gills. Hold it steady; do not move the fish back and forth. The backward flow of water through its gills can suffocate the fish. Don't be in a hurry to release the fish. Oddly, some guides become impatient and want to either release the fish prematurely or kill it. You should be more restrained, for a well-fought salmon may require 6 or 8 minutes or more to recover. Eventually, the fish will begin to move its tail at which time you may release your hold on the tail but continue to support the belly. If the fish darts away, fine. The saddest sensation in salmon fishing is to watch a spent fish roll on its side, unable to be revived.

Most guides don't know how to release fish properly. Some are quite opposed to catch-and-release and deliberately mishandle fish to prove their view that released fish don't survive. Your leadership and assistance are essential under such circumstances. Some years ago, while fishing the Restigouche during the first week of June, I inadvertently caught a black salmon or kelt that had spawned the previous fall and was late in returning to the ocean. My guide promptly stuck his hands into the gills, lifted the fish out of the water, and struggled to remove the hook with his hand. Instantly, I told him to drop the fish into the water, and we proceeded to remove the hook in the proper manner. Unfortunately, the damage to that fish had been done.

Weighing large fish that you wish to release is very difficult. Fish over 18 or 20 pounds often thrash vigorously when netted. Their gills may get caught in the netting, which not infrequently causes bleeding gills, from which no salmon will recover. If your net is large enough to hold the fish securely, the simplest procedure is to weigh the fish in the net, release the fish, and then subtract the weight of the net.[1]

## CORRECTING BAD HABITS

Guides can be very helpful just by observing as you fish. They may spot tailing loops in your cast, which lead

---

1. The best way to weigh and measure large fish is to carry a sling made of soft, knotless cotton mesh and a 48-inch length of cord with loops in each end. The net should be about 36 inches long and 30 inches wide with 3/4-inch dowels fastened along each edge. Place the sling under the fish while it's still in the water. Slip the loops of the cord over the ends of the dowels, attach a scale to the cord, and weigh the fish. The fish will be out of the water less than 10 seconds while it is being weighed.

to knots, or discern drooping backcasts, which often result in broken hook points. I once rose a very large salmon on the Moisie, and while I waited the customary two minutes to recast, my guide politely reminded me to check the fly. I did and was dismayed to find both hook points broken, obviously from hitting rocks on the nearby island. Imagine how dumb I would have felt if I had made that next cast only to lose the fish to a pointless hook. Instead I changed flies, and on the next cast, I hooked the third largest salmon I'd ever caught—all due to Jim's reminding me to follow my usual routine and check the tippet and fly.

I tend to view each of my salmon trips as another field trip or laboratory workshop where I can practice my art to the fullest and hopefully develop new ideas and learn new concepts. This most certainly includes correcting bad habits. A congenial guide is often one of your best critics, politely suggesting how to improve your casting skill, control the float, mend your line, or choose the proper technique for playing your fish. He may even assist you by taking pictures or shooting a video of memorable events or conditions.

Some years ago, concerned with a hitch in my forward cast that was robbing me of distance, I took along a video camera to the Miramichi and asked George to record my casting one afternoon. Since George was behind me with the recorder, I never knew when I was on camera. Rather quickly, I reverted to dropping my back cast, the cause of the problem. I tended to compensate by overpowering the forward thrust, causing ripples and thus limiting my forward cast. Once we viewed the tape, it was easy to correct the problem the very next day.

If you can charm someone else into carrying a video camera, it is a great learning tool. The video camera is especially helpful in analyzing your casting and how you play a hooked fish. Be sure to have the cameraman concentrate on you, the rod, and line, not on the jumping fish.

*Opposite page: Figure 12-7. Guide Agnar Johnson assisting Mollie Fitzgerald with her 30-pounder on the Alta River, Norway. Courtesy of Mike Fitzgerald Sr.*

## LAST CASTS

"Bad guide" is an oxymoron. Bad guides are a paradox. Even though we complain about inept or untrained guides, most of those experiences rapidly fade from our memories. It is the adventures with the good guides we remember and for which we rejoice.

How could I ever forget Stefan Magnusson, who, on my first trip to the Grímsá River, slipped me one of his Collie Dog tube flies on which I eventually caught 20 salmon before it was honorably retired to my box of memories?

My friend George Curtis shall be forever honored for his immobile black net. It taught me much and has served me well.

And Alton Norad on the upper Miramichi who that evening gave John M., Charlie, and me the small Red Butts on which each of us in succession landed a grilse at dusk. Alton certainly knew his water.

Then there was John Edwards at Moisie-Ouapetec, one of the more talented guides I've known, who anticipated the salmon's every move. You never worried about a tangled anchor rope with John at the helm.

And, of course, my friend Jim Lynch on the Moisie, who assisted in landing my first Sixteen-Twenty fish. Jim was truly more excited than I that evening.

More recently, a week with Volund Hermodsson, head guide for the Arnes beats on the Laxá í Adaldal, demonstrated just how valuable a knowledgeable guide can be. Raised on the river, Volle knows every hole in which the salmon hide and every ledge on which they rest.

Finally, I acknowledge with gratitude the most talented canoe guide to accompany me on any salmon water, Agnar Johnson, senior guide on the Alta. In spite of miserable fishing, the week I spent with Agnar was the most enlightening time I've spent on any river. His English was poor; my Norwegian is nonexistent, but Agnar demonstrated an understanding of the river such as few of us ever dream.

My friend John D. is correct. Salmon fishing is addictive.

*Camp in the Woods*
Watercolor
7 3/4 x 11 1/4 inches
Private Collection

# Chapter 13

# Savoring the Catch

My fondest memory from my youth is of canoeing through the wilds of Quetico Provincial Park on the Ontario–Minnesota border. Coming ashore after a long day of paddling, making camp, taking a brief swim in the frigid waters, enjoying a warming campfire that curled enough smoke to discourage the mosquitoes, and, best of all, preparing a balsam bed for the evening. Regrettably, the latter is a luxury that my grandsons may never know. Most of our meals were forgettable, but even then a few were not. Freshly caught walleye, invariably fried; potatoes baked in clay pods; biscuits from the reflector oven; and, in August, fresh blueberries just off the bush. It was luxurious in a simple sort of way.

Luxurious meals in my later years are different in major respects: the time required to prepare and the equipment needed, and the friends with whom and the wine with which to enjoy. For a number of years, a group of friends have celebrated the rites of spring with "Shadfest," that brief period of time during April and May when the shad run up the Delaware, the Hudson, and elsewhere. During this period, the shad roe and firm, oily flesh are to

*Figure 13-1. A platter of gravlax for opening day.*

be enjoyed. Shad in the spring, salmon after your first trip in July, and blini with fresh salmon roe in September all provide a fitting finish to the angling experience.

Because of its rich, oily flesh, no other fish is served in as many ways as is the Atlantic salmon. Many feel it is best uncooked—whether raw, salted, smoked, lightly cured fresh, or more heavily cured, as in gravlax or pastrami. If you prefer your salmon cooked, you may choose poached, grilled, fried, baked in a dozen different ways, or in innumerable prepared dishes, including burgers, mousses, quiches, loaves, and salads. It seems fitting to close this book with a few of my favorite salmon and seafood recipes gleaned over the years from a variety of sources. Enjoy.

## RAW AND CURED SALMON

**SALMON CARPACCIO.** Many argue that salmon coulibiac is the world's greatest culinary adventure, a virtual food for the gods. I happen to agree, but its elaborate recipe and exotic ingredients require two days of preparation. This is beyond the capabilities, if not the patience, of us mortals. For the true salmon aficionado, raw salmon—either as salmon tartar or carpaccio—may be a second choice. Certainly carpaccio is the simplest of preparations and fulfills Ecoffier's dictum that "salmon should be served as plainly as possible."

Remove the skin from a bright filet of salmon and slice it paper-thin. This is best accomplished on your butcher's slicing machine. If the fish has not been

*Figure 13-2. Midafternoon break on the Alta River, Norway.*

previously frozen, freeze the slices for 24 hours as a precaution against parasitic contamination. Allow the thawed salmon to regain room temperature. Combine in a small bowl:

> 2 T. virgin olive oil
> 1 T. fresh lemon juice
> 1 t. fresh basil, finely julienned
> 1 t. fresh cilantro (coriander leaves), finely chopped
> Salt and pepper to taste

For an hors d'oeuvre, brush the salmon slices with the dressing and arrange the slices, overlapping slightly, on a chilled serving plate in several circular rings, working from the rim toward the center of the plate. Season well with salt and pepper. Extra dressing may be drizzled over the slices just before serving.

For individual canapés, the slices may be brushed with the dressing and served flat or rolled on a thin rice or wheat wafer or on rye or wheat bread thinly sliced. Alternatives include omitting the basil and cilantro from the dressing, brushing the slices with only the olive oil and lemon juice mixture, and then sprinkling the chopped cilantro and basil on the slices. Vodka straight from the freezer is an excellent accompaniment.

*Figure 13-3. Lunchtime on the Cains River, New Brunswick.*

**LIGHTLY CURED SALMON**.[1] In Iceland and the Scandinavian countries, salted or cured fresh salmon is an everyday delicacy. The type and extent of curing depends on your taste. Norwegians love salted salmon, which is simply fresh salmon rather heavily salted, sliced, and served as you would smoked salmon.

Salmon lightly cured with salt, sugar, and other ingredients is more generally preferred. This particular recipe for lightly cured salmon originated with Havfruen's Restaurant in Trondheim, Norway, where fresh salmon is available year-round from pen-raised fish. It may be served as an appetizer or presented as a first course.

> 1 lb. salmon fillet
> 2 T. salt
> 4 T. sugar
> 5 oz. virgin olive oil
> Juice of 1 lemon
> 3 T. chopped fresh dill
> White pepper

---

1. Adapted from the *Atlantic Salmon Journal*, Volume 45, Number 2, Summer 1996.

Remove any skin or bones from the fillet and slice it very thin. Mix the salt, sugar, olive oil, and lemon juice and stir until the sugar is dissolved. Brush each slice of salmon on both sides with the mixture and arrange on a suitable plate. Sprinkle the slices with freshly ground white pepper and some chopped dill. Cover with plastic wrap and allow the salmon to cure at room temperature for at least 60 to 90 minutes before serving. In contrast to the traditional gravlax recipes, this preparation includes lemon juice, uses more sugar than salt, and has only a very short cure time. Hence, it presents a different texture and taste.

**GRAVLAX**. Gravlax (also *gravad lax*) is more than just cured salmon; it's a food style. It represents a variety of recipes, all of which are derived from a basic salt and sugar curing, for fresh salmon and other fatty fish. There are almost as many recipes for gravlax as there are chefs. Over the years I have collected dozens of gravlax recipes, each somewhat different, yet all yielding satisfactory cures. This first recipe is the simplest of gravlax recipes.

> 4 T. salt
> 2 T. sugar
> 1 t. white pepper
> 3 T. chopped fresh dill

Fillet a 3- to 5-pound grilse (or similar size section from a larger salmon), but do not remove the skin. For more pleasant eating, remove any rib bones with tweezers or small pliers. Sprinkle the flesh side of both fillets with generous portions of the salt-sugar-pepper mixture. Now cover both fillets completely with chopped fresh dill or dill sprigs. I prefer chopped dill, since it imparts more of the flavor. Dried dill is a poor substitute. Place one fillet on top of the other, skin side out, and wrap them tightly with plastic wrap or insert them in a plastic bag. Place the fillets in a shallow baking pan or dish in the refrigerator and, for at least the first 24 to 36 hours, set a heavy plate or several food cans on top so that the weight centers on the thickest parts of the fillets. Tired of balancing food cans, I found a large flat rock in the Miramichi River that performs this function perfectly. Invert the fillets every 12 hours. As the fillets cure, a small amount of brine will accumulate; as you turn the fillets, this brine self-bastes the fillets and keeps them properly moist.

The formation of the brine is the result of the salt's drawing moisture from the flesh. The time required for curing depends on the amount of salt used, the thickness of the salmon, and your individual preference. Thin fillets from small fish may be eaten after one day, but a longer curing time is better, particularly for thick fillets from a large fish. Three days is the standard cure time in many restaurants. I prefer, as do most gravlax connoisseurs, the fillets to be cured from three to five days. The amount of mix used and the time required can only be optimized by practice.

The best gravlax I've found is in Iceland, where *graflax* (the Icelandic spelling) is almost a food staple, so plentiful that you can gorge yourself on it. I still remember the farewell luncheon at the Veidiheimilid Árnesi lodge on the Laxá í Adaldal River, which included an enormous platter of gravlax, so large that 10 hungry fishermen could not devour it. When my friends request a gravlax recipe, I recommend the following one. It originated with the executive chef at the Hotel Holt in Reykjavik some 20-odd years ago and remains unmatched for flavor.

> 2 fillets from a grilse or similar size section
>    from a 6- to 8-pound salmon
> 4 T. salt
> 1 T. white pepper
> 1 T. powdered fennel seeds
> 1 T monosodium glutamate (MSG)
> 1 T. dried onion, crushed or powdered
> 1/2 T. saltpeter
> 1/4 c. fresh dill, chopped

Mix all the ingredients except the dill, and sprinkle generously over the fillets, covering them thoroughly. Now for my secret ingredient: sprinkle each fillet with 1 or 2 tablespoons of cognac. Others suggest vodka, aquavit, or an anise-flavored liquor such as Pernod. Cover both fillets with generous portions of chopped dill. Press the two fillets together, skin side out; wrap; and process as outlined above.

This recipe yields a delicious gravlax, especially if the salmon is allowed to cure for four or five days. Recently, I have learned that this recipe is well known among restaurateurs in Iceland and is generally considered among the best recipes. The recipe differs from many in that it uses no sugar, although 2 tablespoons may be added if you desire a taste of sweetness. It also uses more pepper than most, as well as crushed onion. My Icelandic friends who recommended this recipe suggest that you may wish to add extra salt, although I do not.

Powdered fennel is readily available in Iceland (as *finkul*) and in Norway (as *fennikel*). Powdered fennel is not usually available in the United States, but fennel seeds powdered in a high-speed coffee grinder produce the identical product. Saltpeter, chemically known as potassium nitrate, is used to cure meats but is not generally available in the consumer food market in the United States. If unavailable, it may be omitted without consequence.

The amount of mixture required is determined by the size of the salmon fillets. The ratio of salt to sugar or other ingredients is strictly a question of taste. Norwegian salted salmon is cured only with salt and perhaps a touch of pepper and brandy. Most salted salmon is too salty for my taste. This Icelandic recipe for gravlax specified an English ingredient called Third Spice (*3-Kryddid* in Icelandic). It took me several years to learn it was nothing but MSG.

To prepare the cured salmon for serving, unwrap the plastic, separate the fillets and scrape off most of the dill adhering to the flesh. Slice the cold fillets on the bias, approximately 1/8 inch thick, just as you would for smoked salmon. Cut it free from the skin and arrange it on a serving plate. Serve with a mustard sauce on toast points, rye bread, or pumpernickel, or thin rye, rice, or wheat crackers. Gravlax is usually presented as an appetizer, but it makes a delicious first course for an elegant dinner.

Gravlax is universally served with a mustard sauce, for which there are also innumerable recipes, and occasionally with condiments such as capers and finely chopped onion. A simple, yet tasty sauce, one we have used for many years, is prepared by mixing 3 tablespoons Dijon-style mustard (Maille or Grey Poupon) with 2 tablespoons clear vegetable oil, and 2 teaspoons white vinegar. Add sugar and white pepper to taste. A variation, which includes dry mustard and offers a slightly sharper tang with a touch of sweetness, was suggested to me by Loretta Maurice, the cook at Camp Ouapetec on the Moisie River, who insists it is the best of all mustard sauces. And when Loretta speaks, you listen.

    8 T. Dijon mustard
    3 t. dry mustard
    3 T. white sugar
    1/4 c. white vinegar
    2/3 c. vegetable oil
    1/3 c. chopped fresh dill

Mix the ingredients together and keep the sauce refrigerated until
ready for serving. Loretta recommends more sugar. I prefer a bit less.
Half a recipe is sufficient for one side of gravlax.

**MARINATED SALMON ALTASTUA**. The Altastua restaurant in Alta,
Norway, offers both appetizers and main courses based on native fish, fowl, and
game. Marinated salmon, reindeer pâté, fresh moose, and salmon prepared three
ways enhance any culinary adventure. Altastua claims its marinated salmon is
not a type of gravlax. On that I disagree, for any salmon cure that commences
with salt and sugar is gravlax in my book. In any event, it is the orange finish that
makes this recipe different and very flavorful.

> 1 fillet from a 4-lb. grilse
> 4 T. salt
> 1 T. sugar
> Dash of pepper, preferably white
> Juice of one large orange
> Several tablespoons of finely chopped orange peel
> 1/2 oz. dry white wine

Prepare the fillet as for gravlax. Combine the salt, sugar, and
pepper, and sprinkle over the fillet. Mix the orange juice and wine and
dribble over the fillet. Wrap the fillet in plastic wrap and marinate for 1
1/2 to 2 days, following which the salmon is ready to be sliced and
served. Altastua serves its marinated salmon wrapped in a thin
homemade potato pancake topped with a dollop of sour cream. This
offers an interesting variation to the more familiar gravlax.

**SALMON PASTRAMI**. Gravlax has been universally popular for so long
that it was inevitable that other recipes for curing salmon would be explored.
One of the more popular alternatives is a pastrami style prepared in a manner
similar to gravlax. Some pastrami cures are quite complicated, requiring a
variety of spices, cayenne pepper, molasses, and even a final cold smoking. This
simple variation has been attributed to Norbert Kostner, the executive chef at the
Oriental Hotel in Bangkok.

> 2 fillets from a 3- to 5-lb. grilse or a similar size
>    section from a salmon
> 3 T. salt

3 T. sugar
4 T. black peppercorns, coarsely ground
7 T. coriander seeds, coarsely ground
6 T. mustard seeds, medium ground

Prepare the fillets as described for gravlax. Grind separately the peppercorns, the coriander seeds, and the mustard seeds. Be certain that the coriander kernel itself is ground after the husks surrounding the seeds are broken. Combine the salt, sugar, 1 tablespoon ground peppercorns, and 1 tablespoon ground coriander; sprinkle evenly over the flesh sides of the fillets.

Place one fillet on top of the other, skin sides out; wrap in plastic; and weight with food cans or a brick as described for gravlax. Place in the refrigerator for 2 1/2 to 3 days, turning every 12 hours. Remove the salmon from the refrigerator and scrape any remaining salt mixture from the fillets.

Mix the remaining 3 tablespoons peppercorns with the 6 tablespoons coriander seeds and the 6 tablespoons mustard seeds. Sprinkle the ground mixture over the flesh sides of the fillets, pressing lightly into the flesh. Refrigerate as before for at least 1 1/2 days, after which the salmon pastrami is ready for serving.

Slice thinly as for smoked salmon or gravlax, and serve with rye bread, toast points or rice wafers, lemon wedges, and a gravlax mustard sauce or condiment of your choice. Salmon pastrami will keep a week in a cold refrigerator.

## OTHER APPETIZERS

**SALMON CAVIAR AND BLINI.** I never think about preparing salmon caviar without remembering that old saw about how to make rabbit stew. First you catch a rabbit—or, in this case, a recipe for preparing salmon caviar. The roe of the hen grilse caught in the fall of the year, after the first of September, is sufficiently ripe for preparing caviar. Remember, no MSW wild salmon should ever be killed for its roe. Caviar from farm-raised salmon is the accepted source these days.

The arduous part of preparing caviar from a wild grilse is separating the eggs from the membrane that surrounds them. The eggs should be removed from the fish as soon as possible, certainly within one hour after capture. Keep the eggs chilled until you are ready to prepare them; it is best not to not mix together roe from different fish if you can avoid it.

Rinse the roe in cold water to remove any blood. Break the roe sacs into small pieces and carefully work the eggs through a piece of 1/4-inch mesh stainless steel screen

Prepare a cold-water brine containing 1 cup of salt per quart of water. Place the roe in at least twice their volume of brine and allow the eggs to soak for 25 to 35 minutes. The proper time depends on the maturity of the eggs and the salinity you desire. The first time you prepare roe, divide the roe into two portions and soak one portion for 25 minutes and the second for 35 minutes. An occasional tasting of the eggs will help you decide. Remove the caviar from the brine and drain well. Wash lightly with fresh water. Transfer the caviar to a strainer, place in the refrigerator, and allow the roe to drain for two hours. When stored in an airtight container, the caviar may be kept at 34°F for one month. For longer storage, remove the roe, drain, repack, and store at subfreezing temperature until used.

The richness of salmon caviar is best savored with well-buttered crepes. The traditional Russian-raised blini require a yeast batter, from which the crepes are often made in advance. An equally satisfactory crepe may be made with a thin baking powder pancake or French crepe. I prefer not to reheat crepes made in advance, for I believe they lose texture. In any event, the key to success is to organize your efforts so that the blini are served as hot as possible.

Allow the caviar and sour cream to reach room temperature before you begin to prepare your crepes. Melt 1/4 pound of butter and set aside. As the crepes are cooked, store them in a warm oven along with the serving plates. Warm serving plates are a must! For serving, remove a crepe from the oven, place on a warmed plate and spread lightly with melted butter. Cover the crepe with 1 1/2 tablespoons of sour cream. Spread 1 to 2 tablespoons of caviar in the center of the sour cream and roll up the crepe into a loose cigar shape. Brush additional warm butter over the crepe and serve immediately.

Since warmth is the essence of the presentation, two blini are often served as an hors d'oeuvre sequentially to the hungry fishermen as they arrive at the dining lodge for dinner. An ounce of ice-cold vodka or Aquavit is a delightful chaser.

**SHRIMP A L'AIL**. Certain spices serve only to whet my appetite. Red peppers, as in a salsa, and garlic in a butter sauce do more to activate my taste buds than any other foods I know. This recipe has both. I have long contended that the popularity of escargot is due to the garlic butter. If you like escargot, you'll love shrimp sautéed in garlic butter. For four servings as an appetizer, the ingredients are:

8 T. butter
8 t. fresh garlic, minced
1/4 to 5/16 t. crushed red pepper
8 oz. raw shrimp, peeled
4 oz. white wine
White pepper to taste

Heat the butter almost to frothing, add the garlic and red pepper, and simmer for 1 1/2 to 2 minutes, taking care not to brown the garlic. Exercise care when adding the red pepper because it tends to spatter in the hot butter. Add the shrimp and sauté for 1 1/2 to 2 minutes on one side. Turn the shrimp over and sauté for another minute. Add the white wine and simmer, but do not stir, for 4 to 7 minutes, depending on the size of the shrimp. Add more wine if necessary.

Serve in shallow sauce dishes with hot French or Italian bread. A dry white wine, such as sauvignon blanc, is the perfect accompaniment. Larger portions served with a tossed green salad make a delightful lunch or light supper. Precooked shrimp may be substituted with an appropriate reduction in the cooking times. This recipe may also be used for scallops, especially small bay scallops.

**MUSSELS IN PERNOD SAUCE (COZZE IN BIANCO).** Shellfish such as shrimp, oysters, and scallops are not my forté, but I dearly love mussels. I first experienced mussels while working in Brussels, where I learned that, from the Netherlands to Brittany, mussels are honored as a gastronomic treat.

The common blue mussel (its shell is black) of the North Atlantic coast is *Mytilus edulis*; on the Pacific Coast it is known as *Mytilus californianis*. These mussels are cultivated in the cool waters of northern New England, the maritime provinces of Canada (particularly Prince Edward Island), and in enormous quantities in the state of Washington. The "off bottom" farming of mussels on ropes or lines was initiated in 1975 by Peter Jefferds in Penn Cove on Whidbey Island, Washington. To this day, Whidbey Island remains the largest producer of mussels in the United States.

For the mussel epicure, the most famous are the green-lipped or greenshell mussels from New Zealand, *Perna canaliculus*. Plump and juicy, these delights are occasionally available in major seafood markets of the East and West Coasts.

Culinary gems are where you find them. Half the recipes in this chapter found me. To find a gem in a modest Sicilian restaurant on the north side of Baltimore is totally unexpected. Carrabba's Italian Grill is unique. It features meats and fish grilled over an open fire fueled with oak and pecan wood. Its proprietary recipes were developed by the company founder. Carrabba's preparation of Cozze in Bianco uses only fresh, live mussels imported form Prince Edward Island. But like many recipes, it's the sauce that makes this creation so exceptional. Pernod is an anise-flavored liqueur that complements perfectly the salty mussel liquor. My adaptation of Cozze in Bianco, which serves four as a main course, is as follows:

> 3 lbs. (about 3 quarts) fresh, live mussels
> 4 oz. lemon butter
> 4 cloves (more or less) fresh garlic, minced
> 1 c. yellow onion, diced
> Zest from 1 lemon
> 1 c. fresh basil leaves, loosely packed
> 2 1/2 oz. Pernod

If you cannot obtain PEI mussels, those from the New England Coast are fine, but make sure that your mussels are fresh and alive. If any of the shells are open, discard them.

Cultivated mussels are usually clean, without beard and free of sand, so that they only need to be rinsed before cooking. Wild mussels should be scrubbed well with a coarse brush. With a small knife, scrape off the beard, which extends from between the closed shells. Place the mussels in a pan of cold water containing a small handful of salt for an hour to allow the mussels to disgorge any sand. Do not leave mussels in fresh water for any length of time; it kills them. Drain the mussels in a colander, rewash, and drain again. Mussels are best served fresh, but they can be stored in a refrigerator for two days. Place the mussels in a flat tray and cover with a damp towel.

Recipes for lemon butter may be found in most cookbooks. I use 1/4 cup of lemon juice, 1/8 teaspoon salt, 4 ounces of butter, and a dash of white pepper. Soften the lemon butter over medium heat, add the onion, and sauté for about 8 minutes. Add the garlic and heat for another 2 minutes. The onion should be soft and translucent, but the garlic should not be browned.

Transfer the onion, garlic, and lemon butter to an 8- or 10-quart kettle with tightly fitted cover. Apply very high heat. Add the lemon zest, Pernod, and the mussels. Every 60 to 90 seconds, lift the kettle from the heat, hold the cover tightly with your thumbs, and toss the mussels with a circular motion to rotate them and allow them to steam evenly. After 4 minutes add the basil. After 5 to 6 minutes, the shells will open, and the mussels are ready to serve.

Transfer the mussels to large soup plates with a skimmer, discarding any whose shells have not opened. Allow the cooking liquor to settle momentarily to separate any sand. Then ladle the liquid over the mussels, sprinkle with parsley, and serve immediately with warm Italian bread and a mixed green salad. (Allow 1/2 to 3/4 pound of mussels per person when served as a first course. As the main course, figure on 1 1/4 to 1 1/2 pounds per person.)

**SHAD ROE**. The firm, immature roe from a fresh spring shad is one of the delicacies of the piscatorial world. Yet shad and their roe are woefully underutilized on the Miramichi and many East Coast rivers, and they are a virtually unknown as a food source on our West Coast rivers. In its basic form, the preparation is nothing but a butter sauté.

  1 pair shad roe per person
  2 strips bacon per roe
  1 lemon wedge per roe
  Butter
  Salt and pepper

I prefer to fry the bacon in a skillet separate from the roe, since I believe roe sautéed in butter is more delicate than when cooked in bacon fat. Better yet, cook the bacon in a microwave oven until somewhat crisp, yet flexible. Drain on a paper towel and set aside.

If the roe are fried at too high a temperature, the eggs will pop excessively, splattering grease everywhere. Even a covered skillet is inadequate. The best solution is to poach the roe for two minutes to set the eggs. Next melt the butter in a heavy skillet over medium heat. Add the roe and prick each several times to allow any steam to escape. Turn the roe every several minutes until they are an even grayish tan inside.

They should not be pink. When done, drain the roe on paper towels.
Place on the serving plate, cover each roe section with a strip of bacon,
garnish with parsley and serve with a lemon wedge. One-half pair of roe
makes an appropriate breakfast serving.

## SOUPS AND CHOWDERS

**THERESA'S SEAFOOD SOUP**. Theresa Lavalle was the cook at Camp Joseph
on the upper Moisie River. A truly delightful lady, she served substantial but
delicious food. This simple shellfish soup was offered occasionally by Theresa as the
prelude to an elegant dinner, often your farewell dinner for that season on the river.

        2 medium onions, chopped
        1/2 green pepper, chopped
        1 stalk celery, chopped
        1/4 t. savory
        1 t. chives, chopped
        1 T. chicken soup base
        1 19-oz. can tomatoes
        2 13-oz. cans chicken broth
        1 c. each of bay scallops, small shrimp, and crab meat

Sauté the onions, pepper and celery until the onions are clear but
not soft. Transfer to a soup kettle and add the savory, chives, soup base,
tomatoes, and chicken broth. Bring to a simmer for a minute or two.
Add the scallops, shrimp, and crab meat, and heat for 3 to 4 minutes
before serving. Serves six as a first course.

**LORETTA'S SEAFOOD CHOWDER**. One of the pleasures of the salmon
camp is making friends with the cook, especially when the cook is as outstanding
as Loretta Maurice, for 15 years the cook at Camp Ouapetec on the Moisie River.
Loretta's skills are like none other I've seen on the rivers of North America.
During the course of a week, her appetizers may include gravlax, smoked salmon,
salmon caviar with blini, crab puffs, and stuffed mushrooms. Her main courses
are certain to include fresh lobster, crab legs, and, of course, a special salmon
preparation or two.

        1/4 lb. bacon
        1/2 lb. lobster

1/2 lb. scallops
1 can baby clams, or 6 oz. chopped fresh clams
2 c. potatoes, peeled & diced
1 c. clam broth plus l cup water
1 c. milk
2 c. light cream
Salt and pepper to taste

Cook the bacon until well browned. Remove the bacon and sauté the onions in the bacon fat until soft. Add the potatoes and sauté for 2 minutes. Add the clam juice and water and simmer for 8 minutes. Add the milk, cream, and seasonings and bring to a boil. Immediately reduce the heat to low, add the seafood and crumpled bacon, and simmer for 4 to 5 minutes. Serve hot with the crackers of your choice. I particularly like hard sea biscuits or authentic Southern beaten biscuits with this chowder.

**RICHARD'S SMOKED SALMON CHOWDER**. This hearty chowder makes an excellent one-course meal, particularly when accompanied by buttered cornbread, a mixed green salad, and a robust red wine, such as a zinfandel or burgundy. Generous quantities of smoked salmon add an earthiness that defies description. You can taste it but not define it. I first used this recipe adapted from a long-lost prototype as a means of salvaging the remains of a 27-pound salmon that inattentively had been hot smoked and thus also cooked. Soft and crumbly, it was useless for serving sliced like the cold smoked variety, and I found that we could consume only so much hot smoked salmon in scrambled eggs and casseroles. This chowder is outstanding; twice it has won my gun club's award as the best soup of the year. Try it; you'll love it.

1/3 lb. fresh salmon fillets, skinned
1/2 lb. smoked salmon
3 T. butter
1 medium onion, diced
2 stalks celery, finely chopped
1 T. flour
1/2 package of frozen corn
2 large potatoes, peeled and diced
3 c. bottled clam juice
1 c. cream plus 1 to 3 cups of water
1 bay leaf

1/4 t. dried thyme
Pepper to taste
Fresh parsley or chives, chopped

Cut the fresh salmon into 1-inch pieces. If you use cold-smoked salmon, cut into 3/4-inch die. Crumble hot-smoked salmon into bite-sized pieces. Melt the butter in a large skillet. Add the celery and sauté for 1 minute. Add the onion and cook over medium heat 3 to 4 minutes until soft but not brown. Form a well in the center of the skillet; stir in the flour and cook for about a minute. Transfer the celery and onion mixture to a large saucepan and add the clam juice, cream, corn, potatoes, spices, and 1 to 3 cups of water. Simmer for 5 minutes. Now add the fresh salmon and any cold-smoked salmon and simmer until the fresh fish is cooked and the potatoes are soft. If you are using hot-smoked salmon, delay adding the salmon until the potatoes are almost done. Hot-smoked salmon requires only a minute or so to heat. Season to taste with pepper. The smoked salmon and clam juice usually provide sufficient salt. Garnish with parsley or chives and serve piping hot. A single recipe serves six to eight.

**CRAB BISQUE.** My wife has the unique ability to read a recipe and virtually taste the finished product. Over the years, her talent has gleaned a few pearls, of which this elegant bisque is one. It has been a specialty of our home for so many years that our grown children still call it "company soup." When you taste this bisque, you would never guess its humble origins. Conversely, if you learned first of the ingredients, you would never anticipate the delicate results. This recipe serves four.

1 can tomato soup
1 can green pea soup
1/2 pt. cream
1 6 oz. can of crab meat
1 T. Worcestershire sauce
1 T. sherry

Mix together the tomato soup, pea soup, and cream in a sauce pan. Heat the mixture to serving temperature. Stir in the crab. Add the Worcestershire sauce and sherry, and taste. You may wish to add 1 or 2 extra teaspoons of each. Served with a fresh green salad and a light white wine, this bisque makes a delightful lunch. For large groups, a portion of the crabmeat may be replaced with the "imitation crab" available as seafood chunks or Krab Delight in most grocery markets.

**CREAM OF FIDDLEHEAD SOUP.**[2] During early salmon season, one of the great delicacies of our northern border states and southern Canada is the fiddlehead fern. More accurately called the ostrich fern (*Matteucia struthiopteris*), the unfurled frond of the fern, somewhat like asparagus tips, is the perfect accompaniment to fresh salmon. Fiddleheads are picked in late May and early June and increasingly may be found in the markets of the northeastern United States. You seldom have the opportunity to relish fresh salmon and fiddleheads simultaneously, but when you do, it's a treat you won't soon forget.

This particular soup has been served to guests of Wilson's Sporting camps for so many years that it is prominently featured on one of their placemats.

> 2 c. fiddlehead fern fronds
> 1 t. salt
> 1 can cream of chicken soup
> 1 1/2 c. milk
> 1 1/2 c. light cream
> 2 T. butter
> 1 1/2 t. basil

Cover the fiddleheads with water, add the salt, and simmer for 20 to 25 minutes. Drain, cool the ferns, and finely chop. If you use a blender, pulse lightly; do not puree the ferns. Blend together in a saucepan the chopped ferns with the remaining ingredients and heat to serving temperature for three to five minutes. Mrs. Wilson cautions against using any shortening except butter. Season to taste with salt and pepper, garnish with parsley, and serve piping hot. (See page 437 for information on additional fiddlehead recipes.)

## MAIN COURSES

**POACHED SALMON.** Perhaps the best, certainly the most comprehensive, fish-and-game cookbook available today is the *L.L. Bean Game and Fish Cookbook* (11). It was from this book that I first learned the secret of successful

---

2. Courtesy of Ethyl Wilson, Wilson's Sporting Camps, McNamee, New Brunswick.

poaching. You determine the time by the thickness of the fish. Measure the thickness of your salmon at its thickest point and poach it exactly 10 minutes per inch of thickness. For example, a salmon 3 1/2 inches thick requires 35 minutes. The thick portion will be properly cooked without overcooking the thinner tail section.

Poaching a salmon is quite easy. It's the preparation that is exasperating. If you do not have a large fish poacher, you will need to exercise ingenuity as to your cooking vessel. With large salmon, you may even need to cut the fish in half, cook each section separately, and rejoin them for serving. The well-cleaned fish should be rubbed inside and out with 2 or 3 tablespoons of lemon juice. Place the fish on a length of cheesecloth long enough to accommodate the fish and to provide handholds on each end. Now lower the fish into the poacher or vessel, just covering it with cool liquid.

The poaching liquor may be salted water, a solution of 1 1/2 teaspoons vinegar per quart of water, or court bouillon (see below). Place an aluminum-foil tent over the fish, even if your poacher has a cover. Apply heat until the poaching liquid begins to boil. Immediately turn down the heat to a low simmer. Time your cooking from the moment you turn down the heat. When the salmon is cooked, carefully remove it from the poacher, drain well, transfer to the serving platter, and garnish prior to serving.

Most people prefer salmon poached in a court bouillon. A typical bouillon is prepared with vegetables and spices, as follows:

> 2 qts. water
> 1/4 c. sliced carrot
> 1/4 c. sliced onion
> 1/4 c. vinegar
> 1/4 c. dry white wine
> 1 bouquet garni
> Fish heads, if desired

The bouquet garni is prepared by wrapping in a piece of cheesecloth several sprigs of parsley, the leaves from two celery ribs, 2 bay leaves, 1/2 teaspoon dried thyme, 3 cloves garlic, and 6 or 8 peppercorns. Combine the ingredients in a saucepan, simmer for 10 minutes, and set aside to cool. Strain the cooled bouillon into the poacher, reserving the vegetables and any fish parts, and add sufficient cool water to just cover the fish. Poach as described above.

**POACHED SALMON STEAKS WITH FIDDLEHEAD FERNS**. A whole salmon almost begs to be poached. Properly seasoned, it's the perfect way to serve "as plainly as possible" a cooked salmon. However, poaching a whole salmon is a production. Many times we crave a similar, but simpler dish. This is it.

> 2 qts. water
> 1 onion, sliced
> 1 carrot and 1 celery stalk, chopped
> 1 T. chopped fresh dill
> 1 c. dry white wine
> Salt and pepper to taste
> 6 salmon steaks, 1 1/2 to 2 inches thick

Combine all the ingredients, except the salmon, in a saucepan, and simmer for about an hour. Strain the broth and discard the vegetables. Place the salmon steaks in a hot skillet and cover the fish with the hot broth. Simmer for 8 to 12 minutes, until the fish is done to your taste. Garnish and serve hot.

One of my favorite vegetables, the perfect accompaniment for poached salmon, is the fiddlehead fern. Steamed and lightly seasoned with butter, salt and pepper, it's pure vegetarian ecstasy. For the fiddlehead aficionado, there is now a very complete fiddlehead recipe book, *Cooking North America's Finest Gourmet Fiddleheads* (41), that incorporates 82 recipes, including 10 soup recipes and 48 dinner dishes, together with instructions for harvesting, storing and freezing fiddleheads.

It is not generally known that fresh fiddleheads may be kept for up to three weeks by covering them with very cold or even ice water and storing in your refrigerator, providing you change the water every day. If you do not change the water, the fiddleheads will turn black.

I learned from my guide Hollis on the Restigouche that fiddleheads also may be canned, or bottled as my Canadian friends say. Hollis' procedure is as follows:

> In a quart jar, place one teaspoon of salt and enough ferns to reach the shoulder of the jar. Fill the jar with sufficient warm, not hot, water to cover the fiddleheads, but leave some space for expansion. Screw the lid onto the jar rather firmly, but not so tightly that the air in the jar cannot escape. Place the jar in enough boiling water to cover the jar one to two

inches. Boil for 18 minutes. Remove the jar and tighten the lid. Stored in a cool place, canned fiddleheads will keep for a year. To serve, you need only to remove the ferns from the jar and heat them for two minutes.

Fiddleheads are very easy to freeze. Wash the fern heads in cold water, trim any heavy stalks, and place them on a cookie sheet in the freezer overnight. Transfer the frozen ferns into plastic bags and store them in your freezer. Frozen fiddleheads will also keep for a year.

**SORREL BAKED SHAD**. The American shad (*Alosa sapidissima*) is a paradox in modern America. The name *sapidissima* means "most delicious." In colonial America, shad were so plentiful that they were not eaten in polite circles, much like the restraints once placed on the serving of the then-ubiquitous Atlantic salmon. Today shad are respected primarily on the northeastern Atlantic seaboard, where the migrating shad are cause for river festivals every April, particularly along the Hudson and Delaware Rivers. Even so, some commercial fishermen shun the shad as fit only for "other people."

The largest member of the herring family, the shad is among the boniest of all edible fishes, with two rows of intramuscular ribs on each side. If you fillet the shad and remove one set of ribs, you still have to open each fillet to remove the second set. As a result, there are two primary ways to prepare fresh shad. One is to bake a whole shad very slowly. The shad is placed in a slow oven at 250°F and baked for 8 to 10 hours, during which time the ribs soften or dissolve. The fish then may be eaten without encountering the troublesome ribs. The second, my way of preparing shad, is to purchase fresh shad fillets at the fish market already boned.

For a number of years, I have baked shad for our annual "Shadfest," using a different recipe each time. We still recall a memorable dinner of shad stuffed with wild mushrooms. However, my favorite recipe is this simple one for sorrel-wrapped shad. The acidic sorrel and lemon juice complement perfectly the oily flesh of the shad.

> 2 shad fillets, deboned but not skinned
> 1/2 t. salt and 1 t. pepper
> 1 lb. fresh sorrel
> 1/4 c. dry white wine
> 1/4 c. lemon juice

Make certain that the shad is fresh. Do not accept a fish more than two days out of the river. Preheat the oven to 325°F. Season the fish inside and out with the salt-and-pepper mixture. Place a layer of well-greased foil in a large baking pan. Since this recipe uses a large quantity of sorrel, you may wish to procure a box of sorrel from a wholesale grocer or restaurateur. Any unused sorrel may be placed in a sealed plastic bag and frozen for use at a later date. Wash the sorrel well, remove the stems, and place about one-third of the sorrel on the greased foil. Lay the shad on top of the sorrel and drape the remaining sorrel over and around the fish, completely covering it. Pour the wine and the lemon juice over the fish. Cover with a tent of foil and bake for 45 to 50 minutes. Serve immediately. Allow 1/3 to 1/2 lb. of shad per serving. I like to complement the shad with steamed asparagus or peapods and saffron rice. A hearty red wine is a must.

**MY MOTHER'S CORNBREAD**. My mother was a superb cook, and this was her recipe. It has been in our family for over a century, modified only in keeping with today's cultured buttermilk. It has become my signature recipe.

I grew up with cornbread as a thrice-weekly treat, and it still holds a prominent place in my household. On a snowy winter's day, nothing can be more satisfying than a hearty soup and wedges of cornbread laced with slices of butter. There is a family tale that as a wee tyke I would appear a day after cornbread had been served with a cornstick in my mouth. My fastidious mother wondered where I secreted them. One day, while cleaning under the sofa cushions she found my hidden treasure. To this day, I still save leftover cornbread for another meal.

Real cornbread does not use flour. You can tell the region of the United States from which a cornbread recipe comes by the amount of flour designated. The farther north you go, the more flour and, hence, the poorer the cornbread. That's probably the reason that Northerners don't fully appreciate cornbread. Theirs is too soft and crumbly.

Place a 9- or 10-inch cast iron or heavy aluminum skillet (or cornstick mold) in the oven and preheat it to 425°F. Mix together:

2 c. buttermilk
2 eggs
1 t. salt
1 t. baking soda
1 3/4 cups corn meal

I prefer to mix the first three ingredients well and the stir in the baking soda just before adding 1 3/4 cups corn meal (stone-ground meal is best).

Place 2 tablespoons butter in the skillet and return it to the oven until the butter melts and froths. You may substitute bacon grease if you prefer the flavor. If so, leave the skillet in the oven until the grease is very hot. Pour the batter into the heated skillet and quickly return to the oven. Bake at 425°F for 22 to 25 minutes. Cornsticks in molds will generally take 10 to 13 minutes.

The texture of cornbread is determined by the type of meal used. I use yellow meal, although many Southern recipes favor white cornmeal. White cornbread tends to be denser and somewhat moister; yellow cornbread is richer and a tad fluffier. Whatever the color of your corn, coarse, water-ground meal is much preferred over the finely ground "commercial" meals.

A heavy cast-iron skillet is essential for forming a good crust. You can adjust the density and moisture of cornbread by the amount of batter in the skillet. In a 10-inch skillet, this recipe will produce bread about 1 1/2 inches thick, which will be firm and crusty. That's my favorite. In a 9-inch skillet, this recipe will produce 2-inch-thick bread, which will be lighter and moister. Try them both and decide.

For extra-rich cornbread, you can replace one-fourth of the buttermilk with whipping cream. My mother often added 1 cup of whipping cream to a quart of buttermilk and allowed it to sour a day before use. Our daughter uses sour cream in place of whipping cream in the same manner.

Powdered buttermilk is now available for those of us who must have a cornbread fix on the trail. It makes an acceptable substitute if you use the recommended amount of buttermilk solids but less water. The equivalent of 2 cups of buttermilk normally requires 8 tablespoons of buttermilk solids and 2 cups of water. This produces a very thin, runny batter that does not bake well. Cut back on the water; between 1 and 1 1/4 cups of water will produce a batter of the same consistency as with liquid buttermilk.

For gracious dining, try serving soup with cornsticks as a first course. For a substantial meal, the large skillet wedges are best.

## A CHILD'S BLESSING

Grant us thy blessing, Dear Lord,
On these and all thy mercies.
For Christ's sake, Amen.

# Bibliography

01. Anderson, Gary. *Atlantic Salmon: Fact & Fancy*. Montreal: Salar Publishing, 1990.

02. Ashley, Clifford W. *The Ashley Book of Knots*. New York: Doubleday, 1944.

03. Bates, Joseph D., Jr. *Atlantic Salmon Flies and Fishing*. Mechanicsburg, Penn.: Stackpole Books, 1970, 1995.

04. ———. *The Art of the Atlantic Salmon Fly*. Boston: David R. Godine, Publisher, Inc, 1987.

05. Bates, Joseph D., Jr., and Pamela Bates Richards. *Fishing Atlantic Salmon: The Flies and The Patterns*. Mechanicsburg, Penn.: Stackpole Books, 1996.

06. Bielak, Alexander T. "Quebec North Shore Atlantic Salmon Stocks" (Ph.D. diss., University of Waterloo, Ontario, 1984).

07. ———. *A Discussion Document on the Implications of Catch-and-Release Angling for Atlantic Salmon*. DFO Atlantic Fisheries Research Document 96/117. New Brunswick Department of Natural Resources and Energy, Fredericton, New Brunswick.

08. Black, James F., Jr., editor. *Black's 2000 Fly Fishing*. Red Bank, N.J.: Black's Sporting Directories, 2000.

09. Borger, Gary A. *Presentation*. Wausau, Wis.: Tomorrow River Press, 1995.

10. Budworth, Geoffrey. *The Complete Book of Fishing Knots*. New York: The Lyons Press, 1999.

11.    Cameron, Angus, and Judith Jones. *The L.L. Bean Game & Fish Cookbook*. New York: Random House, Inc., 1983.

12.    Combs, Trey. *Bluewater Fly Fishing*. New York: Lyons and Burford, 1995.

13.    Cummings, Bill. *Atlantic Salmon Fishing*. Camden, Maine: Ragged Mountain Press, 1995.

14.    Daly, Thomas Aquinas. *Painting Nature's Quiet Places*. New York: Watson-Guptill Publications, Division of Billboard Publications, Inc., 1985.

15.    Doak, Jerry. *The Green Machine, Fly Tyer*, Vol. 10 (Summer 1987): 44.

15b.    ———. Telephone conversation with author, 1998.

16.    Falkus, Hugh. *Salmon Fishing: A Practical Guide*. London: H.F. & G. Witherby Ltd., 1984.

17.    ———. *Speycasting, A New Technique*. London: Excellent Press, 1994.

18.    Fleming, I.A., B. Jonsson, M.R. Gross, and A. Lamberg. *An Experimental Study of the Reproductive Behavior and Success of Farmed and Wild Atlantic Salmon*, J. Applied Ecology 33 (1996): pp. 893–905.

19.    Garcia, L.A. *Handcrafting a Graphite Rod*. Portland, Oreg.: Frank Amato Publications, 1994.

20.    Gingras, Sylvain. *A Century of Sport*. English translation. St. Raymond, Quebec: Les Editions Rapides Blancs, Inc., 1994.

21.    Gingrich, Arnold. *The Well Tempered Angler*. New York: Alfred A. Knopf,1973.

22.    Graesser, Neil. *Fly Fishing for Salmon*. Washington, D.C.: Stone Wall Press, 1982.

23.    Hubert, Joseph P. *Salmon-Salmon*. Goshen, Conn.: Anglers and Shooters Press, 1975.

24.    Jaworowski, E. *The Cast*. Harrisburg, Penn.: Stackpole Books, 1992.

25.    Jonsson, Bror, and Ian A. Fleming. "Enhancement of Wild Salmon Populations." *Human Impact on Self-Recruiting Populations: An International Symposium*. G. Sundes, editor. Trondheim, Norway: Tapir, 1994: pp. 209-242. (Symposium held Kongsvall, Norway, June 7–11, 1993.)

26.    Jorgensen, Poul. *Salmon Flies*. Harrisburg, Penn.: Stackpole Books, 1978.

27.    Karkkolainen, Pekke, editor. *Atlantic Salmon Review*. Ristiniementive, Finland: Atlantic Salmon Publishing Ltd.

28.    Kreh, Bernard "Lefty." *Fly Fishing in Salt Water*. New York: Lyons & Burford, 1986.

29.    ———. Editor. *The American Fly Fishing Symposium: Part Two-Tackle*. Birmingham, Al.: Odysseus Editions,1993

30.    ———. Letter to author, 1998.

31.    Kreh, Lefty and Sosin, Mark. *Practical Fishing Knots*. New York: Crown Publishers, Inc., 1972.

32.    LaFontaine, Gary. *The Dry Fly—New Angles*. Helena, Mont.: Greycliff Publishing Company, 1990.

33.    Lee, Art. *Atlantic Salmon Journal*, Vol. 35, No. 3 (Autumn 1986).

34.    ———. *Tying and Fishing the Riffling Hitch*. Champaign, Ill.: Human Kinetics, 1998.

35.    Lee, Philip. *Home Pool: The Fight to Save the Atlantic Salmon*. Fredericton, N.B.: New Brunswick Publishing Co., Ltd., 1996.

36.    Maxwell, Mike. *The Art and Science of Speyfishing*. Delta, B.C.: Flyfishers' Arte & Publishing Co., 1995.

37.    Marriner, Paul C. *Atlantic Salmon: A Fly Fishing Primer*. Clinton, N.J.: Winchester Press, 1992.

37b.   McKenzie, W. Thorpe. Letter to author, 1998.

38.    McNally, Bob. *Fishermen's Knots, Fishing Rigs, and How to Use Them*. Point Pleasant, N.J.: The Fisherman Library Corp., 1993.

39.    Mills, Derek, ed. *Salmon in the Sea*. Cambridge, Mass.: Blackwell Scientific Publications Inc., 1993.

40.    Mills, Derek, and Neil Graesser. *The Salmon Rivers of Scotland*. London: Cassell, Ltd., 1981.

41.    Nash, J. Mervin. *Cooking North America's Finest Gourmet Fiddleheads*. Oromocto, N.B.: Fiddlehead Canada Ltd., 1995.

41b.   Nemes, Sylvester. *Six Months in Scotland*. Bozeman, Mont.: Privately published, 1998.

42.    Netboy, Anthony. *The Salmon: Their Fight for Survival*. Boston, Mass.: Houghton Mifflin Company, 1973.

42b.   Noorling, Håken. "The Temple Dog Series." *Atlantic Salmon Review*, Vol. 3, No. 2 (Winter 1998/99): 27.

43.    O'Reilly, Peter. *Trout and Salmon Rivers of Ireland*. Shropshire, England: Merlin Unwin Books, 1993.

44.    Randall, Glenn. *Cold Comfort*. New York: Lyons & Burford, 1987.

45.    Richards, Bruce W. *Modern Fly Lines*. Birmingham, Ala.: Odysseus Editions, 1994.

46.    Ritz, Charles. *A Fly Fisher's Life*. Rev. ed. New York: Crown Publishers, Inc., 1972.

47.    Schmidt, William E. *Hooks for the Fly*. Mashpee, Mass.: Piscator Publishing.

48.    Scott, Jock. *Greased Line Fishing for Salmon [and Steelhead]*. Portland, Oreg.: Frank Amato Publications, 1982.

49.    Seiders, Ryan and Smith, Dan. *Start to Finish Fly Rod Building*. Driftwood, Texas: Flex Coat Co. Inc.

50.    Sosin, Mark and John Clark. *Through the Fishes Eye*. New York: Harper & Row, 1973.

51.    Stoddard, Robert. *Atlantic Salmon Journal*, Vol. 23, No. 4 (Winter 1974): 25.

52.    Vincent, Jim. "Steelhead on a Greased Line." *Wild Steelhead and Salmon*, Vol. 3, No. 1, (Autumn 1996): p. 82.

53.    Weeks, Edward. *The Moisie Salmon Club*. Barre, Mass.: Barre Publishers, 1971.

54.    Wood, Robert S. *Pleasure Packing*. Berkeley, Calif.: Ten Speed Press, 1991.

55     Wulff, Joan Salvato. *Joan Wulff's Fly-Casting Techniques*. New York: Lyons & Burford, 1987.

56. ———. "Making It Happen: The Perfect Forward Cast Loop." *Fly Rod and Reel*, Vol. 17, No. 6 (January/February 1996): 82.

57. Wulff, Lee. *Lee Wulff's Handbook of Freshwater Fishing*. New York: Frederick A. Stokes Co., 1936.

58. ———. *The Atlantic Salmon*. Rev. ed. New York: A.S. Barnes and Co., 1983.

59. ———. *Leaping Silver*, George W. New York: Stewart Publisher: 1940.

## REFERENCED TRADE SOURCES

101. Anglers Workshop, P.O. Box 1010, Woodland, WA 98674

102. Boulder Landing Rod Cases, 3728 S. Elm Place, Broken Arrow, OK 74011

103. Cascade Design, Inc., 4000 1st Avenue South, Seattle, WA 98134

104. Dale Clements Custom Tackle, Inc., 444 Schantz Road, Allentown, PA 18104

105. Wallace W. Doak & Sons Ltd., P.O. Box 95, Doaktown, N.B., Canada E0C 1G0

106. Flex Coat Co. Inc., P.O. Box 190, Driftwood, TX 78619

107. Gator Sports, Inc., 3789 South 300 West, Bldg. C, Salt Lake City, UT 84115

108. Godfrey, Ted, 3509 Pleasant Plains Drive, Reistertown, MD 21136

109. Gold-N-West Flyfishers, P.O. Box 41134, Port Coquitlam, B.C., Canada V3C 5Z9

110. Hunter's Angling Supplies, Box 300, New Boston, NH 03070

111. Industrial Safety Co., 1390 Neubrecht Rd., Lima, OH 45801

112. Limited Seasons Company, Inc., P.O. Box 4352, Manchester, NH 03108

113. Pacific Bay Fishing Tackle Inc., 540 Jefferson Street, Placentia, CA 92670

114. J. Peterman and Company, Grand Central Plaza, 107 E. 42nd St., New York, NY 10017 (retail outlet will ship orders upon request)

115. RIO Products International., Inc., 5050 S. Yellowstone Hwy., Idaho Falls, ID 83402

116. The Saltwater Angler, 219 Simonton Street, Key West, FL 33040

117. E. Veniard Ltd., 138 Northwood Road, Thornton Heath, Surrey CR4 8YG, England

118. Watersafe, Inc., P.O. Box 680398, Park City, UT 84068

119. Yerger, Rod, P.O. Box 294, Lawrence, PA 15055

# Index

*NOTE: Italicized numbers indicate pages on which photographs or illustrations appear.*

# About
# the Author

An avid fly fisherman for 50 years and a salmon fisherman
for three decades, Richard Nightingale is the fifth member of
Lee Wulff's exclusive Sixteen-Twenty Club. Membership in
this club is limited to fishermen who have landed a salmon
weighing at least 20 pounds on a size 16 single hook. In 35
years, only six people have qualified for this honor.

Born and raised in Champaign, Illinois, the author
received his B.S. and M.S. degrees in chemistry from the
University of Illinois and his Ph.D. in physical-analytical
chemistry from the University of Minnesota. After teaching
at the University of Minnesota and the University of
Nebraska for seven years, he moved to New Jersey, where he
has since resided. He is the author of some 35 technical and
professional publications and holds 12 U.S. patents.

In his first full-length book, Richard Nightingale
combines his analytical skills with his years of fly-fishing
experiences to offer new insight into the art and technology
of Atlantic salmon angling. He also offers a candid
assessment of the future of the Atlantic salmon, as well as
some practical yet critical measures to reverse the decline
and possible extermination of the wild salmon.